The New Handbook of Administrative Supervision in Counseling

To meet the goal of delivering excellent, culturally responsive services to clients, successful administrative supervisors provide leadership to professional counselors, manage counseling services, and work effectively within their agencies. *The New Handbook of Administrative Supervision in Counseling* is written for practicing, new, or aspiring first line supervisors who work in a mental health agency, private practice, or in a school. It highlights the skills needed to fulfill 18 job responsibilities such as implementing your vision, advocating for services and staff members, navigating the politics inherent in work environments, building a team of staff members, managing budgets and other realities, and maintaining your own professional integrity and development. Useful forms are provided, as are self-directed exercises to facilitate personal reflection. Sponsored by *The Association for Counselor Education and Supervision.*

Patricia G. Henderson has worked as an administrative and clinical supervisor of school counselors for 35 years. She has authored and co-authored 18 books and 26 articles on counseling and guidance. As an active leader in professional counseling at the local, state, and national levels Patricia Henderson has received several awards for work as both counselor and supervisor, as well as for research and writing. She currently heads her own consulting firm.

The New Handbook of Administrative Supervision in Counseling

Patricia Henderson

A product of the Association for Counselor Education and Supervision

Routledge
Taylor & Francis Group

NEW YORK AND LONDON

First published 2009
by Routledge
270 Madison Ave, New York, NY 10016

Simultaneously published in the UK
by Routledge
2 Park Square, Milton Park, Abingdon, Oxon OX14 4RN

Routledge is an imprint of the Taylor & Francis Group, an informa business

© 2009 Taylor & Francis

Typeset in Minion by
RefineCatch Limited, Bungay, Suffolk
Printed and bound in the United States of America on acid-free paper by
Walsworth Publishing Company, Marceline MO.

Library of Congress Cataloging in Publication Data
The New Handbook of Administrative Supervision in Counseling / Patricia Henderson.
  p. cm.
  Includes bibliographical references and index.
  1. Educational counseling—United States—Administration—Handbooks, manuals,
etc. 2. Student counselors—United States. 3. School personnel management—United
States. I. Henderson, Patricia, Ed. D. II. Title: The new handbook of administrative
supervision in counseling.
  LB1027.5.H4365 2008
  371.4—dc22

                                                                    2008022489

ISBN10: 0–415–99583–3 (hbk)
ISBN10: 0–415–99584–1 (pbk)
ISBN10: 0–203–88730–1 (ebk)

ISBN13: 978–0–415–99583–2 (hbk)
ISBN13: 978–0–415–99584–9 (pbk)
ISBN13: 978–0–203–88730–1 (ebk)

Contents

Section V
**Administrative Supervisors: Design, Maintain and Improve an
Effective and Efficient Service Delivery System for Clients**

Section VI
**Administrative Supervisors: Strive Continuously for
Excellence in Fulfillment of Their Administrative Supervision
Responsibilities**

Appendixes

List of Figures

Preface

Like its companion, *The New Handbook of Counseling Supervision*, this *Handbook* is "designed to bridge theory, research and practice" (Borders & Brown, 2005) in administrative supervision in counseling. To date, there is more practice of this type of supervision than there is theory or research. This *Handbook* describes administrative supervisors' job responsibilities, and the skills and knowledge base they need to meet these responsibilities effectively and efficiently. Much of it is derived from experiences of current administrative supervisors in counseling. It also draws from the theory and research of counseling leadership and supervision; and from those of business leadership, management and supervision; organizational and educational leadership; mental health administration; social work administration and supervision; and supervision in government. I have assumed that learning in these related fields transfers to counseling.

An additional purpose of this *Handbook* is to offer definitions and descriptions that will provide a common language base, so important to advancing this dimension of the counseling field. With the dearth of full textbooks on this subject—I am aware of two, Henderson and Gysbers (1998) and Herr, Heitzmann, and Rayman (2006)—a purpose of this *Handbook* is to serve as a "concise reference book" (*Webster's Third*, 2002, "handbook") for potential, new and experienced administrative supervisors. It is rooted in the original Association for Counselor Education and Supervision (ACES) *Handbook of Administrative Supervision* (Falvey, 1987).

The purposes of administrative supervision are to ensure that a counseling department's clients and an agency's mission and goals are well served. To do this effectively, administrative supervisors support professional counselors in the application and development of their professionalism. This *Handbook* is divided into six sections. The first defines basic terms and concepts. Sections II–VI address administrative supervisors' five major responsibilities. In carrying these out, they perform 10 functions, fulfill four roles and draw from seven bases of power in order to meet 18 objectives. Each chapter defines an objective and describes what an administrative supervisor would do to achieve it well. Each chapter ends with an example of a recurring challenge that they frequently face and an effective strategy for responding to it.

Acknowledgements

As someone who has spent 35 years of my counseling career in jobs where my primary professional identity has been as an administrative supervisor in counseling, I worry that, in spite of the fact that there are quite a few of us, there has not been much discussion about this dimension of the counseling profession. The time is ripe to help the profession understand more fully the contributions we make. I am truly appreciative of this opportunity to further delineate this discipline.

First, I congratulate Association for Counselor Education and Supervision (ACES) past, present and (probably) future leadership for their interest in and support of the topic of administrative supervision in counseling, this *Handbook*, and my work on it. Historically, I learned much from Janet Falvey and the first *Handbook* (1987), and from Alan Dye and DiAnne Borders who, as Chairs of the ACES Supervision Interest Network, were inclusive and welcomed me into its work—even though my perspective was quite different. Recent Presidents, specifically, Donna Henderson, Steve Feit, James Benshoff, Harriet Glosoff, have each supported the production of this *Handbook*. And, through it all, Dave Zimpfer, Treasurer and Business Advisor, has, for several years, guided and prodded me through the development process.

Experts outside ACES helped in meaningful ways. Practicing administrative supervisors from counseling centers, agencies and schools in San Antonio shared with me their job descriptions, thoughts and practices for use in this book. Readers will hear, specifically, from Sue Clifford, Debby Healy, Mary Libby, Laurel Malloy, Donna Martin, Patrick McDaniel, Theresa Miller, Kathy Steves, and Eli Zambrano. For 21 years, I provided training and supervision of supervision for several hundred others. Each of them taught me new and different facets of their work.

Robert B. Babcock, Chair of the Department of Counseling and Human Services at Saint Mary's University/San Antonio, helped me immeasurably by providing access to library resources. Beth Durodoye, Associate Professor, University of Texas at San Antonio graciously shared her time and knowledge regarding multicultural perspectives. Katrina Cook, doctoral student at UTSA, shared her insights, perspectives and experiences using the counselor assessment/supervisor response model offered in Chapter 11.

Finally, I acknowledge the openness and generosity of two widely recognized experts in their fields who, through emails, shared their recent work and ideas: Cal Stoltenberg, The University of Oklahoma, and Bertram Raven, University of California, Los Angeles.

Patricia Henderson, Ed.D.
San Antonio, Texas
March, 2008

I
Defining Administrative Supervision in Counseling

- Defining Administrative Supervision

1

Defining Administrative Supervision

Administrative supervision in counseling is a process—a sequence of activities—based on principles of supervision, leadership, management, and administration. To be effective, the process entails reciprocal interpersonal relationships between an administrative supervisor and their counselor and other staff member supervisees (Borders & Brown, 2005; Kadushin & Harness, 2002). The process occurs in the context of a counseling department serving clients from a diverse society in a mental health service-providing agency. The ultimate purpose of administrative supervision is to ensure delivery of the highest quality counseling services to the department's clients in alignment with the mission and goals of the agency by promoting the highest levels of counselor professional development. Administrative supervision is an indirect service to counseling clients, meaning that it is carried out on their behalf but its focus is on the working professionals.

The overarching goal of administrative supervision is to establish and maintain work environments conducive to:

1. Providing efficient, effective and culturally responsive services to diverse clients;
2. Encouraging highest levels of counselor performance; and
3. Contributing to achievement of the agency's goals and adherence to its policies and rules.

Effective administrative supervision entails balancing the interests of clients, professional counselors and other staff members, and their agencies; balancing the priorities of performance quality with the expectations for quantity of services; and balancing effectiveness of services with delivery system efficiency.

CONTEXT

Where Administrative Supervisors in Counseling Work

Agencies that provide administrative supervision for counselors and other staff members may be public or private, and provide outpatient or inpatient services. The "applied counseling settings" (Association for Counselor Education & Supervision [ACES], 1993) include community mental health centers, elementary, middle/junior high and high schools, community colleges, universities, group or individual private practices, general or psychiatric hospitals, federal and state agencies (e.g., veterans affairs, employment services, rehabilitation, defense, education), corrections facilities, managed care organizations, employee assistance programs, substance abuse treatment centers, and gerontological facilities (American Mental Health Counselors Association (AMHCA), n.d.; ACES, 1993; Gaver, 2000; Henderson, 1994; Nelson, Johnson, & Thorngren, 2000).

The Organizational Placement of Administrative Supervision Positions

The basic structure of mental health care agencies is as follows:

Agency Organizational Structure

Governing Body

Administrative Oversight

Professional Oversight

Providers of Services

Consumers of Services (Patterson, 2000).

The primary role of a governing body is to establish policy. Administration translates policies into implementation practices, often through creating rules, regulations and procedures. Although the terminology may be confusing, professional oversight of adherence to these policies and rules by counselors and other staff members is carried out through "administrative supervision." The service providers counsel and do related work in accordance with the policies, rules and professional standards. The counseling clients are the consumers of these services.

Administrative supervisors in counseling may not be "administrators" in their organizations. Typically, they report to individuals responsible for administrative oversight and who are not professional counselors. Example titles of agency administrators are: executives, vice presidents, directors or managers. Example titles of administrative supervisors of counselors are: "supervisor, staff specialist, department head, or program director" (Falvey, 1987, p. 2), or head or lead counselor (Henderson & Gysbers, 1998). They may be called coordinators or team leaders.

Each category of personnel reports to someone in the category above them. Support staff report to professionals; professionals to supervisors; supervisors to managers; managers to executives; executives to senior management; senior management to owners. "In most human service organizations, there are likely to be persistent organizational and status distinctions, such as among managerial, professional, and technical support personnel" (Austin, 2002, p. 75).

An assumption of this *Handbook* is that administrative supervisors in counseling are professional counselors who have shifted their position/job responsibilities, but not their professional counseling identity. Austin (2002) describes this phenomenon in terms of horizontal and vertical differentiation within a field. Horizontal differentiation among counselors is reflected in different specialties that individual counselors pursue, differentiating them from their peers. Vertical differentiation among counselors occurs when a counselor is charged with and accepts more authority and responsibility within a department. He or she moves "up" in the organizational hierarchy.

From the agency perspective, administrative supervisors are "middle managers." "The position of the . . . supervisor in the hierarchy of the agency . . . is clearly a middle management position. . . . A member of both management and the work group, he or she acts as a bridge between them" (Kadushin & Harness, 2002, p. 21). From their supervisees' perspectives, they are their "first-line supervisors" (Drucker, 1974; Hersey, Blanchard & Johnson, 2001; Martin, 2000). They have one or more employees reporting to them (Buckingham & Coffman, 1999). In fact, as soon as someone—from practicum student to counselor at an advanced level of professional development—reports to them, counselors become administrative supervisors.

Individuals in private practice or one-counselor departments in hospitals or centers fulfill these responsibilities for themselves or delegate them to someone else (Martin, 2000). A central agency may have satellite counseling centers; there may be one administrative counselor supervisor centrally housed with responsibility for the counselors and others in the satellites, or in addition to the centrally housed supervisor, there may be designated counseling department leaders at each of the satellites.

The larger the agency and the counseling staff, the more time is required in providing administrative supervision. Individual practitioners supervising themselves spend a fraction of their time on administrative supervision. For counseling department heads with 8–20 counselors reporting to them, fulfilling this role is a full-time job.

Effective administrative supervisors are valuable to their agencies. Successful organizations have one major attribute that sets them apart from unsuccessful organizations: dynamic and effective leadership, and great administrative supervisors (Hersey et al., 2001; Buckingham & Coffman, 1999). They are important to their supervisees: "Exiting employees say that the number one reason they are leaving organizations is their relationship with their immediate supervisors" (Kulik, 2004, p. 4).

The Administrative Supervisee

In their introduction to *Maslow on Management*, Stephens and Heil—the compilers of Maslow's papers on the topic—explain the "new vernacular for people: intellectual capital, human resources, knowledge workers, and all the other terms we have invented to disguise the fact that what we are speaking of are people and their untapped potential" (Maslow, 1998/1962, p. xvi). "Knowledge Workers" is the most widely used term for this category of employees.

Knowledge workers are employees who are well educated. They prepare themselves for a place in the profession: take the course work, earn the licenses/certificates, seek positions based on expectations. They get positions based on what employers' perceive they will bring to an agency. Their competence and commitment levels are their own personal properties. Thus, maintaining these at a satisfactory level and seeking ever higher levels of professionalism are the individuals' responsibility (Henderson & Gysbers, 1998).

Knowledge workers' "value lies between their ears" (Buckingham & Coffman, 1999, p. 23), in what they know and are able to do with that knowledge. They have information about how to do their jobs. Their resources are inherent in their "intellectual abilities, experience, task-knowledge and skills" (Fiedler, 1998, p. 336). Each professional is unique.

When professional counselors leave an agency, their knowledge and skills, their competence and commitment go with them (Buckingham & Coffman, 1999; Drucker, 1998). As such, they have primary responsibility for their own jobs and how they organize them. Knowledge workers:

> are responsible for their own jobs and for the relationships between individual jobs. They are responsible for thinking through *how* the work is to be done. They are responsible for meeting performance goals and for quality as well as for quantity. And they are responsible for improving work, job, tools, and processes, and their own skills. (Drucker, 1974, p. 273)

Knowledge workers are the guardians of their own standards. They can be productive only if they are responsible for their own jobs (Drucker, 1974). A goal for them is that each would "develop the capacity and be given the freedom to self-monitor and self-regulate their performance behaviors" (Martin, 2000, p. 212). To accomplish this, they need to be "self-sufficient. Self-sufficiency requires high levels of confidence, commitment, and motivation" (Hersey et al., 2001, p. 5). They need:

> to know where they stand. They need to know the people with whom they work. They need to know what they can expect. They need to know the values and rules of the organization. They do not function if the

environment is not predictable, not understandable, not known. (Drucker, 1999, p. 90)

True professionals need and want to grow professionally. They "ache to do good work" (Bennis & Biederman, 1997). They "need to experience challenge and opposition to grow and develop, to be well utilized, to be informed, and to be creative" (Covey, 1991, p. 297). When they do not find challenges and opportunities at work, they "go elsewhere, physically or mentally, to find their satisfaction and their sense of growth" (Covey, p. 297). Their motivation is enhanced by autonomy and empowerment. A "high need for achievement surfaces only when people believe they can influence the outcome" (Hersey et al., 2001, p. 48).

Professionals need, want and deserve supervision, leadership, management and administration. "It is important to provide direct supervision to counselors from colleagues who understand what they do" (E. Zambrano, personal communication, June 14, 2005). When they join with counselors in helping them reach their professional goals, both administrative supervisors and their supervisees are apt to achieve the objectives they seek.

The Standards Supporting Administrative Supervision in Counseling

Effective administrative supervisors adhere to established standards for counseling supervisors. While most of these standards focus on clinical supervision, they also inform and guide administrative supervision. Standards are expressed in the *Standards for Counseling Supervisors* (ACES, 1989; *Standards*, 1990) [they are in Appendix A]. Others are in the American Counseling Association (ACA) *Code of Ethics* (2005), especially those directly related to supervision, *Section F: Supervision, Training and Teaching* (ACA, pp. 13–16); *ACES Ethical Guidelines for Counseling Supervisors* (1993) [Appendix B]; *National Board for Certified Counselors (NBCC) Ethical Code* (2005); and the certification requirements and ethical standards for the "Approved Clinical Supervisor" certification, approved by NBCC and managed by the Center for Credentialing and Education [CCE] (2005).

Effective administrative supervisors know and apply the practice and ethical standards of their own counseling specialties (e.g., mental health, marriage and family, substance abuse, group work, school) and those of their supervisees as they are defined by their licenses or certifications. Many of these are published by Divisions of the American Counseling Association.

Every practicing counselor can, and should, benefit from professionally appropriate clinical *and* administrative supervision (ACES, 1993, Preamble). As described in *The New Handbook of Counseling Supervision* (Borders & Brown, 2005), the emphases in clinical supervision are on the details of counseling performance, cognition and thinking about clients and counseling, counselor self-awareness, and ethical standards, regulations and professional guidelines in the context of client work.

While administrative supervision also focuses on the details of counseling, it has additional purposes: establishing interpersonally healthy, productive and satisfying work environments, ensuring staff members' work contributes appropriately to the mission and policies of the agency, and managing the system for delivering the counseling services. Thus, in administrative supervision there is more emphasis on the context in which the counseling service is provided, counselors' specific job responsibilities, compliance with legal standards, policies, regulations and expectations for work habits than there is in clinical supervision.

As demonstrated throughout this *Handbook*, effective administrative supervision is based not only on solid counseling and clinical supervision standards and experience, but also on advanced education/training in the principles of supervision, leadership, management, and administration. Figure 1.1 defines who administrative supervisors in counseling are.

ADMINISTRATIVE SUPERVISORS' JOBS

Five Major Responsibilities

Administrative supervisors in counseling have five major responsibilities. They are responsible for:

1. Promoting client welfare;
2. Ensuring their departments contribute to the quality of their agencies' services and service delivery systems;
3. Supervising, leading, managing, and administering the people who report to them to help each individual advance toward optimum performance, productivity and job satisfaction;
4. Designing, maintaining and improving an effective and efficient counseling service delivery system for clients; and

---

Figure 1.1 Definition of Administrative Supervisors in Counseling

Between the counseling practitioners and the generalist administrators, individuals with counseling as their primary professional identity, background and experience fulfill administrative supervisory responsibilities on behalf of the clients served by their department, the counselors and other counseling department members who report to them, and the organizations in which they work. In overseeing the counseling service delivery system, they have responsibilities for the work of other professional counselors and related non-counseling employees, and have delegated authority and power from the agency's administrative structure. They work with the counselors who report to them as professionals and as agency employees.

5. Striving continuously for excellence in fulfillment of their administrative supervision responsibilities.

These major responsibilities are further detailed in Sections II–VI of this *Handbook*. Section II focuses on administrative supervisors' responsibilities to clients; Section III, those to the agency; Section IV, those to the counseling department staff; Section V, those to the counseling service delivery system; and Section VI, those to themselves.

Ten Administrative Supervisor Functions

In order to carry out these responsibilities, successful administrative supervisors perform 10 functions. They:

1. Identify a moral purpose for the work being done: establishing a vision, values and a meaningful work environment, and ensuring appropriate services for clients.
2. Develop the people with whom they work: building relationships, nurturing professional performance, motivating and communicating with others.
3. Have a global mindset: understanding and contributing to the agency and the community within which the work is done.
4. Lead change processes: planning, designing, implementing, evaluating and enhancing the service delivery system and the performance of the people who report to them, and helping those with whom they work to understand the forces of change.
5. Build a learning community: engendering commitment to continuous learning by all staff members as well as creating and sharing knowledge.
6. Organize and manage people, other resources, and activities: enhancing productivity and achievement and efficient use of resources.
7. Balance being a manager and a career professional: carrying out the management functions on behalf of clients and the agency without losing their professional identity and commitment.
8. Are and hold others for being accountable: monitoring and evaluating the work of the department and each individual in it.
9. Devise and implement systematic approaches to accomplishing the tasks of the department's work: developing systems and setting priorities.
10. Resolve problems related to clients, counselors and other staff members, the service delivery system, and the agency. (Synthesized from Arredondo, 1996; Drucker, 1974; Fullan, 2001; Henderson & Gysbers, 1998; Henderson & Gysbers, 2002; Hersey et al., 2001; Khandwalla, 2004; Tsui, 2005).

Eighteen Objectives

Administrative supervisors apply the 10 functions to the five responsibilities as they aim to accomplish the following 18 objectives. They aim to

I   Promote client welfare
   1. Maintain the clients as the number one priority;
   2. Be responsive to clients' diverse cultures; and,
   3. Uphold relevant legal, ethical and professional standards.

II Ensure their departments contribute to the quality of their agencies' services and service delivery systems
   4. Align the department with the agency's structure, mission, policies and practices;
   5. Communicate effectively within the agency and the department; and,
   6. Advocate for the clients, counseling and counselors within and outside the agency.

III Supervise, lead, manage and administer the people who report to them to help each individual advance toward optimum performance, productivity and job satisfaction
   7. Establish professional cultures that support excellence;
   8. Build healthy, meaningful professional and personal relationships with each staff member;
   9. Nurture continuous improvement of each staff member's performance;
   10. Apply their own models for providing effective administrative supervision;
   11. Organize staff members for effective service delivery;
   12. Implement effectively a performance management system; and,
   13. Evaluate fairly each staff member's performance.

IV Design, maintain and improve an effective and efficient service delivery system for clients
   14. Operationalize the vision for the department;
   15. Acquire and manage human, financial and political resources;
   16. Improve continuously the counseling service delivery system; and,
   17. Lead the process to plan, design, deliver and evaluate the service delivery system.

V   Strive continuously for excellence in fulfillment of administrative supervision responsibilities
   18. Develop continually their own supervisory competence.

Drucker (1974) warned that "unless objectives are converted into action, they are not objectives; they are dreams" (p. 119). Chapters 2 through 18 of this *Handbook*, discuss specific ways administrative supervisors apply their functions in addressing the objectives of their job responsibilities and resolve some of the problems many encounter. Chapter 19 describes competencies that effective administrative supervisors need to develop over the course of their careers.

HOW ADMINISTRATIVE SUPERVISORS ACHIEVE THEIR OBJECTIVES

Fulfilling Four Roles

In carrying out their job responsibilities effectively and efficiently, administrative supervisors fulfill four distinct roles: supervisor, leader, manager, and administrator (Henderson & Gysbers, 1998, 2002). Effective administrative supervisors use these roles intentionally, selecting the role most apt to lead to the desired results. They are clear about each role's purpose and associated tasks. Key tasks often influence the relationship. In each situation, they are aware of their level of responsibility to the clients and the agency, and the related degree of legitimate authority. They are aware of the relevant standards for counseling supervisors' performance (ACES, 1989; *Standards*, 1990), and the balance of power appropriate to a particular situation.

It is important that supervisors and supervisees both understand these roles and their differences. Effective administrative supervisors accept responsibility to "minimize potential conflicts" across these roles by carefully explaining to their supervisees "the expectations and responsibilities associated with each supervisory role" (ACES, 1993, 2.09). When supervisors move from one role to another both they and their supervisees are clear about the role being fulfilled and what the boundaries are. As with clients, shifting from role to role can result in a dual-relationship if either the supervisor or supervisee is not clear about the role being played in the current situation. The characteristics of each role are summarized in Figure 1.2.

Using Their Power Effectively

Due to their positions in their agencies, administrative supervisors have authority over supervisees.

> Authority is the right to issue directives, exercise control and require compliance. It is the right to determine the behavior of others and to make decisions that guide the action of others. In the most uncompromising sense, authority is the right to demand obedience; those subject to authority have the duty to obey. (Kadushin & Harness, 2002, p. 84)

They also have power based on their professional knowledge and experience, and through their representation of their clients and the clients' rights (Henderson & Gysbers, 1998; Hersey et al., 2001; Kadushin & Harness, 2002). Power is defined as the ability to influence others to behave in desirable ways. In order to use their power, effective leaders translate it into influence.

Effective administrative supervisors acknowledge the power they have

Figure 1.2 Administrative Supervisors' Roles

Supervisor

Purpose	Example Tasks	Supervisor Standards	Level of Responsibility	Relationship Characteristics	Balance of Power
Enhance professional practice Maintain good standards of work* Uphold ethical & professional standards**	Provide data-based feedback & opportunities for learning	1. Effective counselors 5. Supervision methods & techniques 7. Case conceptualization & management 8. Assessment & evaluation of clients	Appropriate professional services	Collegiality "Coach or consultant... mutual professional respect and remoteness"****	**Supervisee-**Supervisor

* Kadushin & Harness, 2002.
** Austin, 2002.
*** Bekkers & Homburg, 2002, p. 134.

Leader

Purpose	Example Tasks	Supervisor Standards	Level of Responsibility	Relationship Characteristics	Balance of Power
Influence others to aim for excellent performance Develop supervisee autonomy*	Model excellence Collaborate	4. Supervisory relationship 6. Counselor development 11. Research in counseling & supervision Supervisor development	Professional	Mutuality	Supervisor-Supervisee

* Drucker, 1974.

Manager

Purpose	Example Tasks	Supervisor Standards	Level of Responsibility	Relationship Characteristics	Balance of Power
Achieve organizational goals Adhere to policies & rules Maintain minimum standards Acquire & use resources efficiently	Implement policy-related procedures* Acquire resources Organize work & work place** Hold counselors accountable Manage crises*	9. Oral & written reporting & recording	Link between staff and agency	"Lack of mutual empathy and a quest for control, compliance and obedience"*** "Police officer"****	**Supervisor**-Supervisee

* Khandwalla, 2004.
** Kadushin & Harness, 2002.
*** Bekkers & Homburg, 2002, p. 134.
**** Bekkers & Homburg, p. 133.

Administrator

Purpose	Example Tasks	Supervisor Standards	Level of Responsibility	Relationship Characteristics	Balance of Power
Evaluate quality & quantity of work Advocate for clients & counselors Connect to agency	Formulate policies Set objectives Contribute to agency mission Hire & fire staff members Recommend contract status & pay	3. Ethical, legal & regulatory 10. Evaluation of counseling performance Executive (administrative skills)	Primary allegiance to agency	Delegated authority from agency to supervisor "Networker"*	**Supervisor**-Supervisee

* Bekkers & Homburg, 2002, p. 134.

and are also aware of its limitations. In working with their administrators, supervisees and clients, they learn how far their power goes and into what areas. Although power in the supervisor-supervisee relationship is weighted to the supervisors' side, effective administrative supervisors also recognize that their capacity to influence their supervisees depends in large measure on their supervisees granting them the power to influence them (Raven, 1993, 2004).

Sources of power

Administrative supervisors have resources "to draw upon to exercise influence" (Raven, 1993, p. 232). Seven resources provide different bases for their power: legitimate, information, coercive, expert, referent, reward and connection (French & Raven, 1959; Raven, 2004; Hersey et al., 2001). Effective administrative supervisors capitalize on all seven of these. Figure 1.3 displays the sources of each power base, identifies the administrative supervisors' roles best supported by each, and provides examples of when they are useful.

For a power base to be useful with a supervisee, the administrative supervisor must not only have the capacity implied in the power base, but the supervisee must also perceive that the supervisor has it. For example, a supervisee has to perceive that a supervisor is an effective counselor in order for the supervisor to draw on the expert power base.

Effective administrative supervisors also understand that supervisees perceive some of the power bases as "harsh" and others as "soft." Use of the power bases of impersonal coercion and reward, and personal coercion are more likely to be perceived as "harsh." Use of expert, referent, information, and personal reward power bases are more likely to be perceived as "soft" (Raven, Schwarzwald & Koslowsky, 1998). Use of the harsh power bases is more likely to be perceived by supervisees as supervisors exerting their power *over* them. Use of the soft power bases is more likely to be perceived as gaining power *with* their supervisees. Use of the soft power bases has been found to be more likely to yield compliance and higher degrees of job satisfaction than use of the harsh bases (Raven et al.). "The definitions of harsh and soft factors and their components are, for all practical purposes, stable across cultures and settings" (Schwarzwald, Koslowsky & Agassi, 2001, p. 288).

Good use of power

To be most influential, administrative supervisors are aware of their power and are comfortable with it. Their challenge is to use it well. Appropriate use of power strengthens it. Misuse of it weakens it. Supervisors who abuse their power are "lousy" supervisors (Magnuson, Wilcoxen & Norem, 2000, p. 193). Effective administrative supervisors use their power for the right purposes and in the right amounts. They use power bases that are appropriate to specific leadership situations.

Figure 1.3 Administrative Supervisors' Power Bases

Power Base	Source	Role(s) Supported	Example(s) of Usefulness
Legitimate	Delegated authority Position Supervisees' acknowledgement of legitimacy	Manager Administrator All roles	Holding counselors' accountable
Information	Access to agency & profession Sharing meaningful information	All roles	Helping counselors understand and have input to work-related decisions Helping other agency staff understand counselors & counseling
Coercive: Impersonal Personal	Capacity to mete out negative consequences Judicious use	Administrator	Addressing incompetence or insubordination Forcing compliance
Expert	Expertise in counseling, supervision & administration	Supervisor Leader	Helping counselors enhance their performance levels
Referent	Personal traits Rapport Commonalities	Leader	Attracting counselors to follow
Reward: Impersonal Personal	Capacity to mete out positive consequences: impersonal (e.g., increased pay, better assignments, promotions) or personal (e.g., recognition, approval, acceptance)	Administrator Manager Leader	Encouraging counselors' motivation & commitment
Connection	Ability to accomplish beneficial results by influencing influential people inside or outside the agency	Manager— organizational connections Leader— professional connections	Acquiring resources

Right purposes. The right purposes for administrative supervisors' use of power are those in the best interests of the clients, the agency, and/or the department staff members. Maslow (1998/1962) stated that good power "is the power to do what needs doing, to do the job that ought to be done, to solve the objective problem, to get the job done that needs to be done" (p. 156). Good use of power is using it to ensure that clients are treated well and served by competent staff members.

Supervisors' power is also used well when it is used to empower supervisees. Effective administrative supervisors are empowering when they help supervisees develop their own talents and contributions (Martin, 2000), and when they trust them to become self-managing, independent, and mature workers. Supervisees are empowered by working within structures and systems, and knowing the standards for accountability, thereby allowing for self-evaluation and meaningful external evaluation (Covey, 1991). Empowering administrative supervisors help their supervisees build their own power bases for the good of their departments' clients, services and agency position.

Administrative supervisors abuse their power when they use it to meet their own needs or wants. People who simply want to be boss and have power over other people are not effective supervisors. "Such people are apt to use power very badly; to overcome, over-power, use it for their own selfish gratification" (Maslow, 1998/1962, p. 152). Abuse of power is also seen in supervisors who would impose their beliefs and styles on their supervisees.

Right amounts. Using power well entails exerting an amount of power appropriate to a situation. Effective administrative supervisors recognize that they are neither powerless nor omnipotent. They avoid over- or under-using their power. Over-using power means using more power than is needed in a situation. It is akin to (and may be the result of) over-reacting. If supervisors enter into a supervisory situation and unload "both barrels," they are over-using the power available to them. Under-using power means using less of their power than is called for in particular situations.

Right power bases. An axiom of using power well is being flexible enough to draw from the power base that is most appropriate to a specific situation. Administrative supervisors who are effective at influencing their supervisees make conscious choices about which power base would be most effective in a situation (Henderson & Gysbers, 1998). They use power that fits the developmental level of the supervisee being influenced. It is one of the ways supervisors adapt their behavior to match the supervisory incident.

Effective administrative supervisors draw from the power base that is most directly related to the supervisees' targeted behavior. For example, if feedback is provided that targets counselors' professional performance, supervisors' expert power may be the most meaningful. If feedback is provided that targets counselors' compliance with agency regulations, supervisors' legitimate power may be most meaningful. Selecting power bases that are not appropriate to the situation is another way to abuse or misuse supervisor power. In Magnuson et al.'s (2000) terms, the supervision provided is "developmentally inappropriate" (p. 196), as will be further discussed in Chapter 10.

SUMMARY

Administrative supervisors work in a variety of mental health agencies and are variously placed in their agencies' organizations. As middle managers/first line supervisors of counselors, they are grounded by their counseling identity and accept additional responsibilities for their administrative supervisees' work. Administrative supervisees' are knowledge workers, and as professionals, are primarily responsible for their own competence, commitment and job fulfillment. Administrative supervisors strive for adherence to and promote application of professional standards in carrying out their five responsibilities and applying ten functions as they address 18 objectives. To do this, they fulfill four roles and draw on eight power bases effectively.

II

Administrative Supervisors: Promote Client Welfare

- Maintain the Clients as the Number One Priority

- Be Responsive to Clients' Diverse Cultures

- Uphold Relevant Legal, Ethical, and Professional Standards

2

Maintain the Clients as the Number One Priority

Effective administrative supervisors accept responsibility for ensuring their supervisees hold their clients as the primary focus for their work. They articulate their visions for their counseling departments and model the professional values inherent in this vision. Effective leaders are "vision creators" (Hersey, Blanchard & Johnson, 2001, p. 79) for their staff members. They capture the commitment of their staff members. The collective vision and values of administrative supervisors and supervisees undergird the department's mission. Supervisors' visions are sources of power and energy, "both the energy that empowers others and the energy that results in superior performance. . . . Performance follows vision" (Quigley, 1994, p. 40). A successful counseling practice is built on the practice initiator's passions and followers who share that passion.

Professional counselors agree that helping their clients is the primary purpose of their work, and that it is their primary responsibility "to respect the dignity and to promote the welfare of clients" (American Counseling Association [ACA], 2005, A.1.a). In daily work, however, that focus sometimes gets fuzzy; for example, when other things arise that are important to them distract them at work. They can be preoccupied with their own professional or work-related needs or dissatisfactions. They can have personal issues of their own. Altruism can be displaced by cynicism. Administrative supervisors can lose sight of clients when much of their time is spent in working with counselors. At times, administrative supervisors and staff members alike focus on things, on other people, on regulations, on order, or on procedures rather than on their clients and on what is in their best interest.

ARTICULATE A VISION

To be an effective administrative supervisor, articulate your vision for the department, identifying the moral purpose of its work (Fullan, 2001). The moral purpose of counseling is helping clients make decisions and achieve goals that would enhance their growth and development, and to help them resolve issues or solve problems. A vision is a mental picture "painted by the organization's core values and desires" (Hersey et al., 2001, p. 82). To be complete, picture three interrelated elements: the department's clients, the counselors and other staff members, and the services it provides. One administrative supervisor of school counselors states her premise: "My client is 'the student' and the program that serves them. I support and mentor staff members to that end—and encourage them to seek support and personal growth" (D. A. Healy, personal communication, June 13, 2005).

Clients

To be successful, begin with the premise that clients are at the center of the picture. Ensure that you and your staff members know them in detail as unique individuals and also as members of groups (Locke, 1990). Have a framework for guiding your understanding of individuals' uniqueness, such as Arredondo's "Dimensions of Personal Identity model" (1996, p. 8).

Your vision focuses on specialized groups of clients that fit within the mission of your counseling practice or mental health service-providing agency; for example, if you work in a counseling department within a State's Rehabilitation agency, you envision a different set of clients than those if you work in a private practice that specializes in helping young adult women. In the former, your clients' primary needs are for rehabilitation assistance. In the latter, their priorities are the developmental issues associated with being young adult women.

To be client-focused, you and your staff members are aware of typical patterns of behaviors and issues that are often associated with your group of clients. This includes knowing the typical characteristics of people in their developmental stage. Know about their cultures and the communities they come from and/or live in, but be careful not to impose stereotypes on them. As used in this *Handbook*, the word culture is inclusive (Stone, 1997)—i.e., including race/ethnicity, gender, age, marital status, religion, economic status, abilities/disabilities, etc. Learn the view of counseling in the clients' culture/subculture.

Knowing your clients includes knowing who the "significant others" are in their lives and how they might be helpful in counseling. While this is required for minors and others who are deemed not competent to consent to counseling, it is important for many clients and client groups. Their support networks may include "religious/spiritual/community leaders, family members, friends," or guardians (ACA, 2005, A.1.d).

You and your counseling department staff members learn about your clients' perceived needs, and what additional needs they may have, needs that they may not be aware of. With increasing specialized experience, counselors identify patterns of needs and recurrent issues of their clients; for example, counselors of young adolescents know that people in this age group tend to lose some of their self-esteem; counselors of post-natal women know that they are often depressed; counselors of retiring athletes know that they often lack goals for their next career; counselors of racial/ethnic minorities know that some clients have a history of "mistrust of authority figures that represent the dominant system" (Engels et al., 2004, p. 47). Continually helping your supervisees to identify the recurrent issues presented by your clients and to develop their specialization in responding to these issues is one way to hold clients as the top priority.

You and your counselors should recognize that different portions of your clientele have different levels of needs for counseling services. Clients who struggle to accomplish developmental tasks need *developmental assistance*. Clients who face problems, issues or barriers that threaten their healthy accomplishment of these tasks need interventions that *prevent* them from getting farther off track. Clients whose healthy development has been derailed by their own choices or because of their situations need *rehabilitative assistance*. Clients who are facing situations that are life threatening or that may severely disrupt their continued development need *crisis* responses. Clients at different levels of need require different counseling interventions (Gysbers & Henderson, 2006).

In addition to knowing your clients' needs, be sure you and your staff members know their "wants." Often clients articulate what they want. At a minimum they should be asked, but some of their wants may have to be discerned. Some universal wants are addressed in the profession's codes of ethics as "clients rights" (ACA, 2005; American School Counselor Association [ASCA], 2004a; American Mental Health Counselors Association [AMHCA], 2000) or responsibilities to clients (ASCA, 2004b). Anticipate your clients' "wants" so that they can be readily met. They want "quality service provided by concerned, trained, professional and competent staff" (AMHCA, 2000, Principle 2, B). They want results. They want to be engaged in, and feel comfortable in, the counseling experience. They want good relationships with their counselors and with others with whom they come in contact (Groth, 2004).

Counselors and Other Staff Members

Although each administrative supervisor has his/her own vision, there is some profession-wide agreement as to how client-focused counselors think, feel, and act. They are able to put themselves in each of their client's shoes, and seek to understand others' values, beliefs, identities and orientations, and work within them (Engels et al., 2004). In counseling, their clients' interests supersede their own. Client-focused counselors are genuinely interested in their clients and embrace who they are. They do not impose their values onto them, but empower them by permitting them to express their own thoughts and feelings. By not telling them what to do, giving them quick fixes or superficial advice, counselors (and their supervisors) demonstrate their belief that clients are able to do their own work. They "avoid exploiting the trust and fostering dependency of their clients" (AMHCA, 2000, 1.A., 2). Envision counselors who are engaged and fully present with their clients, and who continually strive to provide excellent services in order to best serve them.

What people talk about and how they talk reflects their thoughts and feelings. When counselors are holding their clients as the top priority for their work, they consider their clients in every discussion, every thought, position taken, and action done. "How will this affect this client?" "What will Sammy do when this happens?" Encourage these conversations.

Client-focused Services

To maintain the clients as your top priority, define what you want the department to look and feel like to the clients. Your vision is "based on cultural relativity, open-mindedness, reciprocity, and continuous learnings" (Arredondo, 1996, p. 5). Strive to establish an atmosphere, procedures, and practices that aim for customer satisfaction.

Client-friendly atmosphere. Clients respond to the physical, professional and interpersonal atmosphere of an office(s) (Harris, 2002). "Clients" include not only individuals with whom a counselor has already established a relationship, but also individuals "seeking or referred to your professional services for help with problem resolution or decision making" (ACA, 2005, Glossary). The atmosphere you want must pervade the department and include all staff members.

The first interaction between clients and the department occurs when potential or existing clients enter the offices. A client-friendly atmosphere is a place where clients feel comfortable. You want them to feel that they are in the right place, that they fit, and that this department is where they personally belong, where they can accomplish their goals. One way to do this is to enter the office and scrutinize it from the clients' perspective. From the entryway through the reception area and into the offices, client-friendly environments exude warmth, comfort and orderliness. Even the décor "speaks" to clients, helps them feel that this is a place where they can relax and focus on the work to come. The pictures on the walls, the plants in the room, the books on the shelves, the magazines on the tables impart both personal and professional messages (B. A. Durodoye, personal communication, December 13, 2005). If the department's work is with children, children's furniture, toys and books help them know that this is a place for them. If you primarily serve a specific ethnic group, the artwork and décor should reflect their ethnicity and contain their cultural preferences. If your work is with senior citizens or disabled clients, you should make accommodations that allow easy access for individuals using wheel chairs, walkers, canes or other assistive devices.

Clients come to a counseling department for professional services, and the physical environment helps set the professional tone. Professional messages may be conveyed by the visibility of licenses and credentials, and pamphlets or other materials on topics relevant to the expertise of the counseling department. Pictures can include counselors working with clients that reflect their primary clients. While some informality suggests comfort, a business-like tone is appreciated—suggesting professionalism.

All the department staff members that clients see and hear set the interpersonal atmosphere. They want to feel welcome. What staff members model is how clients perceive they will be treated. Everyone honoring the worth and dignity of every individual suggests to clients they, too, will be treated well. So, too, do the interactions between staff members and clients/potential clients, and among staff members. They should be pleasant, respectful, inclusive, nondiscriminatory, trusting, positive, and happy. Everyone who comes in close proximity to your clients should smile and acknowledge them. The individual designated to help a client directly should speak to them on first sighting, even if it is to say "Good morning. I'll be with you as soon as I finish helping" another.

Client-friendly counseling practices. In keeping the client as the number one priority of the department, envision ways to make the entry into counseling client-friendly. Taking in new clients entails gathering (often, a lot of) information about them. The ultimate goal for a counseling department is to serve the right clients and to serve them well. The "right" clients are those whose needs and wants can best be met by the counseling department and within the context of the agency's mission. While these may not be identified until the department's mission is clarified, envision how intake procedures will increase the likelihood of success for clients and make best use of the counselors' expertise.

Intake procedures usually entail gathering identification and financial data from clients as well as information about their needs for counseling. Because these are often the first extended interactions between clients and agency staff, determine how the information can best be gathered and documented. Human interactions are friendlier than human-and-form interactions. If this information is being gathered by a counselor, it is, from the clients' perspective, the beginning of the counseling relationship. How it is conducted may facilitate or hinder rapport building.

Registration, intake, informed consent, and clients' rights forms are often developed by an agency to gather the information it needs and to meet its financial, legal or ethical obligations. They are not really focused on the clients. They are agency-focused. They can be carefully crafted to meet an agency's needs *and* attend to the sensibilities of clients; for example, an individual's racial/ethnic identification may be more complex to them than "White," "African American," "Asian," or "Latino." What about Arabs and Indians? "Whites" may think of themselves as Irish or Italian. Some Black people do not identify themselves as "African" based. Some are bi-racial. Initially, forms should be used to gather only the minimum information needed to begin to determine your clients' needs, suitability and eligibility for services. It is your responsibility to ensure that the department's forms are sensitive and "client-friendly."

The same is true for regular practices that are not form bound, but are left to explanation instead; such as, the advantages and limits of confidentiality. It is more client-friendly to explain the advantages than the limits, but it is also legally and ethically important to explain the limits. These conversations are best held when you and your staff members keep the client's perspective in mind—e.g., spending as much or more time on when it does hold than on its exceptions.

If, in clarifying the needs, wants, expectations and goals of potential clients, it becomes clear that the agency is not right for them, you and your professional counselors should be forthright in telling them. The department is still responsible to assist them to get to a more appropriate resource for help. Abandonment is prohibited by counselors' ethical standards (ACA, 2005, A.11. a). It is your responsibility to know about referral sources that are "clinically and culturally appropriate" (ACA, 2005, A.11. a & b) and to ensure that all staff members have and use this information when needed.

Customer satisfaction. Your vision should include goals for customer satisfaction that result from quality services (Hersey et al., 2001; Quigley, 1994). Envision what satisfies your customers. Helping clients clarify their expectations is an essential step toward satisfaction in the long run. Professionals are responsible for helping clients establish attainable, meaningful and realistic goals. In order for their expectations to be reasonable, potential clients need to understand what counselors can realistically help them achieve and how they plan to help them (ACA, 2005, A.2.a & b).

Your clients' (customers') satisfaction is tied to their perceptions of having received not only relevant services but also high quality services. "High quality" is perceived when clients succeed in accomplishing their goals, and, better still, if they go beyond their original goals. Counselors' services may be perceived to be of high quality even if clients do not achieve their goals if the clients accept responsibility for their lack of accomplishment.

To be relevant, a vision includes pictures of effective counseling for the specialization that fits the agency. Assure high quality services by monitoring the services the staff members provide (Chapter 18). Ensuring high quality services may mean your carrying out direct service responsibilities in critical areas. As one long-term administrative supervisor writes in explaining her job description, in order to ensure appropriate services to very needy clients, her duties included such direct services as:

Evaluating the appropriateness of prospective residents [in a temporary residential program for runaway adolescents].

Doing initial danger-to-self assessments on shelter clients and recommending an assessment by a physician if needed.

Developing a program procedure for evaluating and addressing clients who exhibit a danger to self or others. (D. J. Martin, personal communication, July 30, 2005)

After the termination of the counseling process, clients' achievement of results and degrees of satisfaction are evaluated. Example questions you might ask are "Were the clients' expectations met?" "Were their goals accomplished?" "Were they satisfied with the experience?" These evaluations are developed and used for the purpose of improving the client-focus of the department as well as the quality of services (Chapter 18).

Work environment. Counselors are more apt to focus on their clients as their number one priority, when they work in a productive and happy work environment. In their vision for themselves, "the best managers increase the health of the workers whom they manage" (Maslow, 1998/1962, p. 94). Be not only client-focused, but also supervisee-focused.

MODEL PROFESSIONAL VALUES

To set the tone for a client-focused department, begin by articulating and modeling the professional values inherent in your vision. Values are "the guidelines by which the organization expects its members to conduct themselves" (Quigley, 1994, p. 40). As the leader, "take what you believe in, something that flows out of your core values, and make it happen" (Hersey et al., 2001, p. 1). This means being aware of your own vision-related values: those relating to clients, counselors and counseling.

It is critical to make clear distinctions between professional and personal values. The former apply at work, and, of course, should not be incongruent with your personal values. You also hold professional values regarding your own work and that of the agency. The counseling profession has core values, many of which are expressed in its ethical standards (e.g., ACA, 2005; ASCA, 2004a; AMHCA, 2000). Hopefully you endorse the five "moral principles" (Forester-Miller & Davis, 1996) that are well accepted as signposts for ethical counseling practice: autonomy, beneficence, fidelity, justice and nonmaleficence.

To be congruent, your professional values should also align with those of the agency in which you work. Incongruence leads to frustration. If an agency demands that you do things contrary to the profession's values (e.g., that are unethical), the ethical standards suggest that the two sets of values should be in agreement or you should cause change (ACA, 2005, D.1.g).

Good managers acknowledge that they are important to their staff members, and are aware that staff will scrutinize every detail to learn as much as they can about you. Be aware that your supervisees read even your unspoken or unarticulated values and beliefs. Thus, not only must you be aware of your values, you must articulate them so that your supervisees are more apt to understand them and join with you.

Model

Values-conscious administrative supervisors recognize the power of modeling their values. It is through modeling that others develop trust in your authenticity and understand the meaning of your values more fully. As one administrative supervisor wrote, as advice to new administrative supervisors, "Believe in greatness for the clients, counselors, program, and yourself as a leader" (T. E. Miller, personal communication, June 13, 2005). She models that belief in every conversation with counselors and others, and in every decision she makes. She is particularly deliberate about taking every conversation back to the clients, their needs and goals.

Based on practicing adherence to your own, the profession's and your agency's values, develop moral sensitivity and attend to moral issues that arise in your practice (Erwin, 2000). For example, history, research and common practice provide other accepted professional values, such as empathy, client privacy and safety, confidentiality. But even these are not clearly understood or defined in the same way by different individuals. Empathy, for example is a difficult concept—particularly for those counselors who do not come by it naturally. One administrative supervisor, during her staff meetings, held a discussion of its meaning—and was taken aback by her supervisees' lack of depth of understanding. In her supervisory conferences with staff members she began to point out examples of when counselors were or were not empathic with their clients (M. L. Libby, personal communication, December, 2005).

Identify Assumptions

Values and beliefs may be assumptions that individuals make. They are tricky as they are often hidden. They are often thoughts that individuals take for granted, but that others may not have thought about or agree with. You are most effective when you learn to listen to your own and others' assumptions, knowing they shape and guide people's actions.

Positive assumptions are more apt to lead to positive results. Negative assumptions interfere with achievement of good results. If you assume your supervisees want to develop their professionalism continuously (a premise of effective supervision), you are more apt to nurture your supervisees' development than if you do not. If you assume your supervisees must be forced to change, you are apt to engender resistance. Some recurrent assumptions about clients have negative impacts, e.g., our clients—"these people"—cannot really do this work. Our program is underfunded and so will never live up to the profession's standards. Help yourself and your supervisees bring work-related assumptions out into the open for discussion.

CLARIFY THE MISSION

Administrative supervisors' visions include their ideas about what clients would be served best by the counseling department to achieve what outcomes, about how counselors' professional competencies would be used best, and about the most relevant structure of the service delivery system. These constitute the mission of the counseling department. Clarifying the mission allows you to express your vision and provides opportunities for other staff members to blend their ideas into it. By engaging your entire staff in developing the department mission and mission statement, you focus the entire department toward one common vision.

Your mission "provides the foundation for priorities, strategies, plans, and work assignments . . . It specifies the fundamental reason why an organization exists" (Pearce & David, 1987, p. 109). Your mission should be inspiring, enduring, "project a sense of worth, intent, and shared expectations and should state intrinsic value of the . . . services" (David & David, 2003, p. 11). Working with your staff to craft a mission statement begins the process of operationalizing your vision and set of values. This is discussed more fully in Chapter 15.

SUMMARY

To build and maintain an effective department, strive to hold your clients as its number one priority. You accomplish this by clarifying your vision for clients being served well by your staff members. Your vision should be based on knowing your clients in detail, how client-focused counselors think, feel and act, and on what constitute client-friendly practices. Model professional values that lead to client-focused professional work. Your vision and values are the basis for the mission of the counseling department.

SUPERVISORS' CHALLENGE AND RESPONSES

Supervisors' Challenge: Unwell Supervisees

While most counselors are aware of their ethical responsibility to hold clients as their number one priority, their personal issues can get in the way and cause disengagement from their clients. Counselors are human and have their share of emotional problems (e.g., anger, depression, low self-esteem), family problems (e.g., substance abuse, divorce, child rearing), and career problems (e.g., lack of fulfillment, concern about working conditions, sexual harassment). Often, pursuit of further education (e.g., Ph.D. programs) disrupts their client-work centered focus. When these problems become the primary focus for them, counselors slip towards impairment.

Supervisors' Responses

Successful administrative supervisors are aware that counseling effectiveness is correlated to the mental health of counselors, and support counselors and other supervisees in taking care of their own mental health. As one administrative supervisor said it, "I make sure they practice self-care in order to negotiate through the times of burn-out and compassion fatigue that can pop up" (S. Clifford, personal communication, August 14, 2005).

A recommended way to ward off some of the impact of personal issues on employees is for agencies "to support wellness: educate staff and supervisors on the concepts of impairment, vicarious traumatization, compassion fatigue and wellness": develop wellness programs, provide professional and peer supervision, maintain manageable caseloads, encourage/require vacations, do not reward "workaholism," encourage diversity of tasks and new areas of interest/practice, and establish employee assistance programs (EAP)'s (ACA, n.d.e., "What Agencies Can Do to Support Wellness, ¶ 1).

In cases of employees being distracted by concerns about conditions in the work environment, administrative supervisors attend to issues that are within their purview. The more workers care about their work, the more emotional they can become over issues that affect that work. Just as they can feel gratitude, excitement, happiness or pride, they can become angry, fearful, sad or guilty if something is not going right; for example, if a client's complaint is supported by agency administration. The causes of supervisees' emotionalism need to be explored by administrative supervisors, who in turn can work with individuals (or groups) to address the issues (Beck, 2005).

Pro-active administrative supervisors help troubled counselors address their issues when they first arise. Depending on the degree of a counselor's focus on their own problems, supervisors consult about and intervene in the issue. They are careful to avoid dual relationships (e.g., becoming a counselor's counselor). And, recognizing that "it is human nature to react to problems in an emotional way" (Hersey et al., 2001, p. 8), they avoid their own emotional responses and maintain professional objectivity.

Providing administrative supervision skillfully entails using a problem-solving process model (Hersey et al., 2001). Napier and Gershenfeld (2004) suggest a rational problem solving process, with the caveat that:

Figure 2.1 Six Stage Problem Solving Process

1 Identify the problem.
2 Analyze it in sufficient detail.
3 Consider alternative solutions and their probable outcomes.
4 Select the one most likely to reap the desired outcome(s) within existing parameters.
5 Implement the chosen alternative.
6 Evaluate the actual outcome(s).

the study of problem solving by social scientists has shown the process to be not the straightforward one dictated by the scientific method, but rather a nightmare of complexity. . . . The fact is that no one model can account for all the complexity and richness of the human spirit and behavior. (p. 305)

Nonetheless, having an outline that guides supervisors' approaches to these and other problems is useful; one is outlined in Figure 2.1. "The key involves bringing to the surface as many of the existing solutions as possible" (Napier & Gershenfeld, p. 318).

3

Be Responsive to Clients' Diverse Cultures

To best serve the counseling clients, administrative supervisors lead their counseling departments' (and agencies') efforts to be culturally responsive to their clients. People who come for counseling present a wide range of issues and levels of need. They have problems, issues, or situations that they need help to resolve or learn to cope with. They may be struggling with decisions about their jobs or relationships with significant others. Breaking habits of risky behaviors or managing addictions require support. They may feel depressed or suicidal. Any combination of personal or situational issues is simmering within them. They are timid and anxious when they come. They don't know what to expect, but they are hopeful. Added to this is that many of them feel socially marginalized and oppressed, feel they are members of minority groups—groups that are different from those they perceive to be dominant.

When they first interact with a counselor, the counselor is apt to be White, female, well educated, and of the middle class (D'Andrea & Daniels, 1997; Pack-Brown, 1999). While counselors' being of the same race or ethnicity as their clients does not automatically guarantee a successful counseling experience, Pope-Davis et al. (2002) found that "clients who defined themselves and their presenting problem using cultural constructs seemed to prefer racially or gender-similar counselors" (p. 384). The commonality of race and ethnicity is a good place to start a relationship, but differences in educational and/or economic class levels and other factors are often present.

To be inclusive with your clients, you and the staff members respect and work within these differences. You help your supervisees understand the impact of culture on individuals and on counseling, and why cultural responsiveness is essential. You use multiple strategies for deepening counselors' cross-cultural competence and effectiveness. You also strive to attain a counseling staff that is representative of your clients' cultures, and a service delivery system that is culturally appropriate.

BE CULTURALLY RESPONSIVE

Cultural Differences

Strive to ensure that you and your supervisees are aware of the possible differences in the "social and cultural contexts" (American Counseling Association [ACA], 2005, Preamble) in which you and your clients live or have lived. Possible differences occur in racial and ethnic cultures, including their use of languages other than English. Individuals' social and cultural contexts are related to people's genders, and sexual orientations—e.g., gay, lesbian, bisexual, transgendered. Clients may come from a variety of family configurations (e.g., single, married, cohabiting, extended; only children, many children) and life styles (e.g., mobile, migrant, homeless). There may be differences related to economic class. Additionally, social and cultural contexts are defined by an endless variety of other social factors—e.g., levels of education and/or work experience, religious affiliations, physical or mental conditions, family members who are incarcerated or live outside the law.

Clients prefer counselors who they perceive have something in common with them (Esters & Ledoux, 2001; Vontress & Jackson, 2004). Those preferences may go beyond "readily discernible physical characteristics" (Esters & Ledoux, p. 169). In lieu of racial similarities, they may prefer counselors with the "same attitudes and values, same background and socioeconomic status, [and] same sex" (Esters & Ledoux, p. 168).

To be culturally responsive, professional counselors are dually attentive to similarities and differences between themselves and their clients (Carbaugh, 2005). "Counselors' ability to effectively communicate and interact with clients in therapeutic relationships involves the counselors' competence in focusing on both similarities and differences (Miville et al., 1999)" (Constantine et al., 2001, p. 14). To work effectively together, counselors and clients find the commonalities upon which to build their relationship, and they minimize the impact of their differences.

Salient differences exist between counselors who live and have lived as part of the "majority" culture—the dominant cultural group that exercises the most power and influence—and clients who live or have lived as part of a "minority" culture. To be culturally responsive, you and your supervisees understand your minority clients' experiences with dominance, oppression, racism, prejudice, and stereotyping, and their resultant worldviews. You all know that "environmental oppression contributes to psychological distress" (Arredondo & Toporek, 2004, p. 47). "Discrimination, isolation, racism, differential treatment . . . [result] in feelings of confusion, anger, outrage, and discouragement" (Stoltenberg, McNeil & Delworth, 1998, p. 122). This is true for individuals and, collectively, for groups. Effective counselors consider these contextually based feelings and related behaviors in addition to those associated with clients' presenting problems.

Individuals and Group Members

Cultural responsiveness means that you and your department staff members not only accept clients as individuals, but you also reach across cultures and possible cultural barriers to connect with them as members of groups.

The views of persons as individuals or as members of groups must be kept in balance lest the counselor make errors in interactions with the culturally different. The view that the culturally different individual is a unique being whose differences are individual alone will result in a failure to value the culture from which the individual comes. The view that the culturally different individual is a member of a specific group whose behaviors are based on the culture of the group only will result in stereotyping. (Locke, 1990)

Impact of Unacknowledged Differences

When clients perceive that their counselors do not respond to their cultural differences or are insensitive to them, barriers are created that tend to hinder counseling. "One of the most common ways to exhibit racism is to be 'colorblind;' that is, to act as if one's outward physical appearances (e.g., skin color) are not visible (Monson, 1997)" (Pack-Brown, 1999, p. 88). Failure to address racial identity development topics and issues leads to perpetuation of stereotypes, misdiagnosis, racially-based counter transference, and compromises the working alliance, trust, genuineness and emotional bond of both counseling and counseling supervision (Hays & Chang, 2003).

Different cultures "have unique mental health needs. Decades of research have shown that there are important ethnic and racial differences in how people conceptualize mental illness, recognize their own distress, communicate their distress to others, seek help, and participate in treatment" (Hogg Foundation, 2006, p. 3). An additional benefit to counseling responsively is that the "focus on cultural diversity of clients is also fueling an awareness of the larger context of clients' lives" (Quealy-Berge & Caldwell, 2004, p. 310).

Recent research efforts validate that multicultural competence enhances counselors' work with clients whose cultures are different than their own, and offer some guidance for effective counseling across cultures (Constantine, 2002; Constantine & Gushue, 2003; Pope-Davis et al., 2002). Clients of color are more satisfied with their counseling experience, i.e. perceive that counseling is successful, relative to how well their counselors met their needs *and* their counselors' multicultural competence. "The cultural competence of the counselors [provides] an environment within which the client [gauges] the extent to which his or her choices and options for a full range of interventions and opportunities could be reached" (Pope-Davis et al., 2002, p. 385). Pope-Davis et al. (2002) concluded that:

The counselors' role in this process may be to create an environment in which clients feel that the totality of their experience is welcomed and relevant in addressing their presenting issue. . . . This goal may be achieved, in part, by communicating some understanding of the role of culture, affirming of the salience of clients' various identities, and assessing and describing the presenting problem within a cultural context. (p. 388)

Locke (1990) suggests that:

In relation to multicultural intent, one might paraphrase Rogers's sixth condition as: The client must perceive the helping intent as positive, serious, and capable of helping the devalued person or group in the situation not as protecting the dominant group. (¶ 14)

Day-Vines et al. (2007) describe a model for understanding effective and meaningful styles for "broaching or introducing the subjects of race, ethnicity and culture during the counseling process" (p. 401). Their work is based on the premise that:

Broaching behavior refers to a consistent and ongoing attitude of openness with a genuine commitment by the counselor to continually invite the client to explore issues of diversity. . . . In addition to establishing rapport and counselor credibility, a recognition that race *may* contribute to the client's presenting problem functions as a vital element in building a working alliance. (p. 402)

It is not only essential to initiate discussions of the impact of race on the counselor-client or supervisor-supervisee relationship, but also the client's or supervisee's perception of its impact on their issues.

ACCEPT RESPONSIBILITY FOR SUPERVISEES' CROSS-CULTURAL COMPETENCE

Multicultural Competence

You are responsible for your supervisees' being multiculturally competent. Legal cases underscore "the importance of developing a tolerant and non-judgmental attitude, regardless of one's own values. Counselors need to remain cognizant that they are ethically obligated to seek the knowledge, skills, and sensitivity required to effectively counsel a diverse client population" (Hermann & Herlihy, 2006, p. 418). Counselors' lack of awareness, discrimination and being judgmental harms clients, is unethical and illegal, and may be grounds for termination of employment and liability for malpractice.

In addition to ethical standards, the American Counseling Association has published *Multicultural Counseling Competencies and Standards* (Sue, Arredondo & McDavis, 1992, 482–483; Association for Multicultural

Counseling and Development [AMCD], n.d.) and *Cross-Cultural Competencies and Objectives* (ACA, n.d.). The former are included in Appendix C; the latter are available on the ACA website (http://www.counseling.org/Files/FD.ashx?guid=8120574f-e1b2-4605-bd46-f7d459c0d851).

The competencies and suggestions for their operationalization (Arredondo et al., 1996) are those "that need to be integrated into a mental health professional's practice when working with racial, ethnic, or cultural minorities" (Coleman, 2004, p. 58). Middleton et al. (2005) describe competency in multicultural relationships. Durodoye (in Engels et al., 2004) defines competencies for counseling "Multicultural and Specific Populations" (pp. 46–50). Competencies have also been published for working with clients of other cultures; for example, counseling gay, lesbian, bisexual and transgendered clients (AGLBC, n.d.), and gerontological clients (AADA, n.d.).

Cross-Cultural Communication

You are responsible for your supervisees' being effective cross-cultural communicators. Counselors are ethically bound to communicate in culturally appropriate ways (ACA, 2005, A.2). "In every conversation, one or more cultures is at work" (Carbaugh, 2005, p. 1). Communication "is a kind of practical art, infused with people's tastes and habits" (Carbaugh, p. xii). "We should, first of all educate ourselves about . . . moments of communication, and be sure we recognize if, and when, and how there are cultures at work in them" (Carbaugh, p. 94).

"In every moment of talk, people are experiencing and producing their cultures, their role, their personalities" (Moerman, 1988, cited in Carbaugh, p. xi). Interpreting your own and other people's communications is fraught with pitfalls. Words have multiple meanings to different individuals and in different cultures. Variations of tone or register can suggest different interpretations as to intent. There are major cultural differences in such parts of communication as the use of silence, body language, metaphors (Carbaugh, 2005). In a given interaction, individuals hold different assumptions about what other individuals mean by their words, their tone, their style, and the accompanying non-verbal behaviors. The opportunities for misunderstanding are rife.

> As people from different communities come together, they seek to coordinate their actions, and render meaningful those interactions. Typically, participants assume they understand what they are doing and what this means. However, there are times when the understandings of each, while presumably shared, in fact, are not being shared. (Carbaugh, 2005, p. xxii)

Arredondo (1996) cites an example from one of the businesses with which she was working: "We had complaints from clients about service and our employees' style of communication. Apparently it comes across as short and condescending" (p. 49). While the employees were striving for efficiency, the clients wanted understanding. She concludes that "Sometimes I think it is just miscommunication because of language; people don't understand each other" (Arredondo, 1996, p. 50). With this in mind, help your supervisees bring their assumptions to the surface.

Clients' Cultures

You are also responsible for your supervisees' being knowledgeable about the cultures of the departments' clients. Ethically, they must "actively attempt to understand the diverse cultural backgrounds of the clients they serve" (ACA, 2005, A. Introduction). Responsiveness requires counselors and others to be more engaged in this effort than simply being aware or understanding or tolerating. It is based on knowing the clients' cultural heritages, value systems, and socialization processes, on understanding the social, economic and political issues and values of different cultures, and on one's depth of understanding of the clients' cultural norms (Roux, 2001) and practices. It requires understanding the culture's "communication styles, learning styles, contributions, [and] social problems . . . and how to assess clients' levels of ethnic identity development and affiliation" (Gay, 2002, p. 619). These concepts also seem to be true in counseling other groups "that experience oppression and marginalization," such as lesbian, gay and bisexual clients (Salazar & Abrams, 2005, p. 58).

USE A VARIETY OF STRATEGIES TO PROMOTE CULTURAL RESPONSIVENESS

Department Ethos

When you are committed to having a culturally responsive department, you not only ensure your supervisees' basic competence, you carry out a variety of other strategies to foster racially aware and culturally sensitive staff members. You foster "an ethos, a way of thinking and being, that values human rights, diversity and equity, and ultimately facilitates successful" (Johnson, 2003, p. 18) growth for everyone involved. You "instill a philosophical commitment to respecting and celebrating diversity that is consistent with this recognition of human dignity, worth, and phenomenological experience" (Hill, 2003, p. 43).

Cultural responsiveness occurs when counseling practice is based on the belief that pluralism is the "*sine qua non* for democratic relations between people (Batelaan, 1995)" (Johnson, 2003, p. 18). "Pluralism . . . entails looking at the world from different perspectives and accepting other cultures, languages and beliefs" (Johnson, p. 18). Model such a belief system (Ladany, Brittan-Powell & Pannu, 1997; Stone, 1997), and affirm your clients' cultures *and* their human worth (Locke, 1990). Model application of the *Multicultural*

Competencies (ACA, n.d.b; AMCD, 2000) with the clients directly, in consultations with your supervisees, and in your relationships with your supervisees (Chapter 9). Anticipate the issues inherent in such an initiative and anticipate the emotionality that often accompanies the topics. Discussing the profession's ethics (ACA, 2005) and value principles (Forester-Miller & Davis, 1996) within your clients' cultural context is a good place to start.

Counselor Professional Development

Arredondo (1996) points out that "education, mutuality, and dialogue are fundamental to change" (p. 27) in attending to diversity. You provide or provide for the education, set the tone for mutuality of exploration, and lead the dialogues. Agencies support professional development through education, training and supervision. In addition, growth in this area is very personal and may need to be pursued individually. Your supervisees use these strategies most productively when they are driven by professional development goals they have established (Chapter 10).

Self-examination. Ethically, supervisors "must engage supervisees in an examination of cultural issues that might affect supervision and/or counseling" (Center for Credentialing). Therefore, you must examine your own cultural and inter-cultural values and beliefs and then you are ready to lead your supervisees to examine theirs. Together you explore your racial and cultural beliefs and attitudes as they relate to the counseling agency's clientele. Ethical counselors explore their own cultural identity development (Hays & Chang, 2003) and how this affects their values and beliefs (ACA, 2005, A. Introduction). In understanding their own cultural identities, counseling professionals consider such variables in their backgrounds and experiences as socioeconomic status, ethnic identification, and level of acculturation (Stoltenberg et al., 1998). They also learn about their own cultural affiliations and their consciousness of others' cultural identities.

Mutuality. A way to foster self-awareness and enhanced cross-cultural effectiveness is to lead open discussions with your supervisees. Staff members are more apt to be culturally responsive to their clients if their cultural awareness, identity, intervention selection and relationships are open parts of the group's discussions (Locke, 1990). To accomplish this successfully, you set the tone for mutuality of exploration by focusing on the clients. You encourage counselors to be honest about what they do not know about their clients' culture(s), and to be open to learning about it from others, including their clients. You invite staff members to "discuss open-ended questions such as 'What do I do when?'" in addressing sensitive incidents (Locke, 1990, ¶ 22).

Assist counselors to explore their own cultural identity development. The context for this may be set by a workshop presented by a diversity consultant— someone from outside the department. In order to be effective with their minority clients, White administrative supervisors and counselors must acknowledge their membership in a White culture (Hays & Chang, 2003). Many White individuals, including counselors, take for granted (assume) their position in the dominant culture (Pack-Brown, 1999), and are "oblivious" (McIntosh, 1990, ¶ 3) to the detriment and pain of those in an out-group. Speaking from her White cultural upbringing, McIntosh (1990) says:

> My schooling gave me no training in seeing myself as an oppressor, as an unfairly advantaged person, or as a participant in a damaged culture. . . . My schooling followed the pattern my colleague Elizabeth Minnich has pointed out: whites are taught to think of their lives as morally neutral, normative, and average, and also ideal, so that when we work to benefit others, this is seen as work that will allow "them" to be more like "us." (¶ 6)

McIntosh (1990) describes an exercise that raised her cultural consciousness considerably. She identified "some of the daily effects of white privilege in [her] life" (p. 5). A few examples suggest the gist of the exercise:

> 1. I can if I wish arrange to be in the company of people of my race most of the time.
> 2. I can avoid spending time with people whom I was trained to mistrust and who have learned to mistrust my kind or me. . . .
> 6. I can turn on the television or open to the front page of the paper and see people of my race widely represented.
> 7. When I am told about our national heritage or about "civilization," I am shown that people of my color made it what it is. . . .
> 15. I do not have to educate my children to be aware of systemic racism for their own daily physical protection. . . .
> 46. I can choose blemish cover or bandages in "flesh" color and have them more or less match my skin. (pp. 5–9)

You can benefit from using this exercise with all your supervisees, both White and minorities (e.g., listing some of the daily effects of being or not being a minority). They make their lists individually, and, then, discuss them as a group.

You and your supervisees are then ready to discuss individuals' attitudes towards people of other cultural groups; for example, a big step in White cultural identity development is admitting that bias, prejudice, racism, stereotyping and oppression exist, and learning what these look and feel like to individuals who feel marginalized. While not all White individuals are or have been guilty of these negative attitudes or behaviors or experienced advantage, you and your professional counselors must acknowledge your biases, prejudices, stereotypes and racism. These are delicate discussions to lead and need to be done from a position of openness and comfort.

Another effective strategy in the discussion is to encourage White counselors to share their experiences of being in an out-group in some social setting over the course of their lives; for example, in rural areas distinctions are made between farm people and townspeople; in large cities, many White ethnic neighborhoods exist and a pecking order is established among them. These dialogues are meaningful and, typically, enjoyed by the participants. Recollecting their feelings and behaviors in these experiences helps counselors be culturally responsive, but, in and of themselves, they are not enough. They are, at the point of working with clients, well educated and middle class—both of which are ingredients of the main culture that many minorities are still striving to attain. You and your counselors attend to how these impact your clients, both in the experiences they bring to counseling, and those experienced during the counseling relationship.

Ongoing conversations. To help supervisees venture ever deeper into these sensitive, yet essential topics, engage them in ongoing conversations about culture, race, and inter-cultural relationships. Engage staff members who are of the same culture as their clients or who have lived the minority experience and who are part of the staff peer group to help promote discussions. Invite them to share their perspectives as ways to open opportunities to give feedback to their colleagues. As with counseling case conferences, discussions among the whole counseling staff that center around observed discriminatory actions they have witnessed or done themselves are not only eye-opening conversations, they are meaningful ways to promote growth in the participants.

Group consultations about culturally perplexing client cases and ethical issues are also thought provoking. You are also responsible for guiding your supervisees through ethical dilemmas, such as deciding "when it is appropriate, and when it is inappropriate, to refer a [diverse] client" (Hermann & Herlihy, 2006, p. 417) when there are questions about their competence and being judgmental. Conversations can be organized by forming study groups in which staff members read and discuss professional writings on relevant topics. The counseling literature is a great resource! For many counselors who were trained in the past, much of the multicultural literature is new. With the goal of ever-increasing cultural responsiveness in mind, invite feedback from the client representatives on the departments' or agencies' advisory groups.

Individual feedback. Monitor counselors' use of culturally appropriate counseling materials and practices; i.e., those that not only address a client's presenting problem but also consider that problem within the context of your client's culture. Provide individual feedback in supervision (Chapter 10).

Pope-Davis et al. (2002) identified counselor behaviors that clients find important as "cultural knowledge, sensitivity, and receptivity to discussing cultural issues" (p. 388). They identified eight dimensions of client characteristics that cross-culturally effective counselors consider in assessing a client's needs for multicultural approaches (Figure 3.1).

Figure 3.1 Assessing Clients' Readiness for Counseling from a Multicultural
Perspective

1. Initial reasons for seeking counseling
2. Client's expectations of the counseling process
3. Assumptions of cultural similarity or dissimilarity
4. Desired counselor characteristics
5. Salience of cultural identities and the client's acknowledgment of the effect of culture on counseling
6. Assumptions about counselor's expertise
7. Reasons for persisting in counseling
8. Role of family and other support systems in coping with cultural problems

Adapted from Pope-Davis et al., 2002

To establish a culturally responsive practice, encourage your supervisees to apply counseling theories that are relevant to the population you serve (Sue & Sue, 2003), and to understand that true empathy entails "a philosophical shift to cultural empathy" (Hill, 2003, p. 41). Ensure their case conceptualizations (Constantine & Gushue, 2003), assessments and materials are appropriate for each client's cultural identity. Keeping up-to-date is critical for supervisors and supervisees alike as research continues to help improve implementation of the counseling process with diversity in mind.

A Representative Counseling Staff

Another means to promote the departments' cultural responsiveness is to employ staff members that represent your clients' cultures. Ideally, the make-up of a staff reflects the races and cultures of the clients it serves (Johnson, 2003). The profession as a whole has not yet achieved an appropriate cultural mix. Even if it had, creating a balanced staff takes years. It often takes waiting for in-place staff members to leave or retire, or for the expansion of staff due to increased numbers of clients or funding.

To accomplish this, encourage diverse candidates to apply for counseling positions. To do this right, it is essential to strike a delicate balance in recruiting and hiring practices so as not to err on the side of reverse discrimination. The Civil Rights Act (CRA) "prohibits discrimination on the basis of race, color, religion, sex, and national origin" (Kulik, 2004, p. 10). This means that Whites *and* racial minorities, men *and* women are protected from discrimination. Equal Employment Opportunity law identifies two types of discrimination: disparate treatment and adverse impact (Kulik). The first means different practices are used for different demographic groups. The second occurs when different groups are affected differently by employers' practices.

Recruiting practices. One way to diversify your staff is to expand your applicant pool by broadening your recruiting practices. First, identify employee groups that are not well represented within the department, and, then, change your recruiting strategies to reach out to these groups (Kulik, 2004). "New strategies may simply be variations on your existing strategies" (Kulik, p. 42). You may post job advertisements in community-targeted newspapers (e.g., Spanish language or Asian community papers) or websites that reach specific population groups (e.g., http://www.black-collegian.com or http://www.hispaniconline.com), or recruiting at universities that have high minority enrollments.

Kulik (2004) recommends that you emphasize inclusion in announcements (e.g., being an equal opportunity employer; statements regarding non-discrimination), and ensure recruitment materials display a commitment to diversity in words and pictures. "Research suggests that including statements about the organization's commitment to diversity in recruiting materials leads *all* applicants to rate the organization as more attractive—not just the female applicants, and not just the applicants who are members of racial minorities" (p. 45).

At a minimum, the profession's ethical standards are clear that professional "counselors do not condone or engage in discrimination based on age, culture, disability, ethnicity, race, religion/spirituality, gender, gender identity, sexual orientation, marital status/partnership, language preference, socioeconomic status, or any basis proscribed by law. [They] do not discriminate against clients, students, employees, supervisees, or research participants in a manner that has a negative impact on these persons" (ACA, 2005, C.5).

Hiring practices. To be fair and lawful, your selection of employees must be based on established criteria for the job that are associated with job performance. The procedure you use must be the same for all applicants. It usually begins with gathering biographical information about the applicants—application forms, resumés, reference checks, and letters of recommendation. Some agencies use selection tests, which may be more problematic. If tests are used, they must be equally appropriate for all groups of test-takers. Legitimate hiring practices are more fully discussed in Chapter 16.

A Culturally Responsive Service Delivery System

You promote your department's responsiveness by continuously improving the cultural relevance of your service delivery system activities. To do this, conduct periodic self-studies of the system. A list of criteria for ensuring cultural competency in mental health agencies has been developed (Siegel, Haugland & Chambers, 2002) and provides a checklist for considering the cultural responsiveness of the department. Figure 3.2 displays the items.

Additional facets of departmental self-examinations are to assess "customer service perceptions of their distinct customer groups" (Dellana & Snyder,

---

Figure 3.2 Cultural Competency Criteria for Mental Health Agencies

Characterizing your service users
Convening a cultural competence advisory committee
Deciding on culture and language focus
Having a cultural competence plan
Providing language assistance
Adapting services and activities to the different cultures you serve
Training of staff
Representation of cultures among staff members—including administration
and service providers
Hiring and recruiting practices
Evaluating outcomes (e.g., consumer satisfaction, number of missed
appointments/no shows)
Providing consumer and family education
Educating potential service users

Siegel, Haugland & Chambers, 2002

2004, p. 39), and "the cultural appropriateness and relevance of your organizational systems, policies and practices" (Arredondo et al., 1996, p. 8).

As described in Chapter 17, to be an effective administrative supervisor you lead continuous improvement of the counseling service delivery system. You and your staff members identify improvement goals, based on the data you gathered during self-examination. You target discrepancies in services to various groups and/or identified issues with the staff (e.g., projecting stereotypes).

To enhance the department's culturally responsive ethos, the inclusion of the commitment to diversity and intent to be culturally responsive should be included in your vision, values and mission statements. For example, Hyatt (*Diversity*) asserts, "Diversity is one of Hyatt's Core Values." Their goal is "To lead our industry by being an employer and hospitality company of choice for an increasingly diverse population." As described in Chapter 15, a mission statement bridges values and beliefs with a department's operations. Businesses that are intentional in attending to diversity make statements to focus their attention. Hyatt's mission statement that guides their efforts is a good example:

Hyatt's commitment to Diversity is best evidenced by our focus on company-wide Diversity initiatives. Our diversity initiatives, which fall into five key elements: Commitment, Accountability, Training, Measurement and Communication maintain and enhance Hyatt's image as an Employer of Choice, Business, Partner, and Community Ally throughout the communities we serve.

Fully using an advisory group consisting of client representatives helps. They provide important input to the entire delivery system development process (Chapter 18)—from describing the vision and mission through evaluation and ongoing enhancement (Johnson, 2003). Research and experience tell us of "the importance of involving the target community at all stages when developing and evaluating a treatment program for people of color. Without the community's input . . . attempts to develop culturally appropriate services will not be valid and will ultimately fail" (Hogg Foundation, 2006, p. 2).

You also lead assessment of the client appropriateness of the department's activities. Many of the activities and practices used by counselors are based on research and theory that have "not included adequate numbers of people of color. However, emerging research suggests that [many of these practices] can be effective for diverse populations when the provider adapts the delivery of services to reflect the client's culture" (Hogg Foundation, 2006, p. 3). Key to successful cultural responsiveness is finding, adapting and/or developing activities and materials that fit the culture served by the department.

SUMMARY

In order to be responsive to your clients, you understand and help your supervisees understand that clients are unique individuals who are also members of cultural groups. You value and help your supervisees conduct competent culturally responsive counseling. You employ a range of strategies—education, self-exploration, discussion, and feedback—to foster continuing enhancement of your supervisees' multicultural competence and cross-cultural effectiveness. You work to maintain a staff that is representative of your client community, and a delivery system that is culturally relevant.

SUPERVISORS' CHALLENGES AND RESPONSES

Supervisors' Challenges: Biased Supervisees

Counselors have "blind spots" regarding cultural differences. Some find it difficult to admit their biases about others who are different from them. Some individuals cannot see the similarities between individuals, regardless of differences. Some individuals are uncomfortable addressing differences. Some individuals are set in their ways of interacting and counseling with others and remain unaware of their insensitivity. While *overt* racism and prejudice are rare among counseling professionals, *covert* or unintentional racism seems prevalent. Many White counselors feel very comfortable in "colorblindness," reinforcing their ethnocentrism. Some are not oppressive to others, but fail to recognize oppression in society or their institution. Some counselors may not be homophobic, but are not comfortable addressing gay issues with clients. Some members of minority groups feel it is all right to stereotype Whites. Staffs that are made up of people from diverse backgrounds or communities sometimes experience inter-group tensions.

Supervisors' Responses

Sensitive administrative supervisors are aware of individuals' biases. They intervene directly with individuals as soon as they observe prejudicial attitudes or behaviors. Their interventions are over and above what they are doing to enhance the responsiveness of the whole group. In fact, it is often in the group work that individuals' tendencies to stereotype, their prejudices, their lack of awareness of oppression and dominance become evident. While these are "misbehaviors" (Chapter 4), directly disciplining these individuals is best reserved until after some individualized opportunities for growth are provided.

Individual supervision that includes confronting counselors with their behaviors or how others perceive them is a place to start. Before individuals can agree to grow in this very sensitive—and, possibly, volatile—area, they must acknowledge their hidden attitudes and values, both positive and negative. Administrative supervisors help them work through this process from a professionally objective yet engaged perspective. In the effort to uncover an individual's assumptions, they open dialogue with them individually about their background experiences, their similarities and differences from the clients' (or other staff members') culture, their parents' attitudes and values toward others.

Figure 3.3 Constantine's Cultural Development Questions Useful in a Supervisory Relationship

> 1a. What are the main demographic variables (e.g., race/ethnicity, gender, sexual orientation, age, socioeconomic status, etc.) that make up my cultural identities?
> 1b. What worldviews (e.g., assumptions, biases, values, etc.) do I bring to the supervision relationship based on these cultural identities?
> 2a. What value systems, based on my demographic identities, are inherent in my approach to supervision?
> 2b. What values systems, based on my demographic identities, underlie the strategies and techniques I use in supervision?
> 3a. What knowledge do I possess about the worldviews of supervisors/supervisees who have different cultural identities from me?
> 3b. What skills do I possess for working with supervisors/supervisees who have different cultural identities from me?
> 4a. What are some of my struggles and challenges in working with supervisors/supervisees who are culturally different from me?
> 4b. How do I address or resolve these issues?
> 5. In what ways would I like to improve my abilities in working with culturally diverse supervisors/supervisees?
>
> Constantine, 1997, p. 319

Constantine (1997) shared a framework of questions "to facilitate the active discussion of salient cultural issues in the supervision relationship" (p. 320). These "semi-structured questions . . . aid participants in (a) identifying their cultural group identities and (b) acknowledging the extent to which these identities influence their interactions in both supervision and counseling relationships" (p. 319). Both supervisors and supervisees address them. Her questions are presented in Figure 3.3.

After self-awareness has been awakened, and, if they are not impaired in this area, supervisees can be directed to readings, dialogues with others both similar to and different from themselves, and community-based experiences.

If supervisees are not amenable to working with their administrative supervisors, the responsibility shifts to them to work on the issues independently. They must, however, still be held accountable to their administrative supervisor. If they refuse—overtly or covertly—to alter behaviors or attitudes that are detrimental to clients or colleagues, a regular discipline sequence ensues (Chapter 4).

4

Uphold Relevant Legal, Ethical, and Professional Standards

Administrative supervisors are responsible to their clients, to their agencies and to the profession to uphold and ensure their supervisees uphold current legal, ethical and professional standards (Association for Counselor Education & Supervision [ACES], 1993). A standard establishes a baseline for guiding one's practice, for making professional judgments, and for judging the practice of others. Some standards are minimums that have to be followed. Some are guides to best practices. By focusing your work and that of your supervisees on the relevant standards, you keep the quality of work at or above the professional standards and thereby serve clients well.

In order to meet this responsibility, you must know what standards apply in given situations, what the consequences of non-compliance are and how to avoid them, and how to help your supervisees uphold them too. As one administrative supervisor put it, offering advice to new administrative supervisors: "It is your job to maintain the standards of legal and ethical practice and proceed in good faith and high professionalism" (D. A. Healy, personal communication, June 13, 2005).

But, you do not have to become a legal expert. You do have to have a connection to legal services. Larger agencies have legal departments or contract with a law firm. Private practitioners hire lawyers, as they need them, or use legal consulting services provided by professional associations. It is important to have relationships with lawyers who understand and are supportive of counseling perspectives. They not only help weave through the maze of laws, they also interpret ethical and professional standards when needed in areas where laws are relevant or silent. They help you establish proper practices, and help defend you and your supervisees when needed.

Your experience in adhering to the standards in your work with your own clients and clinical supervisees provides a foundation for carrying out these responsibilities. Being already familiar with what they are, in this role you not only apply them to your own work, but also ensure the entire department staff and agency adheres to them on behalf of all the department clients.

KNOW WHAT STANDARDS APPLY

Your first task is to learn as much as possible about relevant standards, where they come from, and how they got there. They are established through laws, professional statements, and administrative supervisors' discretionary power. Their weight is affected by their sources. The heavier their weight, the broader their power base, and the more severe the consequences for non-compliance. Laws are made by representatives of the public at large. Ethics are held by the entire profession, and professional practices are established for segments of counselors who apply them in their specialties. Agency and department policies, rules and regulations are informed by the previous three, and are agency- and department-specific. As a general rule, legal standards supersede professional standards, which in turn supersede those of the agency, which supersede those of the department.

Different kinds of standards may be merged together. Some laws, particularly counselor licensure laws, incorporate or reference ethical or even practice standards in their mandates. Some ethical rules incorporate professional guidelines—for example, the codes' sections on knowing one's boundaries of competence, acquiring new specialties, being multiculturally competent, and recognizing their own personal impairment.

Legal Standards

Legal standards are established by federal, state and local laws and by decisions of the judicial system—Federal, State and local. Except in the instances where states have first rights (e.g., education), federal laws prevail over state laws; state laws over local ones. Local laws and court decisions only apply to the area in which they have jurisdiction. Standards are also set by the administrative authorities charged with implementing laws, e.g., State counselor licensing boards.

Federal laws. There are Federal laws that address client protection, for example, the Health Insurance Portability and Accountability Act of 1996 (HIPAA), Family Educational Rights and Privacy Act (FERPA), Drug Abuse Prevention, Treatment and Rehabilitation Act of 1979, Americans with Disabilities Act (ADA), and Individuals with Disabilities Education Act (IDEA). There are laws that address appropriate services for specific kinds of clients, for example, the Mental Health Systems Act. There may be laws that pertain to the department's particular counseling specialty (e.g., substance abuse, rehabilitation, mental illness), or apply to the agency (e.g., mental health hospitals, schools).

As an employer working with personnel and human resources functions, you must adhere to federal employment and labor laws. "The basis of employment and labor law in the United States is to protect the safety, health and welfare of all U.S. citizens who are engaged in work" (Martin, 2000,

p. 222). There are 25 laws that are administered by the Department of Labor, including the Family and Medical Leave Act (FMLA), the Rehabilitation Act of 1973, Section 503, the Occupational Safety and Health Act (OSHA), and Fair Labor Standards Act. A useful website for basic labor law information is *elaws—FirstStep Employment Law Advisor* (Department of Labor).

There are also laws designed to assure equal employment opportunity (EEO) by seeking to prevent discrimination (Kulik, 2004), and to provide mechanisms for individuals who perceive that their rights have been violated to seek justice. These laws include Title VII of the Civil Rights Act of 1964; the Equal Pay Act of 1963; the Age Discrimination in Employment Act of 1967; Titles I and V of the Americans with Disabilities Act of 1990 (ADA); Sections 501 and 505 of the Rehabilitation Act of 1973; and the Civil Rights Act of 1991. The U.S. Equal Employment Opportunity Commission (EEOC) that administers these laws also has a useful website: http://www.eeoc.gov. The EEOC also administers the Pregnancy Discrimination Act of 1978, the Family Medical Leave Act of 1993, and the Immigration Reform and Control Act (IRCA) of 1986.

State laws. Professional counselor licenses, certifications and/or registries are matters of state law and administration. While you already know the statute and structure of your own license/certification board, you also are obligated to learn about those of staff members who work under different licenses and licensing authorities. Other state laws are also relevant. In the 1990s many states passed laws intended to reform their mental health systems. Among other things, these laws further established boundaries for appropriate practices. There are state laws that interpret applications of federal laws. In order to make them readily accessible, many states compile their legislative codes concerning such relevant topics as education, employment, family, health and safety, and penalties for public offenses into separate codes. Be aware of the laws that apply to your situation and use relevant resources.

Case law. Local, state, district, and federal courts hear cases and make judgments about the cases and issues presented to them. Sometimes these judgments are precedent setting and, thereby, change how we do our business. The most familiar case to counselors is Tarasoff v. Regents of the University of California (1976). Courts in other federal districts or states where the state has the right can make different decisions. The Tarasoff-related rules in Texas, for example, are different than the original case because of a State court decision. What you need to know is what applies in your state.

In counseling, case laws are generated from successful tort claims. These are claims that counselors intended to do harm to someone; malpractice suits are examples. Scott (2000) states that to establish that medical malpractice, including mental health malpractice, has occurred, a suing client is required to prove that there was "a dereliction of duty that directly result[ed] in damages." He explains that "A duty is . . . established when the patient seeks treatment and treatment is provided" (p. 103). The more common examples of "torts in mental health include assault (an attempt to inflict bodily injury), battery (touching without consent), false imprisonment, and violation of a person's civil rights" (p. 102). Sexual exploitation fits under assault and battery.

Local laws and agency standards. In public agencies (e.g., government provided mental health services, rehabilitation and employment services, universities, schools), policies established by the agencies' governing boards are legal statements of the agency. The agency is delegated the state's authority to run the entity, giving their policies the force of law. Agencies' policy-setters are charged with the responsibility of representing the client community and the local or state community at large.

The governance structure of private agencies also establishes policies for ensuring the agency and its staff carry out their legal and other responsibilities. Articles of incorporation are legal charters. They express what these responsibilities are and how they are held accountable.

Regulations. For each law or case decision, administrative agencies promulgate regulations and information; for example, the Substance Abuse and Mental Health Services Administration, a part of the Department of Health and Human Services, or the Education Department. State Licensing Boards develop and implement regulations for ensuring licensees adhere to the policies established in laws. In addition, consumers, their advocates, and citizens at large file complaints about counselors with licensing boards. They hear these accusations and make decisions about them. Many of these decisions end up in subsequent regulations—that have the force of law. Neukrug, Milliken and Walden (2001) surveyed the ethical complaints against credentialed counselors made to state licensing boards. The most prevalent charges were inappropriate dual relationships, incompetence, misrepresentation of qualifications, sexual relationships with clients, breach of confidentiality, inappropriate fee assessments, failure to inform clients about goals, techniques, rules and limitations, and failure to report abuse.

Administrative supervisors establish regulations and related procedures relevant to their service delivery system. For a counseling department these might include job descriptions, establishing priorities and parameters for client services, counselors' use of resources (caseloads and time), and, in some cases, methods of practice. You or the agency establishes regulations and procedures concerning employees' rights, and the expectations for employees' conduct—e.g., work ethics and habits. Operational procedures are often in handbooks or manuals. They explain such things as the compensation system, the performance management system, in addition to guidelines for the counseling service delivery system. If the agency has a human resources or personnel department, consult and collaborate with your "HR" counterparts on all personnel matters.

Professional Standards

Ethical standards. The primary ethical standards for the counseling profession are published in the American Counseling Association [ACA] *Code of Ethics* (2005), and by other associations that represent counseling specialties (e.g., American Mental Health Counselors Association [AMHCA], 2000; American School Counselor Association [ASCA], 2004a). These help professionals know what "*best* [italics added] serves those utilizing counseling services and *best* [italics added] promotes the values of the counseling profession" (ACA, 2005, p.3). The 2005 *ACA Code of Ethics* suggests that these are minimums, but introduces each section with statements of "what counselors should *aspire* [italics added] to with regard to ethical behavior and responsibility" (p. 3). Being an ethical professional not only means adhering to its codes, it also means promoting the profession's values, and following a sound decision-making process when working with clients and facing ethical dilemmas.

Professional practice standards. The ACA and its Divisions that represent counseling specialties publish professional practice standards as well. Examples are listed in Figure 4.1.

Department standards. Finally, you and your staff members alike have professional and job-related personal rules. As the administrative supervisor, you have authority to establish ones that help the department meet its and the agency's expectations. You establish and enforce them for such things as caseload management, work hours, schedules, and the lunchtime patterns for the department. You set them for office coverage, collegiality, and client accessibility. An administrative supervisor of a private counseling practice provides an example:

> From an administrative standpoint, we are all independent practitioners operating under my DBA [*Doing Business As . . .* business name registration] for the name of the center only. We do not co-mingle funds, therefore my oversight is limited. However, I maintain standards of operation and am a stickler that all of us be in full HIPAA compliance. This touches many areas, from record keeping to confidentiality issues. If we were to be audited, there are steep financial penalties that could be incurred (especially non-HIPAA compliance). I find it difficult to be the one to insist that files be maintained properly (triple-locked and papers secured in the file). We have had several in-house training sessions about maintaining these standards as well as keeping "Private Psychotherapy Notes." I have found that from a paperwork standpoint, private practitioners, myself included to be honest, have a tendency to "slide" in areas that are not watched over (no accountability because you are the "boss"). For instance, "Oh, I am in a rush, I will do those case notes later" or leaving a stack of files out on top of a desk not properly locked

Figure 4.1 Examples of Professional Practice Standards

American Counseling Association (ACA)
  Advocacy Competencies (n.d.a.)
  Standards for Internet On-line Counseling (n.d.c.)
American Rehabilitation Counseling Association (ARCA)
  Certification Standards of the Commission on Rehabilitation Counseling
  Certification (n.d.)
American School Counselor Association (ASCA)
  National Standards (1997)
  National Model for School Counseling Programs (2005)
Association for Adult Development and Aging (AADA)
  Gerontological Competencies (n.d.)
Association for Assessment in Counseling and Education (AACE)
(Resources, n.d.)
  Competencies in Assessment and Evaluation for School Counselors
  Responsibilities of Users of Standardized Tests
  Code of Fair Testing Practices in Education
  Standards for Multicultural Assessment
  Standards for Qualifications of Test Users
  Test Taker Rights and Responsibilities
Association for Gay, Lesbian and Bisexual Issues in Counseling (AGLBIC)
  Competencies for Counseling Gay, Lesbian, Bisexual and Transgendered
  (GLBT) Clients (n.d.)
Association for Multicultural Counseling and Development (AMCD)
  Multi-Cultural Counseling Competencies (n.d.)
Association for Specialists in Group Work (ASGW)
  Best Practice Guidelines (n.d.a.)
  Core Group Work Competencies (n.d.b.)
Association for Spiritual, Ethical and Religious Values in Counseling (ASERVIC)
  Competencies for Integrating Spirituality in Counseling (n.d.)
National Board of Certified Counselors (NBCC)
  The Practice of Internet Counseling (n.d.)
National Career Development Association (NCDA)
  Career Counseling Competencies (n.d.a.)
  Competencies for Career Development Facilitators (n.d.b.)

up or a computer that is not password protected. I am teased that I am a stickler for these administrative aspects. (S. D. Clifford, personal communication, August 14, 2005)

LEVY CONSEQUENCES FOR NON-COMPLIANCE AND LIABILITY

Non-compliance

The severity of the consequences for not complying with standards ranges from feedback to loss of licensure, depending on the legal weight of the rule and the specifics of the situation. Specifics include the degree of non-compliance, or the frequency of the employee's non-compliance. The consequences of illegal actions might include costing money (agency funding; liability settlements; fines) and/or reputation. Violating licensure law provisions, including malpractice, could lead to losing one's license. Violating local policies that have the force of law (e.g., School Board policies) could lead to losing one's job. Acting in opposition to precedents established in court cases (case law), opens up the possibility of any of these sanctions, depending on the damage done by one's violation.

In some cases, your responsibility is to levy the consequences for noncompliance. The consequences for employees who do not comply with agency regulations are spelled out in agency policy. Agencies of some size usually "have a discipline policy to assist managers in the proper and legally defensible approach to enhancing the performance of employees by imposing certain work-related sanctions" (Martin, 2000, p. 225). The recommended sequence of disciplinary sanctions to be followed in this process is similar across industries (Hersey, Blanchard & Johnson, 2001; Kadushin & Harness, 2002; Kulik, 2004; Martin, 2000). The typical steps taken with each subsequent violation of the same or a similar rule are:

1. a verbal warning and a reaffirmation of the operational standard or rules;
2. a written reprimand that is placed in the employee's file;
3. inclusion in the performance evaluation;
4. suspension or a "decision-making day" (Kulik, p. 154);
5. demotion/termination.

A rule of thumb for timing the provision of feedback and warnings for serious offenses is within 10 working days of an incident. The mildest oral warnings are *challenges* in the context of feedback conferences regarding supervision incidents, which are recorded on supervision feedback forms or notes. If the misbehavior recurs, the next step entails *oral directives* that are *documented* in your files—as a developing record to be brought out again, if needed.

The next step entails written warnings. The mildest of these are memoranda that address specific incidents. Summary memoranda come next. These "pull together the record of previous deficiencies discussed with the employee as recorded in formal performance appraisals, notes to the file, and specific incident memoranda" (Kemerer & Crain, 1995, pp. 2–4). These memoranda include the dates, and specific facts as you know them. A format I used to guide writing them has four parts:

1. to briefly describe the findings of fact,
2. to state conclusions regarding violations based on laws, policies, administrative directives or ethical/professional codes,

3. to establish specific directives regarding future behaviors (conduct) and remedial activities to be undertaken, and
4. to provide opportunity for the supervisee to respond—also in writing and by what date.

One of the biggest challenges faced by administrative supervisors is writing the documentation to provide to supervisees. Many administrative supervisors find it hard to stick to the facts and to not include emotionally charged words and opinions about sometimes volatile events (M. L. Libby, personal communication, May 6, 2005).

Typically, the consequences of non-compliance with professional and department standards are challenges or receiving negative feedback from supervisors and/or peers. With more severe violations, sanctions might include being found to be insubordinate, being liable due to incompetence, or losing their jobs or licenses.

Liability

Being guilty of not complying with standards opens counselors and their supervisors up to complaints or suits that lead to liability. Simply complying may not be enough to keep you immune from *allegations* of non-compliance. The best way to avoid being *held* liable is to meet three conditions. First, what is/was done is within the scope of the agency's mission and the job the person is employed to do—his or her job description.

Second, the decision made/action taken is similar to the decision that would be made by the "average" professional in the same position. Average implies that the decision reflects individual and collective values of similar professionals and/or is for the general good. Professional ethical and performance standards help define what average counselors and supervisors value and do.

Third, a sound decision-making process was used in applying the known facts of the case (Chapter 19), and the path of that process is documented (Giannatasio, 2005) (Chapter 16). If you work in a public agency, you may be protected by "governmental immunity," meaning that an individual cannot be held personally liable if these three conditions are met.

Supervisors' Vicarious Liability

It is critical to understand vicarious liability: you can be held liable for the work of the counselors and other staff members you oversee. "The supervisor is ultimately responsible for the work that is assigned and delegated. Malpractice complaints and legal decisions have clearly confirmed the principle of the supervisor's responsibility for decisions and actions of supervisees" (Kadushin & Harness, 2002, p. 79). You can be held liable for damages or harm that occur to your supervisees' clients, if it can be proven that you have been negligent in your supervision of that supervisee.

"Supervisors clearly need to attend to statements of ethics, professional standards, and guidelines" (Stoltenberg, McNeil, & Delworth, 1998, p. 178). Knowledge of these, adherence to them, and consistent efforts (documented) to ensure that your supervisees adhere to them, protect you, as much as possible, from charges of negligence, and you and your supervisees from charges of incompetence that result in client damage. You and your supervisees are less likely to be held liable if you can demonstrate your competence. Competence means that you know and adhere to the profession's rules and guidelines for supervisors, and that you are appropriately trained to meet them. Included in these expectations is that you pursue continuous professional development as a supervisor (Chapter 19).

Areas that cause problems for counseling supervisors (as well as counselors) are competence and boundaries of competence, confidentiality and informed consent, dual relationships, due process, evaluations of supervisees, evaluations of clients, representation of credentials, and seeking insurance reimbursement for supervisees' services (Bernard & Goodyear, 2004; Borders & Brown, 2005; Stoltenberg et al., 1998).

A way to help avoid liability for supervisees' ineptness is through conducting continuous assessments of their levels of professional development, and supervising them in accordance with this assessment. Another is standing by and helping counselors work through difficult cases. It supports them as they work, and you are readily available for meaningful consultation and informed debriefing. A third strategy for being a competent supervisor is to consult your colleagues or administrators when working through challenging situations. Acting as others with similar responsibilities would act is one of the best ways to ensure that your supervision practice is solid. It is also a good legal defense. If the agency's insurance policies do not cover you, it is recommended that you carry professional liability insurance.

As mentioned, having a working relationship with a lawyer is critical to an administrative supervisor. Scott (2000) suggests these general guidelines for when legal trouble arises: (a) consult with an attorney when unfamiliar legal issues arise; (b) document the decision-making process (data-gathering, options, and decisions); (c) learn about related statutes and case law; (d) appeal inappropriate denials of care by managed care organizations; and (e) consult with other administrative supervisors of counselors and with the agency's executives.

ENSURE SUPERVISEES UPHOLD LEGAL AND PROFESSIONAL STANDARDS

To do your job right, ensure adherence to standards and priorities. It is your job to defend "institutional integrity . . . [by ensuring] that the organization meets external needs and stays healthy" (Reichard, 2000, p. 189). Meeting external needs and staying healthy, here, means staying in compliance with the laws, policies, rules, regulations, procedures, and values that govern the department's work. But concerns about compliance should not overshadow the interests of clients. It is, thus, your responsibility to balance these priorities for yourself and for the department.

To be most effective as an administrative supervisor, hold high standards for yourself and for your supervisees. The higher they are, the more apt you are to reach the highest levels of self-actualization and professional development in helping achieve the agency's mission. You model their applications day-to-day, moment-to-moment.

Articulate and establish expectations for professionalism, and for everyday practices, tasks and activities. Develop workable procedures for implementation of, and for ensuring compliance with, the rules. Be clear about minimum expectations and what optimum achievement looks like. Include those for work ethics and habits.

Help Supervisees Know the Standards

To help your supervisees know the standards, base your work, as much as possible, on ones that are accepted by larger groups and published. Everyone having resources for learning about them (e.g., reading materials, discussions) helps make the expectations open to everyone, and helps you maintain professional objectivity. It is common for new—and some experienced—administrative supervisors to assume that their supervisees know what they need to know from their pre-service training or their previous work experiences (Bensimon, Ward, & Sanders, 2000). Even when this is true, it is still important to be sure they have essential information. In this case, getting the information more than once is better than never getting it. Additionally, it signals to supervisees that it is important from your perspective.

Provide your supervisees with copies of materials that are basic to their work: relevant laws and regulations, ethical and professional codes. As employees, they also have the right to have copies of the "organization's code of conduct, standards of performance, and appropriate policy and procedures manuals" (Martin, 2000, p. 225). Martin suggests, "the practitioners sign in writing indicating they understand and agree to abide by all of these" (p. 225). This information that they rely on must be kept up to date.

Ensuring they have the information is one step. Teaching and training them in what the information means and how it applies to the department's work follows. An administrative supervisor of a counseling department in an agency that serves troubled youth says that one of her primary responsibilities was "training therapists in issues regarding professional ethics and the juvenile justice system, in understanding and training therapists in family law" (D. J. Martin, personal communication, July 30, 2005).

Learning and applying standards is a task that's never finished for you or your supervisees. It is imperative that you keep your knowledge current. Each policy, regulation, professional statement is subject to change—some more frequently than others. Laws and their interpretations change; for example, "Trying to follow the legal developments that affect human resources decisions [is] challenging" (Kulik, 2004, p. 5). Agency policies and practices change. Regulations change. The profession continues to develop its recommended practices.

It is your responsibility to develop methods for keeping current. As one new administrative supervisor put it, "read everything and ask questions often!" (Y. K. Steves, personal communication, June 16, 2005). Identifying the consultative and legal resources available is also prerequisite to making sound standards-based decisions. There are many means for learning about these and other laws and their implications for the counseling department (Scott, 2000). Coursework, training, books, journals, newsletters and websites are good sources of basic information.

Help Supervisees Understand the Standards

Using this information well also entails a learning process. Ever deeper understanding of standards comes as a result of experience and application. Guidelines are developed to cover a range of agencies and practices. Your responsibility is to make them more specific to the agency and department. For example, the ACA *Cross-Cultural Competencies and Objectives* (n.d.b) apply to all counselors, but if you are providing services in an agency whose clients are primarily African American living and working in the military, help your supervisees by specifying their applications to this clientele. Taking the example to a more specific level: "II. Counselor Awareness of Client's Worldview" becomes counselors' awareness of the range of individual worldviews of middle-class African Americans living the military experience. And, then, a counselor becomes aware of the specific worldview of each individual client based on his/her life experiences.

Most standards, whether they are agency or department rules, ethical or legal codes, are clearly written and fairly easy to read, understand and even articulate. It is their applications that present ongoing challenges. As seen in this chapter, the array is somewhat daunting, and their applications occur multiple times a day in professional work.

Interpreting standards is complex. The distinctions between sets of rules can be blurry. Agency rules are sometimes supported by ethical or legal standards, e.g., attendance policies; ethical standards by legal standards, e.g., confidentiality. Sometimes different ones are in conflict. Dilemmas arise. Clients' situations are usually complex. One set may conflict with others in given situations. Counselors make mistakes. Some counselor mistakes are errors of omission (not knowing); some are errors of commission (intentional). Training counselors how to apply standards entails helping them use a sound decision-making process as they struggle with the issues or dilemmas.

An important step for counselors in a sound decision-making process is consulting with you. In fact, administrative supervisors spend a lot of time consulting with staff members about them. Being readily accessible for consultations is key to your being successful. Consultation amounts to tutoring your supervisees in standards applications. When more than one supervisee brings a similar dilemma for consultation or evidences inappropriate practice, it is advisable to use group supervision to help all the counselors learn.

Help Supervisees Uphold the Standards Independently

As supervisees gain more experience they become less dependent on their supervisors, but the latter are still responsible for ensuring adherence to the relevant standards. In order to hold them accountable, establish methods and systems for monitoring their work. These systems should not be intrusive, but they must provide enough information about counselors' practices so that neither you nor the counselors become negligent.

SUMMARY

Basing counseling practice on established and aspirational standards best ensures that clients will be well served. As an administrative supervisor, your responsibilities for maintaining them extend to the department as a whole. You need to know, work within, and uphold the legal and professional ones that apply to the department's work. Counselors and other staff members need to know and adhere to them as well. The consequences for non-adherence depend on the strength of the standard (i.e. requirement versus recommendation) and the degree of the non-compliant behavior. Counselors and supervisors can be held professionally and personally liable for their misbehaviors. You can be held liable for your supervisees' behaviors. Work to ensure that they know, understand and apply the standards well.

SUPERVISORS' CHALLENGES AND RESPONSES

Supervisors' Challenges: Misbehaving Supervisees

Supervisees do not comply with established standards with surprising frequency. They misbehave. Sometimes supervisors are not sure where supervisees' behaviors fit on the continuum between unintentional and intentional. When confronted with the reality of misbehavior, supervisees often say, "Oh! I didn't know."

In ongoing daily supervision, administrative supervisors "identify signs of underperformance. Signs include showing up late or not at all, leaving early, making mistakes, disregarding safety procedures, being frequently absent, being distracted, and being less involved" (Train Managers, 2006, p. 6), and other signs of slipping into impairment.

In fact, the most frequent examples of non-compliance with agency rules are those that have to do with work habits, specifically attendance policies.

Attendance policies address not only full or partial-day absences away from work, but also tardiness to work or absences away from one's desk (e.g., length of lunch and break times). These rules for professionals are often not rigid, as determining one's own work-time needs is often left to professional judgment. It is clear that counselors need to be at work to meet with their clients. But, how much time before or after clients' appointments should counselors be available in the work setting? How many sick days should a professional counselor take in a year?

Kadushin and Harness (2002) summarize that:

> Supervisors face situations in which workers consistently fail to get work done on time; are consistently late or absent; fail to turn in reports; complete forms carelessly; conspicuously loaf on the job; disrupt the work of others by excessive gossiping; are careless with agency cars or equipment; are inconsiderate, insulting or disrespectful to clients; or fail to keep appointments with personnel of cooperating agencies and services. (p. 124)

A modern issue is employees' misuse of technology. They send emails to clients and supervisors in haste or in emotional moments, without professional thinking or without proofreading. They surf the web for non-work related reasons (How you can stay, 2006).

Part of being professional is having the capacity and the privilege of basing one's work on professional judgment or discretion. It is what guides counselors' work habits, standards applications, relationships with clients, cases management, intervention selection, and more. A reality is that some individuals' judgment is not as good as others', or even as good as minimum expectations. Sometimes agencies or the profession establish protocols to guide professionals' judgment in working with difficult client cases, e.g., suicidal cases (McGlothin, Rainey, & Kindsvatter, 2005); however, in the intensity of complex cases, counselors can lose their professional aplomb and over- or under-react.

Professional counselors usually comply with legal rules. Typically, they are aware of the ramifications of breaking laws, and supervisors are, typically, conscientious about helping their supervisees be aware of them. Non-compliance with ethical standards, however, is more frequent. Some recurrent themes of such non-compliance are fostering dependence of clients, cultural insensitivity, not attending to parents' or guardians' rights, not consulting with other mental health workers serving the same clients, imposing their own values, allowing dual relationships, not screening properly for group work or protecting group members, breaking confidentiality, working outside boundaries of competence, and more (M. Contreras, personal communication, May, 2002). Some counselors have chronic personal problems (e.g., substance abuse, overuse or dependency) that result in their being impaired in their professional performance.

Supervisors' Responses

Ignorance of the rules is not a legally or ethically recognized excuse (ACA, 2005, H.1.a). And, intentional or not, misbehavior is still misbehavior that must be addressed in as timely a manner as possible (Hersey et al., 2001; Kadushin & Harness, 2002; Kulik, 2004). Disciplinary measures are demotivating, not motivating (Drucker, 1974). To be most effective, supervisors tailor their responses to misbehavior, depending on the degree of intentionality of a supervisee's misbehavior, the frequency of the misbehavior, and his/her assessed developmental level (as described in Chapters 10 and 11). When administrative supervisors need responses that draw upon their coercive and other harsh powers (Chapter 1), their responses and related documentation become more and more legally prescribed.

"The origin of the word *discipline* is 'disciple;' a *disciple* is a learner" (Hersey et al., 2001, p. 247). In every case, supervisors educate or re-educate supervisees about the bent or broken standard. Effective administrative supervisors see that "the goal of constructive discipline is to make problem solving a positive, growth-oriented opportunity instead of a punitive experience" (Hersey et al., 2001, p. 263). One supervisor described how apparently difficult it is for some employees to understand that, especially in counseling, an excused absence is not the same as doing one's job. The time missed is work missed, whether the absence was for legitimate purposes or not (M. L. Libby, personal communication, September 5, 2006). Helping them understand this conceptually requires effective teaching.

All discipline should be meted out in private. ("Discipline in private; praise in public" is an old administrators' saw.) The focus should be on the behavior of the supervisees, not on their character or personality, and the behavior should be well documented. The point is to help them change their work-related behaviors. Administrative supervisors are challenged by their work with emotionally or personally impaired or potentially impaired supervisees. Issues, such as chronic substance abuse or dependency, are hard to detect, especially in the early stages of the supervisor-supervisee relationship or in the development of the disabling condition. As professional counselors, it is an administrative supervisor's responsibility to assist them "in recognizing their own professional impairment and provide consultation and assistance . . . and intervene as appropriate to prevent imminent harm to clients" (ACA, 2005, C.2.g). In some of these cases, following the sequence of disciplinary steps is called for.

Effective supervisors avoid having an emotionally charged interaction with their misbehaving supervisees. They do not speak to their supervisees when they are upset with them about the misbehavior. Supervisees often take the feedback personally. It is an administrative supervisor's responsibility to be unemotional and professionally objective. They conduct their conferences "from a caring and compassionate perspective rather than as a punitive maneuver designed to hurt, humiliate and destroy" (Martin, 2000, p. 225). They resist the temptation to apologize for "having to" speak to supervisees about misbehavior, and are direct about what they observed. They approach conferences with confidence, and without defensiveness. They also listen to the supervisee's side of the story before passing final judgment. All of this is handled in light of due process policies of the agency or business. It is a supervisor's responsibility to uphold standards: "Stand your ground . . . make a plan . . . implement it" (D. A. Healy, personal communication, June 13, 2005). (Effectively supervising misbehaving administrative supervisees is also discussed in Chapters 2, 9, 10, 14 and 16.)

III

Administrative Supervisors: Ensure Their Departments Contribute to the Quality of Their Agencies' Services and Service Delivery Systems

• Align the Department With the Agency's Structure, Mission, Policies, and Practices

• Communicate Effectively Within the Agency and the Department

• Advocate for the Clients, Counseling and Counselors Within and Outside the Agency

5

Align the Department With the Agency's Structure, Mission, Policies, and Practices

On behalf of their counseling departments' and agencies' clients, administrative supervisors work continuously to align their agencies, and their departments, structures, missions, policies and practices. An agency provides the purpose and resources for the counseling department. The department provides client services that contribute to an agency's successful accomplishment of its mission. When alignment is working, counselors are able to serve their clients well, and counseling is perceived as an integral, valuable part of the agency. Effective administrative supervisors recognize that agencies are intricate organizations and, to work most effectively and efficiently, each facet of the organization works in harmony with the rest. "We must come together in a constructive way—each bringing a piece of the mural for the greatest good to the [client] and the program" (D. A. Healy, personal communication, June 13, 2005). As the interactive links between their agencies and departments, effective administrative supervisors operate successfully from their middle management positions. They are committed to the success of their clients, departments and agencies, and they accept their share of responsibility for failures in any of these.

You align your department and agency by, first, understanding the department and the agency structures, missions, policies, and practices. As one put it, "I am charged with seeing the BIG Picture—the forest and the trees alike" (D. A. Healy, personal communication, June 13, 2005). Second, you work to ensure these department and agency elements dovetail. You continuously develop your political skills (e.g., influencing others to cause changes in others and/or in your organization; drawing on your power bases; using formal and informal power structures; compromising; negotiating). Often, you are required to make compromises. You manage the tensions of being in the middle, and work collaboratively with your immediate supervisors.

ALIGN WITH THE ORGANIZATIONAL STRUCTURE

Work places "are more than just geographic locations. They are communities" (Drucker, 1974) consisting of individuals with common grounds. Even a private practice of a group of independent counselors takes on characteristics of an organizational community—e.g., sharing reputations, purposes, relationships, facilities, forms, and support staff. Organizations are structured through their components, people, and processes. To be effective, you understand these structures, their subparts, and how they are interconnected in your agency.

Components

Understanding the organizational components allows you and your staff members to understand how the agency functions (Austin, 2002; Reichard, 2000): where and when key activities occur; how and by whom decisions are made; and relationships among components, processes and people. Client service functions are those that provide the basic services of a mental health care agency. These services are the reason the agency exists, and directly produce the client results. Policy-setting and administrative functions establish the purposes and direction of the agency. Financial functions include budgeting and accounting. Support functions facilitate the accomplishment of the other functions, such as human resources, public relations, technology, and clerical support.

As the administrative supervisor of the counseling department, you perform tasks for the department related to each of these functions. In addition to your professional and staff supervision expertise, "mid-level administrators need financial, marketing, production line, and risk-management expertise" (Staton, 2000, p. 13). For example, you interpret established policies and give input into the formulation of new policies on behalf of the department. Through the agency's budgeting processes, you request money to support the department's work, and are accountable for the management of your portions of the allocations. With counseling as a service that is central to the agency's mission, you contribute to the development and implementation of the agency's marketing plan. You oversee your supervisees' compliance with safety regulations.

People

Typically, organizational charts depict the formal, hierarchical structure of authority, accountability, and power. To align the department's work within the structure, understand the charts, accept and use the "chain of command" effectively, learning your own relative positions in the hierarchy and those of others. The charts state titles, and delineate the formal flow of information and decision-making. They imply job responsibilities, and you need to know those for positions that are key to the counseling department (e.g., the purchasing department). It is also helpful to learn from others' perspectives on the agency and on counseling.

Your primary key to the system is your immediate supervisor—usually an agency administrator (Chapter 1). It is imperative that you understand your boss's job responsibilities, perspectives, and goals. It also helps to know where informal power lies, and how to use your own and access the power of others as needed for the good of your clients and department.

In agencies that include counselors and/or other professional specialists, another dynamic comes into play. As a professional specialist, you serve two masters: the organization you work for and your profession. You network with other members of the profession inside and outside of your department as a regular part of your professional responsibilities, and with colleagues outside of the work setting (Austin, 2002). This "can strengthen [your] relative power within the service organization" (p. 76). "The organized profession is also an external force that may be appealed to on issues of ethical standards in program services, or on issues involving the treatment of staff members who are members of the profession" (p. 77).

Because of its interconnectedness, changes in the hierarchy above or below you cause changes for you. Executive and management changes cause changes for everyone under their authority. Coping with changes in management constructively minimizes their negative and optimizes their positive impact on quality counseling services.

Processes

How an agency or a department works is defined by its processes. Using them effectively depends to a large extent on understanding the organizational hierarchy. Key organizational processes are those for setting and implementing policies, making decisions, channeling communications, receiving and sending information, developing relationships, acquiring resources, receiving rewards or sanctions, and accessing professional support services.

A factor that complicates understanding is that these processes vary depending on the issue being addressed. In situations where counseling services are central to the issue, you are involved earlier and carry more weight than when they are only tangentially related. The more you understand these complex mechanisms, the more you are able to use them to the department's advantage—to be integrally involved in issues related to the department. You also can better interpret the processes and your involvement in them to your supervisees. When staff members feel a part of the larger whole, they are better able to understand their place in it. They are more accepting of the opportunities and parameters—the realities—of work within the agency.

You establish these processes within the counseling department to serve its purposes. Ideally, the intra-department processes are established to optimize the department's connections with the rest of the agency. Using and establishing communication channels, receiving and sending information, and developing relationships are described in Chapters 6 and 9. Advocacy through intervening in an agency's policy-setting and decision-making process is described in Chapter 7. Rewarding or sanctioning staff members is described in Chapters 4, 10 and 13. Acquiring resources and accessing support services are described in Chapter 16. Developing a personal style for making decisions effectively is described in Chapter 19. Earning rewards or sanctions for the department's contributions to the agency's program is described in Chapter 17.

ALIGN WITH THE ORGANIZATIONAL MISSION

As Martin (2000) explains,

> Organizational development is the art and science of creating and sustaining a well-functioning organization as a whole. The vision, mission, values, and norms are the glue that holds the structure of the organization together. . . . An organization with a solid culture with support and a clear structure approaches magic. (p. 211)

Culture

In order to interact effectively with the rest of the agency, you, and in turn your department staff members, understand the culture surrounding the agency (Drucker, 1998). The agency itself exists within the contexts of the society and the economy (Drucker, 1974). Perceptions of, and opinions about, mental health vary across society. Many counseling departments are in public agencies that operate within political contexts that are heavily influenced by elected or politically appointed officials. Both society and the economy change and develop. One of the characteristics of an effective organization is that it "responds quickly to environmental changes" (Hersey, Blanchard & Johnson, 2001, p. 2). Strategic planning provides you a means for keeping fluid within a changing environment without losing sight of the department's mission, vision, and values.

To stay viable, you adapt to changes within your agency (Curtis & Sherlock, 2006; Herr, Heitzmann & Rayman, 2006). Fullan (1993) tells us that agency-wide change occurs most successfully when changes are initiated both from the top down and from the bottom up. The department's responsiveness to top-down changes plus its own initiatives in response to societal and economic changes, as seen through your clients, are critical to the success of the agency and department.

Agency Values

Understand and work within the basic beliefs of the agency. As one new school-based administrative supervisor of counselors advises, "Learn the philosophy and pulse of your campus" (K. Steves, personal communication, June 16, 2005). Every business decides "what its business is, what its objectives are, how it defines its results, who its customers are, what the customers value and pay for" (Drucker, 1999, p. 43). In clarifying their moral purposes, agencies articulate values that not only reflect what the policy-makers and executives at the top value (e.g., customer satisfaction, quality and disciplined work, punctuality, productivity), but also what the specialists within the organization value (e.g., quality work, high standards for professional performance, ethical practices) (Khandwalla, 2004). As the link between the professional counselors and the agency administration, you provide the voice for the profession's values to the agency and for the agency's values to the professionals.

Big and small organizations work best when they are based on assumptions that the desire to work is inherent in people, that they can manage themselves and be self-directive, that they are creative and seek to reach beyond themselves and to contribute to the organization. Organizations also work best when they are transparent (Drucker, 1998). In today's work climate, successful organizations are humanistic and democratic. They believe that people work best when they are aware of themselves and their feelings, take risks, and are supportive and facilitative. Such beliefs lead to trust in, concern for, and valuing of individuality (Hersey et al., 2001).

Arredondo (1996) identifies some specific assumptions that are needed for businesses to manage diversity; such as, society is multicultural; organizations have cultures; organizations and people are interdependent. "People are not malleable, and culture is not readily suppressed. Outsiders may adapt to satisfy expected behaviors and norms in the workplace and society, but they find means to express their individuality and cultural identity" (p. 4).

Agency Mission

In order to align the department's missions with those of the agency, discern what the agency's business is and internalize its mission. To be viable to the organization as a whole, the department must contribute to its mission and strategic plan (E. Zambrano, personal communication, June 14, 2005; Herr et al., 2006; Ritt, 2004). Agency goals, objectives and priorities are derived from the mission and addressed through strategic planning for mission accomplishment. These provide direction for the agency's and for the department's work. They guide agency staff to do the right work (The art and process, 2005). They also indicate how the agency and the department measure accomplishment of the mission. The desired results form the basis for accountability for the services provided (Drucker, 1974).

Counseling Department Mission, Goals and Objectives

In leading the department's establishment of its vision, values and mission (Chapters 2 and 15), ensure they "complement the mission of the larger organization" (E. Zambrano, personal communication. June 14, 2005). For example, it is school counselors' ethical responsibility to relate their programs and outcomes to enhancing students' success in school (ASCA, 2004a, D.1.c). Strive to ensure that the agency's mission reflects the values, purposes, and goals of the counseling service. "Clinically informed leadership can enhance the healing environment significantly by facilitating congruence between the organization's mission and the services provided" (Staton, 2000, p. v).

Counseling departments' contributions to mission accomplishment are evidenced by their being accountable for the organizational goals targeted for and by the department (Chapter 15). For example, if an agency's strategic plan has goals related to both physical and mental health, the mental health goals relate to counseling. If there is more than one department of mental health professionals, the relevant goals are the ones targeted for the department as contrasted to goals for other mental health service providers. More specifically, counseling services may focus on developmental and preventive interventions; social work services on case management and in-home services; psychological services on assessment and diagnosis. You set goals and objectives for both quality and quantity of services provided. By being an active participant in the agency's planning process, you ensure counseling-related goals and objectives are in the agency plan.

You "translate the objectives of the organization into the language of the specialist, and the output of the specialist into the language of the intended user" (Drucker, 1974, p. 395). In fact, you:

> may expend considerable energy seeking to understand and interpret the actions and intentions of administrators, with a view toward developing a unit strategic plan that addresses departmental needs and goals while remaining supportive of and related to the [organization's] mission. (Herr et al., 2006, p. 108)

Alignment may be easier said than done. "A far too common mistake with untoward consequences has been for [an administrative supervisor in counseling] to express a narrow goal set that may suit a [counseling department's] purposes, but fails to match the mandates of the institution" (Herr et al., 2006, p. 112). For example, in schools, colleges and universities, counseling departments may target their counseling services toward 10–15% of the student population when the institutions' missions target good mental health of all students. In employment agencies, counselors may focus on helping clients with personal problems, when the agency's mission targets successful job placement.

To be accountable for achievement of part of the agency's mission, you facilitate supervisees contributing to organizational results through planning—establishing objectives and expectations (Chapter 15); organizing—the work and the staff members to do this work (Chapter 12); and evaluating the results—in terms of the objectives (Chapters 14 and 18) (Drucker, 1974).

In large agencies with multiple counseling offices, a counseling department itself should have "a unified mission" (E. Zambrano, personal correspondence, June 14, 2005) that is in place across all agency-connected sites with counseling services. In these cases, the work of each counseling office is focused by the agency *and* the counseling department's mission, and contributes to the relevant goals and objectives. This requires the work of both the site-based and agency-based administrative supervisors. For example, in a multi-church pastoral counseling service, administrative counseling supervisors at each church work within the priorities and parameters established by the administrative counseling supervisor designated as the leader by the area church headquarters.

Professional Counseling Specialists

Accountability to the agency and department mission occurs when individual staff members believe in the mission and are accountable to the targeted objectives. Staff members' professional missions and assignments implement their portion of the departments', and, in turn, their agencies' missions. Ethically, counselors are bound "to maintain the highest level of professional services offered to the agency, organization or institution in providing the highest caliber of professional services" (American Mental Health Counselors Association [AMHCA], 2000, 7.E). They are to do their best work as needed by the clients, and in service to the agency's purpose.

Professional specialists, including you, are able to contribute substantially to improving an agency's work. You "have access to information about program innovations through professional channels" (Austin, 2002, pp. 75–76). By incorporating new professional strategies and methods into your mission-related goals and objectives, the quality of the agency's services is enhanced.

Both you and the agency have vested interests in engaging individual staff members in striving to meet objectives that fit the overall mission (Chapter 15). "Organizations should strive to foster in each individual a sense of responsibility for meeting the organization goals. Only in this way are people infused with the drive and desire to excel" (Rigg, 1992, ¶ 11). As one new administrative supervisor exemplifies, the previous department head "expected us [the counselors] to run the program; her job was to provide structure and support. From that we gained confidence and a working understanding of the overall program. It was OUR program" (L. Malloy, personal communication, June 13, 2005).

When counselors are told what to do, they feel less ownership in the organization, the department or their own jobs than if they feel they have input and some control. "When placed in a subordinate role, most people relinquish their individual control and defer to management authority. Under strong authority, each individual in the organization feels little responsibility or control" (Rigg, 1992, ¶ 10). You mitigate this by being as non-directive as feasible, given individuals' professional developmental levels, as supervisees set their own goals (Chapters 15 and 17).

ALIGN ORGANIZATIONAL POLICIES AND PRACTICES

To act responsibly, you participate actively in the development of counseling-relevant agency policies. You draw from the standards and practices of the counseling profession (Chapter 4). A principle of human service organizations "is that the expertise of professional specialists should be deferred to in areas of professional competency" (Austin, 2002, p. 386). And, it is professional counselors' ethical responsibility to ensure that "institutional policy [is] conducive to the growth and development of clients" (American Counseling Association [ACA], 2005, D.1.g; AMHCA, 2000, 7.E). In agencies that want to do the right things by their clients,

> Professional specialists, because of their identification with ethical traditions and standards established by organized professions, are often viewed as carrying the central responsibility for defining the moral standards that guide service production—that is, as being the conscience of the organization.... [Professional specialists] view themselves as representing and advocating for the interests of [clients] within the organization. (Austin, p. 76)

If employers' policies or practices are inappropriate, ethical counselors are to alert them to these issues, and work to bring change (ACA, 2005; AMHCA, 2000).

Agency Compliance

One of your major responsibilities is ensuring your supervisees comply with agency policies, rules, procedures and guidelines. You also translate those agency policies and rules into the regular procedures and practices of the department (Austin, 2002). Kadushin and Harness (2002) offer some comfort if you are wary of being too dictatorial:

> Though rules and regulations have the negative effect of decreasing worker discretion and autonomy, they have the positive effect of decreasing role ambiguity and increasing role clarity. As a result of a set of formalized rules and procedures and a detailed job description, the worker knows more clearly and with greater certainty what he or she should be doing and how he or she should be doing it. (p. 113)

Professional Ethics Compliance

Whether you are in a stand-alone counseling practice, in a mental health agency, a treatment center for the mentally ill, or in an entity with different kinds of professionals including counselors, the agency has policies and established practices that relate to the ethical standards for counseling. You are responsible for ensuring compatibility between them. In an agency with several disciplines (e.g., schools, hospitals), working to align the practices with both the agency's mission and policies and the profession's standards may be complicated; for example, professionals from other disciplines have less understanding of the counseling profession's standards than of their own; some standards may be in conflict.

As a counseling professional and an administrative supervisor, work to ensure the agency and the department establish policies and/or develop practices that implement the ethical standards of counseling. The most often discussed standards include those for confidentiality, consultation, crisis intervention, direct and vicarious liability, documentation, dual relationships, due process, duty to warn, evaluation of competence, fees, reimbursement, third party payments, gifts, bartering, informed consent, on-line counseling, public statements, record keeping, representation of professional credentials, qualifications, and competence, research, sexual and other forms of harassment, supervision, technology, termination or transfer of clients, transfer—electronic and otherwise—of client information, and treatment plans (ACA, 2005; Association for Counselor Education & Supervision [ACES], 1989; ACES, 1993; AMHCA, 2000; Center for Credentialing & Education [CCE]).

If the agency wisely formulates its rules, standards and procedures, and if it further provides for a periodic critical review of them, the agency, of necessity, must make a systematic analysis of professional practice. The best rules are, after all, merely a codification of practice wisdom—what most workers have found is the best thing to do in certain situations. (Kadushin & Harness, 2002, p. 113)

Department Procedures

Finally, establish procedures within the department that are workable. These procedures relate not only to counseling service delivery system activities, but also to the agency's functions. Workable procedures are those that are as simple as possible to get a task done or meet a requirement. Using the quality circles and quality management approaches that began in Japan in the 1960s, form committees made up of people who will be carrying out the procedures to develop them. This is one way to help keep them practical and doable.

OPERATE FROM A MIDDLE MANAGEMENT POSITION

In describing middle managers, Buckingham and Coffman (1999) state that "the essence of the role is the struggle to balance the competing interests of the [agency], the [clients], the employees, and even your own. You attend to one, and you invariably upset the others" (p. 241). These multiple priorities cause tensions as you attempt to maintain your loyalties to all three, to balance your time appropriately, and to fulfill well your three-pronged responsibilities in different situations.

The three sets of interests may not be in conflict with one another, but rather each vies for your time and attention. Blanchard, Oncken and Burrows (1989) address "managing management time" (p. 111): "Success in management requires that we constantly strike a proper balance among three categories of time: boss-imposed time, system-imposed time, and self-imposed time" (pp. 11–12). Self-imposed time is administrative supervisors' discretionary time for doing what they perceive are their number one priorities. Manage your time to ensure proper balance among the three—particularly not neglecting your own priorities.

You "combine both the function of advisor to top management and the 'conscience' of a business in [counseling and client related matters], with supervisory and administrative responsibility over [the counseling staff]" (Drucker, 1974, p. 394). To do this well, learn to compromise without giving up the integrity of counseling or counselors. Develop methods for dealing with "conflicts between the imperatives of professional expertise and the imperatives of management expertise (Etzioni 1964; Mintzberg 1983)" (Austin, 2002, p. 217). For example, advise top management about what counselors need to contribute to the agency's mission as well as what clients need from counseling and agency services. If you are not trusted by management, they might see you as self-serving or empire building. At the same time, you are responsible to ensure that counselors are delivering high quality services to an agency-appropriate number of clients. When counselors' services are lacking, you may be viewed as an inept administrator and lack credibility. Some administrative supervisors back down from being a "conscience" of the agency lest the department's inadequacies become apparent; when counselors are only serving half the clients intended, administrative supervisors tend to minimize the visibility of their departments.

One recently retired administrative supervisor in a counseling center associated with a larger service organization expressed the difficulties she faced in carrying out this two-pronged role:

> Mixing the duties of counseling supervisor with a position of employment supervisor (Assistant Program Director) placed me in a position to be responsible, on the one hand, to garner trust, help therapists improve their counseling skills and encourage candid communication between them and myself, while, on the other hand, be the one who was expected to give allegiance and loyalty to the Director who had different goals for the therapists. And who had the authority to make immediate, sometimes negative changes in the therapists' daily lives. And, mine as well. (D. J. Martin, personal communication, July 30, 2005)

It is not uncommon in agencies that are grant or publicly funded for administrators to be more focused on meeting the specifications of accountability (e.g., paperwork, numbers of clients served) than on the quality of counseling services. Being caught in the middle of conflicts between those to whom you report and those who report to you is one of your most constant and difficult problems.

A common failing of ineffective administrative supervisors is to focus primarily on what those above them want or want to hear, and to put less priority on representing the interests of counseling and counselors. Again, Drucker (1974) notes that managers say that their job "is to manage the people under them. . . . But, I have yet to sit down with a manager, whatever his [sic] level or job, who was not primarily concerned with his [sic] upward relations and upward communications" (p. 380). On the other hand, another failing occurs when administrative supervisors focus only on their own supervisees and department, and hold themselves and/or their departments back from participating in the agency mainstream (K. Cook, personal communication, May 22, 2007).

As a mid-level manager, you are also challenged to be flexible enough to work in a variety of organizational structures. In some situations you are a member of a team, working as peers with other administrative supervisors or counseling staff members on special projects (e.g., designing a new psycho-educational program for clients' family members). In other situations—perhaps with the same individuals—you are in a position of administrative authority (e.g., working as supervisors with supervisees). In other situations you are the supervisee, working with your organizational supervisor (e.g., developing regulations). In still others, you work side-by-side with your administrators, consulting or collaborating on special agency projects (e.g., developing agency-wide intake procedures) (Drucker, 1998). To be effective, understand these different roles and relative power in different situations and be flexible enough to fulfill them appropriately.

Another reality of being in the middle is that you can feel or be isolated. As Tsui (2005) describes it, administrative:

> supervisors become marginalized in the organization, although they are part of management. They feel lonely, despite their position as leaders of a team, because they do not actively participate in the frontline services. They feel insecure, even though they have authority to monitor and influence frontline [service providers]. (p. 64)

In describing the issues faced by new department chairs in universities, Rezaie and Garrison (2004) state, "When dealing with faculty, chairs are considered administrators, and when dealing with upper administration, they are considered faculty" (p. 14). The same holds true for counselors who become administrative supervisors. Counselors perceive you as an administrator; administrators perceive you as a counselor.

SUMMARY

Working on behalf of counseling clients, you are responsible for establishing and maintaining interactive connections between your department's organizational structure, mission, policies and practices, and those of your agency in the environmental context. You ensure that your staff members understand and adhere to agency policies and rules, and develop related operational policies and procedures for your department. You strive to ensure that your agency's policies and practices adhere to professional counseling standards. You manage the challenges of being a mid-level manager, positioned between your supervisees and your agency's hierarchy.

SUPERVISORS' CHALLENGE AND RESPONSES

Supervisors' Challenge: Getting Along With the Boss

A recurrent challenge for administrative supervisors is learning to get along and to work with their bosses. The style of their leaders affects them (Hersey et al. 2001). According to Drucker (1974), examples of problems of upward relations that worry administrative supervisors are their relationships with their bosses; doubts about what is expected of them; difficulty in getting their points across, their programs accepted, and activities given full weight.

It is not unusual for administrative supervisors to report to someone who is unfamiliar with counseling. Without education they may not understand such values as confidentiality; and, without understanding, "confidentiality is the enemy of trust" (Hurst, 1984, p. 80). It smacks of secrecy and withholding information from someone who thinks she/he has a right to know. Many generalist administrators with authority over counseling specialists do not appreciate confidentiality (e.g., counseling agency vice presidents, school principals).

It is unusual—but not impossible—to work in a situation under an administrator who is ideologically opposed to basic counseling values, who seeks his/her own advantage, who has an authoritarian style based on insecurity, or a situation where nepotism is part of the culture. An experienced administrative supervisor described one of her hardest experiences as:

> working for a director who was 12 years my junior, married to the [agency] director, opportunistic, inexperienced in dealing with people other than a short stint in [the military] where she used military discipline and unchallenged authority to get what she wanted. (D. J. Martin, personal communication, July 30, 2005)

Problems occur when bosses are not supportive, or fail to recognize or appreciate the administrative supervisor or the counseling profession's value. Fiedler (1998) identified "boss stress" as one of the primary stressors in work environments. It:

> is caused by real or imagined interpersonal conflict with the boss.... Stress with one's superior ("boss stress") is usually caused by an immediate superior who is hostile, unfairly critical, unapproachable, or makes unreasonable or conflicting demands. Above all, boss stress diverts the leader's intellectual focus from the task to the anxiety arousing relationship with the boss. (p. 338)

His studies led him to identify this stress as "likely to block or impede the leader's effective use of cognitive resources" (p. 337). The studies "indicate, when stress with the boss is high, leaders typically use their experience but misuse their intelligence; under low stress, leaders use their intelligence but misuse their experience" (p. 340). He makes an interesting point:

> both intelligence and experience are strongly affected by boss stress. . . . Reducing boss stress presumably . . . increase[s] the performance of more intelligent leaders, while high stress . . . increase[s] the performance of the relatively more experienced leaders. (p. 342)

Supervisors' Responses

As Drucker (2005) explains:

> Bosses are neither a title on the organization chart nor a "function." They are individuals and are entitled to do their work in the way they do it best. It is incumbent on the people who work with them to observe them, to find out how they work and to adapt themselves to what makes their bosses most effective. This, in fact, is the secret of "managing" the boss. (p. 107)

To be effective, administrative supervisors adapt their styles to meet their bosses' needs, methods and styles, and, in order to be heard, also communicate in ways that match.

Administrative supervisors recognize that their bosses are a basic source of their legitimate power, and are critical to their effectiveness and success in their jobs. Blanchard et al. (1989) define "boss-imposed time [as] time you and I spend doing things we would not be doing if we did not have bosses" (p. 113). Sometimes these impositions are bothersome, but, "having a boss *requires* some of our time because of the Golden Rule of Management: THOSE WHO HAVE THE GOLD MAKE THE RULES!" (p. 113). To be effective, administrative supervisors need to keep their bosses satisfied. "Always do what your boss wants. If you don't like what your boss wants, *change what your boss wants*" (p. 113). The goals of administrative supervisors and their bosses for the counseling department must be the same. How those goals are achieved may be the bones of contention—or discussion.

The onus of relationship responsibility is on the administrative supervisors. They use both their intelligence and their experience to make these relationships work. To work, they must be based on mutual respect. The basis for administrative supervisors' respect for their administrators is their legitimate authority. The basis for administrators' respect for administrative supervisors is their counseling expertise and their agency-delegated authority. From their different perspectives but with common goals, common ground is usually identifiable. Effective administrative supervisors are properly assertive.

Blanchard et al. (1989) describe, "One of the most important lessons of my career is that good work alone, no matter how much it satisfies *you*, might not be enough to satisfy your boss. Satisfying your boss takes time" (p. 115). Effective administrative supervisors know that it is important from the beginning of the relationship to keep their bosses informed, to protect them from embarrassing surprises, to anticipate their needs and wants and how they want things handled, and to build their trust. Blanchard et al. affirm that "We neglect doing these things at our peril . . . Failing to invest sufficient time to satisfy [the] boss will result in more and more boss-imposed time" (p. 115). Fiedler (1998) suggests the following strategies for reducing stress with your boss:

1. Avoid eyeball-to-eyeball confrontation.
2. Rehearse or role-play difficult interviews.
3. Communicate by telephone, email or memorandum.
4. Compliment your boss for behaviors that lessen your stress.
   (p. 347)

Cottringer (2005b) offers "ten common sense things that all work together to satisfy some very realistic expectations of any employer" (p. 8):

1. Have the right attitude about the job;
2. Solve problems;
3. Be a role model;
4. Be an expert communicator;
5. Learn;
6. Be positive;
7. Ask good questions;
8. Apply common sense;
9. Compromise; and
10. Be real.

Other strategies used by effective administrative supervisors include collaborating with their bosses on agendas that are mutually important, such as those related to good agency-department alignment. Working politically, using their referent power, may also be an effective option; but in doing this administrative supervisors need to consider the potential negative as well as positive ramifications, and do it circumspectly. Insecure bosses tend not to appreciate being circumvented. On the other hand, when bosses are abusive or exploitative, all employees—including administrative supervisors—need to know and exercise their rights (e.g., consulting, reporting, transferring, resigning).

6

Communicate Effectively Within the Agency and the Department

In order for counseling departments to provide optimum client services, administrative supervisors understand and apply the basics of organizational communication. As described in this chapter, they understand and are adept at communicating in different ways, at using a variety of methods, and at working through the communication systems that are in place in an organization. Estimates are that administrative supervisors spend 60–75% of their time at work communicating with other people (Harris, 2002; Hersey, Blanchard & Johnson, 2001).

The experiences you had and the skills you used in counseling, including communication and relationship-building skills, provide a strong foundation for communicating well within an organization. In this role, these competencies are applied not only with your supervisees, and immediate supervisors, but also with those in the larger context of the agency. To be effective, remember that organizational co-workers are not counseling clients. Communications are aimed at understanding others *and* at being understood. More so than in counseling, communicating as an administrative supervisor entails giving as well as receiving information.

UNDERSTAND ORGANIZATIONAL COMMUNICATION

The use of language is one of the most important means for obtaining organizational goals. "Through the use of oral and written language, organizations . . . coordinate, control, lead, and manage individual and group behavior. Verbal communication provides the tools needed to obtain, transfer, and store information and knowledge" (Harris, 2002, p. 117). Language is also used to convey the stories, myths, values, missions, and metaphors that are part of organizational cultures. It is used to exchange ideas and information, lead and motivate, problem solve, and negotiate (Hersey et al., 2001). As a side effect, it influences how people perceive their work place (Kramer, 2004).

Information Sharing

How they handle information signals much about a leader's effectiveness and style. When you are forthcoming with information and providing it in amounts appropriate to your receivers, you appear to be informed yourself, inclusive and collaborative. On the other hand, if you appear to misuse information, i.e. withholding or overloading people with it, it "can result in distrust" (Bekkers & Homberg 2002, p. 140).

In taking responsibility for communications, ask yourself, "Who needs to know this?" "On whom do I depend?" "Who depends on me?" (Drucker, 1999). Be clear about how the information should flow and to whom. As one experienced administrative supervisor of school counselors advises:

> Communication with all who have a "need to know" is essential. Because our (—counselors'—) role supports all facets of the instructional and administrative divisions, we must share as much as we can with all concerned. For example, if I have developed a new document for parents to read and sign for individual or group counseling . . . I must stop and think about who needs to know that . . . my supervisor, the principals, counselors, etc. We cannot work in isolation, and if we do, we will not have the support we need when we need it. (T. E. Miller, personal communication, June 13, 2005)

Not communicating due to errors of omission—not considering who else might need to have the information you have—is one thing. Sometimes, in organizations, people withhold information from others for less than ingenuous reasons—a perception you want to avoid.

> The exchange of information is often a part of game playing between relatively autonomous [entities], and it seems clear that information is rarely a neutral resource. Information exchange affects the positions of [entities] in [organizations], and may be used to preserve autonomy, affect traditional dependencies, et cetera. (Bekkers & Homberg, 2002, p. 140)

To be successful, actively search out the information you need. Sometimes you encounter and need to deal with colleagues who withhold more than share information.

Effective Communication

It is imperative to express yourself clearly and appropriately, and present yourself accurately. Language is used in organizations differently for different purposes. "On the one hand, clarity and directness are required to be effective in giving instructions, making assessments, and dealing with colleagues. On the other hand, language is powerful precisely because it is highly symbolic of much broader meanings (Lee, 1941)" (Harris, 2002, p. 118).

Put your messages "in a way that people can easily understand and accept" (Hersey et al., 2001, p. 295). Analyze what in the information you have or the message you want to send is most useful to your receivers, adapt it to their reception style, and communicate it (Hersey et al.). Communication is most apt to be understood that is concrete, succinct, and clearly thought out. Facts and feelings are sorted out, and over-communicating is avoided. Work to see that what you are expressing is understood correctly. According to Lester and Eaker's study (cited in Hersey et al.) ineffective communication is the number one concern that supervisees have about supervisors. Ineffective communications are either incomplete or unclear.

While accuracy of communication is critical to successful interactions, complete communication is difficult to obtain. Perhaps, to be complete, full "communication requires shared experience" (Drucker, 1974, p. 493), between the expresser and the listener. But, the individual doing the expressing and the individual doing the understanding are each unique, and, therefore, messages pass through different filters. Individuals' use and understanding of language is based on their experiences, their definitions of words, the assumptions they make about the other person in the dyad, and so on. Full communication is impeded by the differing perceptions of the communicators. "As you learn to listen deeply to other people, you will discover tremendous differences in perception. You will also appreciate the impact that these differences can have as people try to work together in interdependent situations" (Covey, 1989, p. 253).

You communicate with many others with very different perspectives and backgrounds from your own. Study carefully the cultural needs and expectations regarding communications of each of your staff members. Arredondo (1996), in helping organizations to better manage diversity, assumes that the interpersonal and organizational communication systems that currently exist are ineffective. With regard to crossing cultural divides, "through communication with others, members gradually reduce their uncertainty about diversity and possible subcultures in the organization" (Kramer, 2004, p. 212).

It is critical to understand that meaningful communications rest on relationships between the communicators. The more essential the relationship to accomplishing the parties' jobs, the more communication is required by the situation. The more discretionary the relationship, the less communication is required. Thus, your relationships need to be strong to support your communications, especially voluntary endeavors. (Healthy relationships with supervisees are discussed in Chapter 9.)

USE THE DIFFERENT WAYS COMMUNICATION OCCURS IN ORGANIZATIONS EFFECTIVELY

Within the organization, you use four kinds of communication regularly, responsively, or reactively. Situations are formal or informal. Interactions occur with individuals and groups. One effective administrative supervisor in counseling—a "Head Counselor" in a high school—reports, "It seems most of my day is spent in conversation/consultation with counselors, teachers, administrators" (M. L. Libby, personal communication, September 26, 2006). She estimates that an average of 75% of that time is spent in individual, informal interactions. 10% is spent in individual, formal interactions; she typically has one of those a day. 3% is spent in informal interactions with more than one counselor at a time, 2% in formal interactions with more than one counselor, and 5% in informal interactions with the whole counseling staff.

Four Kinds

Hersey et al. (2001) describe three basic kinds of communications between you and your supervisees: linear, interactional, and transactional. You make conscious choices about using the kind of communication that fits a situation. Linear is one-way communication and occurs when supervisors tell supervisees something. It is appropriate to use when the information seems to be straightforward, and there is no need for a response. Interactional communication is two-way, but one sided. In this kind of communication, you tell your supervisees your message and invite or allow them to respond (Harris, 2002). Transactional is two-way and two-sided. You use it when you and your supervisees exchange information and thoughts.

The intentional use of motivating language enhances worker job satisfaction and performance (Mayfield & Mayfield, 2002). Three types of motivating language are identified: direction giving, empathetic, and meaning-making. Each is valuable in appropriate circumstances. When you give directions, be straightforward and not ambiguous. Use it when you help your supervisees understand their jobs, tasks, goals, objectives and/or rewards. Use empathetic language when you communicate feelings, such as compassion for a counselor with issues or problems, or appreciation for a counselor for a job well done. Use meaning-making language when trying to help your supervisees understand concepts or abstractions, such as insights into organizational culture, or processes that are happening that cause change. Using the range of motivating language by itself is not sufficient to enhance job satisfaction. Supervisors must also walk their talk; and your supervisees "must understand the intended messages" (Mayfield & Mayfield, p. 91).

A fourth kind of communication is symbolic (Harris, 2002). You use symbolic messages, verbal and nonverbal, when you communicate your organization's and your values, visions and goals. They include "mottoes, visions, and mission statements" (Harris, p. 254), priorities, organization-based stories and metaphors. It includes what you say and do: your nonverbal behaviors, and the role model you present. Understand that what you choose to communicate about is what supervisees perceive to be important. Being aware of what you value and what you want others to value is prerequisite to meaningful communication. Consciously ensuring that your communications relate to important matters is essential to good leadership.

Formal Individual

Your formal work with individuals occurs in work-related conferences. These are most successful when you are clear about the purpose and desired result(s) of a conference, and when you understand the person with whom you are conferencing and respond to that individual in ways that are most likely to lead to the desired result.

Whether you are responsible for conducting a conference or for following the lead of the other party depends on who called the meeting and on the agenda item(s). In either case, it is best to be prepared appropriately for the meeting. This is not to suggest that spontaneity is not good, but it is to suggest that planning is good. Both under-planning and over-planning can lead to negative results. When you are not sufficiently prepared, you may not be able to lead or participate actively in a conference. When you are too prepared, you may become so rigid you are not able to relate well to the other individual.

Your individual conference agenda items may be informative ("There is a new policy related to your work specialty . . .") or corrective ("When you said . . . to—, what kind of reaction did you expect to get?"), include accolades ("You did a great job in that staffing") or reprimands ("I will have to write you up for being late to work for the fifth Monday in a row"), and/or be business related ("Your salary for this year will be . . .") or personal ("I'm sorry to hear of your Mother's illness"). (More information about your individual work with supervisees is discussed in Chapter 13.)

Formal Group

You participate in groups that meet for different purposes. You meet with your staff members in staff meetings that focus on agency and/or department business items, in group supervision meetings focused on case consultations or ethical dilemmas, and when a group requests it. You meet with non-counseling agency colleagues in division meetings, or on agency teams working on special assignments or projects. You meet in groups with agency administrators, such as in agency-wide meetings, committees, or working on specific agency-based tasks. You meet with groups of clients or their representatives on your advisory committees, or with those who are pleading cases or complaining. You meet with community-based groups that are supporters or detractors of counseling.

Again, your roles depend on whether you are the leader or a member of a group. Some groups are regularly scheduled and ongoing (staff meetings). Some are *ad hoc* and end when the project is accomplished. Some are called sporadically; some are one-time, special purpose meetings. You also participate in staff meetings held outside the counseling department. It is through these group meetings that you keep in touch with the rest of the agency and establish professional and personal linkages between the counseling department and the rest of the agency. (Conducting staff group meetings is discussed in Chapter 12.)

Informal Individual

Informal (non-work related) communications occur casually in the work place. Interactions occur not only within offices, but also, for example, when passing in the halls, reception areas, restrooms, mail box areas. They also occur outside of the facility, for example at special events in staff members lives (e.g., weddings, funerals, children's graduations). They occur at work during lunch or break times, or at department social events, e.g., out of work hours parties. They may occur at professional association meetings.

Even in informal contacts, be constantly aware that others are always conscious that you are the leader of your department. One excellent manager identified by Buckingham and Coffman (1999) offered advice to new managers: "Your people watch everything you do, say and the way you say it" (p. 16). Even when in a relaxed atmosphere, be aware that you are a professional role model, and communicate in professionally appropriate ways.

USE THE VARIOUS METHODS OF ORGANIZATIONAL COMMUNICATION EFFECTIVELY

Organizations use five basic methods of communication: reading, writing, speaking, listening, and non-verbal. Increasingly, technology is used to facilitate communication. You operate most efficiently if you use all of them well.

Reading, Writing, Speaking, Listening

Whether paperless or not, organizations rely on lots of reading material, beginning with organizational policies and running through to established procedures. The organization and the counseling profession produce a lot of informative material: handbooks, manuals, memos, letters, newsletters, magazines, journals, and books. Administrative supervisors also write materials: handbooks, guidelines, memos, letters, white papers, brochures, and articles. You write policies, regulations, procedures, directives, job descriptions, performance evaluations, reports, grants, documentation, inter-office agreements, conflict resolution agreements. Written communications are linear communications, although responses may be invited (interactional).

Once communications are written they are more or less permanent. They can be kept and copied. It is advisable to be circumspect about what you write. What is put in writing might end up on public display (e.g., in the newspaper). To avoid misunderstanding, compose each document carefully. When time permits, it is wise to review highly important messages with others to check if you have said what you intended to say. Avoid emotionality and inflammatory words.

Speaking, listening and non-verbal communications are used in individual conferences and conversations, group meetings, and formal presentations. As in counseling, use all your antennae when you communicate with others. Guard against assumptions about what others know, think, feel and do or have done. Administrative supervisors' responses to feelings are different than counselors' responses. They address feelings in ways consistent with a professional, co-worker relationship, allowing both parties to maintain professional decorum and detachment.

Supervisees judge your management style according to how they perceive your effectiveness as a listener (Harris, 2002). Covey (1989) encourages the habit of seeking first to understand, then to be understood. "Most people do not listen with the intent to understand; they listen with the intent to reply" (Covey, p. 239). In listening to reply, people probe, advise, interpret and evaluate. "We have such a tendency to rush in, to fix things up with good advice. But we often fail to take the time to diagnose, to really, deeply understand the problem first" (p. 237). In listening to understand, your goal is to see the world as the expresser sees it. Check, through paraphrasing or other techniques, to ensure that what you are hearing is correct.

Non-verbal

As in counseling, non-verbal behaviors are important in communications. More than half of what is communicated is communicated non-verbally. It is difficult to know what your non-verbal behaviors communicate to others, but such self-awareness is vital to guarding against sending unintended messages. Strive to know, for example, what your facial expressions tell others. Seek feedback regarding both your verbal and non-verbal communications from trusted associates, and be open to criticism when it is offered.

Electronic Communication

In many circumstances, technology facilitates communication. It tends to decrease time and distance between people (Hersey et al., 2001). Technology supports communication through facilitating such activities as email, voice and text messaging, presentations, and videoconferences. The benefits of using technology are multiple, such as, facilitating collaborative work and connections between people, and increasing accessibility of information. It is best when you use technology for appropriate purposes, and avoid using it for communicating sensitive or complex communications. As electronic communications are one-sided and one-dimensional, the possibilities of misunderstanding are increased.

Another downside of advancing communications technology is in the increased number of communications you send and receive. It takes more time to read, listen and respond to an increased number of messages. The potential for information overload is enhanced. And, "beepers, cell phones, and lap tops make it difficult to leave the work behind" (Harris, 2002, p. 419). Workdays for technology users have become longer.

USE ORGANIZATIONAL COMMUNICATION SYSTEMS EFFECTIVELY

No matter how large or small an organization is, there are five internal communications systems (Hersey et al., 2001; Harris 2002). There are three *channels* of communication that are formalized by an agency's structure: downward, upward and horizontal. There are two informal systems: *networks* and *grapevines* that may or may not include individuals from all three levels of the agency's hierarchy. To be fully effective, know what the channels, networks and grapevines are, how they work in the agency, and use them well. The majority of your channel communications are downward with your staff members. Being a member of informal networks and grapevines is often to your advantage.

Channels

Channels are established, formal pathways for communication. The organizational structure defines who must communicate with whom. Additionally, they are used for informal sharing of information and ideas. You communicate "downward" to those who report to you, "upward" to those to whom you report, and "horizontally" to those whose responsibility levels are similar to yours.

Communicating downward. As the leader, you are responsible for the effectiveness of the communications within the department. You are "the therapists' first line of communication" (D. J. Martin, personal communication, July 30, 2005). Be clear about how communication flows between you and your supervisees and among the supervisees (Henderson & Gysbers, 1998). You establish the in-department channels, e.g., who reports to whom about what and through what means. You answer such questions as, do the six counselors who use the same secretary all give her work directly, or does it flow through one person? If one of the counselors is in charge of a special assignment, how do they keep the rest of the department informed?

"Good communication with the employee's immediate supervisor [is directly linked to] job satisfaction in the specific categories of general problems, feedback, salary discussions, career counseling and performance appraisal" (Harris, 2002, p. 13). Your communications with supervisees must be in line with the boundaries set by your differences in responsibility and power. You are not as open in self-expression, self-disclosure, and such (Maslow, 1998/ 1962), but you are open to feedback, information, and suggestions from supervisees. In their massive studies, Buckingham and Coffman (1999) found that employees are more apt to be satisfied when they can answer, "Yes" to the question, "At work, do my opinions seem to count?" (p. 28).

Many employees are dissatisfied with the downward communication they receive (Harris, 2002). Make decisions carefully about what and how much information you pass on to staff members from other parts of the organization. You sometimes filter information down to what you think your staff members want or need to know. This can also be perceived as withholding information that staff members want. On the other hand, some administrative supervisors sometimes pass along all the information they get. This can lead to staff members' feeling overloaded with information that they do not have good perspective for understanding. In striving to be a good communicator, you wrestle with "information adequacy versus information overload" (Harris, p. 236) decisions, and base them on accurate assessment of what information your supervisees need and want. Deliver information in a straightforward manner. (Editorializing might come later, when it is less likely to lead to ambiguity and uncertainty.)

Communicating upward. Upward communications are the means for staying connected with the agency as a whole and clarifying the mission, purposes, standards and needs of the counseling services and staff. Communicating what and how the counseling department is contributing to the good of the whole and how it is doing that is critical to maintaining the viability of counseling in the agency's context. You represent:

> the goals and values of the counseling enterprise to those within the greater organization in positions of . . . administration, in terms they understand. The ability and willingness to *manage up* in this way has become increasingly important if counseling [departments] are to maintain their resource base. (Herr, Heitzmann & Rayman, 2006, p. 324)

Covey (1989) suggests, "When you can present your own ideas clearly, specifically, visually, and most important, contextually—in the context of a deep understanding of their paradigms and concerns—you significantly increase the credibility of your ideas" (p. 257) with others.

In communicating upward effectively, administrative supervisors make suggestions, report what subordinates are doing and their progress toward goals and objectives, discuss unsolved work problems, provide feedback regarding the effectiveness of their bosses' communications and how their subordinates feel about each other and their jobs (Harris, 2002; Hersey et al., 2001). Another function of communicating upward is to ensure executive decision makers understand what professional counselors do, to protect them from being assigned tasks that do not use their expertise.

> It is important to maintain communicative and open relationships with one's own supervisors . . . so that opportunities are taken to share the work and successes of counselors, and to set limits when others would ask counselors to do what is not theirs. (E. Zambrano, personal communication, June 14, 2005)

If administrative supervisors do not take full advantage of upward communications channels, problems occur. Several different reasons (excuses) are cited for being overly cautious about them. Candidness in upward communications can make you feel vulnerable and fear reprisal. Sometimes the solution to a problem you present is delegated back to you. Messages may be taken out of context. Your boss might overreact, exaggerate or minimize a problem. You may feel disloyal in pointing out issues—disloyal to your superiors, or disloyal to your supervisees. Some become cynical and feel it is useless to try to communicate. Some fear that changes will result. Most often, when any of these are used, they result in perceptions of their withholding information.

Communicating horizontally. The size and organizational structure of an agency dictates how many administrative supervisors of departments there are. The more you interact with individuals from the rest of the agency, the more you understand your work setting. One new administrative supervisor advises others to get to know as many of the agency staff members as possible— especially those outside of the counseling and closely related departments (Y. K. Steves, personal communication, June 16, 2005).

Supervisor-to-supervisor communications serve a variety of purposes: sharing and spreading information, task coordination, collaboration, problem solving, conflict resolution, building rapport, and emotional and social support (Harris, 2002; Hersey et al., 2001). They allow for agreeing on methods for communicating across departments, e.g., how information will flow and feedback will be reported. It is critical to clarify how communication with one administrative supervisor's supervisees will be carried out by the other.

An example of interdependent work that is prevalent in mental health care is that of multi-disciplinary teams (Osborn, Dean & Petruzzi, 2004). "Awareness of the complexity of clients' problems promotes interdisciplinary approaches to case conceptualization and management" (Quealy-Berge & Caldwell, 2004, p. 310). Multidisciplinary teams are also used in some agencies for program planning, design, implementation and evaluation (Henderson & Gysbers, 1998; Staton & Gilligan, 2003). Successful communication among multidisciplinary team members is based on understanding and respect for the identity and goals of each profession, and the "differences between the professions, especially in language usage, theory preference, and ethical considerations" (Quealy-Berge & Caldwell, p. 311). Healthy sideways communications allow for "the tending of my own domain and [being] a good neighbor to other domains, with clarity about our counseling imperatives" (D. A. Healy, personal communication, June 13, 2005). Every interaction between you and administrative supervisors of other departments provides opportunities to share information about counseling services, purposes, priorities and results (Henderson & Gysbers, 1998).

Healthy horizontal communications can be impaired by "time constraints, turf struggles, struggles over power and control of resources, secrecy, and indirect communication" (Quealy-Berge & Caldwell, 2004, p. 311). "Empire building, specialization, and a lack of rewards" for cooperating (Harris, 2002, p. 242) also mar good horizontal communications. Where competition is the prevailing spirit, cooperation does not flourish. Agencies may have unwritten— or even written—rules that help or hinder horizontal communication. Being aware of which party has the most responsibility in a given situation may help avert some competition for power.

Networks

Administrative supervisors who are effective communicators recognize the informal and other formal communication mechanisms that their staff members participate in. Developing strategies for accessing the information exchanged and being open to it allows them to capitalize on them when they fulfill constructive purposes, and intervene with your staff members when they are demoralizing or counterproductive. To lessen potential harm from informal communication channels, keep your own information channels open and two-way. Allow individuals to express their personal perspectives and differences of opinion. Be transparent in sharing information.

Networks are usually established informally and operate responsively. They typically consist of individuals and individual contact, although collectively they get and process a lot of information (Kramer, 2004). The communication is traditionally oral, although, today, electronic methods, such as e-mail, are also used. They are based on interdependence, and form around different topics: "tasks (how do I complete my job?), social (who are my friends?), authority (who is really in charge?), political (how do I get things done or changed around here?), and innovation (where do new ideas come from?)" (Kramer, p. 212). Depending on the agency, clients may be part of some of the networks—particularly the political and social ones. When a counselor's social network includes clients, the issues of dual relationships must be addressed.

Grapevines

Grapevines, often called "rumor mills," are informal and formed for satisfying workers' needs for information and providing employees a release valve (Hersey et al., 2001). Often this information is incomplete, but it is, surprisingly, 70–95% accurate (Hersey et al.; Harris, 2002). The news on grapevines travels fast. Harris reports that, on average, 40% of the news is business related, 12% is about sports, politics, personal issues, and 9% is gossip. Typically the information is unverified.

Grapevines may be positive. With access to them, you learn useful information about what is on employees' minds—particularly what worries them (Maslow's, "grumbles" (1998/1962, p. 266). Grapevines, however, can also be negative. The inaccurate 5–30% of the information can distract employees.

The irresponsible information that is promulgated can be damaging to staff morale, to individuals, and to company climate. Information flows inside and outside the work setting through outside activities that your staff members participate in (such as, bowling leagues, bunco games, church functions). Clients also pick up on grapevine information.

SUMMARY

Communicating within the agency and department comprises a large proportion of your job. In communicating formally and informally with individuals and groups, strive for accuracy and completeness. To be an effective communicator, understand that individual differences influence communication. Use appropriate communication methods well. Understand and use well your organization's formal communication channels. Know the networks and grapevines that your supervisees participate in and work to access the information that travels through these informal paths. Strive for openness and transparency in your communications.

SUPERVISORS' CHALLENGES AND RESPONSES

Supervisors' Challenges: Confronting Others' Demands

When communicating with those outside the department, there is less common ground from which to discuss topics than administrative supervisors in counseling have with their supervisees. The chances of ineffective or failed communication increase. The communication topics are often more difficult. Inter-department communications often occur by way of email, meetings, phone calls, or bureaucratic forms. These vehicles also curtail the time and space available for full communication; therefore, they lend themselves to increased misunderstanding. Communicating with colleague administrative supervisors may entail struggles for power or professional jealousy. Such tensions can restrict communication and nurture misunderstanding.

A major job of administrative supervisors is to protect their supervisees from undue demands or assignments from agency administrators and from other departments' supervisors. Examples of non-counseling tasks that other departments try to impose on professional counselors are tracking financial eligibility, making "cold calls" to market the agency, attending public functions as "PR" for the agency, keeping double sets of records.

While collaborating with other departments for the good of the agency is part of all employees' jobs, some tasks are inappropriate for counselors to do as they put them in dual relationships with their clients. Others do not capitalize on their specialized counseling skills. Another consideration is how much of counselors' counseling time is being redirected to "system-imposed" time (Blanchard, Oncken & Burrows, 1989, p. 116).

Supervisors' Responses

Being aware of the possibility for misunderstanding is one way to guard against some of the dangers of incomplete or misunderstood communication. "The single greatest reason for conflict is misunderstanding" (Harris, 2002, p. 284). When administrative supervisors are open to the reality that they might be misunderstood, they listen carefully to the responses they get from their message receivers. They check for both understanding and misunderstanding. They listen especially for erroneous assumptions that might undermine concurrence in discussions. When appropriate a strategy that is useful is to invite other parties in conversations to summarize what they thought they heard.

Some discussions with colleague administrative supervisors become conflicts, based on the different interests of the supervisors involved. Administrative supervisors in counseling are responsible for the appropriate use of counselors' time and talent. Often they find it necessary to confront their peers, based on their differing degrees of responsibility for the counselor supervisees. Confrontation—addressing the issues head-on—may feel uncomfortable to counseling supervisors. In counseling supervision, confrontation is typically cast as being gentle: identifying discrepancies or incongruities so that others may discover them and their ramifications for themselves. Not so here. Administrative supervisors' confrontations with other administrative supervisors require them to be assertive about their positions. Assertiveness requires self-confidence and the courage of one's convictions. Healthy confrontations at work focus on resolving problems, which often entails helping other administrative supervisors or administrators identify alternative ways to meet their needs and responsibilities. Effective administrative supervisors express their opposition to the position taken by others who would misuse counselors. They present their rationale, listen carefully to the others' agendas, and communicate until understanding is achieved. In these sometimes-tense encounters, they keep their emotions in check. If appropriate, they work collaboratively to help others find alternative solutions.

7

Advocate for the Clients, Counseling and Counselors Within and Outside the Agency

To best serve the counseling clients, administrative supervisors advocate for clients, counseling services and perspectives, their counseling departments and staff members, and for their agencies. Advocacy entails working for "a cause beyond oneself" (Glickman, Gordon & Ross-Gordon, 1995). In the American Counseling Association [ACA] *Code of Ethics* (2005), advocacy is defined as the "promotion of the well-being of individuals and groups and of the counseling profession within systems and organizations. Advocacy seeks to remove barriers and obstacles that inhibit access, growth, and development" (Glossary). It is an ethical and professional responsibility of all counselors (ACA, 2005; American Mental Health Counselors Association [AMHCA], 2000; American School Counselor Association [ASCA], 2004a; ASCA, 2005). "When appropriate, counselors advocate at individual, group, institutional, and societal levels to examine potential barriers and obstacles that inhibit access and/or growth and development of clients" (ACA, 2005, A.6.a.). "Advocacy begins with the leadership" (Lopez, 2002, p. 96). Your experiences as a counselor advocating for your clients, your clinical supervisees, and the profession give you a foundation for carrying out these responsibilities.

Advocacy is a political activity. The more politically adept you are, the more effective you will be in influencing others to attain professionally desirable ends. Being intentional enhances your advocacy efforts: know the messages you want to convey, relate effectively to the relevant audiences, and communicate the right messages to the right audiences in the right ways. In fact, formalized advocacy plans are recommended, so that you are properly prepared for opportunities that arise (Henderson & Gysbers, 1998). I spent approximately 15% of my time advocating (Henderson, 1999, 2001).

KNOW YOUR MESSAGES

Being specific about your advocacy agenda is key to successful advocacy. Effective advocacy is based on clear and succinct communications. When striving to influence others, it is important to recognize that, while you have your agenda, others have agenda items also. You and potential allies identify mutual agenda items, or items that individuals in an alliance are willing to support. Then, demonstrate understanding of others' agenda or points through your thoughts, words, and/or deeds, reaffirming the mutuality of the goals. In advocacy situations, silent partners do not contribute much. Silence is welcome, however, when you do not agree with someone else's agenda, but, when it is professionally appropriate, are willing to keep those opinions to yourself.

Knowing the essence of what is being advocated is essential to finding commonalities and making compromises. "In implementing advocacy, administrators [and other decision-makers] appreciate and are more likely to be receptive to supervisor communications that outline the problem clearly and suggest alternative solutions for consideration" (Kadushin & Harness, 2002, p. 71). When you pre-determine what you want to achieve through each of your advocacy efforts you are more apt to get it.

One set of advocacy messages are those aimed at helping your clients get their needs met. Advocacy is "a process for pleading the rights of others who for some reason are unable to help themselves" (Kurpius & Rozecki, 1992, p. 179). Specific agenda items for advocating for clients' welfare are about them as individuals and as members of groups. Individuals have unique needs that may not fit into the patterns established by agencies for diagnoses and related interventions. Groups of clients may have culturally specific needs that are not recognized or understood by others (Chapters 2 and 3). Your messages are based on clear understanding of exactly what those needs are and what you think the agency should do to better serve their interests. Often advocacy is about reminding others that meeting the clients' needs holds a higher priority than meeting the counselors' or the agency's needs.

A second set of messages is those you use in advocating for appreciation of counseling and the enhancement of counseling services. You also advocate to champion ideas, beliefs, or programs that for some reason are under-supported by others. Know and communicate about, not only how counseling helps clients, but also what effective counseling is. Know the profession's standards and what they look like in practice.

Counseling, itself, is often misunderstood. As one administrative supervisor put it:

> It is hard for me to fight the wave of disbelief that flows through society. When I started—prior to the media attention that was given to Postpartum Depression and my belief that women are different creatures—I had respected physicians look me right in the eye and say there was no such thing as PPD. It was difficult to counter such brick walls and often times, mockery. It wasn't that I just had to advocate for counseling—something many still do not give credence to—but then I had to advocate for the existence of a particular disorder! Phew! There were—and still are—some tough days. (S. D. Clifford, personal communication, August 14, 2005)

To be an effective advocate, know what conditions are needed to ensure provision of high quality services, and the quantity of services that are needed by the clients and by the agency. Having an accurate vision of what the counseling service delivery system is and what it could be as it improves allows you to advocate for the conditions that would support its integrity. Conditions include not only the design of the program/delivery system, but also provision of sufficient human, financial and political resources. A lesson learned by a school-based administrative supervisor in counseling was that:

> The decisions campus administrators make are based on their perspectives as to what is in the best interest of the students. It is the responsibility of the Guidance Department and counselors to educate administrators by demonstrating the structure of a comprehensive guidance program and how students benefit because of it. (Lopez, 2002, pp. 99–100)

A third set of messages is those used to incorporate the premises, values and goals of the counseling profession into the agencies' and society's premises, values and goals. You have opportunities to bring the counseling perspective and values to groups outside the department as you work collaboratively on resolving agency, and community problems and issues. The perspectives, values and beliefs about human growth and development, about clients' and society's issues, and about the human services, including counseling, are expressed in the professional standards and knowledge base. For example, the counseling profession's basic premise is that counselors "are dedicated to the enhancement of human development throughout the life span, [and] recognize diversity and embrace a cross-cultural approach in support of the worth, dignity, potential, and uniqueness of people within their social and cultural contexts" (ACA, 2005, Preamble). There are generally accepted professional value principles (Forester-Miller & Davis, 1996, ¶ 2). Advocacy goals often are "to alleviate social, psychological, or educational inequities and to prevent similar circumstances from occurring in the future" (Kurpius & Rozecki, 1992, p. 179). The profession's multicultural "competencies state that environmental oppression contributes to psychological distress and recommend that it is the responsibility of mental health professionals to understand sociopolitical issues and the ways these impinge on professionals as well as on clients" (Arredondo & Toporek, 2004, p. 48).

You advocate for the improvement of "the quality of life for individuals and groups and remove potential barriers to the provision of access or appropriate services being offered" (ACA, 2005, Section C. Introduction). This is sometimes done by being:

> an active participant in the formulation or reformulation of agency policy [procedures and practice]. Having learned from the direct-service workers about client and community needs, having learned about the

deficiencies and shortcomings of agency policy [procedures and prac-tices] when workers have attempted to implement [them], the supervisor should do more than act as a passive channel for upward communica-tion of this information. The supervisor has the responsibility of using his or her knowledge of the situation to formulate suggested changes in agency policy and procedure and practice. (Kadushin & Harness, 2002, p. 75)

The specific agenda items that you advocate are dependent on the specializa-tion of the counseling services provided in your department.

A fourth set of advocacy messages is those you use to establish and protect the image of the counseling department (Henderson & Gysbers, 1998). Image is the result of people's perceptions. Positive perceptions attract people to seek help there, work there, and collaborate there. Examples of characteristics that make a department attractive are perceptions of being informal and approach-able for clients; having a staff that is innovative, exciting, daring, and open to experiences; having staff members who are trustworthy, honest, and accepting of social responsibility, and who do quality work, are successful, and adhere to ethical standards and regulations. An attractive department is one whose adver-tising claims are credible, who are fiscally responsible, and whose administra-tive supervisor manages talent and treats employees well (Davis, Chun, Da Silva & Roper, 2004; Helms, 2005; Resnick, 2004).

Examples of characteristics that have a negative impact on the attractive-ness of a department are perceptions of ruthlessness, arrogance, being control-ling, and/or toughness (machismo), especially in human service work (Davis et al., 2004). Image "is not static. It can change for either the better or the worse" (Resnick, p. 34). Be ever vigilant of key people's perceptions of your department.

A fifth set of messages is those you use for maintaining the professional integrity of counselors and for attaining appropriate working conditions for department staff members. For example, you support professional counselors by advocating "strongly for the integrity of appropriate professional auto-nomy" (Staton, 2000, p. 25), for counselors' professionalism and their need for continuous professional development. Non-counselors, including other men-tal health professionals and generalist administrators (Henderson & Gysbers, 1998), may not be aware of the knowledge and competency bases of the counseling profession. As the links to others, it is incumbent upon you to edu-cate others regarding the appropriate identity and roles of counselors (e.g., not being assigned as paraprofessional aides to psychologists). The success of your advocacy efforts upward is key to your supervisees' satisfaction with your supervision (Kadushin & Harness, 2002). A school counseling administrative supervisor articulates it well:

It is important to articulate and advocate for the appropriate role of counselors. No one in the District or on the campuses knows the guidance and counseling perspective as well as the professionals who are charged with implementing the program. (E. Zambrano, personal communication, June 14, 2005)

You advocate for working conditions that support the efforts of all department staff members. For example, advocate for appropriate pay, benefits, and working conditions. Agencies "get what they pay for" (Martin, 2000, p. 219). It is your job to advocate for appropriate job descriptions and for fair and appropriate treatment of your employees.

A sixth set of messages is those you use, as members of the agency's administrative structure and as employees, in advocating to defend the integrity of, and generate support for, the agency as a whole. You are charged with helping, along with other agency administrators, "to manage the institution's social impacts and to discharge its social responsibilities" (Drucker, 1974, p. 32). You are responsible for "defending institutional integrity . . . [You] ensure that the organization meets external needs and stays healthy" (Reichard, 2000, p. 189). To carry this out appropriately, be able to articulate agency policies, service priorities, and the parameters of its resources. And, be able to explain the rationale behind agency decisions.

RELATE TO RELEVANT AUDIENCES

Advocating effectively requires that you build good relationships with a wide range of people in order to transmit your advocacy messages. You advocate with individuals and groups within and outside your agency, e.g., from advocating with your staff members to advocating with your state legislators or members of Congress.

Within the agency, you use your communication channels, networks and grapevines (Chapter 6) to advocate. In the community, you have contact with others that range from connecting with other counselors to community members who may not have a lot of information about counseling or may have negative opinions about counseling. You represent your agency, the counseling profession and counselors when you work with your colleagues, associates, and clients in the community. It is important to bear in mind that others judge the groups you represent based on your behaviors.

Maintain your connections with the professional counseling community outside the agency. Professional associations provide a primary vehicle for this, as do attending classes, workshops, and participating in clinical supervision groups. Other useful intra- and inter-professional connections are those with counselors in other agencies and with the larger mental health community, e.g., counselors in the same counseling specialty in other practice settings, counselors with other specialties, psychologists, social workers, and psychiatrists.

Build advocacy connections and alliances with clients' community groups and social networks, and, for minors or those who do not live independently, with clients' parents, other caretakers, and teachers. Belong to groups working for systemic changes that seek to remove barriers to clients' enhanced development (ACA, n.d.a).

To advocate effectively in the community, build connections with individuals that have political influence over the profession or the agency, e.g., local, state and federal legislators and their staff members; agency policy setters, regulators, and administrators. Build connections with other groups that may not be directly related to your practice, but who have influence or other resources that might support your work and advocacy efforts, e.g., sitting on other advisory boards, belonging to the Chamber of Commerce or other business or labor groups. Collaborate with community organizations to achieve systemic change (ACA, n.d.a).

You have opportunities to advocate with the public at large through the media. You are asked to provide information to educate the public and to influence public policy (ACA, n.d.a). As stated in the ACA Advocacy Competencies (n.d.a), advocacy-oriented counselors "awaken the general public to macro-systemic issues regarding human dignity" (p. 3) and development. The media tell human interest stories, many of which involve mental health issues. Often they contact counselors when there is a mental health crisis—either involving an individual with a mental health issue, or a group issue such as a teen suicide. These provide opportunities, not only to provide information about the specific incident, but also for helping the public better understand such issues. These opportunities also provide the public with glimpses of counselor expertise. The Code of Ethics of the American Mental Health Counselors Association (2000) informs counselors regarding these opportunities:

> Mental health counselors in their professional roles may be expected or required to make public statements providing counseling information or professional opinions; or supply information about the availability of counseling products and services. In making such statements, mental health counselors take into full account the limits and uncertainties of present counseling knowledge and techniques. (Principle 13)

For example, professionally we have some information about suicide, but we do not have all the answers about it nor what was really at work in an individual circumstance.

Advocacy Relationships

You develop advocacy relationships with a wide and diverse range of people. Working with these ever-widening circles of others when they are significant to the counseling clients, services, and staff challenges you to transfer your rapport-building skills to new levels. It is best if these relationships are built long before you undertake advocacy efforts; however, often you are required to build relationships and your credibility with others in short order. It is helpful to you, as you advocate, if your enthusiasm for your profession is obvious—as exemplified by one who exclaimed, "I *enjoy* sharing with others what we do!" (S. D. Clifford, personal communication, August 14, 2005). "Credibility is built not only on the capacity to articulate guidance [and counseling] agenda, but also on being perceived as having power in the shared environment" (Henderson & Gysbers, 1998, p. 87).

Rapport and alliances are built in relationships that may not be very full. Often they are short term, of limited purpose, and are based on incomplete information. They are formed in the environment of the agency, workplace, and community and are built to accomplish tasks and goals and to solve problems (Henderson & Gysbers, 1998). They are not helping relationships as those words are defined in counseling. They are professional acquaintanceships.

Because the shared information in these relationships is incomplete, the relationships themselves are vulnerable to imperfections and flaws: "Mutual understanding, respect, trust, and credibility are difficult to build in relationships that are only minimally developed and in which common goals may be hard to identify. The [power] of the involved parties may be in conflict, in competition, or simply not understood" (Henderson & Gysbers, 1998, p. 87). One goal in developing these relationships is to form alliances that will support mutual advocacy efforts (ACA, n.d.a).

In advocacy circumstances, maintain your professional detachment and objectivity, keep focused on relevant agenda and goals, and act in good faith. This is particularly difficult when others in the relationship do not do this; for example, when others lose their objectivity and get angry, or when they shift the professional agenda to a personal one, or when their motives are personal and not in the clients' best interest (Henderson & Gysbers, 1998).

CONVEY YOUR MESSAGES EFFECTIVELY

Understand the Situation

To advocate well it is essential to know the context of the discussion. Seek clarity about your position in relationship to that of the person or group with whom you are advocating—the individual or group that will be making the decision. Learn how your position fits either formally or informally with others. And, what the relevance is of the topic being discussed to your position. To be politically effective, work within the operational dynamics and culture of the agency and the community. Learn the intricacies of the dynamics and the nuances of the culture (Henderson & Gysbers, 1998), and the history of the issue. "It is important to know where you have been in order to advocate for a new vision of where you want to be" (Lopez, 2002, p. 97). Understand the issues, the choices involved and the potential ramifications of the decision(s) to be made.

Assess the Situation

To assess a situation, determine how legitimate your stake is in the discussion, and how important the decision-makers think your opinion or information on the issue is to them. It is highly legitimate to offer thoughts about the welfare of clients, about counseling and counselors. It may not be so legitimate to offer thoughts about the value of blood tests.

Key to swaying votes is your ability to garner support for your position. As one Board member says, "Know how to count!"—that is, up to the number needed to constitute a majority of the people voting. On an ongoing basis, foster relationships with key people—those with power to influence decisions that relate directly or indirectly to the counseling agenda. In assessing the odds of success in making a point in a specific situation, learn who else is involved in the discussion and what their positions and messages are. Then, assess your political strength in relationship to the others in the situation. Consider the interpersonal opportunities, boundaries and limits in the situation. Identify those whose values are compatible with counseling standards and values, and build coalitions, sharing your resources and power to further mutual agendas (Henderson & Gysbers, 1998; Rezaie & Garrison, 2004).

It must be determined if the cost of losing a point is worth it. Every conflict that results in a loss damages a leader's power. Thus it is important to recognize others' "bottomlines" or "nonnegotiables" and provide for face-saving—your own and others'. In other words, to be politically effective, pick your battles, and respond with a view to future interactions. Consider the impact of wins and losses on the next debate.

Having a good sense of timing is part of being politically effective. Know when you are being proactive, responsive or reactive, and tailor your interactions appropriately. Know when the time is right to discuss an agenda item, and when it is not. If an item is on your agenda, but not on that of the decision-makers, you have to either wait until it is on the larger agenda or do preliminary work that gets the item on the table. Advice offered by one administrative supervisor is to:

> "Know when to hold 'em, know when to fold 'em, know when to walk away and know when to run" [Schlitz, 1978, track 1]—. . . pick your battles wisely. Counselor and counselor program advocacy can be complicated. Small battles can be won much easier and with far fewer casualties than an all out war. (T. E. Miller, personal communication, June 13, 2005)

Respond Strategically

Identify messages that highlight areas of mutuality with your allies. How you deliver the message depends on the characteristics (idiosyncrasies) of the relationship(s). Recognize that your voice is stronger with more weight behind you. The weight might come through the sheer force of logic. Often you have "to rely on rational arguments, ingratiation, or negotiating some kind of exchange in advocating for acceptance of suggestions. The sophisticated supervisor needs to be able to formulate the suggestion in the most acceptable or the least objectionable manner" (Kadushin & Harness, 2002, p. 71). In situations with elected officials, the weight behind the ideas is often more about the number of people (e.g., voters) that also support the position.

Weight often comes with the power to make relevant decisions in a situation. In your efforts to influence others to support the counseling agenda and to bring competing agenda into closer alignment, use your power bases appropriately. Analyze where your power is based in the situation. For example, if your power rests in your legitimate position, ensure that others are aware that this is your business. If you have information that will enlighten others, provide it as such. If your expertise applies, display it. Most often you rely on your referent power (that based in the strengths of your relationships).

When you are politically astute, you also recognize the power that others in the discussion have. You, then, work within those dynamics (Henderson & Gysbers, 1998). The trick is not over- or under-estimating your own or others' power. By not acknowledging (and seizing) your rightful power, you have a tendency to give it away. Once it is gone, it may be hard to get back.

Perform appropriate function(s). To advocate effectively, educate others at every opportunity, whether in informal conversations, in formal conferences, meetings, or in planned presentations. Each interaction, no matter how short, is an opportunity to raise others' consciousness about counseling clients, services, and perspectives, and/or counselors' professionalism.

There are several functions that you fulfill in advocating. That is, there are multiple ways to demonstrate commitment to a cause. A continuum of functions is available that require different levels of involvement. Indicators of the degree of involvement include the amount of your contribution of resources (e.g., intellectual, time, political, and professional) to an advocacy effort. Levels of involvement range in the degree of participation, energy expended, and commitment you make (Henderson & Gysbers, 1998).

At the lowest end of the participation continuum, you *represent* your counseling department; for example, attending community functions. Your contribution is time. The second level of involvement with a cause is to *provide information* to others; for example, distributing pamphlets describing Licensed Professional Counselors, such as *Who Are Licensed Professional Counselors* (ACA, n.d.d.). Your contributions consist of time and established intellectual property.

The third level is to *welcome* others into the counseling arena; for example, welcoming new clients and clients' significant others into your department or services. Your contribution consists of time and some energy. The fourth level is *reaching out* to others; for example, "attending Precinct Court to sign adolescents up for free counseling, when it was ordered by the Judge" (D. J. Martin, personal communication, July 30, 2005). This advocacy function requires commitment of information, time and energy. The fifth function is to *support* others' work; for example, speaking out on another's behalf. This function requires contributions of intellect and political resources. The last four functions require substantial commitment of intellect, time, energy and resources. The sixth is to *cooperate*—working side-by-side with others. In addition, the last three require initiative and leadership. The seventh function, to *collaborate*; for example, participating in the agency's strategic or ongoing planning. The eighth, to *consult*; for example, consulting with policy-setters as they consider counseling-related policies. The ninth, to *advocate* (Henderson & Gysbers, 1998).

When you are not your department's representative in advocacy situations, carefully select your representatives. The delegate must represent the department well. These occasions are "public appearances," and it is important to put the department's and the profession's best foot forward into the other context.

Remember ACA's Advocacy Tips

Advocacy skills are described elsewhere (e.g., ACA, n.d.a; Trusty & Brown, 2005; Henderson & Gysbers, 1998). The ACA Office of Public Policy and Legislation (2006) offers "Rules for Effective Advocacy." They list 18 basic principles to guide advocates' work:

- Ask for what you want.
- Be specific in your request.
- Be ready to work hard.
- Find a [policy-setting] champion.
- Organize, coordinate, orchestrate.
- Touch all the bases.
- Stay flexible; be opportunistic.
- Keep it simple.
- Assume the perspective of others.
- Build and preserve your credibility.
- Anticipate and deal with your opposition.
- Be prepared to compromise.
- Never burn your bridges.
- Target your efforts.
- Honor the policy-setters' support staff.
- Track your progress.
- Be persistent.
- Follow up (p. 2).

HAVE AN ADVOCACY PLAN

A formal advocacy plan helps you and counselors advocate most effectively (e.g., ACA, n.d.a; Gysbers & Henderson, 2006; Resnick, 2004; Trotter, 2002). Having already clarified what is to be said to whom, you are better prepared to say it when the opportunity is presented. Developing an advocacy plan, like developing other kinds of organizational plans, requires an application of systems thinking. It assists you and counselors to be realistic in your advocacy efforts and to identify available human, material, financial and political resources. In planning, anticipate:

(a) what audiences you might address,
(b) how to approach each of these,
(c) who would be responsible, and
(d) what the time line would be to be proactive. (Trotter, 2002)

SUMMARY

As an administrative supervisor, you spend much of your time advocating for clients, counseling and counselors. You are most effective when you advocate intentionally. To be intentional, determine the messages you want to convey and identify the audiences they relate to. Strive to communicate the messages that are appropriate to an audience in ways that are most apt to be effective in achieving your advocacy goals. Developing a plan for advocating in advance of situations helps guide your efforts.

SUPERVISORS' CHALLENGES AND RESPONSES

Supervisors' Challenge: Complainers

Administrative supervisors are challenged to advocate reactively for the welfare of their clients or their staff members in the face of often emotionally charged, adversarial complainers. Administrative supervisors in publicly funded agencies might be confronted by political activists who do not believe in counseling and who protest the very existence of the services. "Administration looks to the first-line supervisory staff to handle problems relating to services. Consequently, the supervisor performs the function of dealing with clients [or others] who want to discuss a complaint with someone other than the worker" (Kadushin & Harness, 2002, p. 71).

Administrative supervisors and complainers often have different perspectives on and agendas for solving a problem. The relationships between them are incomplete. Prior to resolving an issue, supervisors must discuss the situation, the issue and its possible resolution with their supervisees who are involved. Often, the supervisees react emotionally (e.g., become defensive, are hurt). Some administrative supervisors find this harder than working with people from outside the department. As one counseling administrative supervisor recounts, "It is hard to speak directly to your staff members or others about 'negative' things, even though they are things that need to be said" (M. L. Libby, personal communication, September 5, 2006).

Supervisors' Responses

Effective administrative supervisors listen carefully as people describe their concerns. They take notes on what is said. They paraphrase back what they have heard to ensure understanding. They strive to maintain their professional objectivity, even when the complainers are irrational or emotional. They recognize the power of other individuals. It is essential that they hear both sides of a story before they pass judgment about a situation. They often use their assertion or confrontation skills. Most of these situations are, in fact, negotiations. In searching for suitable compromises, administrative supervisors work to find common ground between the conflicting sides. Their primary responsibility is to do what is in the best interest of clients and the counseling staff members, but they avoid defensiveness.

Dealing with difficult people is not easy. "They might be stubborn, arrogant, hostile, greedy, or dishonest" (Hackley, 2004, p. 3). They "may have an arsenal of weapons, including ridicule, bullying, insults, deception, and exaggeration. In some cases they might attack you; in others, they might avoid confrontation. Sometimes you are taken by surprise; at other times, there might be a chronic problem you need to address" (Hackley, p. 4).

Effective negotiation involves a four-phase process:

1. preparation,
2. information exchange,
3. bargaining, and
4. commitment.

Professional negotiators, such as lawyers, recommend that people prepare for a negotiation, as much as time allows. Experience is a great teacher in responding to complaints. It is important to know what is upsetting, what the bottom lines are, and what is unacceptable. It is helpful to anticipate what the complainer might bring up, so that responses can be anticipated—and suggest the rationale behind keeping their bosses informed.

Effective negotiators help complainers feel heard and understood, without capitulating to unreasonable demands. They, then, move the discussion from confrontation to joint problem solving. A strategy cited by Hackley (2004) for saying "no" is "sandwiching the no between two 'yeses.' First, say yes to your own interests and needs. Then say no to the particular demand or behavior. Finally, say yes as you make a proposal" (p. 4). For example, "This is not sufficient information to fire a typically high performing counselor." Then, acknowledge their point, and "If what you say happened in the way you said, you may have a legitimate concern. I will speak with X and learn her perspective, and get back to you." It is important for administrative supervisors to state their basic positions up front, rather than withhold them. It is also important to be clear about what cannot be done, and then end with providing opportunities to work together toward issue resolution. Effective administrative supervisors allow complainers to save face by hearing their concerns and seeking possible accommodations. "Bring them to their senses, not their knees" (p. 4). When agreement is reached, the results of the discussion are written down, and the administrative supervisor follows up, as promised.

IV

Administrative Supervisors: Supervise, Lead, Manage, and Administer the People who Report to Them to Help Each Individual Advance Toward Optimum Performance, Productivity, and Job Satisfaction

- Establish Professional Cultures That Support Excellence

- Build Healthy, Meaningful Professional and Personal Relationships With Each Staff Member

- Nurture Continuous Improvement of Each Staff Member's Performance

- Apply Your Own Models for Providing Effective Administrative Supervision

- Organize Staff Members for Effective Service Delivery

- Implement Effectively a Performance Management System

- Evaluate Each Staff Member's Performance

8
Establish Professional Cultures That Support Excellence

To best serve the counseling clients, administrative supervisors establish department cultures that aim for excellent client services provided by counselors functioning at the highest levels of professional practice. Employees who work in an entity that has:

> a well defined and motivating vision and who buy into values such as customer service, superior quality, integrity, and excellence are more apt to derive satisfaction from their work. They tend to approach their jobs with a sense of pride, and strive constantly for excellence and superiority. (Quigley, 1994, p. 40)

When staff members do excellent work and are satisfied with their jobs, they provide optimal client services. Being "excellent" means being "meritoriously near the standard or model" (*Webster's Third*, 2002).

When you recognize that "organizational cultures are learned, shared and transmitted" (Harris, 2002, p. 252), you understand that well-established cultures provide values, assumptions, informal and formal ideologies, rules, mores, traditions, attitudes, myths, symbols, rituals, missions, codes of values, behavioral norms, language, jargon, social etiquette, dress and appropriate demeanor (Harris). They dictate roles and performance standards, as individuals define their places within them. These provide direction to the group members through the shared meaning attached to their work.

In order to establish cultures that support professional excellence, you establish high expectations for your supervisees' performance, create conditions that support job satisfaction, and treat them with professional respect. Your experiences in striving for excellence in counseling and supervision give you a foundation for fostering this in the department staff members.

ESTABLISH HIGH EXPECTATIONS
Client Results

By clearly establishing desired client results and guidelines for achieving them, you provide ways for your staff members to evaluate their own work and for others to do the same (Covey, 1991). However, defining quality and productivity in knowledge work "requires the difficult, risk-taking and always controversial definition as to what 'results' are for a given enterprise and a given activity" (Drucker, 1999, pp. 147–148).

> Defining quality mental health care . . . is often difficult. Nevertheless, quality in health care ultimately rests with patient outcomes. . . . Understanding the links between patient outcomes and what we do in [mental health processes] provides a framework for continuous quality/performance improvement—a concept that focuses on improving poor outcomes or maximizing good outcomes through appropriate changes to the processes of care. (Krousel-Wood, 2000, p. 233)

High Professional Standards

As with other knowledge workers, professional counselors want clear values, standards, and rules to live within. They want to work in cultures that are professionally understandable and meaningful (Drucker, 1999). Ensure that those that you and your supervisees hold for high quality professional performance are sound. Base your work on the profession's minimum and aspirational ethical standards (Chapter 4), those for counselors' competence, commitment, motivation and professional identity (Chapter 10), and those that guide employees' work ethics and habits.

Continually connect the department's operations and related performance to these standards. Express values about desirable performance behaviors overtly and consistently, and encourage ongoing reflection by your supervisees on their conformity to them. Engage supervisees frequently, individually and in groups, in discussions about what performing at levels approaching excellent means, providing substantive examples. If you do not keep the desired behaviors at the forefront of their minds and reinforce their applications, some staff members sink to the level of their lowest performing colleague ("She makes the same money I do!"). The lowest common denominator becomes the operational definition.

CREATE SATISFYING CONDITIONS

You help counselors achieve high levels of performance by establishing conditions that build the department "into a great place to work" (Buckingham & Coffman, 1999, p. 29), one that is designed to provide for their satisfaction through supporting the quality of their performance (Drucker, 1974).

Job Satisfaction

When they are empowered to practice according to professional standards, and work in an environment that fosters positive relations based on trust and respect, knowledge workers are more satisfied with their jobs and are more committed to their organizations (Laschinger & Finegan, 2005). This is a two-way street: feeling satisfied with their work supports counselors' efforts to provide high quality services. When they are providing high quality services to clients, they feel satisfied with their work.

From their massive research study, Buckingham & Coffman (1999) identified 12 questions that need to be answered in the affirmative by your supervisees in order to attract, focus, and keep the most talented employees:

1. Do I know what is expected of me at work?
2. Do I have the materials and equipment I need to do my work right?
3. At work, do I have the opportunity to do what I do best every day?
4. In the last seven days, have I received recognition or praise for doing good work?
5. Does my supervisor, or someone at work, seem to care about me as a person?
6. Is there someone at work who encourages my development?
7. At work, do my opinions seem to count?
8. Does the mission/purpose of my company make me feel my job is important?
9. Are my co-workers committed to doing quality work?
10. Do I have a best friend at work?
11. In the last six months, has someone at work talked to me about my progress?
12. This last year, have I had opportunities at work to learn and grow? (p. 28)

Strive to create an environment where your supervisees answer positively to all 12 questions. The researchers also concluded that managers most directly affect the answers to questions 1, 2, 3, 5, and 7. The most powerful questions—those with the strongest links to the most client outcomes—are questions 1–6 (Buckingham & Coffman). (Ways to affect your supervisees' answers to these questions are discussed throughout this *Handbook*.)

Credibility

In order to promote a highly professional department culture, you must establish credibility as a supervisor. By holding high standards for yourself, you model the professional traits you want in your supervisees. The American Mental Health Counselors Association [AMHCA] Code of Ethics (2000) states that supervisors "must have a high degree of self-awareness of their own values, knowledge, skills and needs" (Principle 6). You are to be a role model who accepts personal responsibility—are personally accountable (Miller, 2004).

It is also recommended that you be altruistic, service oriented, and maintain a positive outlook and positive energy. It is effective to demonstrate the "virtues" and "character strengths" identified by Seligman, Steen, Park, and Peterson (2005): wisdom and knowledge, courage, humanity, justice, temperance, and transcendence. Other examples of good character traits that enhance administrative supervision are being honest—true to your word; fair—not judging prematurely, and able to hear all sides of a story; ethical—making choices based on sound principles; open-minded—to others' personal and job-related ideas and choices; and respectful—being courteous, intuitive, unbiased, and caring about others as human beings as well as workers.

What you "say and do provides significant symbolic messages" (Harris, 2002, p. 264). One excellent manager offered advice to new managers: "Remember [you are] on stage every day. . . . These clues affect performance. So never forget you are on that stage" (Buckingham & Coffman, 1999, p. 16). Others echo this. In reflecting on their transitions from counselors to administrative supervisors, Steves wrote, "you find that you lead by example" (personal communication, June 16, 2005); Malloy, a new administrative supervisor, wrote, "The first transitional issue that comes to mind is one of attitude. I am learning that my attitude will be contagious" (personal communication, June 13, 2005). Drucker (1974), too, stated, "the worker's attitude reflects, above all, the attitude of his [sic] management" (p. 379).

Reading symbolic behaviors may be problematic in that they may be misinterpreted, misunderstood, or perceived as lacking substance (Harris, 2002). To ensure you are modeling what you believe is right, monitor how and what others are reading in you. For example, Curtis and Sherlock (2006) highlight the importance of being just. Counselors' perceptions that their organization is just contribute to the quality of their performance and loyalty. You accomplish this "by being consistent, unbiased, ethical, and flexible and by providing ongoing accurate information to employees about all aspects of their work and the agency's goals" (p. 121). To establish trust, one great manager's advice is to "Make very few promises to your people, and keep them all" (Buckingham & Coffman, 1999, p. 16).

The same manager advises, "Never pass the buck" (Buckingham & Coffman, 1999, p. 16). Passing the buck implies that you are not taking responsibility for decisions, but blaming them on someone else. It also implies that you either did not or were not effective in advocating for actions you could support in earnest.

To be a true counselor leader, you also establish credibility as a professional counselor, and maintain counseling as your basic professional identity. As Miller advised,

> Don't ever forget where you came from, i.e., what it is like in the "field"! While leading and managing is a different role, we must remember to not ask others to do what we are not willing to do or have not done ourselves. Model your expectations of others. (Personal communication, June 13, 2005)

Productive and Meaningful Work

To facilitate professional counselors' excellent performance, you make the work itself productive and meaningful. As knowledge workers, professional counselors seek personal satisfaction that comes from work-related achievements: contributing to others, performing well, serving their own personal values, and fulfilling themselves (Drucker, 1974). Administrative supervisees need the "demand, the discipline, and the incentive of responsibility" (p. 308). "Build upward responsibility and upward contribution into the job of each of your subordinates" (Drucker, 1974, p. 309). Clarify the standards for accountability (Covey, 1991). (Establishing goals and objectives is discussed in Chapters 15 and 17.)

Help counselors know, feel and accept responsibility for achievement of the greater good. As Drucker states it, "To make a living is no longer enough. Work also has to make a life" (p. 179). In addition to client service, professional work is tied to being a productive member of society. Part of being a professional is taking responsibility for one's "own job and work group, for . . . contributions to the performance and results of the entire organization, and for the social tasks of the work community" (p. 284). (Establishing visions and missions of the department is discussed in Chapters 2 and 15, respectively.)

Clear Job Responsibilities

Finding satisfaction in their jobs begins with individuals having clear understanding of what their jobs are. Knowledge workers value knowing what their responsibilities are and having autonomy in carrying out those responsibilities. They value being encouraged to be innovative in their work. They like to understand the context of their jobs—the history, and how it fits into the organizational structure. They need to know the standards for them, and that attaining excellence in them is a developmental process. Help your supervisees define their tasks so they can concentrate on them and eliminate everything else—at least as far as is feasible. (Establishing individual job descriptions is discussed in Chapter 12.)

Play

Finally, enjoying one's job is part of finding satisfaction in it. "Maturity and responsibility should never be confused with lack of playfulness. There is always a time and place for both and knowing when to do which is a definite sign of responsible maturity" (Cottringer, 2005b, p. 7). Thus, another challenge is to look for legitimate times and ways to turn work into play or to find the fun in work.

TREAT SUPERVISEES WITH PROFESSIONAL RESPECT

Continuous Professional Development

A hallmark of professionals is their continuous quest to improve their practice. In keeping with established standards for quality performance, establish expectations for your administrative supervisees to pursue professional development. While provision of excellent counseling services is primarily the responsibility of professional counselors, share responsibility by providing them opportunities to experience new learning (Drucker, 1999) to further their capacities to help their clients achieve desired results.

Actively engage in the supervision of your supervisees' professional performance (e.g., Borders & Brown, 2005; Hersey, Blanchard & Johnson, 2001; Martin, 2000). Unfortunately, "the most common approach to high-end knowledge work . . . can by summarized as hire smart people and leave them alone" (Davenport, Thomas & Cantrell, 2002, p. 26). Such *laissez-faire* approaches are not very effective in helping professionals maintain their motivation to learn.

To be supportive, facilitate your supervisees' meeting the continuing education requirements associated with their licenses, certificates and the agency, and their professional goals. Build the department into a professional learning community (Fullan, 2002). "Creating and sharing knowledge is central to effective leadership. Information, of which we have a glut, only becomes knowledge through a social process. For this reason, relationships and professional learning communities are essential" (Fullan, Knowledge Creation and Sharing, ¶ 1). As described in Chapters 10 and 14, effective administrative supervisors establish systems for managing goal-directed performance improvements.

Assumptions

A desirable, basic assumption is to believe that each of your supervisees can become a self-managing, independent, and mature professional (Covey, 1991). Maslow (1998/1962) suggested 36 positive assumptions that encourage supervisees' movement toward excellence; for example, they want to achieve by doing a good job, have good will for all the members of the organization, enjoy teamwork, are psychologically healthy, seek self-actualization, are resilient, want to improve, and prefer responsibility to dependency and passivity most of the time.

Most professionals come to work every day to give 100% of themselves to their work. They want and have the capacity to do well. Sometimes administrative supervisors who face working with impaired professionals find this belief difficult to apply; however, if you lose this belief about an individual or a group, carefully analyze the sources of your disbelief, consult with other administrative supervisors, and confront the supervisee(s). Supervision is not effective when you lose faith in a supervisee's desire or ability to grow.

Talent Development

To achieve excellence, nurture your supervisees' inherent gifts.

Every role performed at excellence, requires talent, because *every* role, performed at excellence, requires certain *recurring* patterns of thought, feeling, or behavior . . . The *right talents*, more than experience, more than brainpower, and more than willpower alone, are *the* prerequisites for excellence in all roles. (Buckingham & Coffman, 1999, pp. 71–72)

Having opportunities to apply theirs is "the driving force behind an individual's job performance" (p. 73).

Buckingham and Coffman (1999) learned that "skills, knowledge, and talents are distinct elements of a person's performance . . . Skills and knowledge can easily be taught, whereas talents cannot. Combined in the same person, they create an enormously potent compound" (p. 83). Help your supervisees identify and build on theirs, and enable them to focus on excellence (Buckingham & Coffman, 1999). You are able to discern gifts as they are:

the behaviors you find yourself doing *often*. You have a mental filter that sifts through your world, forcing you to pay attention to some stimuli, while others slip past you, unnoticed. Your instinctive ability to remember names, rather than just faces, is a talent. Your need to alphabetize your spice rack and color-code your wardrobe is a talent . . . Any *recurring* patterns of behavior that can be productively applied are talents. The key to excellent performance, of course, is finding the match between your talents and your role. (p. 71)

Managers who supervise employees with an eye to their strengths—as contrasted to their weaknesses—believe that "each person's talents are enduring and unique, . . . [and that] each person's greatest room for growth is in the areas of his or her greatest strength" (Buckingham & Clifton, 2001, p. 8). Striving to "place [supervisees] where their strengths can become productive" (Drucker, 1974, p. 309) requires assessment skills on your part.

Professional Self-esteem

Knowledge workers' productivity is affected when they are seen and treated as assets (Drucker, 1999). In order to contribute to excellence, supervisees' evaluations of themselves must be based in reality, i.e., recognizable by others. In order to feel professional self-esteem, they need such things as to be prime movers, to have control over their own fates, to make plans and carry them out, to expect success and to succeed, and to have others acknowledge their capabilities fairly (Maslow, 1998/1962). As their administrative supervisor, you are in position to help them feel valued. As one experienced administrative supervisor in counseling recommends to others:

Acknowledge/appreciate the work of others. Take a moment to email them a "thank you" for the work they do. Recognize the contribution to the success of the department. Everyone deserves a pat on the back. It only takes a second [and is] well worth it in the end. (T. E. Miller, personal communication, June 13, 2005)

Empowerment

Autonomy is important to professionals. In today's work world, they are responsible for managing themselves and their career development. In Drucker's (2005) words, "Now, most of us, even those of us with modest endowments, will have to learn to manage ourselves. We will have to learn to develop ourselves. We will have to place ourselves where we can make the greatest contribution" (p. 100).

Some of your administrative supervisees need to be empowered to manage themselves. Personal empowerment stems from individuals' beliefs that they are competent, possessing valuable knowledge and skills, and having the:

capability to take action required to overcome problems and to succeed under the stresses and pressures of life. . . . They need evidence that they can contribute to worthwhile endeavors and that they have the ability to influence events in [their] lives. (Sutton & Fall, 1995, p. 331)

You empower supervisees by helping them be aware of their strengths and talents, how they perform, what their values and motivations are, where they belong in the work world, and what they should contribute (Drucker, 2005).

Empowerment also stems from:

the processes by which a person in a superior power position increases the sense of social power of his/her subordinates. Empowerment may be accomplished by supervisors' formal granting or delegating of authority (that is, using their legitimate power to grant legitimate power to others). It can also be accomplished by other means, such as increasing subordinates referent or expert power, delegating ability to mediate rewards and punishments, demonstrating how information power can be used successfully, etc. (Raven, 2004, p. 7)

BUILD EXCELLENCE IN YOUR SUPPORT STAFF MEMBERS

Regardless of size, almost all counseling departments employ non-counseling personnel, such as administrative assistants, technicians, paraprofessionals, clerks, and receptionists. They, too, are your responsibility. The principles described above for nurturing excellence in professional counselors apply for nurturing excellence in support staff members.

When you believe in your employees, you understand that non-counseling supervisees are loyal to their own work ethics and standards; to the values of their employing agency—the provider of their livelihood; and to their bosses. Support staff members seek partnership roles in a department (DeMars, 2006). Buckingham and Coffman's (1999) 12 questions apply to them as well. Support staff members care about their relationships with the professional staff members. These are best cultivated in a culture of high professionalism and open, honest communication. You are responsible for their training about and adherence to the boundaries of their work and their business (American Counseling Association [ACA], 2005).

Burge (2006) offers some ways to build a highly productive relationship between administrative supervisors and their support staff members. In building a team approach, you:

- Give them plenty of discretion.
- Set realistic deadlines for projects.
- Develop trust over time.
- Avoid micromanaging.
- Share information in a timely manner.
- Listen closely.
- Include them in goal setting.
- Hold formal and informal reviews.
- Co-develop their careers by supporting professional growth opportunities. (p. 8)

You attend to some of the differences between them and counselors. Support staff members may not be trained and educated as professionals, but this does not mean that they do not strive for excellence in their work. It does mean that their needs and motivations are different than those of professionals. As Cebik (1985) pointed out, their levels of career-related ego development tend to fall in the "conformist" and "conscientious" stages (p. 230). They are influenced by environmental factors, rules, intra-office relationships, external rewards and consequences. They are interested in things, appearances and reputation. These are keys to you helping them perform well and find satisfaction in their jobs.

Typically, support staff members' relationship with you is their top priority. Treat them as extensions of yourself and the professional staff. Burge (2006) also suggests four strategies for maintaining healthy, meaningful relationships with support staff members:

1. Schedule time together;
2. Share your expectations;
3. Depend on each other; and
4. Openly discuss differences.

SUMMARY

To be an effective administrative supervisor, you establish a professional culture that supports excellence. You establish high expectations for results achieved by clients and for professionals' performance by helping your supervisees adhere to standards of the profession and those of your agency. You create conditions that enhance professional counselors' job satisfaction by helping them understand and carry out meaningful work. You treat them with professional respect. You fully engage your support staff in the department's culture of excellence.

SUPERVISORS' CHALLENGES AND RESPONSES

Supervisors' Challenge: Taking Over Supervisees' Work

Administrative supervisors undermine their supervisees' excellence in performance by taking over their responsibilities or problems. Oncken and Wass (1974) and Blanchard, Oncken and Burrows (1989) use a monkey-on-the-back analogy. "A monkey is the next move" (Blanchard et al., p. 26) to be made in working on a task or solving a problem or handling a case. Supervisees come to their administrative supervisors with questions or issues about handling their "monkeys." When supervisors promise to look into it, or think about it, or do something with it themselves, they are trying to rescue their supervisees. As in counseling, rescuers do something people could (and probably should) do for themselves. In these cases, rescuees often feel that their rescuers think they are not capable of handling the problems. They increase their dependence on the rescuers. "In the process, their self esteem and confidence are eroded" (Blanchard et al., p. 49).

Supervisors' Responses

Effective administrative supervisors leave supervisees' responsibilities to their supervisees without abandoning them. "The best way to develop responsibility in people is to give them responsibility" (Blanchard et al., 1989, p. 72). Oncken and Wass (1974) describe five levels of initiative that supervisees can exercise, from lowest to highest:

1. *wait* until told;
2. *ask* what to do;
3. *recommend*, then take resulting action;
4. *act*, but advise at once; and
5. *act* on own, then routinely report. (p. 79)

Rather than doing their work for them, empowering administrative supervisors want their supervisees initiating at levels 3, 4, and 5.

In working with their supervisees to help them carry out their responsibilities well, administrative supervisors follow "four rules of monkey management" (Blanchard et al., 1989, p. 94):

1st: Supervisors and supervisees discuss the issue. "The dialogue must not end until appropriate 'next moves' have been identified and specified" (p. 94).

2nd: In the discussion, the next moves are assigned for handling at the lowest organizational level needed for their accomplishment.

3rd: Administrative supervisors insure supervisees' recognize they have their support by asking them to make recommendations about the course of action and then act, or to act and then advise the supervisor.

4th: Administrative supervisors follow up with their supervisees on their progress. The follow-ups occur at appointed times established at the end of the discussion.

9

Build Healthy, Meaningful Professional and Personal Relationships With Each Staff Member

To best serve the interests of their counseling clients, effective administrative supervisors build healthy, meaningful relationships with each of their staff members. In leadership, "if moral purpose is job one, relationships are job two" (Fullan, 2001, p. 51). Supervisor-supervisee relationships are fundamental to the success of supervision (Borders & Brown, 2005; Pearson, 2000; Popper, 2004; White & Queener, 2003). Good relationships do not *guarantee* successful supervision, but bad relationships do guarantee its failure (Pearson, 2000)—40% of new managers fail. They fail most often due to not establishing effective interpersonal relationships, and/or not being compatible with their agency's culture (Harris, 2002).

How long employees stay with their employers, and how productive they are while they are there are determined by these relationships (Buckingham & Coffman, 1999; Kulik, 2004). Their levels of job satisfaction are dependent on whether "my supervisor, or someone at work, seem[s] to care about me as a person" (Buckingham & Coffman, p. 28). Maslow (1998/1962) concluded, "everyone prefers or perhaps even needs to love his [sic] boss (rather than to hate him [sic]), and that everyone prefers to respect his [sic] boss (rather than to disrespect him [sic])" (p. 28). At the same time, effective administrative supervisors "maintain appropriate boundaries with supervisees" (American Counseling Association [ACA], 2005, p. 13).

This chapter describes making a successful transition when you become an administrative supervisor. In relating with individuals as an administrative supervisor and supervisee, you make changes that impact these relationships. You need to work to develop personal qualities that enhance them. To build relationships intentionally, you manage relationship responsibilities, and select leadership styles appropriate to your supervisees. Your experiences in building rapport and relating with individual clients and colleagues give you a foundation for carrying out these responsibilities. Previous leadership experiences, in counseling associations or other settings, also provide experiences for developing leader-follower skills.

MAKE THE TRANSITION FROM COUNSELOR TO ADMINISTRATIVE SUPERVISOR SUCCESSFULLY

Shifting from counselor to administrative supervisor causes changes in your responsibilities and perspectives. Your responsibilities expand from attending primarily to your assigned clients to attending primarily to counselors' competence in, and commitment to, working with their clients; their morale and job satisfaction, professional development, and job suitability. You also add responsibilities for counselors' contributions to or detractions from the work environment, the counseling service delivery system and the agencies' goals; and adherence to agency policies, procedures, people and norms. You add responsibility for promoting and protecting the welfare of each of your employees and all of the clients.

With these shifts in focus, you have a different perspective on each of your supervisee's work than they themselves have, or than you had when you worked side-by-side with them as peers. Your individual supervisees' perceptions of themselves are subjective (first person). A professional supervisor is more objective (third person). Both sets of perceptions are incomplete. Supervisees only know what they intended to do or say or be, or what they thought they did or were or said. On the other hand, you are in position to help them see and hear themselves as others see and hear them, allowing them a glimpse into the "Known to Others/Unknown to Self" pane of the Johari Window (Luft & Ingham, 1955). Many supervisors see this as the primary gift they have to give their supervisees.

Your perspective also changes as you observe, over time, a wide range of different counselors' behaviors and attitudes. With enlarged samples of professional behaviors, your understanding of a myriad of applications of professional standards becomes deeper and more textured. Your grounds for making comparative judgments among counselors become sounder.

RELATE WELL TO YOUR SUPERVISEES

Dimensions

Administrative supervisor-supervisee relationships are complex. They are a condition of employment, and as such not completely voluntary. The blending of two complex beings into one harmonious and growth-producing relationship makes each relationship unique. The two people involved are different individuals. You each bring the infinite details of your genetic and psychological makeup, learnings, experiences, cultures, and belief systems (Borders & Brown, 2005). Cultural and personal differences abound! "Consistently demonstrate respect and acceptance of [these] differences" (Fong & Lease, 1997, p. 399). At the same time, you and your supervisees have different jobs. While each has power, the power differential is weighted on your side. You are dependent on each other for success in your careers. Part of the essence of the success of these relationships is "that [you] understand one another" (Drucker, 2005, pp. 107–108).

These relationships have professional and personal dimensions that are intertwined during the course of each day's work. The professional dimension is primary. It is formal and centers on the supervisees' job performance, and their work ethic and habits. Its base is rational. At a minimum, your supervisees want to know who you are professionally. They want to learn about your levels of expertise, limits, personality, and capacity to manage. They have rights to know your administrative supervisory credentials and professional status, the conditions of supervision, the ethical standards, the supervision process and goals, case management procedures, how to handle crises, and your expectations of them (ACA, 2005; Center for Credentialing & Education [CCE], 2005; National Board for Certified Counselors [NBCC], 2005).

The personal dimension is informal and centers on your supervisees as people (e.g., eating lunch together, commuting together, sharing day-care arrangements). Friendships do develop among colleagues. When counselors are promoted to administrative supervisors these friendships do not end—although, they usually change. You make relationship transitions successfully when you realize that many supervisees test their supervisor's mettle, either professionally or personally by challenging your authority or skill or personality.

Effective administrative supervisors are cautious about developing personal relationships with their employees, as there are many boundary issues that can and do arise. Your supervisees need to know the opportunities and limits of the relationship, such as when it is bound by the standards of confidentiality and when it is not. Some boundaries are addressed in ethical standards, such as, maintaining professional detachment/objectivity in the work relationship, not harassing or engaging in sexual relationships, avoiding supervising relatives, and not counseling their administrative supervisees, but rather providing them with appropriate referrals when they need or want personal counseling (ACA, 2005; Association for Counselor Education and Supervision [ACES], 1993; American Mental Health Counselors Association [AMHCA], 2000; CCE, Ethics). As one administrative supervisor describes:

> I think it is most difficult for me to keep the boundaries of teacher/ student, supervisor/intern, managing director/friend. I can do it, but sometimes I want to be "one of the guys" and hang out and be pals. But there is a boundary, and the relationship works best if this is kept in place. I am getting better at establishing and maintaining these limits. We have other counselors with us that have a professional history, so back history and politics do come into play. Therefore, if I stick to my role as owner, I can navigate these disagreements and bumps in the road. (S. D. Clifford, personal communication, August 14, 2005)

Contexts

The contexts surrounding you and your supervisees also impact your relationships. You relate within the contexts of your department, agency, and each person's life outside of work. You (and your supervisees) consider what the climate is around you as you address your relationships.

Department. Intentionally or not, leaders set the tone for the interpersonal climates within their departments. If you set a tone that is open, friendly, warm, positive and harmonious, there is a stronger likelihood that individual relationships will reflect that. On the other hand, if the climate you establish encourages staff members' isolation and secrecy, is unfriendly, negative, cold and there is disharmony, individual relationships are apt to reflect that. Individual staff members, especially informal leaders, also impact the department climate, positively or negatively. Although you work to maintain a positive climate—e.g., one that supports honesty, inclusivity, collegiality, and trust—departments' climates fluctuate along a continuum because of the many variables involved.

Relationships among staff members affect a department's climate. Bear in mind Buckingham and Coffman's (1999) finding that being able to answer "yes" to the question "Do I have a best friend at work?" (p. 28) indicates a higher probability that workers will be satisfied with their jobs than if they cannot. Creating a climate that supports the development of friendships among workers tends to make for a happier work climate, which leads to higher employee retention (Davenport, Thomas & Cantrell, 2002).

Relationships among staff members who work together for extended periods of time tend to stabilize, and people find ways to get along (or peacefully coexist) with their co-workers at least in the work environment. Successful interpersonal relationships in organizations are based on interdependence (Arredondo, 1996), and "require *co-orientation* of behavior" (Harris, 2002, p. 305). Changes in organizations affect the balance of relationships among the players. "Leadership situations are always changing" (Fiedler, 1998, p. 335). "The leader may report to a new boss. Key subordinates are promoted or forced to take a leave, task assignments change, and the leader gains experience" (Fiedler, p. 335).

Agency. Similar ingredients at the agency level impact your supervisory relationships. "Organizational membership means more restrictions on our behaviors. Essentially, we are giving up the freedom to do whatever we want in order to be rewarded in some fashion for doing what the organization wants" (Harris, 2002, p. 305). The agency's missions, goals, rules, and demands impact the interpersonal climate. Other agency factors impact your supervision environment as well: the services provided (crisis, short term, long term), the clients (healthy and seeking growth, mentally disturbed, needing hospice), the overall service delivery system (collaborative and connected, isolated departments), resources (budgets, salaries, facilities, equipment), size (numbers of employees), attitudes (professional, political, social), and support for professional development (Dye, 1985).

Your agency's performance management system impacts your relationships, as it defines the philosophies and processes for how employees' jobs are defined; supervision is provided; performance evaluation is conducted; and professional development is or is not supported (Chapter 13). Since summative performance evaluation is a central part of your work, all of these interconnected activities affect your relationships. How you conduct them and what they signify to your supervisees may contribute to, or detract from, as examples, their job security, professionalism, anxiety, or frustration.

Personal lives. While each of you have lives outside of work that may influence your work relationships, you understand that these influences only matter as they relate to your work relationships or work behaviors. Your supervisees' personal lives are beyond the boundaries of your influence. Using your regular supervision processes (Chapter 10), you address only the degrees to which your supervisees' personal lives interfere with their work.

MAINTAIN RELATIONSHIP ENHANCING QUALITIES

The same personal qualities that supported your effectiveness as a counselor and clinical supervisor support your effectiveness as an administrative supervisor. In supervision, "personal traits [coupled with] relationship factors are considered as significant as technical prowess" (Borders, 1994, p. 23). The thoughts of many and diverse writers converge to identify some of the qualities basic to establishing healthy supervisory relationships (e.g., Borders & Brown, 2005; Cottringer, 2005c; Covey, 1989, 1991; Harris, 2002; Maslow, 1998/1962; Stoltenberg, McNeil & Delworth, 1998).

A partial list suggests some characteristics to nurture in yourself: charisma, common sense, high standards, integrity, multicultural competence, psychological health, and a sense of humor. Successful administrative supervisors are self-actualized, accept reality, are consistent, handle ambiguity, know their own strengths and limitations, and manage their own lives. They act like leaders (Harris, 2002), and can handle being, at times, unpopular, unloved, laughed at, and/or attacked (Maslow, 1998/1962). When it is called for, they are good followers. " 'What separates effective from ineffective leaders,' conclude Kouzes and Posner, 'is how much they really care about the people [they] lead' (p. 149)" (Fullan, 2001, p. 55).

DEVELOP RELATIONSHIPS INTENTIONALLY

To best ensure healthy and meaningful relationships with your administrative supervisees, you develop them intentionally. Begin developing rapport from your first encounters with potential supervisees, through induction and ongoing work together, and ending with termination. For better or worse, every interaction contributes to or detracts from the relationships. They blossom or disintegrate through interactions, and should strive to make each of them healthy and meaningful.

First Encounters

With an eye to hiring new supervisees, begin your relationships when potential employees come to your office to introduce themselves, learn about the job or pick up applications. Your first formal conversation is usually during the job interview. Having selected someone, guide new supervisees through the mechanics of the hiring process—which in large agencies may be complicated and possibly intimidating to eager, but anxious, new employees. You assign each of them a work placement and responsibilities (Chapter 16).

Getting Started

Throughout their orientation and induction, consciously and carefully set the tone that is the basis for the rest of your relationship with them. You establish employment and supervision contracts. The former are developed by the employing agency that also sets guidelines for how they are to be initiated.

In developing supervision contracts ethically, follow the principles of informed consent (ACES, 1993). Explain the requirements, expectations, roles and rules of the performance management system, and address due process rights and procedures (ACES, 2.14). Inform supervisees about the goals, policies, and theoretical and institutional orientations toward counseling, training and supervision (ACES, 3.07). Typically, these are augmented through handbooks, procedural guides, forms, and oral history. Address this complex content so that it is manageable for the supervisee and conveys the messages and attitudes you want. When presented properly, all of these rules and guidelines provide a sense of security to new employees. If there is a structure in place, they know that they are more apt to be treated fairly, not arbitrarily or capriciously.

In initiating development of their relationships, effective administrative supervisors make conscious efforts to learn about their supervisees as individuals:

> They talk with each individual, asking about strengths, weaknesses, goals, and dreams. They work closely with each employee, taking note of the choices each makes, the way they all interact, who supports who, and why. They notice things. They take their time, because they know that the surest way to identify each person's talents is to watch his or her behavior over time. (Buckingham & Coffman, p. 149)

Invite your new supervisees to share their previous experiences with supervision—whether they were good or bad impacts your relationship and situation. Open up discussions about potential differences, especially related to culture. Try to learn early on "about the values, traditions, and worldview of persons from different backgrounds" (Daniels, D'Andrea & Kim, 1999, p. 202). Discuss together "ways in which [you] will resolve cultural misunderstandings, disagreements, and potential conflicts . . . [and] ways in which unintentional forms of racism and ethnocentrism might be manifested" and addressed (Daniels et al., p. 202). In these initial discussions, raise the subject of potential power issues as well (Borders & Brown, 2005).

Ongoing Work

Time and opportunity. You and your administrative supervisees have time and many opportunities to develop relationships fully. The ongoing nature and variety of types of interactions cause increased texture and depth in them. You learn a lot about each other. Time allows for careful attention to building solid relationship foundations. In addition to being long term, lasting the tenure of both parties in an agency, your relationships play out nearly every workday—minute-by-minute, hour-by-hour. Unless one of you is part-time, you typically work together 8 hours a day, 5 days a week. Typically, you work side-by-side—your offices are in the same geographic area. In these circumstances, you and your supervisees interact frequently—in some circumstances, almost constantly.

Be continually vigilant to avoid the "fatal flaws" of ineffective administrative supervisors. Leaders impair their relationships by being insensitive—the most frequently found flaw; aloof; untrustworthy—the worst flaw; or over ambitious. Other flaws to avoid include having your own performance problems, overmanaging, hiring ineffective people, or being unable to think strategically, being unable to adapt to a boss, or being over-dependent on a mentor (McCall & Lombardo, cited in Hersey, Blanchard & Johnson, 2001, p. 91).

Termination

Administrative supervisor-supervisee relationships are not terminated until one or the other leaves the current department. Terminations may be in positive circumstances, e.g., people being promoted, achieving a desired job change, or retiring. They may be in negative circumstances, e.g., people's contracts being terminated for such reasons as incompetence, judgment errors, or losing their position due to staff reductions. Strive to maintain the health of the relationship. Keep in mind that individuals lose their jobs because of their behaviors or because of the situation, not because of their personhood (terminating individuals is discussed further in Chapter 14). While it is difficult and somewhat unusual in negative circumstances, work to end your relationships on positive and supportive notes.

MANAGE RELATIONSHIP RESPONSIBILITIES

As the administrative supervisor, you are responsible for relationships with your supervisees. You manage them intentionally by striving to conduct each interaction appropriately, even informal ones. You "engage in an ongoing assessment of the dynamics of the relationship" (Pearson, 2000, p. 286), analyze how *you* contribute to and detract from it, and change your behaviors to improve the situation. In each interaction you are clear about which role you are fulfilling (supervisor, leader, manager, administrator). You clarify what, if any, links there are between roles (ACES, 1993, 2.09). For example, supervisees often assume all supervision functions directly impact performance evaluation, which may not be true. You monitor if your supervisees are fulfilling complementary roles. When they are not, they may not understand the role you are in, including the power bases that support it.

The dynamics are different in different interactions as you have different purposes (e.g., morning greetings vs. negative feedback). Your and your supervisees' comfort and anxiety levels vary in interactions (e.g., supervision vs. evaluation). Relationships shift as the dynamics between the individuals change (e.g., positive recognition vs. confrontation). Many of these variables are also tied to supervisors' and supervisees' professional developmental levels (Chapters 10 and 11).

Recognizing the impact that your power has on your relationships, manage consciously your use of it. Be aware of the power differential between you and your supervisees. Use different power sources, depending on the situation. Intentionally use them to empower or weaken others. When you exercise your power on behalf of counselors, the counseling department, or the department's clients, your supervisees experience the use of power vicariously. They feel powerful when their administrative advocates, acting on their behalf, are powerful. In some instances, administrative supervisors intentionally disempower supervisees (e.g., incompetence, insubordination). Avoid misusing your power, as you can unintentionally disempower supervisees by eroding their sense of their own capacity to influence others (e.g., ignoring supervisees' expertise can erode their confidence).

Issues

"When cultural, clinical, or professional issues threaten the viability of a supervisory relationship, it is the ethical responsibility of both you and your supervisee to make efforts to resolve the differences" (ACA, 2005, F.4.d). When they become aware of issues, effective supervisors take the lead in bringing their discussion to the table. Issues arise related to individual differences, supervisor-supervisee relationships, supervision processes, job satisfaction, satisfactoriness of performance, and relationships among staff members. These issues are well-described in the literatures that inform relationship development from other disciplines (e.g., Harris, 2002; Hersey et al., 2001; Kulik, 2004; Raven, 2004), and those that inform supervisory relationships and the supervision process in the helping professions (e.g., Bernard & Goodyear, 2004; Borders & Brown, 2005; Kadushin & Harness, 2002; Stoltenberg et al., 1998). Some frequently recurring specific issues deserve attention: multicultural issues, parallel process, resistance, and supervisees' acceptance of relationship responsibility.

Multicultural issues. Take responsibility for the impact of multicultural issues in your supervisory relationships (e.g., ACA, 2005, F.2.b; Ladany, Brittan-Powell & Pannu, 1997; Leong & Wagner, 1994). Taking advice from professional counseling supervisors, explore, preferably proactively, your differences and their effects, and make them an important part of your work.

"It is the supervisor's cultural competence and openness that will dictate whether the [supervision] experience will be positive" (Bernard & Goodyear, 2004). Supervisees who are culturally different from you or who are in situations where they are in the minority do have thoughts, feelings and issues to discuss. They often struggle to assert their unique needs and to help others know of their perspectives and issues. They need your help in advancing their own racial/cultural identity development, in processing their cross-cultural experiences, and in improving their cross-cultural competence (D'Andrea & Daniels, 1997). You, too, have to be aware constantly of your biases, experiences with privilege and discrimination, and your ever-advancing racial identity development.

Parallel process. Parallel process occurs in administrative supervision, as it does in clinical supervision. As supervisees struggle with challenges with clients, with their responsibilities (e.g., procrastination), with their colleagues (e.g., competition), they often unwittingly present these struggles in administrative supervision. They may bring client-like issues forward, seek parental-like approval or reprimands, and the like. You may also slip into countertransference. When you recognize these symptoms, bring the behaviors up for discussion and processing in supervision conferences. Ultimately, you help your supervisees understand that such struggles are normal and part of the developmental process (Stoltenberg et al., 1998).

Resistance. Address the problems that generate resistance. "When an otherwise close supervisor/employee relationship has become strained, extra effort must be made to reconnect with the employee" (Stanley, 2005, p. 12). Try to anticipate the discomfort or conflict these situations might bring forth, and embrace the notion that a "relationship that is free of stress is one which is contemptuous of the . . . counselor's strength and does not extend [him/her] so that [he/she] can grow maximally" (Kell & Mueller, 1966, p. 108). "Always ask both sides of the question: How is the counselor contributing to the problem, and how am I contributing?" (Pearson, 2000, p. 292).

Supervisees' responsibility. To relate successfully, assist your supervisees to take their share of the responsibility for making your relationships healthy and meaningful. As knowledge workers and professionals, effective administrative supervisees manage themselves, which "requires taking responsibility for relationships" (Drucker, 2005, p. 107). Being self-aware, they conduct self-supervision (Henderson & Gysbers, 1998), and strive for continued development of their own professionalism. They contribute to the psychological safety of your relationship by being open, honest, trustworthy, and good communicators. They appreciate your power bases, and use their own appropriately.

Supervisees who do not take relationship responsibility may need to be taught how (Drucker, 1999). To do this, identify when your supervisees are not appropriately self-aware, reflective, analytical, honest, trustworthy, accepting responsibility for their problems, or actively participating in their own professional development. Help them further understand their responsibilities as sole owners of their work-related competence, motivation and commitment.

SELECT APPROPRIATE LEADERSHIP STYLES

My experience in working with hundreds of administrative supervisors in counseling suggests that their personalities are as varied as any other group of individuals. They may be introverts or extroverts, pessimists or optimists, cautious or risk-taking, or detail-oriented or global conceptualizers. Their effectiveness is not tied to their personalities or personal styles, but it is tied to their leadership styles. Your leadership style "is the behavior pattern, as perceived by others, that [you exhibit] when attempting to influence the activities of those others" (Hersey et al., 2001, p. 117). Whether your choice of style in supervisory interventions is appropriate is not only in your own perception, but also that of the supervisee or others who observe it (Hersey et al., 2001). Often it is the response you elicit that indicates the appropriateness of your choice. Also, "leaders are judged by the accomplishments of their followers" (Harris, 2002, p. 406); therefore, it is incumbent on you to use styles that work for your supervisees.

Different Styles

Administrative supervisors' leadership styles have been described as falling on different continua: from supervisor-centered to supervisee-centered, from autocratic to democratic, from task- to relationship-centered. Drucker (1998) summarized two ends of the continuum of styles used by managers, leaders, and administrative supervisors. "'Theory X' . . . assumes that people don't want to work, so must be coerced and controlled. ['Theory Y'] assumes that they really do want to work and require only proper motivation" (p. 9). Similarly, Hersey et al. (2001) phrase it:

Leaders influence their followers in either of two ways: (1) they can tell their followers what to do and how to do it or (2) they can share their leadership responsibilities with their followers by involving them in the planning and execution of the task. (p. 108)

A *laissez-faire* leadership style "permits the members of the group to do whatever they want to do" (Hersey et al., p. 109).

Popper (2004) characterizes three types of emotional relationships between leaders and followers that describe leadership styles: "regressive, symbolic, and developmental" (p. 112). Regressive relationships are those in which the leader oppresses the followers. They are focused on content, tasks, or ideology. They tend to be used in crisis situations and are used to respond to followers' needs for safety and survival. Symbolic relationships are also content- or task-based, and are used when the followers need to better form their identities or when changes are occurring. They help followers improve their self-concepts and feelings of self-worth. Developmental relationships focus on individual followers and help them " 'to be more' than they were before their relations with the leader" (Popper, p. 117). They help followers develop their competence, and are characterized by autonomy, trust, and positive identification with a role model—often the leader. They promote self-confidence, self-realization, achievement orientation, and a sense of security.

Style Selection

With the objective of developing healthy, meaningful relationships, intentionally adapt your leadership style to fit specific individuals *and* situations (e.g., Fernando & Hulse-Killacky, 2005; Glickman, Gordon & Ross-Gordon, 1995; Tannenbaum & Schmidt, 1973). "The concept of adaptability implies that the effective leader is able to use the right style at the right time" (Hersey et al., 2001, p. 267).

Maslow "showed conclusively that different people have to be managed differently" (Drucker, 1998, p. 9). Tailor your style for influencing others' behavior based upon understanding and predicting a supervisee's behavior (Hersey et al., 2001). It is through relationships that you learn to understand others well enough to predict their responses to your actions. Also adapt your leadership styles to fit different situations. Situations include you— the leader—and your power, authority, and chosen role; your followers and their power, authority and chosen role; your relationships; and the degree of structure required by the circumstances (Fiedler, 1998; Popper, 2004). (This is discussed further in Chapters 10 and 11.)

SUMMARY

To be a successful administrative supervisor, you are responsible for building healthy, meaningful supervisory relationships. You do this based on understanding the shifts in responsibility and perspective that accompany your transition from counselor to administrative supervisor. In relating with individuals, you learn to operate within the complexities of these relationships, and develop your relationship-enhancing traits. Acknowledge that these relationships develop in every interaction and activity, and manage your relationship responsibilities. Adapt your leadership style to fit your individual supervisees and each situation.

SUPERVISORS' CHALLENGE AND RESPONSES

Supervisors' Challenges: Resistance

Administrative supervisors face resistance from their supervisees. Pearson (2000) identified "two common signs of resistance . . . worth noting: discussing a long list of safe issues and using excessive self-criticism" (p. 290). Supervisees resist supervisors and supervision primarily to decrease their anxiety levels. Their anxiety has several sources: the need to change, the need to leave behind beliefs and behaviors learned in past experiences, the need to be dependent on a supervisor—threatening their independence and autonomy, fear of inadequacy, the supervisor's power to reward or sanction their status. Resistance is a defensive tactic. It takes different forms, and, with some consistency, makes supervisors uncomfortable.

Kadushin (1968) described four strategies that supervis*ees* use to try "to keep losses to a minimum and maximize the rewards that might derive from the encounter" (p. 24): "manipulating the level of demands made on the supervisee" (Kadushin & Harness, 2002, p. 266), "lessening the demands made on the supervisee by redefining the supervisory relationship" (p. 267), "reducing the power disparity between supervisor and worker" (p. 269), and "controlling the situation" (p. 271). Each of these strategies is described by "games."

> Supervis*ors* also may get defensive based on felt threats to their position in the hierarchy, uncertainty about their authority, reluctance to use their authority, a desire to be liked, a need for supervisees approbation— and out of some hostility to supervisees that is inevitable in such a complex, intimate relationship. (Kadushin, 1968, p. 30)

With these feelings, they abdicate both their administrative and professional responsibilities by passing the supervisees on to somebody else (e.g., upper level management, members of the professional counseling staff). They use strategies to assert (often, over-assert) their power (Tsui, 2005).

Supervisors' Responses

Effective administrative supervisors are alert to the potential that they or their supervisees might be playing games. "A manager should remember that aggression, rationalization, regression, fixation, and resignation are all symptoms of frustration and may be indications that problems exist" (Hersey al., 2001, p. 28). Borders and Brown (2005) remind supervisors that supervisees' resistance is usually not to growth and learning, but to a threat to their psychological or professional safety. As Maslow (1968/1992) picturesquely describes it, "When these passive, sneaky, underhanded, behind-the-back retaliations come, they come out of anger, anger generally about being exploited or dominated or being treated in an undignified way" (p. 62).

Resistance most often occurs when a supervisor has not assessed a counselor's developmental level accurately or has responded with an inappropriate approach. Effective administrative supervisors reduce resistance by providing supervision that is balanced (Magnuson, Wilcoxen & Norem, 2000), and provides both support and challenge. They generate other alternatives for communicating with the supervisee and for helping the supervisee communicate with them (see Chapters 10 and 11).

Supervisors often have an intuitive ("gut") reaction to defensive behavior that should not be ignored, but it should also not cause a defensive response. "Although such defensive games help the supervisee cope with anxiety provoking stress, they may be dysfunctional and subvert the purposes of the supervisory encounter. Consequently, the supervisor may be required to break up the games" (Kadushin & Harness, 2002, p. 274). The simplest and most direct way of doing this "is to refuse to play" (Kadushin & Harness, p. 274). If it suits some of their own needs, supervisors sometimes play along or get entangled in the supervisees' games. They may have to give up some of the benefits they get from playing. In order to break up a game, effective administrative supervisors use their power appropriately and comfortably, and are self aware and self-accepting. "The less vulnerable the supervisor, the more impervious he or she is to game playing" (Kadushin & Harness, p. 274).

A second way to interrupt a game is through "gradual interpretation or open confrontation" (Kadushin, 1968, p. 32). Confrontation entails exposing and making explicit what the supervisee is doing. Effective administrative supervisors handle such situations compassionately and gently, as supervisees in these cases feel vulnerable. Another game-ending strategy is for the supervisor "to share honestly with the supervisee one's awareness of what he or she is attempting to do . . . and to focus on the disadvantages for the worker in playing games" (Kadushin & Harness, 2002, p. 275). The largest disadvantage is that they will not get the assistance they need and deserve from supervision.

10

Nurture Continuous Improvement of Each Staff Member's Performance

To ensure the best services are provided to their counseling clients, and to enhance their contributions to the overall effectiveness of the department and the agency, administrative supervisors nurture counselors and other supervisees to perform at ever-higher levels of professionalism in their jobs. As one experienced administrative supervisor put it, my primary responsibility is "to help counselors be better counselors by continually challenging them to develop professionally" (M. L. Libby, personal communication, May 6, 2005).

To help counselors most effectively, you use a systematic process model consistently, develop your own model for conceptualizing counselors' developmental levels and how to help them, and develop your own model of administrative supervision. Experiences in continuously striving to improve your own professional developmental levels, in assessing your clients, and in finetuning your own personal counseling theory provide the foundation for carrying out these responsibilities.

This chapter describes why attending to each staff member's continuous improvement is important, and outlines a systematic process for carrying out daily supervision. Chapter 11 suggests questions you answer in clarifying your own staff supervision models, and provides an example of a conceptual model for assessing supervisees' developmental levels and responding appropriately.

PURPOSES

For Counselors

"Professional competence requires a commitment to lifelong learning, self-assessment, and excellence" (Pinsky & Fryer-Edwards, 2004, p. 582). Ethical counselors "strive to maintain the highest level of professional services" (American Mental Health Counselors Association [AMHCA], 2000, 7.E), and are to be qualified for the positions they fill (American Counseling Association [ACA], 2005, C.2.c). They "monitor their effectiveness" (C.2.d), recognize that professional growth is ongoing throughout their careers, and take personal initiative to maintain their competence and currency (ACA; American School Counselor Association [ASCA], 2004a). It is also professional counselors' ethical responsibility to be "alert to the signs of impairment from their own physical, mental, or emotional problems," and "seek assistance for problems that reach the level of professional impairment" (ACA, C.2.g).

Employees want or need to know what others think of their work. "If professionals try to analyze their own productivity, they need a clear idea of how others, especially managers, view their performance" (Kelley & Caplan, 1993, p. 137). As one administrative supervisor stated, "everyone should feel important. We do that when we empower them to do what they do best and challenge them to stretch in areas in which they are not as comfortable" (T. E. Miller, personal communication, June 13, 2005).

Four of the 12 "elements needed to attract, focus, and keep the most talented employees" (Buckingham & Coffman, 1999, p. 28) pertain to nurturing their professional development:

> In the last seven days, have I received recognition or praise for doing good work?
> Is there someone at work who encourages my development?
> In the last six months, has someone at work talked to me about my progress?
> This last year, have I had opportunities to learn and grow? (p. 28)

For Administrative Supervisors

Ethical administrative supervisors facilitate the professional development of their supervisees (AMHCA, 2000) by encouraging and cultivating their "adaptability and growth toward self-direction" (ACA, 2005, D.2.c). They nurture them by providing performance improvement-directed supervision. No one sees themselves as average (Gray, 2002, p. 16). In fact it has been estimated that 80% of workers think of themselves as being in the top 25% (Coens & Jenkins, 2000). The relative quality of their work is nearly impossible for individuals to judge.

"The exemplary supervisor has a blueprint of what the well-trained [and well-practiced counselor] looks like and how supervision can contribute to developing that picture in a systematic way" (Bernard & Goodyear, 1992, p. 169). Based on this conceptualization of the highest levels of counseling practice—The Ideal Professional Counselor (as discussed in Chapter 11), you are able to help supervisees have clear information about the relative status of their own performance and suggest areas for learning and growth (e.g., Glickman, Gordon & Ross-Gordon, 1995; Hersey, Blanchard & Johnson, 2001; Stoltenberg, McNeil & Delworth, 1998). You:

> focus/attend to needs of counselors regarding their knowledge and skills development. [Counselors] can easily get distracted with the everyday routine of their work and lose sight of their own need to grow continually. Assessing what they need is key. (E. Zambrano, personal communication, June 14, 2005)

Performance improvement-directed supervision is the means for identifying and "defining the difference between top performers and average workers [—an] essential for improving professional productivity" (Kelley & Caplan, 1993, p. 128). Identifying star performers helps you identify potential leaders and supervisors. You do well to support their proud accomplishment of meaningful work and goal attainment (Fullan, 2002). In some ways, you can help give "people a sense of accomplishing what they never thought they could in the first place" (Bielous, 1998, ¶ 1).

Additionally, you identify marginal or low performers and can help them in concrete ways to improve their functioning (Bielous, 1998) or to leave the counseling department (Henderson & Gysbers, 1998). You are ethically responsible for assisting others recognize "their own professional impairment" (ACA, C.2.g). To avoid vicarious liability for supervisees' actions, conduct continuous assessments of your supervisees' performance levels and respond appropriately by knowing when or where a supervisee is impaired and by monitoring client welfare.

To establish such an improvement-focused system, foster a climate that normalizes feedback; that is, one in which feedback is a part of the day-to-day process of supervision. Create multiple opportunities every day to observe your supervisees' specific work behaviors, establish a feedback-rich environment by providing it frequently, specifically, and consistently. Daily supervision targets specific incidents. In clinical supervision, Stoltenberg et al. (1998) labeled these as work samples, e.g., sessions with clients, reports of case conceptualizations, psychological reports, case notes. In administrative supervision work samples also include such behaviors as participation in staff or team meetings, engagement in professional development, attendance and in-office behaviors, consultations with colleagues, and accountability reports. They range from formal observations of counseling activities to informal observations of behaviors or conversations in hallways.

Performance improvement-directed feedback includes both positive (support) and negative (challenge) comments (e.g., Borders & Brown, 2005; Pinsky & Fryer-Edwards, 2004; Stoltenberg et al., 1998). To be a growth-producing supervisor, "spend sufficient time reinforcing positive actions so that any criticism is seen as the ongoing coaching and development process between the supervisor and subordinate" (Harris, 2002, p. 299). Remain "open to discussion of feedback and areas of clarification or disagreement from supervisees" (Stoltenberg et al., p. 142).

These responsibilities require a lot of conscientious administrative supervisors' time, for me approximately 16–20% (Henderson, 1999, 2001). If sufficient time is not appropriated for this dimension of supervision, you could feel frustrated, as indicated by another experienced agency-based counseling administrative supervisor: "One of the hardest parts of the job was being accountable for well-trained therapists, but being given no time or proper opportunity to develop them" (D. J. Martin, personal communication, July 31, 2005).

THE SUPERVISION PROCESS

Using a system for ongoing assessment, analysis and feedback provision helps you be consistent in your daily approaches to your supervisees. The recommended process for doing that includes steps that, when used with each supervisee in each supervised incident, support legitimate and fair supervisory interventions. These steps are captured by the acronym OARS: Observe, Assess, Respond, Steps.

Summary of the OARS Process

You *observe* a supervisee's work behavior. Through analyzing what you observed, you *assess* the motivation and professionalism levels of the supervisee in that particular incident. You *respond* by providing this feedback intentionally in a conference. Feedback conferences or interactions end with your assisting supervisees identify the *steps* they will take *next* to continue to improve in the noted area, and to build their areas of strength.

This process describes how to think and act on the job. When you have internalized it, you always observe-assess-respond-envision improvements. You conduct the process informally and formally, spontaneously and with careful planning. It requires systematic, conscious thought, especially in the early learning stages. You apply it not only every day, but even moment-by-moment. You notice small performance samples and big ones. "Effective performance rarely happens by accident. Effective performance is the result of predictable, planned actions that can be learned and applied" by others (Hersey et al., 2001, p. 1).

OARS Process Steps Described

Observe

Observations you or others make provide data that support your supervisory interventions. They provide "direct access to therapists' working skills and behaviors" (Stoltenberg et al., 1998, p. 138). There are two basic ways to gather information.

> We can either ask the person or observe the person's behavior. We could ask a person such questions as, "How well do you think you are doing at such and such?" or "How do you feel about doing that?" or "Are you or are you not enthusiastic and excited about it?" (Hersey et al., 2001, p. 234)

As much as possible, observe from a neutral, unbiased perspective. Direct observations provide the most reliable data. "Observations" include what you see, hear, or read from your supervisees. You make them by "walking in their shoes" (C. E. Henderson, personal communication, March, 2006), shadowing or working side-by-side with them, and observing their processes and thoughts.

Realistically, you receive a lot of second-hand information—a third way to get data—about your supervisees from clients, from other supervisors and supervisees, and from administrators. While these secondary sources do not provide very full pictures of your supervisees' behaviors, they do shed light on how they are perceived by others.

What you observe or otherwise learn about your supervisees' work behaviors provides a snapshot of their performance levels. Ideally, it is an accurate picture, and one that a supervisee and you agree on. These snapshots provide useful data to use in comparing and contrasting the supervisees' behavior with standards for performance. Use observed behaviors or other work samples as springboards to discussions. "Supervisee perceptions and self-reports yield some of the richest and most important data regarding therapists' attitudes, thoughts, feelings, and behaviors" (Stoltenberg et al., 1998, p. 140). Discuss your perceptions with them. The purpose of these discussions is to bring your two perspectives of reality closer together, to arrive at a "clear understanding" of what occurred (ACA, 2005, D.2.b).

In diligently striving for accuracy, record your observations as completely as possible. Live observations are, perhaps, the most complete form of observation, but they also require scripting or some form of note-taking. Tapes provide a fairly complete set of information for you and a supervisee to work from, but they are only one- or two-dimensional. The *Ethical Guidelines for Counseling Supervisors* (Association for Counselor Education & Supervision [ACES], 1993) state, "actual work samples via audio and/or video tape or live observation in addition to case notes should be reviewed by the supervisor as a regular part of the ongoing supervisory process" (2.06). These are methods you use with the longer, more formal observations. Informal observations—what you notice—are typically captured in your and your supervisees' memories and notes, and may be less complete than an actual recording.

Assess

Assessing the quality of a work sample is complex. Each reflects a supervisee's motivation, feelings, skills, knowledge, and thoughts. Some of these are directly observable (skills); others are implied (thoughts, feelings); still others are deeply buried within the individual (motivation, knowledge). It is best to conceptualize motivation and competence as two separate factors. These factors also intertwine. "If motivation is low, employees' performance will suffer as much as if their ability were low" (Hersey et al., 2001, p. 13). If competence levels are low, counselors are not motivated to perform.

Analyze Performance Data

It is essential to make assessments by carefully comparing and contrasting your supervisees' work samples in light of the standards you have established for these two factors. A "key is to have some objective measure that compares actual behavior with some standard, and a nonevaluative means of providing the feedback" (Harris, 2002, p. 300). Then, you cautiously draw conclusions about a supervisee's need for growth.

This process is ongoing throughout the tenure of your supervisor-supervisee relationships. In practice, every conversation, every interaction, every observation contributes information to supervisors' perceptions. "In practice, a supervisor goes through quite an interactive process of assessment and intervention" (Loganbill, Hardy & Delworth, 1982, p. 15). However, to be fair, focus on the specific incident recently observed. The data you rely on is that from the observation of this single event. Performance evaluation, on the other hand, focuses on patterns of behaviors that are evident across many activities. Base it on aggregated data from multiple observations. To provide supervision effectively, do not over generalize from one event. In providing performance evaluation, give feedback regarding patterns you identified that indicate either good or less-than-good performance.

Assess motivation levels. "If you want to influence another person's behavior, you must first understand what motives or needs are most important to that person at that time" (Hersey et al., 2001, p. 30). Analysis of a counselor's motives entails having a conceptual understanding of work-related motivations and a valid process for learning about an individual's motivations in a given circumstance. Useful "standards" for measuring work-related motivation levels have been described by Maslow (1954) and Herzberg, Mausner, and Snyderman (1959). Maslow's familiar hierarchy of needs that motivate people is: survival, safety, security, belonging, status, esteem, and self-actualization. Herzberg et al. identified a hierarchy of need-related motivational factors: impact of work on personal life, job security, working conditions, salaries, opportunities to change the work environment, technical supervision, relationships, status, challenging work, achievement, responsibility, recognition, and opportunities for advancement and growth.

When you are observant, you see supervisees' motivation as reflected by their "interest, investment, and effort expended in clinical training and practice" (Stoltenberg et al., 1998, p. 16). The need to perform well and make important contributions through work are part of self-actualization, and what drives individuals to seek job mastery, work achievement, and professional growth. You motivate others by helping them satisfy their needs and wants, achieve their goals, and express their values. Maslow (1998/1962) concludes, "There are many kinds of pay other than money pay. . . . [:] Status, success, self-esteem with which to win love, admiration, and respect" (p. 72). Consider the breadth of these motivating factors and motivators, and make full use of the ones that fit a specific supervision situation. Fear is not much of a motivator. As early as the 1970s, "behavioral psychology [had] demonstrated that great fear coerces [and *may* cause changes], while remnants of fear cause only resentment and resistance. . . . The lesser fears . . . destroy motivation" (Drucker, 1974, p. 237).

There are no assessment tools readily available that probe the needs and wants of your supervisees. You "cannot presume to decide which motives are most important to [them]. If we are to understand, predict, and control behavior, we must know what our employees really want from their jobs" (Hersey et al., 2001, p. 54). Again, one way to gather this information is by asking them and listening carefully. Through dialogue, you and your supervisees share perceptions about what need/want/value/goal is being most strongly felt by a supervisee at a given time.

Maslow (1998/1962) offered a useful insight. Needs that have been gratified fade from an individual's consciousness, and "what the person is craving and wanting and wishing for tends to be that which is just out ahead of him [*sic*] in the motivational hierarchy" (p. 267). He reminds us, "human beings will always complain" (p. 268). "The level of complaints—which is to say the level of what one needs and craves and wishes for—can be an indicator of the motivational level at which the person is living" (p. 267). He describes "Low Grumbles, High Grumbles, and Metagrumbles" (p. 266) that relate to the safety, social, and self-actualizing needs. Thus, listening to what your supervisees complain about gives you hints about what is motivating them and what you might attend to in response.

Probe carefully into what affects the work of your supervisees. When you have built meaningful relationships with them and established a professional climate that encourages openness, probe to learn about how their life contexts impact their work, and about what dissatisfies them (Herzberg et al., 1959). Together, identify the work-related needs/wants/values/goals that can be addressed at work. With this input from your supervisees, determine what motivator/incentive might be helpful to stimulate job satisfaction and continued professional development. Typically, you can enhance their motivation by inviting them to suggest what specifically they want you to provide positive and negative feedback about and to what ends.

Assess competence levels. Assessing supervisees' competence levels—their skills, knowledge and thoughts—is supported by the counseling profession's standards. Although the profession has a way to go in delineating and verifying standards for effective counselor performance (Erickson & McAuliffe, 2003), it has begun to define effective counseling, consultation, referral, client assessment, and so on. Objective statements of standards, like those listed in Chapter 4, facilitate analysis of performance behaviors, in identifying strengths and weaknesses of supervisees' competence.

As you reflect on your increasing experience, you refine your criteria base. Establishing criteria for making administrative supervisory judgments is also informed by developmental models in clinical supervision; however, much of that literature and research targets trainees, and *may* not apply to experienced practitioners functioning at different levels.

The reality is that much of "the work of knowledge professionals happens inside their heads. And managers can't directly observe, let alone accurately [assess] these mental processes or strategies" (Kelley & Caplan, 1993, p. 129). At the same time, "many people have a hard time describing what goes on in their minds when they work or even determining whether or not they've been productive" (p. 129). "Supervisees may not be sufficiently self-aware or resistance free to respond to questions in an accurate manner" (Stoltenberg et al., 1998 p. 140).

Draw Conclusions

After analyzing the observed or gleaned data, you make judgments about a supervisee's motivation and performance levels in a specific incident. Much is left to your professional judgment. To be discriminating in drawing your conclusions, and, in addition to using the standards, "compare the regimens of star performers to those of the also-rans and then target the differences" (Kelley & Caplan, 1993, p. 129). You identify your objectives for supervisory interventions: strength(s) to build on, and weakness(es) to improve.

To be cautious in drawing conclusions, avoid making judgments prematurely. Your data may be flawed by the recording mechanism (e.g., memory). Remember at all times that your recordings of data can be flawed by omissions, misperceptions, or assumptions. Avoid making assumptions about the motives or causes behind a supervisee's behavior. The focus is on counselors' behaviors, not on their characters. Humility is an essential quality in ensuring accurate assessment. "The importance of a leader's *diagnostic ability* cannot be overemphasized. It is the key to adaptability" (Hersey et al., 2001, p. 266).

Respond

To best guide your supervisees, respond by helping them see their strengths *and* their weaknesses. In a growth-producing supervisory environment there is nothing *wrong* with placement at any level of motivation or performance. Rather, it "is a reflection of the individual's development to date" (Stoltenberg et al., 1998, p. 142). In trying to overcome the historical tendency of managers to correct their employees' behaviors, there is much emphasis in today's management literature on capitalizing on employees' strengths (e.g., Bielous, 1998; Buckingham & Clifton, 2001; Drucker, 1999; Hersey et al., 2001).

Maslow (1998/1962) asked the question, "Shall we accentuate the positive?" (p. 47), and answered with a "yes, but . . .":

Absolutely, yes—but under the conditions where this is objectively called for, i.e., where it will in fact work. . . . To be realistic we must also accentuate the negative in whatever proportion is realistically and objectively called for by the existing facts. (p. 47)

Bielous (1998) also explains that, when faced with subordinates who are not doing well, you must provide support and guidance to help get them back on track.

Adapt Response Styles

To nurture each individual's professional development, you intentionally adapt your response style to the one that is most apt to promote the growth of each supervisee. Being a great manager "demands discipline, focus, trust, and perhaps most important, a willingness to individualize" with the real challenge being in "how you incorporate these insights into *your* style, one employee at a time, every day" (Buckingham & Coffman 1999, p. 12).

In addition to the motivational and competence levels of your supervisees, you consider relevant contextual variables, such as client-related issues; cross-cultural issues, including age and gender (Granello, 2003); your supervisor-supervisee relationship; and the organizational climate, and your own role requirements (Schwarzwald, Koslowsky & Agassi, 2001). Bearing in mind all the variables, you, then, begin the process of deciding on the appropriate response style for the supervisee in your intervention. You clarify goals for the particular supervisee, and decide on what seems to be the appropriate approach, power base, empowerment strategy, intervention modality, leadership function, and behavior to use.

The logic of matching your supervisory responses to supervisees' performance levels in different situations is clear. Applying it, however, is complex. One administrative supervisor of counselors with several years of experience still sees it as the hardest part of her job, but also the most important (M. L. Libby, personal communication, May 6, 2005). Like learning to apply any complex thought process, the more you use it, the more it becomes internalized and automatic. Discussing application examples in supervision of supervision helps develop competence and confidence in your processes and judgments.

Select approach. Your supervisory approach is the degree of directiveness that the supervisee needs from you in order to make desirable changes. The continuum of response approaches ranges from non-directive to controlling. Appropriate approaches allow supervisees appropriate levels of autonomy (ACA, 2005, D.2.C). The supervision literature is clear about the level of directiveness that supervisors take with supervisees at different levels (e.g., Bernard & Goodyear, 2004; Glickman, 1981; Henderson & Gysbers, 1998; Hersey et al., 2001). Essentially, the higher the performance level, the less controlling you need to be. The lower the performance level, the more controlling you need to be. The higher the supervisee's level, the more supportive you are. The lower the supervisee's level, the more challenging you are.

Being too directive (oversupervising) or not directive enough (undersupervising) are both errors—"lousy supervision" (Magnuson, Wilcoxen & Norem, 2000). According to Maslow (1998/1962), "Everybody seems to be aware ... that authoritarian management outrages the dignity of the worker. He [sic] then fights back in order to restore his [sic] dignity and self-esteem" (p. 56). It is also true that *laissez-faire* management demeans workers. They sense their supervisors' lack of belief in their ability to handle constructive criticism, or, worse, they feel ignored and that their work does not matter.

Select power base. Raven's (1993, 2004) research tells us that supervisees with different developmental levels respond best to different power bases. For supervisees who are at higher developmental levels, use softer power bases; for those at lower levels, use harsher ones (Raven, Schwarzwald & Koslowsky, 1998). The continuum of power bases ranges from expertise (non-directive) to coercive (controlling).

Libby considers using the power bases consciously the hardest facet of responding to apply. "Answering the question, 'Which power base could be most useful (powerful) here?' is especially difficult in uncomfortable situations" where it is most helpful (personal communication, May 6, 2005). Without conscious thought, your choices of power bases are apt to be unduly influenced by your own self-confidence and self-efficacy (Raven, 1993). If these are low, you are apt to use a power base that is too harsh.

Select empowerment strategy. Devising an empowerment strategy involves targeting a supervisee's power base that is most likely to help him/her build on an identified strength; for example, if a supervisee is competent, but undermotivated, you empower the supervisee's expertise. Empowerment supports improvement by helping supervisees feel "a sense of personal power, confidence, and positive self-esteem. [It] involves a process of change that can be achieved in relation to specific goals" (Arredondo, 1996, p. 17).

Select intervention modality. Loganbill et al. (1982) described five types of supervisory interventions that are useful with counselors at different developmental levels. From least directive to controlling, intentional supervisors are facilitative, conceptual, confrontive, catalytic, or prescriptive.

Select function. The range of functions you fulfill with supervisees at different levels is, from most supervisee-driven to most supervisor-led: mentoring, consulting, coaching, teaching, counseling and judging (Bernard & Goodyear, 2004; Henderson & Gysbers, 1998; Kulik, 2004). In the counseling function, you are clear about the distinctions between supervision and therapy. Therapy often addresses causes, reasons *why* individuals do things or have personal issues.

Supervision addresses behavior, cognition, and attitude—*what* you observe in work performances. In rare instances, when supervisees' issues are tied to their emotions or values, some exploratory counseling may be warranted to help them identify their issue (Henderson & Gysbers, 1998; Hersey et al., 2001). After this initial discovery, you provide them appropriate referral sources (ACA, 2005, D.2.a; ACES, 1993, 3.18, 3.19; AMHCA, 2000; CCE, Ethics). In working with an alcohol-abusing administrative supervisee, for example, the reasons *why* they drink to excess is not your business; but rather, how their behaviors are perceived and their impact on their clients and co-workers is. In these and similar instances, you might use your counseling skills from a consultant perspective to help them examine their problems sufficiently to own them or acknowledge the need for outside help. Short of entering into a counseling relationship with them, you, instead, use supervisory strategies. A delicate balance at best!

Select behaviors. When you are self-aware, you choose behaviors that are consistent with the directiveness of the selected response style. Examples of behaviors you use, from non-directive to controlling, are modeling, active listening, presenting ideas and information, problem-solving, negotiating, demonstrating, directing, standardizing, and referring (Glickman, 1981). Raven (1993) also suggests that the manner in which you communicate with a supervisee should be intentionally selected. Supervisees perceive statements made in a friendly, light-humored way as soft, and statements made in a loud, forceful, threatening, or sarcastic way as harsh.

Select Specific Feedback

Select the best examples. The more intentional you are in providing feedback, the more it is likely to lead to supervisees' performance improvement. In a supervision incident, review your recording of the observed event and select key phrases and other supervisee behaviors that exemplify what you want them to learn about their own motivation or performance. "Behaviorally grounded impressions and observations provide the specificity that supervisees most often desire" (Stoltenberg et al., 1998, p. 138). Use these examples so that supervisees can understand for themselves how near or far they are from the standards for excellent performance.

Deliver feedback. Feedback is best that is specific, descriptive, concrete, accurate, factual, and given in amounts that can be managed and used productively. Balance positive ("support") and negative ("challenge") feedback. Your timing of the feedback presents interesting issues. You are ethically responsible to provide it in a timely manner (ACES, 1993; AMHCA, 2000). Feedback is best heard when it occurs so that both you and your supervisee can remember the situation, and provided at a time as close to the actual event as possible (AMHCA, 2000, Principle 11, F). On the other hand, it is your responsibility to reflect on the feedback you want to give and to plan how to give it. Both are equally important, but resurrecting history is not useful. Some feedback can and should be given "the instant you see, hear, learn about something" (M. L. Libby, personal communication, May 6, 2005). In more difficult situations or with lengthy observations, you need some time to process the information. Twenty-four to forty-eight hours seems to be a maximum time delay.

Plan/Conduct the Supervision Conference

In anticipation of supervisory feedback conferences, you have determined *what* the goal is for supervisee learning and *what* examples will be used to identify strengths and weaknesses. The final step is to plan the conference process—*how* the conference will flow. Planning time varies depending on the amount/intensity of data; the complexity of a supervisee's performance level; and the context of supervision (e.g., the quality and length of the relationship, the depth of the issues, supervision history, client or agency needs and requirements). Your selected response style dictates whether you solicit supervisees' thoughts before or after providing your own. Except in very rare instances where you choose to be highly directive, supervisees' active participation is desirable.

"Working in conjunction with [supervisees], [you] attempt to develop a clear definition of the problem, goals for change, and predicted consequences of interventions that are culturally responsive and appropriate to the needs of [supervisees]" (ACA, 2005, D.2.d). Asking questions engages supervisees in the reflection and analysis process. Increasing their self-reflection has been found to increase their self-awareness (Smith & Agate, 2004). And, "Skovholt and Ronnestad (1992) concluded that critical self-reflection was the most important distinction between counselors who continued to develop and grow professionally versus those who faced professional stagnation and burnout" (Guiffrida, 2005, p. 202).

"How do you think the session went?" is a legitimate way to start most feedback conferences. Other questions to help heighten supervisee awareness include, "What happened here?" "What were you thinking when . . .?" "What were you feeling when . . .?" Remember that, except in situations that are harmful to clients, your focus in supervision is on the supervisee and not the client. In conference planning, develop tentative questions you might ask. Figure 10.1 displays a generic conference planning agenda.

Take special care in planning supervisory responses in difficult situations, such as those with impaired professionals, marginal performers, or people who are defensive or insubordinate. Consulting about your work with a difficult supervisee with other supervisors is a good practice. When you know you are feeling unsure or uncomfortable about an upcoming supervision conference, you might plan actual words to use, role play with a consultant, or "dress rehearsal" in some way (M. L. Libby, personal communication, May 6, 2005). Libby also stresses the importance of being sure staff members know the exact consequences for doing or *not* doing what you expect.

Figure 10.1 A Generic Post-Observation Conference Planning Agenda

I. Review the information about the observed event
    A. The context
    B. The highlights of what happened
    C. Ask questions to fill in missing data

II. Discuss strengths
    A. Ask questions to elicit supervisee's perceptions of strengths
    B. Report those observed by supervisor in event

III. Discuss area(s) for improvement(s)
    A. Ask questions to elicit supervisee's perceptions of area(s) for improvement
    B. Report those observed by supervisor in event

IV. Discuss strategies for improvement
    A. Next steps to shore up weaknesses
    B. Next steps to build on strengths

Next Steps

At the end of supervisory conferences, you assist your supervisees identify the *steps* they will take *next* to continue to shore up the weaknesses identified in the observed behavior and to build their areas of strength. "Supervisees should be encouraged and assisted . . . to establish supervision goals for themselves, and to monitor and evaluate their progress toward meeting these goals" (ACES, 1993, 3.08). As much as possible, allow your supervisees to make their own choices about *how* they will meet their targets.

Specify Next Step Improvement Goals

Supervisees are more motivated to improve if they have choices and can exercise some power over their own work situations. "Controlling environments . . . restrict individual choice, gain compliance, and create resistance. Informational environments expand individual choice, promote autonomy, and encourage commitment to improve" (Glickman et al., 1995, p. 190). To raise levels of motivation, invite supervisees to participate in their own decision-making (Tannenbaum & Schmidt, 1973).

These "next steps" improvement goals are smaller in scope than counselors' year-long professional development goals (discussed in Chapter 13). They are related to the supervisory feedback and are very specific: "I will learn ____X____;" "I will do ____X____." At least two improvement targets and plans should emerge from every feedback conference: one related to a strength and one related to a weakness. Building on their strengths helps workers focus on and hone their talents (Buckingham & Coffman, 1999). Addressing their weaknesses helps workers learn to meet the requirements of their jobs in a satisfactory manner (Fullan, 2002). Many such improvement targets are to "remedy one's *bad habits*" (Drucker, 1999, p. 167).

Shift responsibility. At this point, supervisees take primary share of the responsibility for their own work, and you relinquish much of yours. "A goal, to be effective, must be appropriate to the need structure of the person involved" (Hersey et al., 2001, p. 30). This, added to the reality that they own their own professionalism, makes the supervisee's commitment to the targets and the plan virtually essential. Goal setting, itself, "is viewed by most executives and behavioral scientists as a motivational technique" (Seijts & Latham, 2005, p. 125). "These studies show again and again that a performance goal influences choice, effort, and persistence to attain it—the three cornerstones of motivation" (Seijts & Latham, p. 127).

In rare cases when counselors evidence impairment in an incident, and when you are not convinced they will set appropriate paths toward improvement, you attempt to limit or take away their autonomy. You choose a more controlling response style, relying on your coercive power, being prescriptive, and teaching your expectations for behaviors that are least apt to lead to client harm. One administrative supervisor recounted a story of a counselor who worked with emotionally disturbed teenagers, but who was unable to handle their suicide threats—a chronic issue. The agency had established a standard protocol to follow in these cases that the counselor did not follow. After observing such an incident, the supervisor mandated the counselor's next step improvements: (1) memorize the protocol, (2) place it under the glass on top of her desk, (3) tell the potentially suicidal client what the protocol requires, and (4) follow it. If the counselor found herself not following it, she was to consult with the administrative supervisor immediately. If she did not follow the protocol, she would be written up and, after two more such incidents, be released from her contract (M. L. Libby, personal communication, May 6, 2005).

If you have a working alliance with your supervisee (Bordin, 1983), you both understand and agree to the targets. After planning, you reach mutual agreement on the tasks needed to accomplish them. This shifting of responsibility is complicated or compromised when supervisees are unwilling or unable to be autonomous in improving their own professionalism.

Guide action planning. Even with small next steps that are relatively easy to take, a systematic action planning process is useful in assisting your supervisees think about how they will achieve these changes in their behaviors (Mackenzie, 1997). What they will do. An action plan delineates the *tasks* needed to accomplish the objective, a *time frame* for accomplishing the tasks, and what *evidence* will demonstrate accomplishment of each task. Monitor your supervisees' implementation of their plans, again choosing response styles that match the supervisees' needs for oversight.

At the end of the planned timeframe, you and your supervisees separately and together evaluate completion of the action plan. Supervisees report to you the actual completion dates of each task, actual evidence of completion, and assessment of the quality of task accomplishment. Finally, they assess the overall accomplishment of the objectives, and the level of attainment of the broader goal. You concur or provide more feedback. Forms are useful in guiding this process (Henderson & Gysbers, 1998) (an action plan format is provided in Chapter 17).

Reflect and Document

After a feedback conference, reflect on its successful and not-so-successful elements. At a minimum, it is a way to improve your work with a particular supervisee, or, as you notice your own patterns, to work more effectively with all your supervisees. As Raven (1993) puts it, after the "influence attempt" supervisors assess the effects of the strategy, and the effects of the specific feedback (pp. 240–241). Also teach your supervisees to reflect on the experience and provide you feedback, as appropriate.

Finally, you document the supervision incident; and file the forms and notes in secure personnel files and other appropriate places. You plan how you will follow up with them as supervisees take their "next steps."

SUMMARY

As professionals, counselors are expected to continuously improve their performance. You are expected to help them. One way you do this is by using a consistent process in ongoing supervision when responding to specific incidents of supervisee work behaviors. OARS, a performance improvement-driven supervision process, entails your **o**bserving supervisees work behaviors, **a**ssessing their levels of motivation and performance in the work sample, and **r**esponding intentionally to each counselor's developmental level. The process ends with your facilitating counselors' setting of meaningful "next **s**tep" performance improvement goals, and developing action plans for meeting those goals.

SUPERVISORS' CHALLENGES AND RESPONSES

Supervisors' Challenge: Poor Performance

Administrative supervisors are challenged when they observe poor performance. Although it is universally recognized that supervisors should confront poor performance head-on and in a timely manner (Buckingham & Coffman, 1999), they often shy away or cringe at these "opportunities." It is hard to say negative things to supervisees, even in a positive, feedback rich environment.

Supervisors' Responses

Poor performance adversely affects counseling clients. It must be addressed, but carefully and with an eye to the due process rights of employees (Chapters

3 and 4). A first question to consider is the cause of the poor performance. If it is due to a system problem—e.g., insufficient technical support—administrative supervisors may have to look to themselves or the agency for solutions. If it is due to individuals' problems, it is their challenge to resolve and alter its impact on their own work. Administrative supervisors can address other causes of poor performance, such as supervisees' needs for training or inadequate supervisor support.

If non- or poor-performance is still observed in an area, "the nonperformance is probably a talent issue. The person is struggling because she [sic] doesn't have the specific talents needed to perform" (Buckingham & Coffman, 1999, p. 167). Further clarification of the problem is required. Applying the 80/20 Principle may be useful in these situations. It is a "method of inspection and analysis . . . [for] identifying that vital few [work behaviors] to which corrective action can be applied where it will do the most good, the most quickly" (Napier & Gershenfeld, 2004, p. 315).

The role demands on counselors are wide ranging. Not all people have talent in all areas. Non-talents become performance weaknesses when they are expectations of their jobs. Administrative supervisors are challenged to help supervisees determine if their lack of talent is critical to job success. Buckingham and Coffman (1999) identified some strategies great managers use in "managing around a weakness" (p. 164): "devise a support system, find a complementary partner, or find an alternative role" (p. 168). The latter, which includes helping them move out of counseling services, is the last resort. To help supervisors get to this point, they explain that:

> You will have to manage around the weaknesses of each and every employee. But if, with one particular employee, you find yourself spending *most* of your time managing around weaknesses, then know that you made a *casting error*. At this point it is time to fix the casting error and stop trying to fix the person (p. 174).

The person is cast in the wrong role. Career redirection is the best help administrative supervisors can give to some supervisees.

11

Apply Your Own Models for Providing Effective Administrative Supervision

To ensure the best services are provided their counseling clients, effective administrative supervisors apply their own personal models for nurturing the continuous improvement of their supervisees' performance. To be most effective, they use them consciously and consistently. Your model (whether it is conscious or not) guides your thoughts and behaviors as you respond to each work sample, whether it is a supervisee's treatment of clients, counseling performance, role in the department's service delivery system, or responsibilities to their agency.

> Having a model to operate from is really helpful. I always go back to that with individuals and in supervision case consultations. It really is useful when your peer group applies the same model, so when you consult you are talking the same language. (M. L. Libby, personal communication, May 6, 2005)

Your supervision model has two dimensions: process and conceptual. Chapter 10 described the prevailing model for a supervision process. This chapter addresses conceptual models. Standard 6 of the professional *Standards for Counseling Supervisors* (Association for Counselor Education & Supervision [ACES], 1989; *Standards*, 1990) speaks to nurturing counselor development. The *Curriculum Guide* for training counseling supervisors (Borders et al., 1991) outlines as major topics for training: the stages of counselor development, the characteristics of the stages, the critical transition points, and the supervision environment recommended for each stage of counselor development.

This chapter describes what a conceptual model consists of, suggests questions to answer in clarifying your own process and conceptual models, and provides an example of a conceptual model and its application in a supervision process. Your experiences in developing personal counseling and clinical supervision theories support this endeavor. Similar to counseling theories, the theory that guides your administrative supervision work describes key concepts, effective processes, the roles of the supervisor and supervisee, and useful techniques and procedures (Corey, 2001). One goal of this *Handbook* is to help you articulate your own such theory. And, like counseling and clinical supervision theories in practice, your theory is "always evolving" (Riley cited in Collie, 2001, p. 112). You develop depth and texture in it with every supervisor-supervisee interaction and every supervisory learning.

DEVELOP YOUR PERSONAL ADMINISTRATIVE SUPERVISION MODELS

Conceptual Models

To conduct administrative supervision intentionally you conceptualize counselors' professional roles and responsibilities, and levels of counselor development, and how to best apply them in supervision. Conceptualizing counselor development in the workplace is a part of the counseling field that has not yet been fully addressed. You can be informed by theories and research in development of counselors-in-training, professional development within other human service disciplines, and follower development within leadership studies.

There is not profession-wide consensus as to the stages or levels of counselor development. You might agree that development is defined by chronological maturity (20- . . . years old), or tenure in the field (pre-service trainee to excellent professional), or quality of professional performance (impaired counselor to "star" performer), or some combination of these or other factors of human diversity. You define concretely for yourself the "Ideal Professional Counselor" and the factors of the professional self that contribute to achieving optimal levels of counseling performance. An example of this is provided in the last section of the chapter.

Your model of the Ideal provides the standards for your assessment of individual counselors' levels of development, and guides your determining supervisory responses that are most apt to nurture supervisees' performance improvements. "In order to set the context for ongoing assessment and feedback, supervisors need to conceptualize for supervisees the overall process of development" (Stoltenberg, McNeil & Delworth, 1998, p. 141). It must be concrete enough to explain to other people, particularly your supervisees.

Existing conceptual models. There are models that offer conceptualizations of the factors of professionals or knowledge workers that indicate their developmental levels. Loganbill, Hardy and Delworth (1982) identified developmental issues of supervisees: competence, autonomy, emotional awareness, professional identity, respect for individual differences, purpose and direction, personal motivation, and professional ethics. Stoltenberg et al. (1998) describe "overriding structures" (p. 16) as self and other awareness, motivation and autonomy as applied across "domains of clinical practice" (p. 17). Based on the work of Bernard and Goodyear (2004), Borders and Brown (2005) describe the "discrimination model" (p. 7) in which supervisors focus on counselors' performance skills, cognitive skills, self-awareness, and professional behaviors. This model is widely used in counseling supervision.

Hersey, Blanchard and Johnson (2001) identify the major factors of workers' developmental stages as "ability and willingness" (p. 176). Ability includes knowledge, skill and experience. Willingness includes confidence, commitment and motivation. Glickman (1981) identified levels of commitment and abstraction as the factors. Glickman, Gordon, and Ross-Gordon (1995) re-labeled commitment to motivation and redefined the second factor to include "cognitive, conceptual, moral, and ego development" (p. 77). Henderson and Gysbers (1998), in the model described at the end of this chapter, use competence and commitment as the factors that describe counselors' professionalism. Although different words are used, the themes across these models that you might consider are that counselors' levels of knowledge and skills, motivation, and commitment to things outside of themselves are basic ingredients of their professional developmental levels.

ANSWER QUESTIONS ABOUT YOUR MODELS OF ADMINISTRATIVE SUPERVISION

To develop your administrative supervision models that guide your thoughts and resultant actions, you answer the following questions.

Process Model
> *What process do you use for determining how you can most effectively facilitate growth in an individual supervisee?*
> *What steps do you take to ensure the most meaningful interaction between yourself and a supervisee?*
> *What thought process do you go through to have a meaningful interaction?*
> *How do you identify a counselor's improvement needs?*
> *What data-gathering methods are useful to you?*
> *Where do the data come from to support your conclusions?*
>> *Do you use first- and second-hand data?*
>> *Do you use data that are informally and formally gathered?*
>> *How do you record your observations?*
> *How do you assess the developmental level of a counselor?*
> *How do you analyze that data?*
> *How do you determine how to respond appropriately to a specific developmental level of a counselor?*
> *How do you make use of the differences in perspectives between yourself and your supervisees?*
> *How do you adjust a conference with a supervisee in order to influence him or her?*
> *How do you begin and end a successful conference with a supervisee?*
> *What do you do after a supervision conference?*

Conceptual Model
> *What are a counselor's roles with clients, within the department, within the counseling service delivery system, and within the agency?*

Are employees improvement-oriented by nature?

What causes people to change?

What are the purposes of administrative supervision?

What are a supervisor's roles with clients, with counselors, within the counseling delivery system, and within the agency?

What are the differences in perspectives between supervisors and supervisees?

Whose responsibility is job performance?

    If it is shared, what are the proportions of responsibility held by the supervisor and the supervisee?

What makes for effective supervision?

What are the roles and responsibilities of supervisors and supervisees in supervision?

What factors are demonstrated in a work sample?

    What label do you use to summarize this concept?

    If there is more than one factor, how are they reflected in a counselor's behavior?

    How are they related to each other?

What standards describe these factors?

    How do you know what the Ideal Professional Counselor would think, feel and do in a particular situation?

How do you define counselors' developmental levels?

How do you conceptualize a counselor's needs for supervision?

    How do you determine a counselor's developmental level in a performance?

    What criteria do you use to analyze the data and base your judgments on?

How do you most effectively influence your supervisees?

What motivates employees?

    How do you consider a supervisee's motivation?

What is the purpose of having a conference with a supervisee after observing an example of performance (work sample)?

How do you decide which strengths and weaknesses to address?

What contextual variables do you consider in planning for an interaction?

How do you decide what supervisory intervention strategies to use?

How do you assess a counselor's level of motivation?

How do you determine the best communication strategy for working with a supervisee?

What options are available to you in responding appropriately to a counselor at a specific developmental level?

What bases of power are available to you?

    How do you best use each of them?

How do you empower counselors?

What results suggest a successful administrative supervisor-supervisee interaction?

How is your counseling model reflected in your supervision model?

CONSIDER MY MODEL FOR CONCEPTUALIZING AND RESPONDING TO SUPERVISEES OF DIFFERING DEVELOPMENTAL LEVELS

An example is offered here from my experience as an administrative supervisor. This model is not only based on research and theory, but also on practical experience, as it was used for 20+ years by over 100 administrative supervisors nurturing the professionalism of several hundred counselors (Henderson & Gysbers, 2006). What is described here is the model we use for conceptualizing counselors' developmental levels, described as their levels of professionalism, and using this concept to assess individual counselors' performance behaviors. It describes the thought process for applying the concept that suggests appropriate supervisor responses for counselors at different developmental levels. Generalized patterns of supervisor responses have been identified for each developmental level.

Factors of Counselor Development

Supervisees' developmental levels are characterized as their levels of professionalism. Professionalism has two factors: competence and commitment. Competence includes supervisees' levels of cognitive knowledge, their thought processes, skill development and use of techniques. It describes their level of ability to carry out their jobs. Commitment includes their levels of dedication to their clients, their job and role, their agency, their profession and their colleagues. It includes their work- and profession-related values, interests, attitudes, feelings, belief systems and motivation. It is evidenced by their sense of purpose, professional identity, and ethics. Commitment to the client takes precedence over other commitments.

Individuals vary in their functioning within each factor. These functional variations represent places along a continuum. There is a continuum of behaviors that describe different functional levels of competence, and a continuum of behaviors that describe different functional levels of commitment. Developing a vocabulary of words that describes the range of functional levels of competence and commitment is a critical skill in applying this model. It clarifies supervisors' understanding and precise communication with supervisees. Examples of words used to discriminate among different functional levels along the competence and commitment continua, from lowest to highest, are displayed in Figure 11.1.

A premise is that these functional variations in competence and commitment are not the result of a counselor's tenure in the field. Any reasonably sized group of counselors will include new counselors who are well-trained,

Figure 11.1 Competence & Commitment Continua: Sample Discriminating Vocabulary Words

Low Points →   → High Points

Competence

Negative Side: Incapable → inept → unskilled → ineffective → awkward → fumbling → apprentice → novice → trained → prepared
Positive Side: → qualified → efficient → apt → capable → proficient → adroit → accomplished → expert → artist → virtuoso

Commitment

Negative side: Lethargic → apathetic → bored → impassive → disdainful → indifferent → detached → disinterested → pre-occupied
Positive side: → enthusiastic → engaged → excited → spirited → responsible → passionate → involved → dedicated

Word Source: Microsoft Windows 97, Word, Thesaurus

more technically competent and more highly committed to the profession than some of the more experienced counselors in the group, and vice versa. So, this model is "developmental" in that it is "designed to bring about improvement by gradual training adapted to the learner's . . . development" (*Webster's Third*, 2002, "developmental"). Performance improvement-driven administrative supervisors using this model help their supervisees move up both continua. As described by Kelley and Caplan (1993) in their study with Bell Labs, the differences between star and average performers were at the strategy level—the little ways they go about their work. Individuals move up and down either continuum depending on the specifics observed in an activity, the client, and whatever else affects each piece of work.

Assessing Professionalism Levels

Administrative supervisors, first, make judgments about where a supervisee's behavior falls on each of these continua. They analyze supervisees' work samples and compare and contrast their behaviors with the standards established for competence and commitment. In using standards, administrative supervisors clearly define, for themselves and their supervisees, what the minimum expectations are and what the optimums look like.

The convergence of the two factors results in one level of professionalism (Henderson & Gysbers, 1998). Supervisees' professionalism levels are reflections of their levels of competence *and* commitment. That is, in each work sample observed a counselor demonstrates a level of competence and a level of commitment, a specific point along each continuum. Administrative supervisors, second, determine a supervisee's level of professionalism in a work sample by combining the two dimensions.

The two continua can be lined out, one horizontally (competence) and one vertically (commitment), and depicted as intersecting axes, defining four quadrants. As displayed in Figure 11.2, descriptive labels have been applied to each of the quadrants. When counselors' behavior reflects high competence and high commitment, they are labeled "Star Workers." When counselors' behavior reflects low competence and high commitment, they are labeled "Unfocused Workers." When their behavior reflects high competence and low commitment, the label is "Disengaged Workers." When their behavior reflects low competence and low commitment, the label is "Impaired Workers." (More detailed descriptions of these categories of workers can be found in Henderson and Gysbers, 1998.)

For example, a counselor may be qualified (mid-level competence) to initiate a session, but be indifferent (low-level commitment) to the client. The point within a quadrant where lines drawn from each continuum point meet identifies the professionalism level of the counselor *in the specific instance*. In plotting the example, the behavior of the counselor, demonstrating mid-level competence and low-level commitment, falls in the Disengaged Worker

Figure 11.2 Categories of Professionalism Matrix

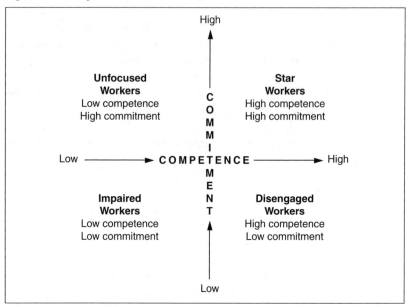

Adapted by Catherine Somody from Henderson & Gysbers, 1998

quadrant. Applying this model requires training and practice, but it has been found to be highly useful. One relatively new administrative supervisor in counseling includes in her advice to new administrative supervisors, "Take hold of the four quadrants of commitment and competence and use that as a tool to identify the strengths and weaknesses of each staff member" (Y. K. Steves, personal communication, June 16, 2005).

A word of caution is required. While "a common ground of terms and labels . . . enrich the language and basic communications by which professionals interact with one another" (Loganbill et al., 1982, p. 15), their application must be done with care. There is a big difference between generalizations that help focus thinking and stereotypes that over-generalize and force people into inappropriate pigeonholes. Levels of competence and commitment are identifiable only by using accurate descriptions of *standards* for behaviors that reflect certain levels of competence and commitment, and with sufficient *data* supporting judgments about a staff member's performance in the specific instance (Henderson & Gysbers, 1998).

In addition, there are gradations of placement within each quadrant, points at which supervisees are nearer to or farther away from another quadrant. Counselors' behaviors in three of the corners of the quadrants are a breath away from a neighboring quadrant. A behavior sample plotted in the middle of a quadrant looks very different from one plotted near the highest end of the continua for that quadrant. Following the earlier example, the behavior of the counselor demonstrating mid-level competence and low-level commitment—would be plotted near the lower left-hand corner of the Disengaged Worker quadrant—a step away from the Impaired Worker quadrant. If, however, the counselor's competence level is near the high end of the continuum, and the commitment level only a little below par, the intersecting point between the two would be at the middle of the top of the quadrant, near the border of the Star Worker quadrant.

In working with this concept effectively, administrative supervisors clarify what being in the uppermost corner of the upper-right hand quadrant (highest competence + highest commitment) looks like. Their vision of the Ideal Professional Counselor includes pictures of what competence looks like at its highest levels, and what commitment looks like at its deepest levels. Many new administrative supervisors mistakenly think that is what they represent, and want others to match their behaviors. But, open-minded administrative supervisors allow people to work in their own ways (Drucker, 1999). Supervisors and supervisees alike need to stretch their vision by looking at examples of "stars" in the profession as a whole, at counselor practitioners, theorists and researchers that are legendary counseling professionals—e.g., Carl Rogers, Fritz Perls, Rudolf Dreikurs, Albert Ellis, Donald Super, William Glasser, and the like. Their notions of Ideal Professional Counselors need to stretch beyond the confines of their specific department or even their acquaintances. At the same time, the more examples of professional counselor behavior they have observed, the more textured their vision of degrees of excellence in counseling performance becomes.

Responding Appropriately

The professionalism assessment model is applied by administrative supervisors to assist all their supervisees, including non-counseling staff members. What changes for different types of supervisees are the standards that describe competence and commitment. Effective administrative supervisors use standards that are relevant for each employee category. The assessed professionalism level suggests appropriate administrative supervisory responses, as described in Chapter 10.

In this model, the response planning process begins with identifying as precisely as possible the professionalism level of supervisees, their strengths and weaknesses in areas of competence and commitment. Patterns of supervisor responses have been identified for workers whose behavior patterns fit in each of the quadrants (Henderson & Gysbers, 1998; Northside Independent School District, 1997).

Generalizations of how the response selection process flows for workers in each of the four professionalism quadrants are:

Responding to Star Workers:
  Assessment rating:
    High Competence: (specific from observation)
    High Commitment: (specific from observation)
  Supervisor Goal(s) (improvements): Increased commitment or increased competence (specific to individual)
  Supervisee—Considerations:
    Strengths: Commitment or Competence (specific to the individual)
    Motivators/Needs: self-actualization, esteem; achievement, responsibility, recognition, opportunities for advancement and growth
  Supervisor Responses:
    Approach: non-directive; collegial
    Power base: expert, information, referent
    Empowerment strategy: applications of commitment + competence; expertise; referent
    Modality: facilitative
    Leader functions: consulting, mentoring; delegating
    Leader behaviors: listening, clarifying, encouraging, reflecting, modeling by example

Responding to Unfocused Workers:
  Assessment rating:
    Low Competence: (specific from observation)
    High Commitment: (specific from observation)
  Supervisor Goal(s) (improvements): Increased competence (specific to individual)
  Supervisee—Considerations:
    Strengths: Commitment (specific to individual)
    Motivators/Needs: belonging, status; recognition, advancement, growth, challenging work, supervision, relationships
  Supervisor Responses:
    Approach: collaborative; collegial with confrontation
    Power base: information, referent, legitimate, reward
    Empowerment strategy: application of commitment (specific to individual's strength)
    Modality: conceptual
    Leader functions: mentoring, coaching, teaching, participating
    Leader behaviors: presenting ideas & information, problem solving, negotiating, building relationship

Responding to Disengaged Workers:
  Assessment rating:
    High Competence: (specific from observation)
    Low Commitment: (specific from observation)

Supervisor Goal(s) (improvements): Improved commitment (specific to individual)

Supervisee—Considerations:

Strengths: Competence (specific to individual)

Motivators/Needs: belonging, security; challenging work, status, relationships, supervision, opportunities to change the work environment

Supervisor Responses:

Approach: directive informational; autonomy with normative structure

Power base: information, referent, legitimate, reward, connection

Empowerment strategy: applications of competence; referent, information (specific to individual's strength)

Modality: confrontive, catalytic

Leader functions: consulting, coaching; selling

Leader behaviors: building relationship, standardizing, directing

Responding to Impaired Workers:

Assessment rating:

Low Competence: (specific from observation)

Low Commitment: (specific from observation)

Supervisor Goal(s) (improvements): Increased competence; increased commitment; career redirection (specific to individual)

Supervisee—Considerations:

Strengths: (specific to individual)

Motivators/Needs: survival, safety; impact of work on personal life, job security, working conditions, salaries

Supervisor Responses:

Approach: directive control; normative structuring with increasing autonomy

Power base: legitimate, connection, coercive

Empowerment strategy: (specific to individual's strength)

Modality: prescriptive

Leader functions: teaching, counseling; telling, judging

Leader behaviors: reinforcing, standardizing, instructing, referral

These patterns of responses offer supervisors places to *start* their thinking about how to respond effectively to specific individuals. Ranges of choices vary by individuals and circumstances, and by individuals' relative placement *within* quadrants.

SUMMARY

Recognizing the conceptual part of administrative supervision is essential to your effectiveness. To improve services to your clients, you articulate a vision for what your counseling department provides and how. Because your supervisees are the providers of those client services, you must also have models that guide your work with them. Supervisees want meaningful supervision, and to be treated consistently and fairly; your operating from consciously articulated conceptual and process models better ensures that. Chapter 10 described a process model that is widely used for helping counselors continuously improve their performance.

Two facets of conceptual models that serve you well are those regarding the specific characteristics of The Ideal Professional Counselor, and various Counselor Developmental Levels. Your Ideal Professional Counselor model establishes your standards for professional counselors' work. It is the basis for your assessing fairly each counselor's degree of closeness to the Ideal—how close his or her performance is to excellence. Your model of Counselor Developmental Levels defines the factors of performance and describes various levels counselors fall into in their development of these. It is the basis for your consistency in assessing individuals who are neither Perfect nor Imperfect.

In order to practice intentional supervision and make fair evaluations (Chapter 14), you consciously use these models and articulate them to your supervisees and your supervisors. By answering the questions offered in this chapter, you have developed your model. The model of counselor developmental levels that I use in my administrative supervision practice, and its applications within the model supervision process, were described.

SUPERVISORS' CHALLENGES AND RESPONSES

Supervisors' Challenges: Assessment Complexities

Assessing counselors' levels of professionalism in the assessment phase of the OARS process is one of the most difficult parts of administrative supervisors' jobs. It is also one of the most important. Lester and Eaker (cited in Hersey et al., 2001) found that four of the top 10 concerns of supervisees about their supervisors related to insufficient help with performance: "lack of feedback on performance," "no or inappropriate goal setting," "lack of opportunity for advancement," and "rewards not related to performance" (p. 10).

New, hurried or harried administrative supervisors tend to overreact to and over-generalize about their supervisees. Too often, they see each supervisee in black-and-white, all good or all not good. Their analyses are not based on sufficient data. Their conclusions are not sound. It is difficult to discern whether individuals are "Unfocused" or "Disengaged," or "Disengaged" or "Impaired." For many, "Unfocused Workers" are most fun to supervise—eager, but lacking knowledge or skills. It is tempting for supervisors to think of supervisees they like personally as unfocused, when in fact they may be disengaged. For some, "Disengaged Workers" are tough to work with—not needing competence development as much as they need to boost their commitment levels. It is tempting for supervisors to think of supervisees they find off-putting as disengaged, when in fact they may be unfocused.

Effective administrative supervisors may spend as much as 75% of their time in spontaneous supervisory interactions with supervisees. "Spontaneous" entails making a lot of choices in deciding how to respond to each appropriately in a short period of time. A look at the math entailed in choosing among the variables demonstrates how complex the ethically required thought process is for each supervision incident.

For each supervisee administrative supervisors consider information about their personal and situational contexts. In applying the process and conceptual models exemplified in this chapter, there are nine categories of *variables* to be processed within each event, requiring 65 choices. There are two factors, and, for each, counselors' long term goals and "next step" improvements. Consideration of a supervisee's motivation entails choosing among the seven needs (Maslow, 1954) and 14 factors (Herzberg, Mausner & Snyderman, 1959). Then, they choose from four approaches (Glickman et al., 1995), seven power bases for two uses—influencing and empowering (Raven, 2004), five intervention modalities (Loganbill et al., 1982), six functions, and nine behaviors. Some of the variables have subparts (e.g., the two factors, competence + commitment, are each described by a continuum, consisting of an infinite number of increments). (The number of increments depends on the size of the vocabulary of the supervisor.)

Figuring how many times they do this in a year underscores its importance. To keep it simple, the example is for one supervisee that participates in one interaction with the supervisor per hour. For a typical workweek, that equals 2000 interactions a year (8 hours/day × 5 days/week × 50 weeks/year = 2000 interactions/work year). Making choices among nine variables in 2000 interactions equals 18,000 choices. If the choices among the 65 variable subcategories are taken into account, the total is 130,000. Of course, the numbers increase exponentially with each additional supervisee, and shorter periods of time.

Supervisors' Responses

To be an effective administrative supervisor, you consciously develop and internalize your models for processing counselor assessment information and for conceptualizing supervisees. To assess someone's professionalism accurately and fairly, you rely on data, particularly your recorded data. You treat each incident as a unique "work sample," and guard against allowing the impression left by one event to contaminate your next impression. Very few people are competent or incompetent all the time. Very few are committed or not committed all the time. It is the aggregation of professionalism levels in specific incidents that support summary judgments—performance evaluation (Chapter 14). And the more discretely each single incident is analyzed, the sounder the summary.

A key skill of responsive administrative supervisors is developing their vocabulary for use in counselor assessment. As an example, using precise words to describe exactly a counselor's competence and commitment levels in an incident can lead the supervisor to exact locations on each continuum. The plotting of quadrant placement, then, may be intuitive, but it will not be capricious. It may be mathematical, but it will not be rigid.

Internalizing the decision tree outlined in the example model for selecting appropriate responses takes time and experience. Using our example as the model, the decision tree includes making choices among the factors (dimensions), goals (targets), strengths, motivations, approach, power base, modality, function, and behavior. Supervisors have created many ways to remember the variables and their choices. To get themselves started, they have developed "cheat sheets." These typically consist of a handout with one category of worker quadrant per page, listing the generalized decisions—the "places to start" their thinking. Some have put these in notebooks that sit on their desks; others have shrunk them to fit in drawers. They have laminated them and taped them to their sliding desk shelves. Some, creatively, have made up acronyms (which is not easy in this model): f-g-s-m-a-p-m-f-b = For goodness sake, make a professional move for betterment. (!)

12
Organize Staff Members for Effective Service Delivery

To best serve the counseling clients and the mission of the department, effective administrative supervisors have smooth working departments that perform their tasks effectively, efficiently and in line with the highest standards of quality. "Productivity of the knowledge worker will almost always require that the *work itself* be restructured and be made part of a *system*" (Drucker, 1999, p. 154).

A system, here, is defined as several functionally related elements or processes that serve the accomplishment of one end (American Heritage Dictionary, 1982). That means seeing the department's services not as disconnected or loosely connected, but rather as parts of one whole, organized collection of staff members, services, activities, procedures, resources, and clients focused on helping the clients (Herr, Heitzmann & Rayman, 2006; Henderson & Gysbers, 1998). All functions and tasks of a department "should have some connection or relation to other tasks being performed" (Hersey, Blanchard & Johnson, 2001, p. 443). Envisioning the system can be especially challenging when the primary service is individual counseling, or for new administrative supervisors whose primary focus has been on their own work in their own offices and, perhaps, feeling isolated from others in a counseling practice or a multifaceted mental health agency.

This chapter addresses the staff members' element of the service delivery system. To be a systems thinking administrative supervisor, you begin by identifying the essential functions that must be performed in order to provide desired client services, and the linkages between them. Related to those essential functions are "processes, roles, responsibilities, [and] accountabilities" (Linder, 2005, p. 24). Examples of processes are decision-making, sharing information, communicating, and problem solving. Examples of roles of staff members, in addition to their counseling roles, are those of planner, leader, resource manager, and colleague. Examples of responsibilities include conducting specific services and activities, maintaining documentation, managing their time, being professionally autonomous, setting and working toward goals. Examples of accountabilities are those related to client outcomes, services provided, and professional performance.

This chapter describes how to organize your staff members' work within a service delivery system, clarify each staff member's job responsibilities, build a team of the staff, and conduct effective staff meetings. Experiences in designing your own organizational systems for carrying out your counseling practice, in group counseling and supervision give you a foundation for carrying out some of these responsibilities.

ORGANIZE THE SERVICE DELIVERY SYSTEM

A department's mission suggests the structure for the work and the workers' responsibilities (Abernethy & Lillis, 2001). In organizing the work and the workflow, you consider several perspectives: the clients, the services, and the logistical support activities. Systematic management of your department's clients means tracking their progress from the time they enter the system—at reception and greeting—through orientation, initial assignment to a counselor or an activity, making progress toward goal achievement, to termination and follow-up. Systematic organization of the services means identifying them (e.g., individual counseling, group counseling, assessment, psychoeducational offerings), and determining when and where they are provided, by whom, and how (or if) they are related to each other. Logistical support services include having and scheduling the use of facilities, furniture and equipment; record-keeping (forms, systems), communication vehicles (e.g., phones, computers), accountability systems, and clerical and other non-counseling support services (e.g., accounting, word-processing). All of these facets are, then, arranged in a design that supports effective and efficient client service delivery, and staff members assigned to carry out each of the activities. You plan, assign, delegate and coordinate the work (Kadushin & Harness, 2002).

To be clear, you communicate what the organizational structure of your department is. Organizational structures include lines of authority, channels of communication, and movement of people and ideas. Typically, there are both formal and informal structures in place. Your plotting this on paper facilitates your precision and understanding, and helps others see it as well. In striving for optimum effectiveness, Mintzberg and Heyden (1999) suggested metaphors that you can use to describe "*how* a place works, depicting critical interactions among people, products and information" (p. 88). They described sets, chains, hubs and webs.

Sets are people or machines that have little connection with other sets. You see this pattern in professional service firms, such as private counseling practices:

> with professionals working almost exclusively with their own clients. . . .
> They are loosely coupled as a collection, [or] a group. . . . These sets usually share common resources—facilities, funds, overall manage-
> ment—or else they would not be found in the same organization. But otherwise, they are on their own. (Mintzberg & Heyden, 1999, p. 89)

Chains are linear connecting processes that you see in organizational charts or flow charts. *Hubs* are coordinating centers that "depict movement to and from one focal point" (p. 89). One shared computer and the technician that operates it is often a hub. *Webs* "are grids with no center; they allow open-ended communication and continuous movement of people and ideas" (p. 89). The organizational pattern for designing and implementing a big project or a new activity is often a web. To be effective, create organizational structures that best suit your purposes in different situations. Explaining how the department works in a circumstance allows all of the staff members to operate more effectively.

Each of these organizational structures calls for use of different management styles. "Sets suggest that managers stay away from the action, watching and comparing.... Their job, basically, is to decide who gets what resources" (Mintzberg & Heyden, 1999, p. 93). As the owner of a group private practice, you probably have to decide who gets to use the one conference room and when. As an administrative supervisor in a chain pattern, you are at the top of each link in the chain. "The chain of command is laid over the chain of operations. The chain of operations is clear and orderly, and the chain of management exists primarily to keep it that way—for control" (p. 94). If you work in a local office of a statewide agency, your accountability to the state-level office entails your being at the top of the chain of your department.

"In the hub, management appears in the center, around which activities revolve" (Mintzberg & Heyden, 1999, p. 94). You coordinate the people and the activities, but the workers are empowered. For example, if, in developing your department's budget request, you ask your staff members to develop their individual budget requests and you merge them, you are using a hub pattern. A web pattern is fluid: you move around to the different parts of the web, facilitating collaboration and infusing energy at different points. This is a useful organizational structure if your department is planning an event with multiple activities, where a different group within your department is conducting each activity. To be most effective, you not only understand the organizational pattern in use, you change it if it is not working. In this last example, if the different groups have different ideas about what the theme of the event is, you might switch to a hub pattern by meeting with all of them to arrive at a consistent definition and focus.

CLARIFY STAFF MEMBERS' JOB RESPONSIBILITIES

To organize for efficiency ("Organize for efficiency," 2004, p. 25), you help staff members "operate at their highest potential [by] letting them know what their duties are and how they fit into the scheme" of the department (Diamond, 2006, p. 68). What their duties are, their job descriptions, are derived from the scope of practice permitted by your staff members' licenses, certificates and training (e.g., Licensed Professional Counselor Act, 1999, §003; *Texas*

Administrative Code, §681.31). They describe how this knowledge and these skills are to be applied in a licensee's work. Agency job descriptions do the same for non-licensed staff members, and specify the duties for licensed staff members. Heed what is and is not permitted within the various licenses your staff members hold. These are issued by state commissions and agencies, and vary for different categories of mental health workers (e.g., counselors, psychologists, social workers, psychiatric technicians, and so on).

For the delivery system to work most systematically, you specifically describe each staff member's job duties, coordinate their activities and tie them to a calendar. Legal (non-discriminatory) job descriptions begin with a list of the required essential functions (e.g., counseling, assessment, referral). These are the "primary duties associated with a job; duties that are critical to job performance" (Kulik, 2004, p. 244).

When the essential functions of each of the jobs are laid side-by-side, they comprise the essential functions of your whole delivery system. Figure 12.1 provides a partial example of such a layout. This allows you to ensure that each employee's responsibilities are related to those of others, and that one employee's work is not in conflict with nor overlaps another's.

It helps you make "clear to employees who is responsible for what" ("Organize for efficiency," 2004, p. 25). Individuals' specific job descriptions address each staff member's unique roles and responsibilities. Each has "a work program and specific and concrete work assignments with defined goals, with deadlines, and with clear accountability" (Drucker, 1974, p. 119). Each counselor applies his/her competencies differently; for example, they are each responsible for an identified caseload of clients, are assigned different tasks in implementing services, have unique styles and ways of doing things, and different objectives (Henderson & Gysbers, 1998). To maximize efficiency, periodically review "the work of all employees to make sure employee and manager have the same understanding of each job" (Drucker, 1974, p. 119).

In assigning work in your department, bear in mind that job satisfaction relates to a staff member's being able to answer "Yes" to the question, "At work, do I have the opportunity to do what I do best every day?" (Buckingham & Coffman, 1999, p. 28). To be most effective, assign staff members responsibilities that make optimum use of their talents and strengths, and minimize their weaknesses (Gysbers & Henderson, 2006). Great managers advise other managers, "If you want to turn talent into performance, you have to position each person so that you are paying her [*sic*] to do what she [*sic*] is naturally wired to do" (p. 148).

Making good use of staff members' talent includes using people in roles, jobs and tasks appropriate to their training and competence. Over-relying or under-relying on support staff members not only wastes their expertise, it also wastes the expertise of whoever is doing the clerical or technical work instead—often the professional staff members. For example, some professionals

Figure 12.1 Example Sequence of Essential Client Services Functions

Staff member	Secretary	Administrative Assistant	Counseling Intern	Administrative Supervisor	Scheduling Secretary	Professional Counselor	Administrative Supervisor	Billing Clerk	Administrative Assistant
	↑	↑	↑	↑	↑	↑	↑	↑	↑
Functions	Greeting Reception Recordkeeping	Orientation Registration Recordkeeping	Intake interview Initial assessment Recordkeeping	Assignment to specialist Recordkeeping	Setting appointments Phoning reminders Recordkeeping	Counseling Ongoing assessment Intervention through termination Recordkeeping	Monitoring client progress Recordkeeping	Develop & distribute bills Maintain ledger Deposit payments Follow-up on non-payers	Closure interview Follow-up Record-keeping

prefer to produce their own handout materials and by-pass the secretarial services available. It is most economically efficient when an individual doing a task has the lowest salary required by that task: freeing up others to do what they are not only specially trained to do, but also paid to do. To be efficient, avoid overloading employees, delegate authority along with responsibility, and clearly define the lines of authority.

Members of departments with one coherent delivery system are inter-dependent. "One of the realities of organizational behavior is that we must work with others to accomplish our aspirations" (Hersey et al., 2001, p. 317). You are responsible for helping staff members understand not only their own work responsibilities, but also those of their co-workers. The more each understands the whole system and the role of each individual, the smoother the operation works. As administrative supervisor, you develop procedures to ensure that staff members fulfill their responsibilities.

> In prescribing and proscribing, in monitoring what should be done and what cannot be done, the supervisor is ensuring predictability and reliability of performance. Workers doing different things, whose work needs to be coordinated, can be assured that the work their partners are doing will be in accordance with some uniform expectations. (Kadushin and Harness, 2002, p. 112)

Worker satisfaction is also linked to the answer to the question, "Are my co-workers committed to doing quality work?" (Buckingham & Coffman, 1999, p. 28). Knowing others' work requirements, standards and values supports development of trust among staff members.

BUILD A TEAM OF YOUR STAFF

Because your staff members work in a system that is interdependent, it is best when they work together as a team. You accept responsibility for building the collection of individuals into a high functioning team, and for building your group's development of the characteristics of successful groups, as well-described in group literature (e.g., Building Team Performance, 2005; Hurst, 1984; Katzenbach & Smith, 2005; Napier & Gershenfeld, 2004). However,

> the founding principle here is that excellent teams are built around *individual excellence*. Therefore the manager's first responsibility is to make sure each person is positioned in the right role. Her [sic] second responsibility is to balance the strengths and weaknesses of each individual so that they complement one another. Then, and only then, should she [sic] turn her attention to broader issues like "camaraderie" or "team spirit." (Buckingham & Coffman, 1999, p. 173)

You begin to build a team by helping your counseling and non-counseling staff members recognize that they have an ethical responsibility to "develop positive working relationships and systems of communication with colleagues to enhance services to clients" (American Counseling Association [ACA], 2005, D, Introduction), and to honor their colleagues' and co-workers' dignity and be respectful (American Mental Health Counselors Association [AMHCA], 2000, Principle 8, Introduction, & C; American School Counselor Association [ASCA], 2004a, C.1.b).

The stronger your staff members' feelings of affiliation for, and cohesion within, the group as a whole, the more individual competitiveness is replaced by the healthy competition that is fostered by their desires to perform well in order to earn the respect of the other members (Bennis & Biederman, 1997). "The truth is that human interests especially when people know each other and love each other are pooled rather than being mutually exclusive" (Maslow, 1998/1962, p. 122).

> Something happens in ["Great Groups"] that doesn't happen in ordinary ones . . . Some alchemy takes place that results . . . in a qualitative change in the participants. [They] seem to become better than themselves. They are able to see more, achieve more, and have a far better time doing it than they can in working alone. (Bennis & Biederman, p. 196)

They become "more than the sum of [their] parts" (Riley in Collie, 2001, p. 111).

Collectively, they learn more, make better decisions, collaborate more, and develop more commitment to the work of the whole department and agency (Harris, 2002). By planning together they build more solid delivery systems. Problems in the delivery system or the office are more readily identified and resolved. "Employees who work in teams report that they experience greater job satisfaction, collaborate better with others, have increased pride and ownership in their jobs, and experience higher self-esteem" (Hersey et al., 2001, p. 321). You will probably see decreases in absenteeism and turnover. Even in a "set" organizational pattern, individual counselors grow and learn from their office-mates when there is a feeling of professional cohesiveness and shared professional identity. Sharing space and other resources can lead to growth-producing consultative relationships and help address the isolation issues of single practitioners.

Work to Build Your Team

Building a team of your staff members requires more than just labeling the group a "team." It takes diligent work, attending to the individual team members, keeping the team on task, and monitoring the developmental progress of the team as an entity of its own.

Team leadership is simple, because effectively functioning teams tend to harness a natural synergy that gives them motivation, allowing you to step aside and let the team work on its own. Team leadership is complex, because your relationships with the team members are dynamic and constantly changing, depending on the situation, goal, and the environment. (Hersey et al., 2001, p. 322)

As an effective leader, you fulfill different roles in the group depending on the situation. At times you are the department head, the team leader or a member (Blanchard, Carew & Parisi-Carew, 2000). You may be the lead producer, being action-oriented and knowledgeable; or the administrator, supervising the system, managing details, providing appropriate facilities, equipment and materials; or an entrepreneur, creatively taking risks as a "pragmatic dreamer" (Bennis & Biederman, 1997, p. 199); or an integrator, bringing people and ideas together (Hurst, 1984). No matter what your functional role, you are always the leader with the institutional power. Even in social situations, your staff members are aware of this differential. Clarify for your staff members the role you are fulfilling in a situation, and define your boundaries carefully.

Attend To Your Individual Staff Members

In attending to the individuals in your group, strive for staff members to embrace the personal, cultural and professional diversity of individual staff members. You and your staff members recognize that synergy is based on valuing differences (Covey, 1989). Lead your group by enhancing the strengths and talents of individuals, while minimizing their weaknesses (Cottringer, 2005a; Drucker, 1974; Henderson & Gysbers, 1998). You and the team members encourage others to maintain their uniqueness, and at the same time develop the ability to work together in spite of each individual's idiosyncrasies (Bennis & Biederman, 1997). Teach individuals to give up some of themselves for the good of the group and to compromise, believing that between two people's opinions is a third opinion—often the one that works (Covey, 1989).

A part of your challenge is that, most likely, your administrative supervisees will represent diverse mental health professionals (e.g., social workers, psychologists, psychiatrists) with different professional belief systems. They may also be from different professional backgrounds (e.g., business/finance, technology, human resources). There will be those with different educational backgrounds (e.g., interns, paraprofessionals, clerks, administrative assistants, bookkeepers). Each individual's experiences are different and are to be valued.

Attend To Your Team As An Entity

As with individual supervisees, groups at different times and in different circumstances fall into different levels of functioning and do best when you change your leadership style. Your group may have times of impairment and need a leader who is highly directive. They may lose their commitment to the goal or a task, and need you to provide information and structure their work. They may lose their focus and need task direction and designed collaborative approaches. They may function as a "Star Team" and need collegiality.

In maintaining your group as a team, help your staff work through the stages of group development: form, storm, norm, perform (Tuckman, 1965) and adjourn (Tuckman, 1977); or beginning, confrontation, compromise and harmony, reassessment, resolution and recycling, and termination/adjournment (Napier & Gershenfeld, 2004). Because your perspective is different than that of your staff members, it is your responsibility to provide feedback on the stage of team development that you see happening at a given time, as well as on individuals' functioning within the team.

Form. In the formative stage, your goal is to get off to a good start. It is a time to re-state the overall department vision, values and mission. Your responsibility is to bring into focus the purpose of the group. Typically, they take on collective work products, (e.g., developing new activities or products, solutions to identified problems, group spirit). As the team leader, one of your goals is for the group itself to feel responsible for its work and for individuals and the group to be mutually accountable. You want "every person . . . to take upon his [*sic*] own shoulders all the responsibilities of the whole enterprise" (Maslow, 1998/1962, p. 86).

Storm. As with all developing groups, the storming stage is the least comfortable, consisting of much confrontation and, in some instances, hostility. During it, your leadership skills are tested. As the administrative supervisor, you manage group difficulties and guide problem solving. Be decisive, but not arbitrary. Some administrative supervisors mistakenly try to avoid or deny the existence of this difficult stage. Over the long haul, your group will be damaged if you ignore issues, or pretend that differences have been resolved when they have not. "Focusing on the end result before difficulties in team dynamics have been ironed out can be detrimental to the team's performance" (Seijits & Latham, 2005, p. 129).

Issues arise for all teams. They erupt over plans, projects, or assignments, professional perspectives or external (e.g., organizational, community) factors. Some apparently prevalent specific "turf" issues are those caused by sharing clients in different activities, or budget money, facilities or other resources (Henderson & Gysbers, 1998). The most emotional issues are interpersonal issues, such as professional jealousy, competition for position with peers or supervisors, assigning blame rather than fixing mistakes or solving problems, personality or value differences, interpersonal or cultural differences, and the inability to differentiate the personal and the professional. Severely impaired or disengaged staff member(s) can derail staff groups. All groups consist of individuals whose work ethics are different from others (e.g., those striving for excellence, and those comfortable with being satisfactory or some who only do the bare minimum). Some individuals are willing to work 24/7/365; others' work parameters are described by clocks and calendars.

Every group of staff members that I have seen has had individuals among them who are unprofessional in their behaviors (e.g., some who unwittingly and others who wittingly violate ethical standards). The examples provided below with the rules categories give you a glimpse of the kinds of issues that arise (i.e., individuals who are judgmental, hold back, or shun new staff members; bosses who dictate too much or do not provide enough leadership; individuals who do not face others when they have a problem, or who work to split the loyalties of staff members, dividing the team into different factions). In managing these issues, address them individually or with your group depending on how widespread the difficulty is. Whether with individuals or groups, also lead those involved through re-norming (i.e., recasting or recommitting to the operational rules).

Norm. In the norming stage, you guide your group to establish operating rules, guidelines for working together. These are the foundation for the group's ongoing work. The categories of rules to be discussed and agreed to by all the group members are listed below with examples that emerged during my work with actual counseling department staff groups.

Communication: *"We will be open and non-judgmental."*
Participation: *"We will each give input."*
Interpersonal climate: *"We will welcome new-comers."*
Leadership: *"The leader will maintain 2-way communications."*
Decision-making: *"Top-down and bottom-up decision making processes will be used according to the situation."*
Problem-solving: *"We will, first, address a problem at its source."*
Conflict management: *"When in a conflict with another staff member, we will not seek allies or try to build coalitions."*
Individual's behavior: *"I will listen to and respect the rights of others."*
Group behavior: *"We will laugh, lighten up and have fun."*

Establishing guidelines takes time, but it is time well spent. Issues will arise. It is much harder to reach consensus on behaviors when a group has individuals in it who are hurt or lack trust, for example. A successful exercise that I have used with storming teams is to have individuals reflect on the best team of any kind they have ever been part of (e.g., sports, service groups, work), and list the ingredients they think made them so good. Next, you organize their discussion of these particulars around the nine categories listed above, recording them on nine separate sheets of easel paper (one for each category). You strive for consensus on specific behaviors that the entire group (all the individuals) is willing to abide by.

Perform. Blanchard et al. (2000) use the acronym, P-E-R-F-O-R-M, that suggests the characteristics of well-functioning teams in this stage of group development. Each of the members is committed to the **P**urpose of your group. Each "has introjected the goals or directives or objectives in the . . . situation and . . . is so identified with them that he [*sic*] wants them done in the best possible way" (Maslow, 1998/1962, p. 158). Pat Riley, legendary NBA coach, describes how a successful team is built from individual players:

> We understand that . . . it's about the relationship of each part as it fits into the whole. We had guys coming in from different cities, and they had to come together quickly to understand the mission, grasp the system, work hard, be unselfish, respect one another, meet the idiosyncrasies of 11 other players, and aim for a common goal—to win. If team members don't get with the program, we fail. (Collie, 2001, p. 111)

Their common purpose is to win. Yours is to help your clients most effectively and efficiently.

In a well functioning team, each member feels **E**mpowered, as does the group as a whole. You help empower them by sharing your power. You provide them the information they need and leadership, direction, and training. You help them know their authority and limits, give them permission to be independent, delegate to them, trust their work and their products. You support each individual's participation and growth. Highly functioning groups help individual members achieve their own goals.

For your team to perform well, **R**elationships and communication among them must be healthy (Chapter 9). The more your individual staff members care about other staff members, the stronger your group. You encourage open, transactional and democratic communications, having open-ended discussions and promoting active group problem-solving. You encourage—within reason—non work-related conversations about common experiences (e.g., hobbies, sports, other outside interests, shared historical experiences, common/different family stages). These "ease the way for more effective work-related communications" (Kulik, 2004, p. 236).

As the group member with the most legitimate power, your degree of **F**lexibility contributes to your team's effectiveness. You are advised to share responsibility, using individuals' talents and strengths, and to be open to new ideas and taking risks. **O**ptimal performance comes when individuals and the group establish high standards, seek continuous improvement, are productive and achieve results. One success leads to another and to another. You also help individuals and your group as a whole learn from their mistakes, resolve conflicts and solve problems. As administrative supervisor, you are in position to **R**ecognize and appreciate accomplishments of individuals and the team itself. Effective performance supports your group's **M**orale as you encourage optimism, confidence, enthusiasm, pride, and satisfaction. Your giving them voice in discussions also heightens their morale.

Adjourn. Adjournment of a whole group is rare in the work setting.

Complete adjournment only happens when a practice or a department closes down or the people relocate. However, you have to anticipate re-forming, re-storming, re-norming, and re-achieving optimal performance with each change in assigned task, and in staff membership. In some ways you adjourn one group and re-develop another when individual staff members leave and new members join. When your people change, your group's dynamics change. It is always a work-in-progress. Adjournment and new starting does occur when a new leader takes over (i.e., when you are the new department administrative supervisor).

CONDUCT EFFECTIVE STAFF MEETINGS

Katzenbach and Smith (2005) distinguish between teams and working groups. To be effective, you use both kinds. Each serves a different purpose, requires you to alter your leadership style, help your staff members fulfill different roles, and use different communication patterns—circles in the team, stars in working group meetings (Hersey et al., 2001). Working group meetings are business meetings. In a working group, be a strong and clearly focused leader, run efficient meetings, allow for discussion, but make decisions, and delegate responsibility as appropriate. Each individual focuses on his/her individual work products and is accountable for him/herself. Communications occur in a star pattern, with you in the middle, and each other individual communicating with you. The structure is autocratic and efficient.

Much of your work as an administrative supervisor is conducted through staff meetings. Preparing for, holding and following up on staff meetings absorbs a lot of your time—between 8% and 15%, depending on the size of your staff. Ensure the value of staff meetings.

> Many meetings with groups or teams, instead of being a good use of our time, feel repetitious and boring. It is not unusual to leave with a sense not only that our abilities have not been well utilized, but that the time and energy we exerted will not result in real value. Leadership begins with a responsibility to see each meeting as an opportunity to build successes, good will, and future commitments. That means that leaders need to be accountable for how they utilize the time and resources of others and that everything they do is carefully designed for maximum impact. (Napier & Gershenfeld, 2004, p. 225)

In planning, consider the purposes of the meetings and carefully attend to logistics. The purposes of staff meetings are to provide opportunities for conducting the business of the department, for communicating, collaborating and being collegial. In a group approach to service delivery, they are the medium for planning, designing or evaluating work, and for addressing office logistics and resources (Curtis & Sherlock, 2006). They provide opportunities for the group to assess its developmental stage in both team and working groups, and to discuss adherence or lack thereof to the established operational rules.

These meetings, however, are not counseling or encounter group sessions. They are *not* retreats or play time. They are not times for in-depth staff development or work on major projects. Those should be scheduled separately.

You call the meetings, set the agendas, establish the form of the meetings, locations, times, and so on.

> It is important to meet with counselors in a scheduled and thoughtfully planned format so that communication can happen—upward and down. It is necessary to insist on this, as any member of the [group] can always find (or others can find for them) reasons not to attend. (E. Zambrano, personal communication, June 14, 2005)

Staff meetings are most useful when you hold them regularly and schedule them consistently, so that they are an automatic entry on everyone's calendars. The days and times of the meetings follow the same pattern from week to week or month to month. When possible, the place is consistent as well. The day and time are originally selected with attention to everyone's client and work schedule. Attendance is required. Out of respect for everyone's calendar, you announce the beginning and ending times before meetings and adhere to that time schedule.

For staff members within one service delivery system, hold staff meetings weekly. Even administrative supervisors of independent practitioners who share an office space (e.g., the owner) are advised to meet often enough to ensure harmony in the shared facility, become better acquainted, and have opportunities to consult with each other. If your staff is very large, hold additional meetings of smaller groups. Smaller groups help facilitate two-way communication. You also meet regularly with the non-professional members of the department staff.

Your agenda should also have a place for staff members to raise topics of concern to them. These items may be spontaneous, submitted before the meeting, or a combination. The agenda should be published ahead of time so members can come adequately prepared. Your flexibility in changing the order of items attends to the needs of the group. A sample weekly staff meeting agenda is provided in Figure 12.2.

SUMMARY

To be an efficient and effective administrative supervisor, you organize your department's work into an integrated and efficient service delivery system. You ensure that each staff member understands his/her own job responsibilities and place in the system. Your staff members understand the job responsibilities of their co-workers and the interrelatedness of their work. Building a highly functioning team of your department staff members best ensures

Figure 12.2 Staff Meeting Agenda

COUNSELING DEPARTMENT STAFF AGENDA WEEK OF _____

1. Service Delivery System
   a. Debriefing of last week's activities
   b. Planning for next week's activities
   c. Case consultation(s)
2. Improving Services
3. Agency news
4. Resource management topics
5. Inservice moment (e.g., reports from conferences, articles read)
6. Group/Team topics
7. Individual staff members' news
8. Summary of individual's responsibilities in meeting follow-up

provision of quality services to your clients, and counselors' job satisfaction. Holding effective and efficient staff meetings is the means for strengthening your working group and for managing the delivery system.

SUPERVISORS' CHALLENGES AND RESPONSES

Supervisors' Challenges: Intra-Staff Conflicts

Conflicts among staff members often begin between individuals. "Bickering, quarreling and outright hostilities will distract employees and drain the organization of its dynamics" (Stanley, 2006, p. 6). If left unchecked, conflicts between individuals can infect a whole group. By definition, conflicts are emotional (Harris, 2002), and people behave irrationally (Stanley). They "get the facts confused with their highly-charged feelings" (Stanley, p. 6).

Supervisors' Responses

Effective administrative supervisors intervene in staff member conflicts, but it is not easy.

> The manager plays a key role in setting the tone and modeling effective conflict management behavior. Peter Block (1991) advocates "moving toward the tension," since most people avoid it. As a person, you too may wish to avoid conflict in the organization. As a manager, you have a responsibility to move toward it and manage it. (Reichard, 2000, p. 186)

Department members need to understand that "conflicts are a normal part of the work place, but resolving them successfully is the main goal" (Cottringer, 2005a, p. 4). Group operational rules establish how conflicts between staff members or among the group as a whole will be handled. "Research has shown . . . that fostering an environment in which respectful conflict can occur actually enhances organizational effectiveness (Schermerhorn, Hunt & Osborn, 2000)" (Curtis & Sherlock, 2006, p. 122). This is especially true of ideological or profession-based conflicts. Interpersonal conflicts are usually more complicated and more volatile. It is imperative that supervisors not choose sides or "play favorites" in such conflicts, and facilitate the needed problem resolution conversations from a position of neutrality.

The strategies administrative supervisors use in these conflicted situations are best when they are carefully designed (Napier & Gershenfeld, 2004). Stanley (2006) suggests a 5-step process as a basis for resolving conflicts between individuals. Step 1 is for a supervisor to convene an introductory meeting with the employees involved, where it is made clear that the conflict needs to be resolved, and that the "employees must re-focus their individual energy toward accomplishing organizational goals and objectives" (Stanley, p. 6). Based on ground rules, each party is asked to express his/her thoughts and feelings. The supervisor takes responsibility for separating "actual objective facts . . . from the subjective feelings" (p. 7). To be successful, the meeting allows for involved individuals to express themselves, but does not allow a shouting match.

In step 2, a supervisor independently generates a "fact finding page" (Stanley, 2006, p. 7). Stanley recommends using one piece of paper, with four columns (if there are two people in conflict). In the first column, the supervisor lists the problem issues as discovered in the introductory meetings. The next two (or more) columns are labeled with the name of each individual involved in the conflict. In this column, the supervisor writes "a brief statement as to how each employee feels about the issue" (p. 7). In the last column, a list of "workable alternatives" (p. 7) for resolution of each issue is begun.

In step 3, the administrative supervisor meets with each employee separately to go over the fact-finding page. More is learned about the issues and individuals' thoughts. The employees contribute to the workable alternatives column, which is used to work out a resolution that each of the parties can live with. This step may take more than one meeting with each person involved (shuttle diplomacy). Step 4 is a joint meeting to "discuss the agreement and affirm their commitment to resolve the dispute" (Stanley, 2006, p. 7). Step 5 occurs if a workable agreement cannot be found. An outside professional is brought in to mediate an agreement. If that fails, then disciplinary action is called for.

13

Implement Effectively a Performance Management System

Effective administrative supervisors assist their supervisees to best serve their clients by implementing a performance management system that connects the activities that target counselors' and other staff members' professional development (Falvey, 1987; Latham, Almost, Mann & Moore, 2005). As discussed in Chapter 4, fair employment practices and federal and state statutes require employers to provide employees with accurate job descriptions, to conduct fair and meaningful evaluations of their staff members, and to promote their continuing professional and career development. The counseling profession's standards stress the value and importance of professional supervision in providing quality client services. Worker satisfaction with their workplace is related to two questions: "Do I know what is expected of me at work?" and "In the last six months, has someone at work talked to me about my progress?" (Buckingham & Coffman, 1999, p. 28).

A performance management system folds into one continuous process the activities that define individual counselors' jobs, provide them supervision and performance evaluation, and help them set goals for performance improvement. This chapter describes your responsibilities in conceptualizing, managing and implementing such a system. In addition to your experiences in each of these activities, and in devising your own system for assessing individual clients and clinical supervisees, planning and tracking treatment and supervision, and recordkeeping provide a foundation for this systematic approach. Your experience in counseling and providing clinical supervision supports your conducting the private and confidential conferences this responsibility entails. As an administrative supervisor, you do not counsel your supervisees, but you do approach the sessions with the same professional demeanor.

DEFINE YOUR PERFORMANCE MANAGEMENT SYSTEM
More than Performance Evaluation
Traditionally, the event with the most emphasis among the system's activities has been performance evaluation. "An organization that wants to build a high spirit of performance recognizes that 'people' decisions—on placement and on pay, on promotion, demotion, and firing—are the true 'control' of an

organization" (Drucker, 1974, p. 460). Performance evaluation and its ramifications produce anxiety in supervisors and supervisees alike—to the point that they are often not done effectively or not done at all. Recently, it has been recognized that "the annual appraisal process is necessary, but not sufficient" (Martin, 2000, p. 213). "The focus of current best practices in [personnel] evaluation is to provide the supervision and guidance needed to address the problems of individuals who can benefit from such interventions, as well as to promote positive growth and development" (Bunch, 2002, p. 193). By aligning the series of activities with the same targets, the power of the one summative evaluation activity is mitigated. "Organizations with strong performance management systems are nearly 50 percent more likely to outperform their competitors" (Parallels between, 2005, 1st ¶). Ninety-one percent of organizations use performance management systems (¶ 3).

Interrelatedness

Through building the interrelated activities into one system, each activity is more meaningful than when it is done as an isolated event (M. L. Libby, personal communication, May 6, 2005). You and your supervisees can see that the activities are interrelated. One activity provides the basis for the next. The job description sets standards for supervision and performance evaluation. Supervision activities provide information that supports fulfilling the job description, and performance evaluation. Evaluation conclusions suggest professional development goals. Professional development goals become targets for supervision. It is your responsibility to maintain the continuity from one activity to the next (Northside Independent School District, 1997).

All of the activities center on counselors' and other staff members' performance.

> Performance represents the constellation of attitudes, behaviors, cognitions, and perceptions that are focused on achieving a specific work-related goal or set of goals. Similarly, a well-designed therapeutic system depends upon a constellation of practitioner attitudes, behaviors, cognitions, and perceptions focused on achieving a defined clinical outcome using as few resources as necessary and ethical given the unique demands of each therapeutic encounter. Diagnosis and treatment are basically ways that practitioners perform in mental health organizations. Thus, enhanced performance results in improved outcomes, increased productivity, and greater satisfaction. (Martin, 2000, pp. 211–212)

Your goals for your supervisees are to help them perform at levels as close to perfect as they are able to get. Advancing their performance levels and, thereby, increasing the results their clients achieve is the purpose of all of the activities. In the context of your supervisory relationships, you and your supervisees do these activities together. Under a performance management system:

the individual employee plays a more active role. In contrast, under the traditional annual performance appraisal model, the manager plays a more active role than the employee, who typically is the recipient of information to be refuted, defended, or challenged. (Martin, 2000, pp. 214–215)

Responsibility for the activities is shared. You are responsible for seeing that they get done. Supervisees are responsible for their own professional development. "The ultimate goal of the developmental process . . . is to shift people toward self-management so that they can eventually assume responsibility for motivating their own behavior" (Hersey, Blanchard & Johnson, 2001, p. 245).

The balance of responsibility within the activities is different with different supervisees, depending on each one's professional developmental level and the related degree of supervisor directiveness called for. It also varies by the performance management system part. In general, the job description and performance evaluation activities are more supervisor-directed. Setting and committing to professional development goals is more supervisee-directed. Supervision is most often a shared responsibility, but varies depending on the situation.

Different performance management system parts and activities are more important to facilitating growth in counselors at different developmental levels. High functioning staff members benefit from emphasis and time spent on professional development goal setting. Unfocused staff members benefit from emphasis and time spent on supervision. Moderately functioning staff members benefit from clarity and emphasis on their job descriptions and performance evaluations. Impaired staff members need time spent on all four parts.

The activities of the performance management system are based on the same professional standards: those that reflect your Ideal Professional Counselor (Chapters 10 and 11). "The performance standards provide the basis for everything we do in the performance improvement system" (M. L. Libby, personal communication, May 6, 2005). They are each based on your assessments of staff members' developmental levels, which in turn suggest your responses. In supervision, you base assessments on behaviors in one incident at a time. In the job description, performance evaluation, and goal-setting parts, your assessments are based on identified patterns of counselors' job behaviors. In making professionalism assessments based on behavior patterns, be alert to changes in counselors' developmental levels.

Independent Counselors

Effective performance management for individual counselors in a group practice includes some management by peers if they are all equal. Owners' or managing partners' responsibility for managing other staff members is best spelled out in the initial contract for working together. Continuous feedback, consultation, and accountability are important stimulants for professional development. Professional counselors seek out supervision that will enhance their learning.

Performance management for individual counselors in independent practice is essentially self-directed. Isolation is not only lonely; it can also lead to unintentional impaired performance. Without feedback and without being stimulated to learn new things (e.g., ideas, strategies, competencies), expertise stagnates, becomes ineffective, and wanes. New learnings of the profession can slip by. Without someone providing feedback on how individuals are perceived by others and on how their performance compares and contrasts with standards, they do not have a full set of information to spur their professional development. "People need pressure to change" (Glickman, Gordon & Ross-Gordon, 1995, p. 422). Learning on one's own certainly happens, but feedback, challenging ideas, and collaboration support improvement. Peer assistance as individuals manage their own performance is one effective way to avoid having one's potential to improve "blocked, slowed down, or even reversed" (Glickman et al., p. 77).

MANAGE YOUR PERFORMANCE MANAGEMENT SYSTEM RESPONSIBILITIES

Develop a Plan and Schedule

To be responsible for managing the flow of the performance management system activities, plan your interventions for a year. Your efficiency is enhanced if you develop an Annual Performance Management Plan that guides both your administrative supervision approaches, the activities to be emphasized, and the approximate dates for the related conferences (Henderson & Gysbers, 1998). Figure 13.1 displays a format for these Plans.

Discipline yourself to focus on these responsibilities every day, and do not let your days be swallowed up with other, less important administrative supervision tasks. Exemplary managers follow "a 'performance management' routine. This routine of meetings and conversations, [forces] them to keep focused on the progress of each person's performance, even though many other [work-related] demands [compete] for their attention" (Buckingham & Coffman, 1999, p. 222). It is best when this routine is simple, but which forces frequent interactions between you and your supervisees, focuses on the future, and assists each supervisee to "keep track of his [sic] own performance and learnings" (Buckingham & Coffman, pp. 222–223). Conscientious administrative supervisors interact with each of their supervisees daily.

Conduct Individual Conferences Professionally

The activities of the performance management system are carried out through a series of individual conferences. These require you to prepare for them,

Figure 13.1 Annual Administrative Supervision Plan: Performance Management System Activities & Approximate Dates

Counselor	Developmental Level	Supervisory Approach	Job Description	Goal Setting	Goal Monitoring	Planned Supervision	Formative Evaluation	Self Evaluation	Goal Attainment Level	Summative Evaluation	Professional Development Goal Setting
						Approximate Dates					
"A"											
"B"											
"C"											
"D"											
"E"											

manage the time spent, to keep records of them (Herr, Heitzmann & Rayman, 2006), and to conduct them formally (Henderson & Gysbers, 1998). Schedule conferences in advance, allowing enough time so that both you and your supervisees can be well prepared. Make and honor appointments, and allot sufficient time in your schedule to allow them to be full—not aborted or interrupted—meetings. Manage the time in each conference to assure accomplishing the agenda and yet not prolong the interaction.

To be effective and appropriate, conduct these conferences with a serious and professional demeanor. Maintain professional objectivity, keeping in mind that you are carrying out your job responsibilities and protecting client welfare. Your mission is not a personal one. The ultimate focus is on helping clients by helping your supervisees. Carry out the conferences with integrity, and follow protocols established by the performance management system of the agency, by law, or by best practices.

Distinguish Among System Parts

The parts of a performance management system are interrelated, but each has a distinct purpose and goals, consists of different formal activities, and is documented differently. The system is always in process, but the highlights of each phase are the conferences between you and your individual supervisees. You maintain personnel files on each supervisee that contain all of the notes, records and other forms used in the system (Chapter 16).

Orientation/Training

In order to establish a joint approach to performance management, orient and train your administrative supervisees in the system (McMahon & Simons, 2004). Through training, provide information about your performance standards, the system, its parts, and its processes. Educate your supervisees about the purposes of each part, how they relate to each other, the focus on continuous improvement, and the role of performance standards. Understanding how the system works and its activities is one means to ensure fairness. In the training, describe your conceptualization of developmental levels, and how, when and where you will gather data that provide the basis for your assessments, and how you provide feedback. Teach supervisees about their responsibilities and yours.

Training provides a common language. It not only enhances communication, it also allows for deeper mutual understanding of the expectations and the work involved in meeting them.

> Two things occur when people who work together all have a common language. First, they are able to give each other feedback and help in a very rational, unemotional way that affects behavior. . . . Second, when followers start to realize that if their manager is using [a supervision

model,] it is not the manager, but their behavior that determines the leadership style to be used with them. (Hersey et al., 2001, p. 468)

Informed Consent

Orientation and training comprise one element of the professionally required informed consent by supervisees for supervision. Ethical standards state that supervisees have a right to know about the rights and responsibilities of the supervisor and the supervisee, the purpose of the services being provided and the nature of the relationship, their risks and benefits, and the limits of confidentiality (American Counseling Association [ACA], 2005, D. 2.d; American Mental Health Counselors Association [AMHCA], 2000, 6.B). Under the National Board for Certified Counselors [NBCC] Ethical Code (2005), supervisors are required to ensure "that supervisees are informed of all conditions of supervision as defined/outlined by the supervisor's practice, agency, group, or organization" (pp. 5–6).

The employment contract is also part of the supervisory contract, and incorporates the counselors' assigned jobs and work responsibilities. Through other activities, describe objectives and standards for individuals' work. Ideally all of this is also in writing. Agencies of some size have personnel handbooks that contain much of the information legally required for employees. These, too, meet some of the requirements of informed consent.

Job Description

The job description is the basis of a performance management system. Its purpose is to clarify expectations for each counselor in his/her specific assignment (Chapter 12). Job descriptions for staff members are determined after development of the annual service delivery plan at the beginning of the calendar work year (Chapter 17). The conference discussion includes specifying counselors' caseloads and task assignments, job priorities, and the data sources you will use to support supervision and evaluative judgments. Reaffirm the counselors' professional development and service delivery system goals. Your supervisees identify any constraints they see that will keep them from meeting their job expectations (Henderson & Gysbers, 1998). An individual's specific, detailed job description is written down for you both to agree to and sign. Putting these in writing provides precision and facilitates communication between you throughout the year (Diamond, 2006; Gysbers & Henderson, 2006). They are contracts.

Supervision

Supervision helps staff members improve their work performance. It is ongoing, focuses on *specific* work samples related to job expectations, and provides them feedback about what they do well and about areas for improvement (Chapter 10). Your feedback is related to the standards referenced in orientation and the performance evaluation. You individualize it for each staff member, and address specific behaviors and incidents. It is forward looking (Pinsky & Fryer-Edwards, 2004).

You and your supervisees develop specific supervision plans for the year. You may develop these together, or separately; they are brought together in conferences. Supervision activities occur throughout the year and on a daily basis. They comprise the majority of your work together.

You observe your supervisees' work, and monitor their performance. You have an ethical responsibility to "meet regularly with supervisees to review case notes, samples of clinical work, or live observations" (ACA, 2005, F.1.a). You consult with supervisees about the implementation of their goal-related action plans, and formally or spontaneously about cases and ethical issues. You also are together in staff meetings, in-service training, professional association conferences and meetings, and mentoring. You delegate tasks to them.

Your administrative supervision records and notes include forms and process documentation. Some examples are annual supervision plans; treatment plans; progress, process and case notes; supervisees' session plans; observation records or notes; data-analysis documentation; consultation notes; formal case study write-ups; and "Next Step Improvements" goals and action planning forms. You store these in individual personnel files (Chapter 16).

Performance Evaluation

The purpose of performance evaluation is to rate the quality and quantity of each of your employees' work for the evaluation period. You make summative judgments about a staff member's performance based on the standards established for the job in the job description. It also reflects your judgment as to how an employee stacks up against other workers in jobs with similar expectations. It is static (Pinsky & Fryer-Edwards, 2004). It looks back.

It is also advisable to conduct performance evaluations formatively (or tentatively or as a status update). Staff members conduct self-evaluations. To be a performance improvement-driven administrative supervisor, conduct evaluation conferences periodically throughout the year. Conferences regarding supervisees' self-evaluations and your formative evaluations are held on a regularly scheduled basis. For most of your supervisees, you hold only one summative performance evaluation per year. Probationary employees are either new to your setting, or have demonstrated unsatisfactory performance. They may be summatively evaluated quarterly, semiannually, or on some other interval. Performance evaluations are delivered orally and in writing.

An agency has a legal obligation to provide approved performance evaluation forms that fit the job expectations for specific positions. To ensure they are meaningful activities, formative and self-evaluations use the same forms. Notifications of recommended employment status and compensation levels are typically filed with an agency's human resources department. How performance evaluation is carried out is described, and an example form provided, in Chapter 14.

Goal Setting for Professional Development

Purpose

Goal setting for professional development provides focus for staff members' efforts to improve the quality of their work. Service delivery system goals focus on their quantity of work (Chapters 15 and 17). In Seijts and Latham's (2005) terms, professional development goals are learning goals, i.e., goals for knowledge and skill acquisition. "It takes between ten and eighteen years before world-class competency is reached" (Buckingham and Coffman, 1999, p. 185). If you want your supervisees "to approach world-class performance, you must find ways to encourage them to stay focused on developing their expertise" (Buckingham and Coffman, p. 185).

By implementing a system that supports goal-based pursuit of professional development you help your supervisees make changes. It is your responsibility to "set up social conditions so that the goals of the individual merge with the goals of the organization" (Maslow, 1998/1962, p. 57). Accomplishing work-related goals entails using resources to accomplish something in the future.

Goal-setting Process

Although the targets are much larger, the process for setting professional development goals is similar to the process for setting "next step improvement" goals (Chapter 10). A gap is discovered between what is and what could be. A work-relevant goal is selected for closing that gap. Meaningful goals target the continued development of each staff member's strengths and talents as well as the improvement of their performance weaknesses. They should be "set high enough so that a person has to stretch to reach them, but low enough so that they can be attained. . . . People are not highly motivated if a goal is seen as almost impossible or virtually certain to achieve" (Hersey et al., 2001, p. 31). If they are to be fully accomplished, two or three goals per year are sufficient. Using leadership styles that match the developmental levels of your supervisees, collaborate with them as they set priorities for their goals.

Action planning. Administrative supervisees develop action plans for attaining each goal (Chapters 10 and 17). It is your ethical responsibility to be reasonably certain your supervisees have the competencies and other resources needed to implement their plans (AMHCA, 2000, Principle 6.C). Additionally, you may recommend that supervisees participate in personal growth experiences or personal counseling, but you may neither provide them nor force them to participate (Association for Counselor Education & Supervision [ACES], 1993, 3.17–3.19).

Monitoring goals and plans. To be most effective, monitor your supervisees' progress in implementing their plans and taking steps toward goal attainment. Encourage, support and redirect their progress or lack thereof. As one administrative supervisor explains:

> Because I market myself as well as the Center as a whole, and therefore pass along many referrals to other clinicians, I also insist on a level of professional development. All of us have specialties that we work hard to maintain by tripling the required CEU standards set by the [LPC] Board. I keep track of our certifications and specialties. (S. D. Clifford, personal communication, August 14, 2005)

The amount and structure of your monitoring activities depends on a supervisee's developmental level.

At the end of the work year, you and your supervisees assess their levels of goal attainment. The standards for these assessments are the goals set and action plans they developed in collaboration with you. If you want your staff members to continue to pursue goals that make them stretch, you must recognize that some goals are harder to attain than first appeared. An alternative is to set interim goals, and lengthen the timeframe for accomplishing a larger goal. It is wise to give credit to supervisees who make legitimate efforts toward goal attainment.

Formal Activities

Hold formal conferences with your supervisees to help them select goals, and to establish, monitor and assess action plan implementation, and finally to assess their overall level of goal attainment. These conferences may be separate from or joined with conferences held in implementing other parts of the performance management system. In some performance management systems assessments of goal attainment become part of the summative performance evaluation.

To be most timely, tentative professional development goals are established soon after the performance evaluation conferences. Conferences to reaffirm the goals might coincide with the job description conferences. Hold monitoring conferences, at a minimum, at mid-year. They might coincide with the mid-year formative evaluation. If it is a part of their summative evaluations, your and your supervisees' assessments of action plan completion and overall goal attainment levels occur prior to the summative evaluation conferences. Forms for writing out selected goals, tracking action plan progress, and ascribing levels of goal attainment facilitate this part of the system (Henderson & Gysbers, 1998).

CLARIFY YOUR PERFORMANCE MANAGEMENT SYSTEM PROCESS

Sequence of Activities

As the administrative supervisor you are responsible for linking the activities in a performance management system, so that it is continuous and cyclical over the course of an employment year, and across years. Professional development goals are established at the end of one year for the following year. Job descriptions are typically similar but not identical from year to year. The information gathered and previous analyses made support professional assessment from one year to the next year. After the first year, supervision targets do not exist in a vacuum, but continuous progress can be measured and recognized.

On the other hand, each year is unique. Changes occur in the delivery system. Individuals and their circumstances change. Each year begins with training and orientation for all staff members. Each year the service delivery plan for the year reflects modifications from previous years' learnings (Chapter 18). Within the revised delivery system, individuals' jobs are defined. The OARS process (Chapter 10) is applied freshly to each supervision incident. Supervisees' professional development goals and action plans are different each year.

Performance evaluations reflect work done during the one year that is ending. They are not an accumulation of ancient history. You develop anew your overall plan for providing performance management assistance to your supervisees. While these are built on previous knowledge, the plans should also be freestanding at the beginning of the year. Work diligently to avoid classifying and stereotyping your supervisees.

Patterns of Activities

A performance management system's parts are interrelated. Each part consists of multiple activities, and these activities crisscross throughout a work period (e.g., a year-long contract, a 6-month trial period). Figure 13.2 presents an example year-long calendar of the activities conducted in a performance management system.

It is easy to see how the activities of different system parts crisscross. By combining topics from different system parts in one conference, you might confuse your supervisees; or yourself, especially if you are a new administrative supervisor. Not unlike clarifying what roles you are fulfilling in different circumstances, you ensure your own clarity and clarify for your supervisees what each activity or part of an activity relates to. Another way to avoid confusion is to hold separate conferences for different activities.

SUMMARY

To be an effective administrative supervisor, you implement a performance management system that aligns the activities conducted to help your

Figure 13.2 Sample Calendar of Performance Management System Activities

Employment Month*	PMS Activity	PMS Part
January / 1st	Annual service delivery plan developed	All
	Annual performance management plan (supervisor)	All
	Orientation to PMS	All
	Professional development goals reaffirmed	Goal setting
	Action plans for goal achievement reviewed	Goal setting
	Job description conference	Job description
	Supervision plans (supervisee)	Supervision
	Professional assessment	All
	OARS	Supervision
	Consultations	Supervision
February / 2nd	Professional assessment	All
	OARS	Supervision
	Consultations	Supervision
March / 3rd	Formative evaluation	Performance evaluation
	Self-evaluation	Performance evaluation
	Professional assessment	All
	OARS	Supervision
	Consultations	Supervision
April / 4th May / 5th	Professional assessment	All
	OARS	Supervision
	Consultations	Supervision
June / 6th	Formative evaluation	Performance evaluation
	Self-evaluation	Performance evaluation
	Professional assessment	All
	OARS	Supervision
	Consultations	Supervision
July / 7th	Goal-related action plan progress update	Goal-setting
	Professional assessment	All
	OARS	Supervision
	Consultations	Supervision
August / 8th	Professional assessment	All
	OARS	Supervision
	Consultations	Supervision

September / 9th	Formative evaluation	Performance evaluation
	Self-evaluation	Performance evaluation
	Professional assessment	All
	OARS	Supervision
	Consultations	Supervision
October / 10th November / 11th	Professional assessment	All
	OARS	Supervision
	Consultations	Supervision
December / 12th	Assessment of goal attainment	Goal setting
	Summative self-evaluation	Performance evaluation
	Summative evaluation conference & filing of form	Performance evaluation
	Tentative professional development goals and action plans established	Goal setting
	Professional assessment	All
	OARS	Supervision
	Consultations	Supervision
*Depends on fiscal year		

supervisees advance their performance levels. The parts of this system are orientation to and training in the system, describing individuals' jobs, providing supervision, evaluating their performance, and establishing professional development goals. Implementing these activities requires you to conduct effective individual conferences. You understand and help your supervisees understand the interrelationship of the system activities, their distinctions, and their year-long flow. You manage your responsibilities in the system by scheduling and planning them for the year.

SUPERVISOR CHALLENGES AND RESPONSES

Supervisors' Challenges: Empowering Supervisees

Effective administrative supervisors are aware that empowerment is a key to helping supervisees advance their developmental levels. Selecting empowerment strategies appropriate to each supervisee is a three-pronged challenge. First is the challenge of identifying a supervisee's power base that is most likely to help her or him build on a talent or strength. The second is for the supervisor to identify his or her power base that matches the supervisee's, and that she or he can share. Third, a supervisor identifies or creates a strategy that facilitates the supervisee's feelings of empowerment. This is a complex concept to understand and idiosyncratic to implement.

Supervisors' Responses

To respond appropriately, effective administrative supervisors are self-aware and have command of a repertoire of relevant empowerment strategies. They also know each supervisee well enough to know his or her motivators and talents, even if the supervisee is not aware of them.

Some generic examples of supervisor empowerment strategies are offered. Legitimate power can be shared by delegating administrative supervisory responsibilities to a responsible supervisee, expanding the supervisee's leadership knowledge and skills. Legitimate power can also be shared by delegating to a good conceptualizer responsibility for developing intra-office procedures for smoothing out a wrinkle in the service delivery system. Information power can be shared by sending individuals who want to better understand "the big picture" to attend and report back on agency-wide professional meetings. Information power can also be shared by sending an individual with vision to study and report back on the values, vision and mission of the agency. Expert power can be shared by assigning counselors to provide peer clinical supervision to other counselors or by sending a supervisee to professional association workshops or conferences. Referent power can be shared by using a supervisee's relationship building skills in providing opportunities for them to "meet and greet" potential clients and consumers or by assigning a supervisee to mentor a new staff member. Reward power can be delegated to an individual to mete out recognitions to colleagues on staff, or by assigning a supervisee to recommend criteria for rewarding staff members. Connection power can be shared by supporting a supervisee's involvement in leadership positions in professional associations, or by assigning a supervisee to meet with other authorities (agency administrators, political figures) to advocate for a counseling agenda item.

14

Evaluate Each Staff Member's Performance

To best serve the counseling clients, effective administrative supervisors help their supervisees carry out their jobs well by providing summative evaluations of their performance (Waugh, 2006). These are the primary means for holding employees accountable for what they do, and for helping agencies ensure quality staff performance. Through summative evaluations, administrative supervisors communicate judgments about their supervisees' levels of professional performance, and their value to their clients, the department service delivery system, the agency, the profession, and the public. In some agencies, this part of performance management systems is labeled "annual appraisals" or "annual reviews."

To be an effective administrative supervisor, you recognize the importance of performance evaluations to yourself and your supervisees; develop ones that are relevant, just and fair; engage your supervisees in the evaluation process, and to make their own judgments about their performance levels; and communicate your evaluative judgments in writing and through well-planned conferences. The same principles and procedures apply for evaluations of your professional counselors and non-counseling staff members. Your experiences in evaluating clients and clinical supervisees, measuring their progress, giving them feedback and final ratings give you a foundation for carrying out these responsibilities.

> Summative performance evaluation in administrative supervision is defined as the objective appraisal of the worker's total functioning on the job over a specified period of time. . . . It is a process of applying systematic procedures to determine with reliability and validity the extent to which the worker is achieving the requirements of his or her position in the agency. An evaluation should be a judgment based on clearly specified, realistic and achievable criteria reflecting agency standards. It is job related and time limited. It is concerned with both the quality of performance and the quantity of accomplishment. (Kadushin & Harness, 2002, p. 329)

(Evaluations based on client outcomes and the service delivery system are discussed in Chapter 18.) The performance evaluation form, a legal document, supports performance evaluation. This form helps guide your thought processes as you develop and communicate your professional judgments.

RECOGNIZE THE IMPORTANCE OF YOUR EVALUATION RESPONSIBILITIES

Central Responsibility

Administrative supervisors in all counseling settings are delegated performance evaluation responsibilities by their agencies (Curtis & Sherlock, 2006; Falvey, 1987; Henderson & Gysbers, 1998; Kadushin & Harness, 2002). Evaluating each of your staff members fairly is key to your job success. It is the culminating activity of the performance management system, the centerpiece of fair employment practices (Chapter 4), and what distinguishes your administrative supervisory role. To be effective, you carry out this responsibility with utmost professionalism because of its summary nature (relying on the full range of standards for professional developmental levels and all data sources); its multiple purposes (from identifying leaders to terminating impaired employees, from implementing sound personnel practices to legal compliance); and its broad array of potential audiences (from the evaluated individual to the general public and the mass media in an open, public hearing).

To carry out these responsibilities professionally, acquire the competencies needed. Standards for "knowledge and competency in the evaluation of counseling performance" (Association for Counselor Education and Supervision [ACES], 1989; *Standards*, 1990, p. 31) are spelled out in the *Standards for Counseling Supervisors* (Standards) and in the *Curriculum Guide for Training Counseling Supervisors* (Borders et al., 1991) For example, the first competency underscores the need to shift your perspective from that of a counselor evaluatee and to be able to "interact with the counselor from the perspective of evaluator" (*Standards*, p. 31, 10.1). Be sensitive to the reality that performance evaluation has high-stakes for you and your supervisees.

High Stakes for Administrative Supervisors

Conducting summative evaluations is pivotal to your relationships with your supervisees. Its purposes can be perceived to conflict with each other; for example, goals of terminating employees who are not performing at acceptable levels can conflict with the goals associated with professional development (Kulik, 2004). Learn to manage these trade-offs, especially by delivering honest evaluations. Generally, supervisees appreciate the support and encouragement of their supervisors, and get a clearer sense of their contributions to the organization (Waugh, 2006) In fact, your employees' perceptions of whether you treat them justly is based on your being consistent, unbiased, ethical, and flexible, and by providing ongoing accurate information about all aspects of their work and agency goals (Curtis & Sherlock, 2006). Your most impaired supervisees often do not intentionally hurt their clients; they need you to point out their behaviors that have that effect. One of my former supervisees used to fall asleep in counseling sessions and denied that he did that! Your best performing supervisees do not know how good they are unless you tell them their strengths, and point out areas where they could still improve.

There are some supervisees, who focus only on the negative dimensions of their ratings and need as much help to see the positive dimensions. If you do not use the standards well or use the wrong standards, you create dissonance with your staff members. Some supervisees fear unfair treatment, discrimination, or arbitrary and capricious actions by individuals with power over them. They might see your coercive power at the forefront of their minds. Some supervisees might blame you, the messenger, for pointing out their weaknesses, failings or loss of position. In fact, some may have had experiences that validate these fears. Ineffective administrative supervisors evaluate their supervisees based on hearsay rather than solid information.

The agency holds you accountable for carrying out the evaluation process appropriately. If the decision-making process you use in arriving at your summative professional judgments is flawed (e.g., too hasty, too specific), you can inadvertently hurt people. If your process is inappropriate, you can make yourself and your agency vulnerable to grievances, lawsuits, and charges of non-compliance with legal or ethical standards. You can put your own job or your agency's status in jeopardy. You could lose the support of your funding sources. You are already aware of supervisors' potential for vicarious liability for errors of omission or commission. To maximize your effectiveness, consult with your counterpart in the agency's Human Resources Department or your legal advisors as you develop and implement your evaluation processes, especially those used with problematic staff members.

High Stakes for Supervisees

For supervisees, how they are rated—above average, average, below average—has positive or negative ramifications on their employment status. You make recommendations regarding further employment: contract extension, termination or promotion; increases or decreases in compensation and benefits; merit pay; and endorsement for licensure or certification. Ethically, you only endorse for licensure, initial or continuing employment supervisees who you perceive are qualified (American Counseling Association [ACA], 2005; ACES, 1993). You should not endorse those who are "impaired in any way that would interfere with the performance of counseling duties" (ACES, 1993, 2.13).

Your feedback impacts your supervisees' career development. On one hand, "explicit feedback helps the worker get a sense of meaningful achievement, reduces the tension associated with role ambiguity, and provides positive reinforcement for good work well done" (Kadushin & Harness, 2002, p. 329). It "is one means to help counselors feel good about their work, especially if it's done in terms of legitimate, professional standards" (M. L. Libby, personal communication, May 6, 2005). Their professional competence, identity, pride, self-esteem, and self-efficacy may be enhanced. On the other hand, their career self-esteem is vulnerable, especially when it is based on inflated self-perceptions. Remember, "Few, if any, workers would describe their own performance as average" (Gray, 2002, p. 16). Low ratings require extra effort on remedial work for both you and your supervisees.

Evaluation Anxiety

"Nothing creates more anxiety in managers and employees than performance reviews" (Waugh, 2006, p. 16). Kulik (2004) describes supervisees as experiencing "sweaty palms, upset stomach, pounding heart—these are symptoms frequently associated with performance appraisals in organizations" (p. 91). And, "managers report that *giving* performance feedback is one of the most difficult parts of their jobs" (Kulik, p. 91). Some of this stems from tradition and history when evaluations were conducted from a deficit model aimed at pointing out what workers were doing wrong or were not doing (Bunch, 2002; Harris, 2002). It led to over-supervision, overly harsh responses that were punitive and faultfinding. Little training was done to help new supervisors learn how to carry out this role (Gray, 2002). As with learning how to do many difficult tasks, they learned to do it the way it was modeled to them.

On the other hand, supervisors who undersupervise are reluctant to give negative feedback, but "avoiding the appraisal process undermines organizational effectiveness through lack of accountability, and undermines staff morale through the lack of constructive feedback" (Falvey, 1987, p. 47). "It is often the failure in identifying areas of weakness during the evaluative process that inhibits the development of therapists" (Stoltenberg, McNeil & Delworth, 1998, p. 136).

To lead the evaluation process effectively, overcome your own insecurities and self-consciousness, focus on the possible (sometimes probable) negative consequences, and negative prior experiences. Some new administrative supervisors' discomfort relates to the shift from the counselors' non-judgmental role to the supervisors' judgmental one, from a role of letting clients select their own goals to one of imposing goals on some of their supervisees (Borders & Brown, 2005).

"Admirable as it is to be nonjudgmental and possessed of unconditional positive regard, it is essential for effective managers to be judgmental, critical thinkers and to confront destructive, inappropriate and unprofessional behavior when it is exhibited by employees" (Herr, Heitzmann, & Rayman, 2006, p. 325). A surprising number of staff members do not exemplify excellent professional or employee behavior. Recurrent themes we found included not keeping current and thereby losing essential skills, focusing on wrong job priorities, not attending to work all day every day, being consistently overwhelmed by assigned responsibilities, exercising poor judgment, and losing zest for their work.

ENGAGE YOUR SUPERVISEES

Effective administrative supervisors nurture their supervisees' active participation in the performance evaluation process. You help them understand the role of evaluation in the performance management system, and that its primary purpose for most supervisees is directing future professional development. It is wise to require them to fulfill roles and responsibilities that parallel yours, making the interactions more productive. To enable their full participation, you ensure their understanding of the performance evaluation form and the procedures entailed in sound evaluation.

Conducting self-evaluations enhances the quality of employee participation in the process (Kulik, 2004). To develop them soundly, they go through the same activities and thought processes you do. They "develop mental images of successful performance and then make a self-evaluation determination of their ability to perform the desired behavior (self-efficacy)" (Martin, 2000, p. 215). One administrative supervisor of counselors observed that her staff members learn a lot about their own performance by using the performance evaluation form as their self-assessment tool: "It allows them to understand their own performance needs and wants and to focus on areas for growth" (M. L. Libby, personal communication, May 6, 2005).

To work optimally, both of you maintain professional objectivity and integrity, and acknowledge that you each are operating from different perspectives and data. Your supervisees understand that the purpose of self-evaluation is not self-promotion or for covering-up inadequacies or gaps in their practice, and that "self-assessment skills are integral to being a good" practitioner (Pinsky & Fryer-Edwards, 2004, p. 584). They maintain a file in which they "track their own performance" (Waugh, 2006, p. 17), and record their learnings, accomplishments, and setbacks. They project applications of their learning in their future work (Zubizarreta, 2004).

Supervisees who take advantage of summative evaluative feedback are eager to learn and seek continuous improvement. They maintain their integrity and accept constructive criticism. They strive to avoid becoming defensive, to recognize it when it occurs and own it honestly with their supervisors. They know their rights and responsibilities, and are assertive.

To improve your own competence, listen to their perspectives and openly consider contextual variables that might impact your judgments. Your supervisees may be in circumstances that ought to be brought to your attention, such as perceiving that they generally receive insufficient direction or training. They may be accurate. Ultimately you have to "decide whether failure to meet performance standards was due to a lack of follower performance or to managerial, organizational, or environmental problems" (Hersey, Blanchard & Johnson, 2001, p. 356).

DEVELOP RELEVANT, JUST AND FAIR EVALUATIONS

Use a Sound Process for Making Evaluative Judgments

Evaluation is determining the value, significance or worth of something. To be sound, an evaluation process should entail "careful appraisal [rating] and study" (Merriam-Webster *On-Line Dictionary* retrieved March 4, 2008 from http://www.merriam-webster.com/dictionary/evaluation). The performance evaluation process consists of a series of evaluative judgments about how near or far an individual's performance is relative to established standards. An administrative supervisor's goal is to be relevant, just and fair in making these judgments. *Relevant* judgments relate logically to your supervisee's specific job description and implementation priorities (Synatschk, 2002). These are job-specific standards (Chapter 12 and 15). Judgments that are *just* are based on standards for what is right (*Webster's Third*, 2002) that are accepted by your agency and by your supervisees' profession (Abernethy & Lillis, 2001; Henderson & Gysbers, 1998). To be *fair*, they are based on legitimately acquired data and sound reasoning, free from fraud, prejudice or favoritism (*Webster's Third*, 2002).

Begin the process by distinguishing between two performance evaluation questions: How *well* your staff members apply their competencies in accordance with standards; and, how *completely* they fulfill their job descriptions. Successful use of the empty chair technique in counseling sessions is an example of "how well" supervisees perform, reflecting the *quality* of work. Seeing 25 individual clients and conducting three small groups a week is an example of "completeness" behaviors, reflecting the *quantity* of work.

Review the established standards, including the expectations for the individual's job performance. Using overtly expressed standards makes comparison possible, facilitates communication, drives learning, fuels creativity, and enables collaboration and discovery (Buckingham & Coffman, 1999). These are the same standards that are applied in supervision. Hopefully you have expressed your expectations for performance "concisely and without questionable interpretations . . . The more specific you [have been], the less misinterpretation that is likely to occur" (Peters, 2002, p. 13). For example, it is clearer to have said, "be at your desk and working at 8:00 a.m." than "be on time to work."

Review the data you gathered throughout the evaluation period. As contrasted with supervision, the data you use now are those you gathered in supervision (Chapter 10), but they are drawn from multiple observations, aggregated, and analyzed to identify *patterns* of behaviors evident across many specific incidents. The more performance examples you have to work with, the easier it is to be discriminating and confident in your judgments. When you consistently maintain a separate file for each of your supervisees, "preparation for the performance review consists of pulling out that working file and other supporting documentation" (Waugh, 2006, p. 17).

You are then prepared to make the series of evaluative judgments that are required in studying performance in the counselor's complex role. "Chunk" the data by analyzing, studying and appraising one performance category at a time. This requires answering the question, "What do these data indicate the proximity of the counselor's performance is to the standards for this category?" These individual and related summative judgments represent a balance between subjective opinion and objective evaluation (subjective objectivity). Check your professional opinions against the standards (Barratt, 2006). In complicated cases, consultation with other supervisors is also useful for checking the validity of your professional opinions.

Usually, agency's evaluation procedures include a rating scale or system that provides the means for reflecting your judgments. Ratings may be expressed in words (e.g., Clearly outstanding or unsatisfactory) or numbers (e.g., 4–0), or both (e.g., 4 = clearly outstanding). Avoid significant misunderstandings by explaining, preferably in the system orientation, to your supervisees where you start thinking about your ratings; that is, whether you start in the middle of the scale and use the data to move individuals up or down the scale, or at the top and use the data to move down the scale, or start at the bottom and move upwards.

Avoid Evaluator Bias

Sometimes it is a struggle to avoid evaluator bias and appraisal errors (Gray, 2002; Kulik, 2004). Your bias as an evaluator might stem from the history of your relationship, your supervisee's past evaluations, insufficient information for supporting your conclusions, extenuating circumstances, and personal, cultural or professional differences. You might make premature judgments about supervisees based on hearsay from third parties.

The most common rating errors are unwarranted strictness, unwarranted leniency, rating everyone in the middle range, halo effect, basing judgment on most recent events, contrasting one employee with other employees rather than the standards, assuming the reason/cause of a person's behavior—and forgiving or blaming too much. Counselors are used to helping clients explore why they think, feel or do things. What matters most in administrative supervision, especially in deriving evaluative judgments, is that individuals *do* things; *why* they do them is usually not within an administrative supervisor's purview (Kulik, 2004).

Use a Sound Performance Evaluation Form

If your agency has a sound performance evaluation form, it should guide you through the evaluation thought process, document your judgments, and support your communication with your supervisees and others who have access to the information (e.g., agency administrators). To ensure its relevance and support for just and fair judgments, the categories of items to be rated must be professionally appropriate, and the format must provide an understandable means for aligning your data-analysis, and for assigning your ratings of staff members' performance.

Some examples of categories appropriate to professional counseling are knowledge base, technical skills, relationship development (Krousel-Wood, 2000), professional judgment and ethical behavior. Other more specific categories are those directly related to the counselor license. Some examples of appropriate work setting-related categories are work ethics and habits, attendance standards, communication skills, teamwork, and co-worker relationships.

Several different formats are used. Some agencies choose to use detailed checklists that appear to be very objective. Some use a narrative or anecdotal approach. Some use holistic scoring of objective criteria. Typically, the judgments made for individual categories are aggregated into a summary rating. You may choose words to describe the status of employees (e.g., clearly outstanding, proficient, unsatisfactory), or numerical symbols for the words (e.g., 1 (lowest) to 5 (highest)) to facilitate aggregation. You need to anticipate that some evaluatees focus on the numbers and do not give due consideration to the words they symbolize.

Some evaluation systems apply weights to the various roles fulfilled by counselors and other staff members (Texas Counseling Association, 2004). These weights are useful when different workers fulfill similar roles, but balance them differently. For example, some counselors in a practice might do more individual than group counseling, and vice versa; or some counselors might spend more time conducting formal assessments than doing psychoeducation. By using a weighting system, you recognize these variations in role applications.

Other requirements. Finally, performance evaluation forms provide places to record your recommendations for an evaluatee's employment and contract status (e.g., renewal or termination). All formal evaluation forms have places for the signatures of the evaluator and evaluatee. It is your evaluatees' employee right to see the documents that are in their official personnel files.

Designing a Performance Evaluation Form

You may find that your agency does not have an appropriate form for evaluating counselors. And, as yet, the counseling profession has not developed a research-based, valid and reliable instrument for evaluating counseling skills (Ericksen & McAuliffe, 2003). A counselor performance evaluation form must match the philosophy, structure, rating scale and application of the form used for other professionals in the agency (Bunch 2002; Henderson & Gysbers, 1998, 2002; Synatschk, 2002). You may have to create one that is professionally appropriate and adheres to the agency's personnel policies.

When a form and recommended evaluation process are first designed, it is advisable to involve a team of people who will be users of the form (e.g., counselors, other relevant administrative supervisors, human resource department professionals, agency executives, and other experts in counseling [e.g., counselor educators or professional counseling association leaders]) (Bunch, 2002; Henderson & Gysbers, 1998, 2002; Synatschk, 2002). Some of the relevant questions to discuss are suggested in Figure 14.1.

There are some other topics that often come up in these discussions. In implementing the use of a new form, you benefit from having the group's recommendations about what the best process is for evaluators (administrative supervisors, counselors) to follow. What are essential or appropriate data to consider and how (e.g., information gleaned from clinical supervision)? What is the best point on the scale at which to start making evaluation ratings (lowest, middle, highest)? What should be the minimum qualifications of counselor evaluators (background, license, specialized training)?

An example of a generic (i.e., not agency specific) counselor performance

---

Figure 14.1 Some Questions to Answer in Designing a Summative Performance Evaluation Form

Categories and delineations
  Categories of competencies to be rated that are central to the counselors' jobs and that provide the structure for the form
  The level of detail describing these categories to be delineated on the summative evaluation form or in supporting documents (e.g., competencies, indicators of each competence, descriptors of each indicator)
  At what level of detail evaluations will be made

Rating system
  How the ratings will be expressed (e.g., in numbers or words) and how many rating categories there will be
  How the ratings made at the more detailed levels will be combined to provide for summative evaluation of each major category, and, ultimately, for all categories combined
  How these summative judgments will reflect differences in individuals' specific job responsibilities (e.g., weighting)

Contextual information
  What, if any, information is needed to provide context for this evaluation (e.g., job tenure, agency or personal issues)
  If and how evaluative information gathered in other performance management system activities will be reflected in the summative judgment and on the form (e.g., improvement, implementation and professional development objectives and progress; self evaluation)

Format
  What the format will be (checklist, open-ended, anecdotal)

Figure 14.2 Professional Counselor Performance Evaluation Form

Name_____

Assignment:_____

Evaluator Name:_____ Review Period:_____ to_____

Date of Form Completion:_____ Date of Evaluation Conference:_____

Directions: Rate each competency within a standard. Average these ratings to derive the mean for the standard. Average the six standard means to derive the Summary Evaluation Rating.

Rating Scale: Clearly outstanding = 4; Exceeds standards = 3; Meets standards = 2; Below expectations, requiring consultation and targeted improvement = 1; Unsatisfactory = 0. If a competency is not expected in a counselor's job description, it is marked NA (for Not Applicable), and is not figured in the rating.

Evaluated Standards, Competencies & Ratings:

Ratings

1. Demonstrates knowledge needed to facilitate human development and adjustment.	
A. Applies principles of mental health.	
B. Applies principles of counseling and psychotherapy.	
C. Applies principles of human development.	
Standard 1 Mean Rating	
Comments:	

2. Implements interventions to prevent, assess, evaluate, and treat mental, emotional or behavioral disorders and associated distresses.	
A. Conducts individual and small group counseling.	
B. Conducts assessments and evaluations to establish appropriate treatment goals and objectives. C. Plans, implements and evaluates treatment plans.	
D. Provides guidance to facilitate clients' normal growth and development and aids their understanding and solving of current and potential problems.	
E. Provides consultation to facilitate clients' normal growth and development and aids their understanding and solving of current and potential problems.	
F. Identifies needs for and carries out referrals to other specialists.	
G. Is appropriately trained in specific methods, techniques or modalities used.	
Standard 2 Mean Rating	
Comments:	

3. Accepts responsibilities for implementation of department's annual service delivery plan (calendar).	
A. Contributes actively to design of the service delivery system.	
B. Serves the planned number of clients.	
C. Provides the planned number of services.	
D. Is accountable for efficient use of resources.	
Standard 3 Mean Rating	
Comments:	

4. Develops professional relationships.	
A. Establishes and maintains appropriate relationships with	
1. Clients and their significant others.	
2. Co-workers and colleagues.	
3. Supervisors and administrators.	
4. Community members.	
B. Advocates on behalf of clients.	
C. Uses effective communication skills.	
Standard 4 Mean Rating	
Comments:	

5. Adheres to professional standards.	
A. Adheres to legal standards expressed in Federal and State statutes, rules, or regulations.	
B. Adheres to ethical standards published by Texas State Board of Examiners of Professional Counselors, including the general and specific requirements regarding sexual misconduct, testing, drug and alcohol use, confidentiality and required reporting, licensees and the Board, and assumed names; and those of the American Counseling and American Mental Health Counselors Associations.	
C. Adheres to accepted standards for counselor performance and practice (e.g., multicultural, group work, assessment).	
D. Demonstrates commitment to clients as first priority.	
E. Pursues continuous performance improvement.	
Standard 5 Mean Rating	
Comments:	

6. Meets employee responsibilities.	
A. Adheres to agency standards expressed in policies, rules, regulations, procedures and protocols.	
B. Demonstrates commitment to the mission of the counseling department and the agency.	
C. Exercises sound professional judgment.	
D. Demonstrates professional work ethics and habits.	
E. Maintains good physical and mental well-being.	
Standard 6 Mean Rating	
Comments:	

Summary Evaluation Rating (Average of Mean Ratings, Standards 1–6 ÷ 6)	

The Summary Evaluation Rating represents an overall average evaluation and means:

_____3.5–5.00 = Performance is clearly outstanding

_____2.5–3.49 = Performance consistently exceeds standards

_____1.5–2.49 = Performance consistently meets standards

_____0.6–1.49 = Performance is below expectations; consultation is required, and improvement is needed in specified areas

_____0–0.49 = Performance is unsatisfactory; little or no improvement has resulted from consultation; employment status is in jeopardy

---

Evaluator signature, Title   Date

I have discussed this evaluation with the evaluator and received a copy. A copy will be retained by the evaluator and the original is to be placed in my personnel file.

Counselor signature   Date

If I do not agree with this evaluation, I understand that I may submit a letter in duplicate stating my position and rationale. A copy will be retained by the evaluator and the original is to be placed in my personnel file.

---

evaluation form rooted in Texas professional counselor licensure (Texas Occupations Code, Chapter 503, §503.001–.003; Texas Administrative Code, Rule §681.31, .41–.47) is provided in Figure 14.2, above.

COMMUNICATE YOUR EVALUATIVE JUDGMENTS WELL

Having carefully developed your evaluative judgments (*what* you want to tell them), you plan *how* best to communicate them so that your supervisees understand and learn. You communicate in two ways: (1) in writing through the performance evaluation form, and (2) orally through the evaluation conference.

In Writing

Avoid ambiguity by selecting precise words and writing succinct, simple declarative sentences. Guard against using inflammatory language. Where evaluative judgments are above or below average, or as you deem important, include or reference specific behavior-based examples. Your recommendations for remedial assistance or termination "should be clearly and professionally explained in writing to the supervisees who are so evaluated" (ACES, 1993. 2.12).

By tentatively completing the form prior to discussion with an evaluatee, you go through the thought process for clarifying and explaining your evaluative conclusions. It also allows a supervisee to have a valid role in the conversation. As an example, if you fill it out it in pencil, a supervisee's points or data can be added or other changes made easily.

Orally

Planning. Your summative evaluation conferences go best when they are planned. You begin by knowing what you want to accomplish. After the conferences, you want your evaluatees to be goal-directed, make better decisions for themselves and their clients, and to be loyal to your clients, their jobs and their employers (Abernethy & Lillis, 2001). Ultimately, you want to:

> help each person find the right fit . . . For one employee, this might mean promotion to a supervisor role. For another employee, this might mean termination. For another, it might mean encouraging him [*sic*] to grow within his [*sic*] current role. For yet another, it might mean moving her [*sic*] back into her [*sic*] previous role. (Buckingham & Coffman, 1999, p. 177)

To be most effective, decide your priorities for your supervisees' understanding. Bear in mind how much information they can absorb. A basic goal for your conference is mutual understanding and, ideally, agreement regarding your summative judgment. "First you want to make sure that your employee understands the reasons for the rating(s) and feels fairly evaluated. And second, you want to motivate the employee to strive for better performance in the future" (Kulik, 2004, p. 106)—to grow. Identify the specific standards you want to reference, and the goal-targets for strength building and weakness remediation.

In successful evaluation conferences, you express yourself clearly, and your supervisees understand what you tell them. Many effective administrative supervisors prepare explicit statements to clarify the judgments they think are important to discuss. Often these statements are also recorded on the form. They carefully select typical examples of behavior to illustrate their points. When supervisees get defensive, they typically quibble with the examples, dissecting them to rationalize their behaviors and choices.

As with the assessments and responses described in daily supervision (Chapter 10), your summative assessments of counselors' and other staff members' developmental levels and motivations suggest appropriate approaches, power bases, modalities, functions, and behaviors, to use—those that are most apt to spur a supervisee's learning. Identify the appropriate leadership style and consider how you will apply it. Remember that in this activity your primary power base is your legitimate power (it is your job), supported by other power bases, especially those of expertise, reward, and coercion.

Schedule these conferences in advance, allowing sufficient time for both you and your supervisee to be properly prepared. There is a tendency for administrative supervisors to hold the summative conferences with all their supervisees in the same timeframe. Spread them out so that you have the time you need to feel fully prepared and be fully attentive to each supervisee. It is your responsibility to ensure that these one-on-one conversations (unless the evaluatee requests a third party) are held in private places with the door closed. Do not allow interruptions.

Conducting. In summative evaluation conferences, effective administrative supervisors maintain their professional demeanor, are fair-minded and straightforward. Work from the guiding principle—and legal safeguard—to "do unto others as you would have them do unto you" (Kemerer & Crain, 1995). You shift from working side by side with your supervisees to working across the table from them. Yet, strive to help each individual relax and see him- or herself more accurately.

Peters (2002) offers tips for delivering performance feedback:

1. Create the right setting.
2. Use the supervisee's learnings.
3. Address problems honestly and directly.
4. Communicate expectations clearly.

Establish the tone you think will be most effective in allowing your supervisees to be open to learning and reducing their anxiety. The conference consists of a dialogue. Let your supervisees do as much of the work as possible—sharing their thoughts and learnings from completing their self-evaluations. Discuss the contextual considerations from both points of view. In striving to help evaluatees avoid the perception that criticisms are personal affronts

(Kulik, 2004), bear in mind that helpful messages focus on behaviors or problems, "defensive-producing messages focus on the other as a person" (Harris, 2002, p. 299). "Defensiveness should be addressed openly" (Bernard & Goodyear, 1992, p. 107).

A good evaluation form provides an efficient means for structuring your conversation. The agenda includes discussion of identified strengths and areas for improvement for each standard or group of standards, with each summarizing your evaluation findings. Having the structure of the specific standards is an anxiety reliever (Stoltenberg et al., 1998). It is useful, however, to start with general observations that focus on positive points. On the other hand, if a supervisee is impaired or for some reason facing negative consequences, starting in a neutral position better serves your objective.

End the conference with clarity about the final rating, and the beginning of a discussion about possible professional development goals for the next year/ performance management system cycle. If the agency's performance management system includes the performance improvement action plan accomplishment and goal attainment in the summative evaluation, they are discussed in the context of setting supervisees' next professional development goals (Chapter 13). Remind your supervisees that personal evaluation information is private and held confidential by the few agency people who have access to it, and who those people are. Discourage them from sharing their ratings with others.

Post conference activities. Following a conference, reflect on both its process and results. Consider the role you played, and your level of success in helping the supervisee feel comfortable, open to learning, and understand their ratings. Supervisees, too, are encouraged to reflect. As soon as feasible and by any official deadline, complete the final, official copy of the performance evaluation form.

Then meet with each supervisee to point out the changes that were made and other reflections either of you have had. Both parties sign the form. Signatures verify that both of you reviewed the form before it was filed in the official, agency personnel file. Although many employees misunderstand this, signing the form typically does not signify agreement with the judgments. It only verifies their having seen them. When you and a supervisee are unable to reach agreement on the ratings, your final ratings prevail, based on your legitimate authority and administrative responsibility.

You are responsible for distributing confidentially (no laying them uncovered on others' desks!) the original and copies of the completed form. Agencies—small and large—have official procedures detailing who gets copies of individuals' evaluation forms. At a minimum, the evaluatee and evaluator get one. Often the human resources department and perhaps other agency executives get them. They are a part of an employee's official personnel file and record. They are kept for as long as the supervisee is employed there and five years after that (Campion & Campion, 1995), or however long the employing agency specifies in their policies. (More rules for administrative supervisors to know!)

Some time subsequent to the summative performance evaluation, follow up with your supervisees as they develop their goals and action plans, and any plans for immediate changes in performance behaviors.

CONDUCT FORMATIVE EVALUATIONS

To be fair, you and your supervisees also conduct formative evaluations periodically throughout an evaluation cycle. They are a means for sharing your approaches to evaluative thinking, drawing some tentative conclusions, and paving paths to summative evaluations. By normalizing the evaluative process, they help reduce the tension and anxiety associated with summative evaluations. If there has been ongoing, honest and straightforward day-to-day supervision and periodic formative evaluations, "both parties should see the [summative evaluation conference] as a review of what happened" (Hersey et al., 2001, p. 355). There should be no surprises (Curtis & Sherlock, 2006; Henderson & Gysbers, 1998; Hersey et al.).

SUMMARY

Evaluating each staff member's performance is central to administrative supervisors' responsibilities. To do it well, you recognize its importance, and assist your supervisees to engage in evaluation processes by making clear their own judgments about their performance levels. You make evaluative judgments that are relevant, just and fair; and you communicate them both orally and in writing in ways that ensure they are understood.

SUPERVISORS' CHALLENGES AND RESPONSES

Supervisors' Challenges: Impaired Supervisees

Perhaps the most difficult challenge administrative supervisors face is supervising and evaluating impaired supervisees. However, according to an ACA survey, "63.5% of counselors have known another counselor they considered impaired." In 77.8% of these cases "the impaired counselor did not receive disciplinary action," and in 73.7% of these cases, "the impaired counselor did not receive therapeutic intervention" (By the numbers, 2005, p. 3)

The very fact that supervisees' performance behaviors support the impaired diagnosis (Hersey et al., 2001) means that they are problematic. Impaired supervisees are not competent, not committed and not as motivated as they need to be. They have stagnated (Loganbill, Hardy & Delworth, 1982) and continue to decline.

They have blind spots as to their own limitations and tend to operate with a false sense of security and of their own stability. They are vulnerable to categorical thinking and rigid thought patterns, and they lack insight. They demonstrate a lack of interest or intensity in counseling, often mechanically going through the motions. They are not creative in identifying solutions to problems. They may have low personal and professional self-concepts. (Henderson & Gysbers, 1998, p. 163)

They might suffer from compassion fatigue, "have problems with the supervisors, problems with co-workers, suffer burnout, boredom" (Hersey et al., 2001, p. 248), or be physically or emotionally ill. In many cases, ineffective counselors have work personality types that do not match those of counselors (Wiggins and Weslander, 1986).

Telling supervisees that they are impaired in or are not suited for the work presents the most difficult scenarios in administrative supervision. Administrative supervisors frequently become frustrated with or angry at misbehaving or impaired workers. The fuel of negative emotions increases the odds that what is said is inappropriate. Too, "a worker's incompetence is an indictment of the supervisor" (Kadushin & Harness, 2002, p. 80). However, they harm clients, distract their co-workers, and hurt the services of the counseling department, and the agency.

Too frequently, administrative supervisors try to avoid addressing the issues inherent in impairment. They do not respond in a timely manner, making or allowing excuses to be made for their supervisees' ineffective performance (E. Zambrano, personal communication, October 5, 2006). They sometimes do not even record negative feedback on annual performance evaluations (Gray, 2002)—one of the recommended steps in the discipline process (Chapter 4). Avoidance is only one harmful delaying technique used by administrative supervisors, another lies in:

deciding to keep all their employees at arm's length. With this neat trick they hope to diminish the tension and the pain inherent in giving bad news to a friend. Unfortunately, as Phil Jackson pointed out, by refusing to get to know their employees, they also diminish the likelihood that they will ever be able to help any of these employees excel. (Buckingham & Coffman, 1999, p. 206)

Chronic impairment should lead to termination of employment. Managing the firing of staff members presents challenges also. Supervisors are often uncomfortable. Fired supervisees are usually emotional.

Supervisors' Responses

The ethical standards are clear as to what administrative supervisors (and other counselors) should do about impaired supervisees (ACA, 2005, F.5.b.).

The presence of any such impairment should begin a process of feedback and remediation wherever possible so that the supervisee understands the nature of the impairment and has the opportunity to remedy the problem and continue with his/her professional development. (ACES, 1993, 2.13)

Impairment is not difficult to see. By using consistently process and conceptual models to guide their supervisory interventions (Chapters 10 and 11), administrative supervisors are well grounded to carry out this unpleasant, but important dimension of their responsibilities. "There comes a time when employees will simply not respond to interventions designed to enhance their performance without the imposition of sanctions" (Martin, 2000, p. 225).

Some impaired supervisees can be helped; some cannot. Effective administrative supervisors believe that poor performers know that they are performing poorly, especially if the standards for performance have been clearly set out. On some level they want the help of their administrative supervisors. Seemingly, they expose their weaknesses in order to be saved from their misery (Buckingham & Coffman, 1999).

In order to respond effectively, administrative supervisors "have many decisions to make: What level of performance is unacceptable? How long is too long at that level? Have you done enough to help . . . ?" (Buckingham & Coffman, 1999, p. 206). Very effective supervisors adopt a tough love approach to managing these situations. Buckingham and Coffman describe toughness as:

> using excellence as their frame of reference when assessing performance. *Tough* love simply implies that they do not compromise on this standard. So, in answer to the question, "What level of performance is unacceptable?" these managers reply, "Any level that hovers around average with no trend upward." In answer to the question, "How long at that level is too long?" Great managers reply, "Not very long." (p. 207)

In counseling, clients' welfare is at stake.

Buckingham and Coffman (1999) describe love as focusing on poor performers' lack of talent to carry out the job they have successfully. The supervisee is not to blame.

> Great managers don't have to hide their true feelings. They understand that a person's talent and nontalent constitute an enduring pattern. They know that if, after pulling out all the stops to manage around his [*sic*] nontalents, an employee still underperforms, the most likely explanation is that his [*sic*] talents do not match his [*sic*] role. In the minds of great managers, consistent poor performance is not primarily a matter of weakness, stupidity, disobedience, or disrespect. It is a matter of miscasting. (p. 209)

As Drucker (1974) phrased it, "The nonperformer is often . . . not a 'dud.' He's [*sic*] only in the wrong place. It is the manager's job . . . to think through where a nonperformer might be productive and effective and to say that to him [*sic*]" (p. 311).

Termination. Firing supervisees is not easy to carry out. When administrative supervisors have followed the guidelines for disciplining employees (Chapter 4) termination is relatively straightforward. Impaired supervisees will have been warned not only by their direct administrative supervisor, but also by a representative from the human resources department that it is the logical outcome of their apparent inability or unwillingness to improve their job performance.

Termination procedures vary in different settings. In agencies, they are usually prescribed in employee handbooks. Private practices offer "employment at will" (Kulik, 2004, p. 183), meaning that with "good cause" they can end an "employment relationship at any time" (Kulik, p. 184). People employed in public and other large agencies typically have written or implied contracts for employment. Most contracts are contingent on employees performing their jobs well. Termination or firing signifies the end of the contract. There are rules established by states for handling premature canceling of contracts. Administrative supervisors must know the laws in their states, and to consult attorneys when considering firing someone (Martin, 2000). It is also good practice to ensure that employees be told at the outset of their tenure what the termination process is. There are different rules for downsizing that also need to be explained (Kulik, 2004).

It is administrative supervisors' responsibility to tell staff members of their impending termination, although they should already have gained the support of their administrators. In places where leadership responsibilities are shared by more than one administrative supervisor (e.g., the administrative supervisor in counseling and the principal of a school), the two might be there, but the primary communicator should be the direct supervisor. Termination should be handled in a face-to-face conference in a private setting, preferably on neutral territory. The communication should be very clear and to the point. The tendency to want to soften the blow only adds confusion to the message. Maintaining professional detachment and minimizing emotionality are especially important during these conferences (Kulik, 2004).

People should not be told of their firing on Friday afternoon at 5:00 p.m. They should be allowed some time to adjust to the thought. Kulik (2004) advises that firings be done at 8:00 a.m. on Monday, so fired employees have time to adjust to the news themselves before they face family and friends. She also suggests that:

termination meetings should usually last only 15 minutes or less. There are only three things you need to do during this meeting: Present the fact that the employee no longer has a job, explain why (is it a disciplinary decision? A downsizing situation?), and plan the next step. (p. 195)

Supervisees need to know how to handle the details of their leaving: the deadline for cleaning out their desks and offices, how to get their final paycheck, and such. They are not ready to process a lot of information. There should be no need to rehash details regarding the staff member's lack of performance or talent. The soon-to-be-former employee will be emotional. Effective administrative supervisors are aware of their emotionality and plan how they will end the conference without prolonging the discussion.

V

Administrative Supervisors: Design, Maintain and Improve an Effective and Efficient Service Delivery System for Clients

- Operationalize the Vision for the Department

- Acquire and Manage Resources

- Improve Continuously the Counseling Service Delivery System

- Lead the Process to Plan, Design, Deliver, Evaluate, and Enhance the Service Delivery System

15

Operationalize the Vision for the Department

To best serve their counseling clients, effective administrative supervisors create a vision for their departments and articulate "this vision so it turns into concrete strategies, solid management systems, and informed resource allocations that enable [the] organization to accomplish results" (Hersey, Blanchard & Johnson, 2001, p. 79). Your vision includes how counselors promote the mental health/well-being of their clients (Chapter 2), and how the services you deliver are organized most effectively and efficiently (Chapter 12). The administrative supervisor of a successful private counseling practice exemplifies this: "From my days in graduate school, I had a vision of a center or several centers where counselors could each have their private practice but under the umbrella of a center with a common theme" (S. D. Clifford, personal communication, August 14, 2005).

For that to be accomplished, you translate your vision into reality. Typically, this involves making changes. "Change is a process that requires vision, persistence, leadership, collaboration, systems analysis, and strong data" (American Counseling Association [ACA], n.d.a, ¶ 4).

> Three key aspects of managerial leadership [(administrative supervision)] are the following: (a) managerial leadership involves influence because it is concerned with how the managerial leader affects followers, (b) managerial leadership also typically occurs in groups because groups are the context within which managerial leadership takes place, and (c) managerial leadership includes attention to goals because a key measure for managerial leadership effectiveness is goal attainment. (Curtis & Sherlock, 2006, p. 120)

This chapter describes what you do to align your department's work with your vision. You provide leadership for change, making your vision operational by leading your supervisees to articulate the mission of your department and establish goals for achieving the mission; by analyzing what the department is currently doing; by designing the work to best meet your mission and goals; by assisting your supervisees to set implementation objectives; and by considering making major changes. Your experiences in leading groups and participating on staff teams give you some foundation for carrying out these responsibilities.

LEAD CHANGES

Change is constant, and you need to be adept at leading and managing changes and their ripple effects. "The rate of change in organizational environments requires that the development of organizational change strategies become an ongoing part of the functioning of the human service change-adept organization" (Austin, 2002, p. 447). "A change at any one point [in a system] will eventually have an impact on the total system and upon its various subparts" (Napier & Gershenfeld, 2004, p. 251). The "points" in a counseling department that may change include the people, organizational structure, service delivery system, process for developing the service delivery system, and resources.

Some changes are caused by external situations. Managements, organizational structures, resource providers, regulations and colleagues change. Some are caused within the department. As reflected in the Baldridge National Quality Program criteria, service agencies value "1] delivering ever improving value to customers; and 2] improving total organizational performance" (National Institute of Standards & Technology, n.d., p. C7). By continuously striving for better services for your clients and more effective and efficient organizations, you establish conditions for making continuous change.

There are two kinds of changes. First order changes are "essentially technical, uncontested incremental changes" (Austin, 2002, pp. 446–447). Examples of incremental changes are improvements within existing services or structures. Second order changes are fundamental, or often "highly politicized transformational changes" (Austin, pp. 446–447). Examples of these are changes in mission, organizational structure, or goals (Reichard, 2000). How you address changes depends on the magnitude of the change.

In order to operationalize your vision, you lead your supervisees through the changes required. You "become [a] *change manager*" (Hersey et al., 2001, p. 377) by planning, directing and controlling the change process. There are several change processes that are well described in the literature, for example, long range planning, strategic planning, and systematic planning (Art and process of strategy, 2005). These are processes that help you and your supervisees step back from your immediate work, and "define the organization's mission, vision, and values and translate them into tangible action" (Art and process of strategy, p. 11). A combined approach serves to focus "strategically for the long run based on factors that are universal and relatively unchanging, yet be responsive to those factors that change from year to year or even month to month" (Herr, Heitzmann & Rayman, 2006), or day to day, and moment to moment.

In preparing to lead a process for change, anticipate as much of the process flow as possible. Plan the steps to take. As Covey (1989) advised, "Be proactive. . . . Begin with the end in mind. . . . Put first things first" (p. 65). Laying out a tentative timeline is valuable so that you and others know how it will unfold (Gysbers & Henderson, 2006). The length of time it takes to complete the process depends on the scope and depth of the changes you seek. Three to five years are often projected. Finetuning a system of services does not take as much time as making systemic changes in it. Processes are unpredictable, but when you know the direction you are headed, you are better able to manage the unexpected—like changes in the political climate or in the level of support by agency executives.

Document

Design and change processes involve group work and thinking together. In making changes, the value of writing, publishing and disseminating the work for the participants and interested bystanders to read is inestimable. Writing forces you to precisely refine thoughts (Gysbers & Henderson, 2006). It records the data collected, decisions made and policies established. It supports institutional memory, and effective policy implementation. It better ensures common understanding, facilitates communication, and provides a means for monitoring and measuring the department's work and that of each staff member.

As the leader, you are responsible for ensuring that the writing is done well, and reflects the work accomplished through the process. Even if you delegate the actual recording to others, you must carefully review and edit the written products. The products of this part of the change process include statements of the department's shared values and vision, mission statement, goals, the results of the analysis of the current situation, the established design priorities and parameters, and implementation objectives.

Prior to publishing and disseminating them widely, you acquire approval of the documents from your agency administrators and policy-setters. You, also, internalize them and "refer to them often" (Y. K. Steves, personal communication, June 16, 2005). You encourage your supervisees to do the same.

Involve People

One way to help your supervisees manage change and the related stress is to involve them in the process.

> John Kotter, a Harvard Business School professor who has studied dozens of organizations in the midst of upheaval [says], "The central issue is never strategy, structure, culture, or systems. The core of the matter is always about changing the behavior of people." (quoted in Deutschman, 2005, ¶ 6)

Often it entails positive reframing (Deutschman, ¶ 14). To manage change successfully, involve all the members of your department in the process in some way. Their daily work will be affected by the outcomes of the process. It also includes other people within your agency and, perhaps, outside it, whose work may be affected by the changes, e.g., other department administrative supervisors, executives, and policy setters (Lees, 2004).

For staff members to commit to your ideas, they also have to commit to your leadership—to follow you through the process, in thinking together, and ultimately to change. Such commitments cannot be made until you have built trust with them. Even if you were a member of the staff and were promoted, it must be rebuilt within the dynamics of your new relationships. You spend your energy wisely if you focus on the 20% of your supervisees who seem amenable to improvements (Koch, 1998). Their participation will help bring most of the 80% along: 20% may never come around.

Manage Resistance

Recognize that "progressive, innovative administrators often have difficulty getting supervisees to accept changes in policies and procedures" (Kadushin & Harness, 2002, p. 76). All but a few of your supervisees will probably resist any changes you propose. "Expect it!" (Y. K. Steves, personal communication, June 16, 2005). They will want "to maintain the status quo" (Connor, Lake & Stackman, 2003, p. 151). Resistance is an integral part of the change process (Reichard, 2000, p. 198), and you should not underestimate it (Lopez, 2002). Like resistance in counseling, it is complicated. Anticipate and prepare to address it. It occurs when supervisees perceive their situation as ambiguous, causing them to be uncertain.

You are best apt to manage their resistance by identifying its causes, which are often anxiety or fear. You can see anxiety in supervisees when (if) you work in crisis management mode—the second highest concern of supervisees (Lester & Eaker cited in Hersey et al., 2001). It disrupts (changes) their workflow, patterns of behavior, and feelings. They wonder *Who Moved My Cheese?* (Johnson, 1998). You can see their fear when you make decisions in the present situation with an eye to the future—as you are advised to do in order to successfully improve your department's work (Drucker, 1974, p. 399). It can be the result of implementing changes before they are ready (Reichard, 2000, p. 197).

It should comfort you to know that "resistance to change and . . . innovation are *not* inherent in human nature. . . . [It] has its origin in fear of loss of job" (Drucker, 1974, pp. 286–287). Some of your supervisees will fear that having to change their job behaviors might in turn lead to their inability to do their jobs. They may feel victimized. Some resist because they have not yet grasped the concepts in the vision, values and mission; some because they do not agree with the changes; some are cynical and doubt real change will ever occur; some don't want to change, period. Often, resistors seek support from others to join them in their refusal to move (Gysbers & Henderson, 2006).

As the change process unfolds, your supervisees will have different excuses for not coming along with your desired changes. In the initial phase of change they blame:

1. Time: "We don't have time for this stuff" (p. 4).
2. Help: "We have no help" or "We're wasting our time" (p. 4).
3. Relevance: "This stuff isn't relevant" (p. 4).
4. Walking the talk: "They're not walking the talk" (p. 4).

In the phase of sustaining change, they express such positions as:

5. Fear and anxiety: "This isn't good" (p. 5).
6. Measurement: "This stuff is not working" (p. 5).
7. True believers ("We have the way") and non-believers ("They are acting like a cult") (p. 5).

And, in the redesigning phase, they suggest other impediments to change:

8. Governance: "They (the powers that be) never let us do this stuff" (p. 5).
9. Diffusion: "We keep reinventing the wheel" (p. 5).
10. Strategy and purpose: "What are we here for?" (p. 5).

(Senge & Kaeufer, 2000)

It is your responsibility to help your supervisees move through their resistance to acceptance of desired incremental and transformational changes. People are prompted to change when they feel dissatisfied with their current situation, have a concrete and specific vision of how things would be better after changes occur, and believe that the benefits of their changing are worth the costs of giving up current practices (Beckhard & Harris, 1987; Gysbers & Henderson, 2006; Reichard, 2000). Supervisees are usually dissatisfied when they feel under-, over- or mis-used. Developing a clear vision of what is desirable requires imagination and creativity, and being able to get a realistic mental picture of what will be. Not all your supervisees will come to this naturally. To help them, you might take them through a guided meditation script or other such technique, or take them, physically, to visit facilities that are doing what you want your department to do. They have to be able to put themselves into the picture and see improvements in their work over that of the status quo. They have to feel that, after changes, their jobs will be better, and more aligned with what satisfies them.

The primary processes to use to address resistance are "communication, education, participation, and training" (Reichard, 2000, p. 198). Through a combination of these, you help your supervisees learn the lessons described in the parable, *Who Moved My Cheese* (Johnson, 1998):

Change happens—They keep moving the cheese
Anticipate change—Get ready for the cheese to move
Monitor change—Smell the cheese often so you know when it is getting old
Adapt to change quickly—The quicker you let go of old cheese, the sooner
  you can enjoy new cheese

Change—Move with the cheese
Enjoy change!—Savor the adventure and enjoy the taste of new cheese
Be ready to change quickly and enjoy it again and again—They keep moving
the cheese (p. 74).

Above all, be patient. As one administrative supervisor advises, "Don't give up. Change is slow" (Y. K. Steves, personal communication, June 16, 2005). As with many other aspects of supervision, appreciate that individuals take different paths to the same end, and work with them not only collectively, but also individually. Once resistance weakens, ongoing changes continue.

DEVELOP A SHARED VISION AND MISSION

Find Meaning

In order to help your supervisees envision how their work will be more meaningful when changes occur, you lead them in creating a productive, coherent and shared mindset (Fullan, 2001; Hersey et al., 2001). Finding meaning in a department's work is fundamental to sharing a mindset (Fullan, 2001; Hersey et al., 2001). "The dominating need of human beings is to find meaning, . . . to control one's destiny, . . . [and] to be an expert in the promotion and protection of values" (Peters & Waterman, 1982, cited in Hersey et al., 2001, p. 24).

> All human beings prefer meaningful work to meaningless work. This is much like stressing the high human need for a system of values, a system of understanding the world and of making sense out of it. . . . If work is meaningless then life comes close to being meaningless. (Maslow, 1998/ 1962), p. 116)

Your supervisees need help making sense out of new approaches to their work (Weick, 1995).

Develop a Shared Vision

To develop a shared mindset, you and your supervisees strive to blend your individual visions for your counseling work (Fullan, 2001; Hersey et al., 2001). Your supervisees need not only to hear about your thoughts, they must be educated and have opportunities to align theirs with yours. A shared culture consists of common beliefs, values and norms (Hersey et al., 2001). You "define an image, then cultivate it, and get it into everyone's psyche" (Riley as cited in Collie, 2001, p. 112).

As described in Chapter 2, you begin by clarifying your own values and making your own vision concrete. With this basis, you are ready to engage your staff members. With them, you begin by communicating your values and vision. "The vision has to be articulated so that others see in it the possibility of realizing their own hopes and dreams" (Hersey et al., 2001, p. 435). An example vision statement is that by Clifford (2005), who summarizes succinctly the purpose of the center she administers as providing "quality counseling services to women and their families across the lifespan" (personal communication, August 14, 2005). To fully engage your staff members, you must be aware that "creating and communicating a vision will succeed only insofar as others are able to internalize and pursue the vision with you" (Napier & Gershenfeld, 2004, p. 245).

You attract followers with your vision. "The leader who offers a clear vision that is both coherent and credible, and who lives by a set of values that inspire imitation has a fundamental source of power" (Quigley, 1994, p. 39). Fullan (2001) describes the drawing power of sharing visions and moral purpose as "strange attractors" (p. 115). These "attractors involve experiences and forces that attract the energies and commitment of employees" (p. 115). Volition—"the absolute commitment to achieving something" (Ghoshal & Bruch, 2003, p. 51)—is "the decisive driver of effective implementation of change initiatives" (Ghoshal & Bruch, p. 52). It is a convergence of intellect and emotion. Solid commitment comes from each individual choosing to commit to the values, vision, mission, goals and decisions of the group and the leader.

You lead the discussions that result in the development of shared values, vision, mission and goals. Having five skills helps you do this effectively:

1. Encourage personal visions.
2. Communicate and ask for support.
3. Conduct visioning as an ongoing process.
4. Blend extrinsic and intrinsic visions.
5. Distinguish positive from negative visions. (Senge, 2004a)

Define the Mission

The next step in this foundation-building stage is for you to lead your staff members in clarification of your department's mission, the expression of the shared mindset (Fullan, 2001; Hersey et al., 2001). In order for workers to be highly satisfied, they need to answer "Yes" to the question, "Does the mission/purpose of my company make me feel my job is important?" (Buckingham & Coffman, 1999, p. 28). Successful enterprises make a "concentration decision" (Drucker, 1974, p. 104). They decide on their specialty. Again, an example from Clifford:

> When I started, I specialized in Postpartum Depression counseling. Through referrals, I found that women as a whole were grossly underserved—especially when faced with acknowledging the role of our unique hormonal make-up. Therefore, we expanded to include adolescents, pregnancy and infertility issues, parenting and families, PMDD [Premenstrual Dysphoric Disorder], and menopausal issues as our core. We needed a strong foundation in the most common themes we had found

in this population: anger, anxiety, depression, undetected learning disabilities, stress, substance abuse, trauma, and lack of positive coping skills. I needed clinicians in the center that were strong in these areas as well as shared my view of the mind-body-spirit connection. (Personal communication, August 14, 2005)

You must recognize the purpose for which your counseling program and services exist (Reichard, 2000). The "mission is going to determine and inspire people's behavior. A mission is an image of a desired state you want to get to" (Riley cited in Collie, 2001, p. 112).

Write a mission statement. You lead your staff group to write a mission statement as a means for focusing the entire department toward the common vision. This provides opportunities for you and your supervisees to blend ideas. It, then, "provides the foundation for priorities, strategies, plans, and work assignments . . . It specifies the fundamental reason why an organization exists" (Pearce & David, 1987, p. 109).

Hersey et al. (2001) suggest that mission statements include the known clients, the services provided, a brief description of the delivery system and the staff members. A simple formula for writing the mission statement is to include who (e.g., professional counselors and other staff members) does what (e.g., assists clients achieve specified results) for whom (e.g., specific clients) and how the department is organized (i.e., your counseling services delivery system) (Gysbers & Henderson, 2006). Doing this as a group by first making lists for each of the four units and not worrying about sentence structure works well. After deciding on the details, you pull it together into one, coherent statement.

Others recommend that statements answer three questions: 1. What are the needs we exist to address? (purpose); 2. What are we doing to address these needs? (work); 3. What principles or beliefs guide our work? (values) (Radtke, 1998). Some research suggests that mission statements should include nine components that identify the clients, services provided, geographic markets, resources, philosophy (values, ethics, beliefs), public contributions, service delivery staff members, and distinctive competence. Your mission statement provides the bridge between the ideals of your department and its operations. An example of a mission statement that includes the nine components is provided in Figure 15.1.

It is agreed that a "mission statement needs to be longer than a phrase or a sentence, but not a two page document" (David & David, 2003, p. 11). As the leader, select the mission statement style that makes most sense for you and aligns with that of the agency.

CLARIFY GOALS

The next step is to lead your supervisees in establishing goals that result in mission achievement. These are statements about what you and your supervisees

Figure 15.1 Counseling Center Mission Statement (Example)

> The mission of the _____ Counseling Center is to provide highest quality counseling and referral services that help displaced older adolescents and young adults from the Bexar County area develop and implement plans for being self-sufficient. The Center is funded by donations from private agencies and individuals who believe in the values and standards of the counseling profession. It is the aim of the Center to help our clients to be fulfilled and productive citizens, and, therefore, the County community to be a safer place to live. The Center's staff consists of professional counselors and support staff who assign the highest priority to the clients we serve, and are dedicated to excellence in culturally responsive services and professionalism. Our services are built to meet the identified needs of alienated youth from diverse cultures by applying appropriate theories and using techniques that are supported by professional research.

would like to see as results of your work. Goals in this context guide operations, but they are general statements. They are written for each dimension of a practice's service delivery system: clients served, outcomes achieved, use of counselors' and support staff members' competencies, types of activities provided, for resource acquisition and use, and for the operation of the delivery system. Some examples of goals are:

Our clients will feel satisfied with their relationships with their therapists.

Each professional counselor will perform at a "clearly outstanding" level.

Each support staff member will demonstrate warmth and respect for the counseling clients.

The resources appropriated to the counseling department will be used efficiently.

You make these more specific later on through implementation objectives. Review your mission statement and goals annually to ensure their relevancy and accuracy. Review them in detail when you hire new staff members or when an issue arises that brings the mission or people's belief in it into question. Renew (re-write) it every 3–5 years, or more frequently as expected by the agency or funding source(s).

ANALYZE THE CURRENT SITUATION

At this point, you and your engaged supervisees may be eager to start making improvements. The people that promoted or hired you may be impatient and applying some pressure. However, the change process entails your clearly understanding the problem, gathering information about it, analyzing that information, and developing suggestions for future actions (Connor et al., 2003). To clearly understand your situation, you and your supervisees thoroughly analyze the system that is in place before you start tinkering with it.

Lead your supervisees to gather information about what your department is currently doing to address the stated mission and goals. This requires time and energy; however these expenditures are worth it in the long run. The data provide the baseline for the future (Art and process of strategy, 2005). Data are gathered about the *clients*, their family members, and significant others, and about the numbers of clients you serve. Within these, identify subgroups of clients (e.g., by demographic groups, by issues presented, by interventions used). You gather data about the kinds of *activities* and interventions experienced by your clients, and the proportion of each within the total service delivery system. These indicate what *competencies* of the counselors and your other *staff members* are being used, and their proportions within the total delivery system. You gather data regarding the *results* achieved by your clients or others through the activities and interventions and the applications of your staff members' competence (Gysbers & Henderson, 2006).

You and your staff members gather information about what *resources* are available and how they are currently used. "Chunking" the resources into three categories helps make that data manageable: human, fiscal and political (politics *and* policy-makers) resources (Gysbers & Henderson, 2006). Finally, you see how the services are currently organized—the functions and activities and their relationships.

After the rather large quantity of data is gathered, you and your supervisees analyze it and draw conclusions that describe the alignment of your current work with the newly established or re-established mission. You identify current priorities and how the resources are used within those. In examining the design of the current system, you and your supervisees may be satisfied with the current structure. You may want one that is similar but fine-tuned, or one that is completely different. These questions are best answered after the design is clarified for what would work best to carry out your mission for your clients within the resources available.

DESIGN THE SERVICE DELIVERY SYSTEM

At this point, you and your supervisees are ready to operationalize your vision, mission and goals. You accomplish this by establishing priorities for service delivery and parameters for the use of resources. Designing your department's services is akin to building a house. Owners' priorities are reflected in their choices about the style of the house; the colors to be used in the house; the flooring materials; the placement of windows, their styles and treatments; and so on. Parameters are set by the size of the lot and the foundation, and the height of the structure. Building codes and standards establish rules that must be followed in the construction of the house. The rooms comprise the house's organizational structure.

Three basic questions that you and your supervisees ask and answer here are: What should be done for whom for maximum effectiveness? How should our resources be used for optimum efficiency? How should the various things we do with and for clients be organized for effective and efficient service delivery? (Gysbers & Henderson, 2006). "Efficiency is concerned with doing things right. Effectiveness is doing the right things" (Drucker, 1974, p. 45).

Set Priorities

Doing the right things entails your setting priorities—a difficult task. Clients' needs are many. The contributions that counselors and your other staff members can make to help them meet their needs are multiple. But, "no business can do everything. . . . It has to set priorities. The worst thing is to try to do a little bit of everything. This makes sure that nothing is being accomplished" (Drucker, 1974, p. 119). The criterion here is how to help your clients with the highest priorities achieve the most highly desired results by making the best use of the resources available. Again, it helps when you structure activities to facilitate the setting of priorities.

You and your supervisees set priorities for the *clients* you will serve. You prioritize the various subgroups of clients, and differentiate between primary (e.g., those seeking counseling) and secondary clients (e.g., their significant others). You determine the number of clients in each category to be served. You prioritize the results you want these clients to accomplish (for example, is the mission of your agency to help clients work through their depression or to help them progress in their career development?). You clarify the priorities for using counselors' and other staff members' competencies and skills. This means deciding the relative importance of such competencies as individual and group counseling, guidance/psychoeducation, consultation, assessment, and referral. It means clarifying who does the tasks that do not require graduate degrees in counseling.

You identify the relative importance of the *categories of services* to be offered and describe how they will be organized. A relevant organizational structure incorporates all the appropriate functions and tasks of staff members (Chapter 12). The daily activities are the essence of the delivery system (Hersey at al., 2001). Your structure organizes the interactions among clients, counselors, and resources through activities and services (Mintzberg & Heyden, 1999). Too often this "architecture" is the result of "a largely tacit process—more or less 'in the back of the minds' of managers" (Hemre, 2006, p. 10). You want to bring your vision of the desired structure to the forefront and solicit input about its viability from your supervisees.

Work Within Resource Parameters

Having identified the resources available, you and your supervisees determine the parameters that are set by the resources. They describe and define the limits to the department's capacity to provide activities/services. They are incontrovertible, finite, and reality. Resources are about time, numbers, budgets, space size, and standards (Chapter 16). In order to be realistic you ensure that the design fits within parameters set by the budgets available for materials, supplies and capital outlay; the numbers, sizes and configurations of the rooms in your facility.

You and your supervisees have discretion about your use of time. Time considerations include counselors' work time, and clients' availability. The most valuable resource in a counseling agency is the talent and time of its counselors and other specialists. The critical resource allocation question to be answered is: What should be the balance of time spent on each grouping of services provided by counselors for which clients? And, for other specialists? (Gysbers & Henderson, 2006).

Ultimately, it is your administrative supervision responsibility to ensure the compatibility of the service delivery design with the resources available. In shifting the delivery system design from what it is to what you want, your counseling department starts by making efficient use of the resources already appropriated to your department, and ensure they are targeted toward making the department's work most effective and efficient. When this is successful, you may be better able to acquire additional resources. On the other hand, this is the same process that allows you to manage shrinking resources.

Develop Implementation Objectives

You lead your department in development of implementation objectives. They are developed to assure maintenance and ongoing refinement of the department's fundamental services. Individual staff members develop their assigned objectives with your collaboration. Objectives need to be SMART (Drucker, 1974), as displayed in Figure 15.2. Examples of implementation objectives aimed at maintaining and improving elements in the current service delivery system of the example Counseling Center in addressing its stated mission are:

Figure 15.2 SMART Objectives

Specific
Measurable
Acceptable
Realistic
Timely
Drucker, 1974

In order to continuously assess clients' satisfaction with our services, I will conduct 30-minute exit interviews within the last three days prior to clients' termination from the Center. I will continue to follow the established interview protocol and enter their responses into the recording spreadsheet.

In order to maintain competent professional performance, I will continue to counsel 3 small groups of my clients weekly, according to professional standards and whose purpose is to engage the 15–18 year olds in processing their relationships with others in the residence hall.

In order to maintain a warm and respectful client environment, I will make eye contact and speak to each individual within 2 minutes of their entering the reception area.

In order to continue to ensure my 10 administrative supervisees' accountability for their time use, I will continue to review and analyze their weekly time logs and monthly summaries by comparing and contrasting them with their appointment calendars.

Development of objectives is empowering to staff members. It helps them see their responsibilities in relationship to the mission and to the whole department. It gives them the ability to direct their own work—as long as they are working effectively (Drucker, 1974). Action plans (Chapters 10 and 17) are developed subsequently to project how the objectives will be met.

Full implementation of the operationalized vision takes time, and even then it is an ongoing process. You establish procedures that also support achievement of the mission, goals, and objectives. You re-establish implementation objectives every year. Administrative supervisors develop methods (rules, procedures, systems) for monitoring and measuring service delivery (Chapter 18).

CONSIDER MAJOR CHANGES

Through the course of data gathering and analysis, administrative supervisors and supervisees often identify major gaps in their current design or resources. These require major, systemic changes—i.e., second order or "transformational" change (Austin, 2002). They have far-reaching ramifications. They cause changes in an operation's culture, or go deeper into changing the department, or farther out to changing the agency or even the community. They usually require large acquisitions of or shifts in resource use. Accomplishing such changes usually takes many years, yet follows the process described here and in Chapter 18. Implementation of major changes is guided by establishing improvement objectives and action plans. If the department's delivery system is serving clients and the agency mission reasonably well, some time can be allowed for making major changes.

SUMMARY

It is your responsibility, working with your supervisees, to understand change, and to "ensure that the organization is delivering the right programs, moving in the appropriate direction, and effectively using resources" (Herr et al., 2006, p. 320). "Right", "appropriate", and "effectively" are defined as being related to the department's and the agency's vision, mission and goals. Your department's mission is part of a shared mindset established by you and your staff members. Implementing the mission effectively and efficiently entails designing your service delivery system by setting priorities and working within parameters set by the resources available (Chapter 16). Your supervisees develop implementation objectives and action plans to guide their continuation of mission-related services.

SUPERVISORS' CHALLENGES AND RESPONSES

Supervisors' Challenges: Uncertainty

Human beings become uncertain when changes occur or are in the offing.

Questions arise about what is going on and what the result will be. They try to determine appropriate ways to function in their new situation, maintain good relationships, and make good decisions (Kramer, 2004). Not all supervisees are creative about their work, but "creativeness is correlated with the ability to withstand the lack of structure, the lack of future, lack of predictability, of control, the tolerance for ambiguity" (Maslow, 1998/1962, p. 220). Effective administrative supervisors nurture their supervisees' creativity.

In order to manage their uncertainty, individuals first make cognitive attempts to reduce uncertainty without seeking information (Kramer, 2004). They strive to understand. Next, they become motivated to seek information to reduce the stress. Some methods of information seeking are direct inquiry, observation, indirect inquiry, writing, or guessing (Kramer, 2004). "Gaining information generally reduces uncertainty and improves attitudes and actions in response to the uncertain situations" (Kramer, p. 63).

Competing motives affect how they manage information seeking. Curiosity, and the need to get along in their environment are examples of motives that increase information-seeking behaviors. Fear of negative consequences (social appropriateness, social costs, others' negative impressions of them) decreases their willingness to seek out information.

When they do not manage their uncertainty—i.e., not understanding, not gathering either the right or the right amount of information—individuals are less fluent in their communications, more apt to perceive unfairness or injustice, and to be less effective in decision-making (Kramer, 2004). They try to build coalitions with others who seem to think and feel like they do.

Supervisors' Responses

Administrative supervisors who successfully make changes help their supervisees manage their uncertainty. They recognize that "overall, the experience of uncertainty relates to ambiguity in the communication or context" of work (Kramer, 2004, p. 74). They primarily use two strategies. They help their supervisees process their uncertainty. The first step might be to address the causes of resistance directly. They listen carefully to hear what is on the minds of their supervisees and discern their real concerns (e.g., "If this change happens, I will have to work harder, or otherwise change my ways"). They treat them respectfully, acknowledging the validity of their concerns. At the same time, they hold firm that improvements will occur, and work with their supervisees to help them determine what they can do to improve to meet the challenges.

Second, they recognize that supervisees benefit from having information about the changing situation. When they "feel they are receiving sufficient information, they experience certainty, and as a result will experience satisfaction and confidence in their organizational role" (Kramer, 2004, p. 42). When possible, administrative supervisors provide the information, knowing that supervisees also get incomplete or inaccurate information from their networks and grapevines (Chapter 6). As much as possible, they involve staff members in collecting and interpreting data, and in planning, implementing and monitoring changes.

In order to respond to them appropriately, administrative supervisors consider each of their supervisees individually. They avoid feeling unduly threatened by apparent coalitions, as individual supervisees have individualized needs. For each individual, they determine the underlying cause of their uncertainty, their motives and styles of gathering and processing information, and adapt their own communication and leadership styles accordingly.

16

Acquire and Manage Resources

Efficient administrative supervisors acquire, allocate and manage the human, fiscal and political resources that support their work with clients, the work of counselors and other staff members, and the department. You are responsible for acquiring sufficient resources to implement the service delivery system as designed (Chapters 12 and 15); or to redesign the delivery system to use the resources available (Gysbers & Henderson, 2006). When supervisees can answer, "Yes" to the question, "Do I have the materials and equipment I need to do my work right?" (Buckingham & Coffman, 1999, p. 28), they are apt to feel satisfied with their jobs. Many resources flow through systems established by your agency. Your ability to acquire resources and manage them well is symbolic of your power and perceived effectiveness within the agency as a whole.

Your experiences as consumers of resources and followers of the systems and procedures required for accessing and being accountable for them provide a foundation for carrying out the responsibilities of establishing and enforcing these systems. To be efficient, you identify the essence of what needs to be done, and do it well by making it as simple as possible (Koch, 1998). You also consider this as you develop procedures for your staff members to follow.

HUMAN RESOURCES

The primary resources of any mental health care organization are the human resources (Falvey, 1987; Henderson & Gysbers, 1998; Martin, 2000). You strive to optimize each supervisee's talents. For example, if a minority of counselor activities currently contributes to a majority of the successful client results, increasing those activities will improve the number of successful results. If a majority of counselor activities currently contribute very little to improving client welfare (e.g., completing paperwork), those activities should be stream-lined or displaced (Gysbers & Henderson, 2006).

Some minimum standards for fair employment practices are established in federal, state and local laws and regulations (Chapter 4); however,

employment laws generally emphasize what you *cannot* do as a manager. As long as an organization's practices don't violate EEO law, it's left up to the organization's management to decide how to best recruit, select, and just generally manage employees. (Kulik, 2004, p. 8)

You are responsible for establishing or knowing your agency's human resources policies and practices, and operating within them. If the practices do not suit the best interests of your department or staff, you negotiate for appropriate changes in the system. As their administrative supervisors, you are responsible for your staff members after they are hired; therefore, you actively engage in staff acquisition and management processes.

ACQUIRE

Know Your Job Openings

Knowing how many positions you have available is a prerequisite to hiring. You determine how many staff members will be funded by your agency or practice. Counseling positions are usually tied to predicted numbers of clients. In large agencies (e.g., hospitals, school districts, state mental health care agencies, universities), staff allocations are often determined based on formulas related to counselor-client ratios. In that circumstance, you develop the staff allocation formula and work to align that formula with professional standards. Similarly, if you are in an independent counseling practice, you discern when your current clinicians are working at capacity, and identify how many additional ones are needed to meet the apparent client needs, and that will generate the revenue to pay them. Other openings for staff members occur when people leave your department or practice through job moves or retirements.

Recruit Qualified Applicants

Recruiting qualified and desirable applicants is an ongoing job. You are always aware that openings will become available, and reach out to ensure a high quality applicant pool. It is a regular part of your work. If your goals are to hire staff members that reflect your diverse client population, you recruit applicants from specific groups intentionally (Chapter 3).

Use an Effective and Legitimate Hiring Process

Hiring effective counselors and other staff members is one of the most important jobs you do. "Faculty are the most valuable and expensive asset of colleges and universities. Consequently, in hiring and managing faculty development, department chairs have one of the most challenging institutional responsibilities" (Bensimon, Ward & Sanders, 2000, p. xvi). These responsibilities call for new administrative supervisors to make a difficult shift in perspectives: from applicants to employers. The purpose of the hiring process is to find individuals who have the skill, talent, and ability you need and who seem likely to fit well with your department or group (Buckingham &

Coffman, 1999; Train Managers, 2006). In striving "to turn each employee's talent into performance, [the first key] is to select for talent" (Buckingham & Coffman, p. 213).

You manage the many steps in the hiring process: posting a job announcement, receiving applications, pre-screening, interviewing apparently qualified applicants, selecting, and hiring. Your carrying out the selection process is akin to working a jigsaw puzzle. You arrange multiple pieces of information within the frame of the available job responsibilities and your work environment. Thorough as your process may be, the picture is never complete.

Your process must follow both legal regulations and agency policies and procedures. Following the *Uniform Guidelines on Employee Selection Procedures* (1978) helps ensure that you conduct the process fairly. The *Guidelines* express the Federal government's position regarding discrimination, and have been adopted by the Equal Employment Opportunity Commission, the Department of Labor, the Department of Justice, and the Civil Service Commission. Your "policies must be applied uniformly to all" (Train Managers, 2006, p. 6).

The posted job announcement is the first step in hiring and orienting a new person to a specific job. There is a distinction between a job announcement or posting and an individual's specific job description (Chapters 12 and 13). Job announcements offer a generic description of available positions, including a summary of the job duties, the education and licensure requirements, a list of duties and responsibilities, the terms of employment, and how to apply.

The application form and related documents (e.g., letters of interest; resumés; essay on a relevant topic) must meet the agency's legal requirements and those of the counseling department. Other information you gather must be job related. Pre-screening aids efficiency, in that it helps narrow down the number of applicants to interview. When you do it well, interviewing is time and labor intensive. Pre-screening may include paper screening of application materials, including credentials and experiences, letters of recommendation, checking references, reviewing indicators of competence and work ethic (e.g., attendance records). If you use tests, they must be valid to predict levels of competence related to the job requirements and not have an adverse effect on minorities, women or other protected groups (Agard, 2005).

Interview. In interviewing, you try to discern if the interviewees have the talent needed for the available job, and would fit with the staff members in place. To be legally sound your "interviewing practices should start with a job description and specifics about the job requirements and expectations. . . . [You] should avoid all personal information and the protected characteristics" (Train Managers, 2006, p. 6). If you ask a few simple, open-ended questions, you are able to listen for the specifics in the applicants' answers that exemplify their past behaviors (Buckingham, 2005).

Past behaviors are the best predictors of future behaviors. Buckingham (2005) offers two questions that have worked for him. "To identify a person's strengths, first ask, 'What was the best day at work you've had in the past three months?'" (p. 75). "To identify a person's weaknesses, just invert the question: 'What was the worst day you've had at work in the past three months?'" (p. 75). Your asking questions that address key areas of job expectations are also worth hearing the answers to, such as "Describe the most successful/least successful team you've been on, and your roles on them;" "What ethical dilemma did you encounter recently, and how did you handle it?"

In conducting good job interviews, you get acquainted with applicants, and get information far beyond what you learn from paperwork and assessments. These are also part of the beginning of your relationships with new employees. On the other hand, they are not really representative samples of people's work. Increasingly, administrative supervisors are taking opportunities to see live performance by their potential employees. Some hire them as temporary workers, or on a limited part-time basis, or invite them to volunteer to work for several days or to earn internship hours there. As one explains,

> I have been drawn to other clinicians who have their dreams as well and seem to be determined to provide high level of quality care while pursuing their vision. I usually offer part-time space until I am sure a clinician will be the right "fit" to our program. I look for someone who has that eagerness and passion for what they do. (S. D. Clifford, personal communication, August 14, 2005)

Select and hire. You elect to hire the highest ranked applicants, and offer them positions. If (when) they accept, the logistical steps to becoming an employee ensue. Contracts or other types of agreements and benefits are explained and signed. In large agencies, Human Resource departments typically carry out these functions. Even then, you are responsible for seeing that potential or new employees' questions are answered, and that they do not fall through bureaucratic cracks. Keeping in touch with them during this process is key to helping them get started on the right foot. You also notify unsuccessful applicants when positions are filled.

MANAGE

Allocate

Allocating human resources entails your placing them in specific jobs. Jobs may be available that require different specialties or are at different sites. To be most effective, you place new hires where they are most apt to be successful. For placements at different sites, you include site-based supervisors in the selection process. Currently placed counselors may pursue opportunities to transfer to different positions. As with new hires, the process for transferring staff members laterally from one position to another must be formalized and systematic. It, too, needs to be a fair practice.

Provide Professional Development

To maintain quality performance of staff members, you systematically provide for their job-related professional development. This has two phases: orientation/induction of new staff members, and continuing development beyond the first year (Bensimon et al., 2000).

Orient new staff members. You attend to new staff members' uncertainty systematically. They are uncertain about mastering their roles, jobs and tasks; about establishing their own identity; about building their relationships with others; about the organizational culture, structure and procedures; about what they will be evaluated on; and, about politics and the power structure (Kramer, 2004). It is important for you to note that members of minority cultures experience more relationship uncertainty than do members of the majority culture (Kramer).

"Newcomers focus on learning the details of their job initially" (Kramer, p. 48). You help new supervisees get off on the right foot by carefully orienting them to your work place—the physical arrangements as well as to the day-to-day operations of your office, and about basic procedures. As they master many of their new tasks, new supervisees "begin to focus on broader issues such as how they are being evaluated" (Kramer, p. 48).

New staff members have the right to know the policies and procedures related to employment, compensation and benefits, attendance, formal relationships, standards for conduct, dress and grooming, consequences for not adhering to policies, and what to do in crises or emergencies. Many agencies have personnel handbooks that detail these for the agency as a whole. You address specific applications that apply to your department, such as information about the vision, mission and goals of the department, the service delivery system design, and the performance management system.

In some situations, you provide formalized training to new-hires, whether they are experienced counselors or new professionals. Remembering that assumptions can be dangerous, you acknowledge that even experienced counselors need orientation to and training about "how we do things around here." Data aggregated from my calendar, as an experienced administrative supervisor responsible for approximately 200 counselor positions in a growing agency, show that I spent approximately 10–15% of my time during a year in hiring, orienting, inducting, and training new employees (Henderson, 1999, 2001).

You provide a lot of the information that new supervisees need and help them make sense out of their new situation (Weick, 1995). You guide them through the induction period (3 months to a year), until they are comfortable in and confident about their new job responsibilities and work place. Peers and senior co-workers contribute too. Assigning trustworthy mentors has been an effective adjunct to supervisor orientation (M. L. Libby, personal communication, May 6, 2005). There are, however, dangers that result from negative mentoring experiences (Eby, Butts, Lockwood & Simon, 2004). If you use them, you monitor these relationships.

The initial period of employment is the most critical to ongoing success, and the first day is the hardest challenge! Ramsey (1998) offers an extensive and practical "check list for helping new employees succeed" (What supervisors can do, ¶ 2). Some highlights that administrative supervisors too often neglect are displayed in Figure 16.1.

Continue staff members' development. You are responsible for "developing the human resources for which [you] are responsible" (Hersey, Blanchard & Johnson, 2001, p. 229). Your primary system for doing this is the performance management system (described in Chapter 13). Methods for developing staff members' competence are inservice training, continuing education, and supervision. In general, you provide inservice training for all staff members in the same content. You support individuals as they pursue continuing education in accord with their professional development goals and plans. Supervision is tailored for each individual (Chapter 10).

Administrative supervisors are often held accountable for retaining good employees. Bethune, Sherrod and Youngblood (2005) offer 101 "tips to retain a happy, healthy staff" (p. 25). You benefit from following such tips as striving for a positive work environment, empowering your employees, allowing for clinician-directed care, being flexible, providing for meaningful continuing education, integrating your staff, valuing your staff members, being personally available, recognizing staff members' contributions, developing means for staff members to recognize each other, and holding celebrations.

Figure 16.1 Some Tips for Helping New Employees Succeed

The first day is the most important; be there.
Have basic materials ready to give them.
Arrange for accommodating any handicap or disability and for needed training.
Conduct a walk-through of the facility, introducing them to key players—for
  their jobs and roles.
Learn their preferred name, arrange for them to have lunch with a co-worker.
Encourage questions; listen carefully—i.e., don't do all the talking.
Demonstrate department professional and social values.
Check with them at the end of the first day, the first week, the first month.
Give positive feedback as early on as possible.
Give constructive or negative feedback carefully and gently.
Make the atmosphere fun.
Care about them.

Ramsey, 1998

Keep Personnel Records

As managers, you maintain personnel files for each of your staff members. These files house your records and notes. You best ensure privacy and confidentiality by keeping them in a locked file cabinet (Greengard, 1996). No matter how small, your agency needs to "adopt a written policy on personnel files and records" (Fago, 2004, p. 9). You know and adhere to the relevant Federal and state laws and policies that govern your employment and counseling practices for recordkeeping. These vary from state to state, and agency to agency.

Records. In larger agencies, human resources departments often guide completion of and house official, legally required personnel records. Where you *are* the human resources department for your staff members, you keep the legal records. It is recommended that you keep hard copies of records (Campion & Campion, 1995). You keep copies of all records housed in the HR department in your secured personnel files. When questions arise, you consult your HR counterparts, the written policies and regulations, and lawyers who are experts in interpreting them. A list of basic individual personnel records and how long they are to be kept are listed in Figure 16.2.

Reprimands and warnings are records that are also kept in your personnel files. You are advised also to "put recognition and praise about good performance into the personnel files" (Train Managers, 2006, p. 6). If there are more than 10 employees in your agency, records must be kept about injuries and illnesses (Busick, 2006). Medical information is kept in another separate file cabinet (Greengard, 1996). Purging your files of "paperwork that is outdated, redundant, useless or ill-advised to keep on file in today's litigious environment" keeps them streamlined (Campion & Campion, 1995, p. 13; Record Retention, 2006). You are advised to establish a record purging policy and use consistent procedures for carrying it out.

Notes. To be responsible, you keep personal notes on supervisees—your personal recordings of supervisee-related events and thoughts. By definition, these are private and kept in your sole possession, and are for your use only (similar to counseling notes). Keeping track of performance management activities is an important adjunct to a systematic approach to helping your supervisees grow. Many of the forms used in the system are "notes." These include job descriptions, supervision plans, observations, assessments, response planning and feedback conferences, specific improvement goals and action plans, notes from consultation conferences, formative evaluations, and self-evaluations.

Good recordkeeping and notetaking support your effective supervision (Borders & Brown, 2005). Most of the documents and their uses in the performance management system are centered on the professional development of your supervisees. Given the ongoing nature of most of your supervisee relationships, such records and notes are valuable to your reflection and

---

Figure 16.2 Rules for Filing and Keeping Individual Personnel Records

---

Permanent Records
   Employment application
   License/certification information
   Work history information, including work history within current
      organization
   Other work history information
   Other official information:
      job descriptions
      work assignments
      temporary assignments
      leaves of absence
      termination

   Educational information:
      internal and external education and training records
      educational assistance forms
   Indicators of policies communicated
   Any other signed forms:
      compensation
      IRS forms
      benefits
      legal information
      emergency notification information
      equal employment opportunity
      citizenship

5 Years or Until Termination
   Letters of reference
   Job performance information:
      summative performance evaluations
      letters of commendation
      absenteeism

2 Years
   Test results

                    Campion & Campion, 1995; Fago, 2004; Record Retention, 2006

---

insight. You use them as support for careful thinking about supervisee development or decline, and identification of their behavior patterns.

Summative performance evaluation forms. The performance management system records and notes, however, are also linked to summative performance evaluation (Chapter 14). In the relatively few cases when counselors' performance ratings are unsatisfactory or unacceptable, summative evaluation is at the heart of the system for forcing individuals to make seriously needed changes. This potentiality requires that you be precise, complete and professionally appropriate in your record keeping and notetaking. They provide a paper trail.

As in counseling, your records and notes may be needed to respond to complaints or grievances, or in legal proceedings—or worse yet, find their way into media coverage of highly-charged events. Typically, you know well in advance when your notes in such cases are needed, and are allowed time for ensuring their relevance and appropriateness.

Maintain Accountability for Service Delivery

As a manager, you develop and implement systems for holding your staff members accountable for their work. This dimension of your job entails developing forms and procedures for their use that are simple and workable. Procedures include the timeline for form dissemination, collection and review, and use of the data. To be practical and useful, all the systems you establish are meaningful (have a valid purpose), congruent (collect information in a way that is consistent with the purpose), appropriate (provide data relevant to the purpose), timely (match the department and agency's operational calendars), simple (take a reasonable amount of time to complete, and gather only needed data), workable (fit smoothly into work processes), and economical (not cost an undue amount of money to implement) (Drucker, 1974).

In developing forms and procedures for accountability—whether for tracking clients' progress, job implementation or time—you are wise to collaborate with your staff members as they entail both your work and theirs. Ideally, they should serve a meaningful function for both. Develop one format to serve a purpose for all relevant staff members to use to ensure your being able to aggregate the data easily. Educate supervisees about the purposes of your various accountability systems, and train them in proper use of forms, and how to follow the procedures.

To be organized, you have efficient and relevant filing systems for storing and processing collected information. Where possible, you use computer-based systems. Examples of systems that are useful to administrative supervisors are those that track and monitor client progress, staff members' fulfillment of their job responsibilities, and their use of time.

Client progress. You monitor clients' progress from initial contact to termination. The agency may already have forms and policies in place that guide client documentation and record keeping, but you need the case notes and progress notes to serve your purposes as well. Your client record keeping forms are one method for monitoring and measuring both clients' and counselors' performance.

"Clinical record keeping plays a key role in providing good mental health care" (Kapp & Mossman, 2000, p. 128). It allows "clinicians to succinctly document their thoughts and decisions at crucial points during a patient's care" (Kapp & Mossman, p. 135), and supports their adherence to ethical standards (American Counseling Association [ACA], 2005; American Mental Health Counselors Association [AMHCA], 2000; American School Counselor

Association [ASCA], 2004a). It may be used to report measures of effectiveness with clients to funding sources. As one administrative supervisor explains:

> In addition to overseeing the clinical aspects of the Counseling Center, one of my responsibilities was to review therapists' progress notes to ensure they were done according to grant specifications and to ensure they were done in a professional manner. (D. J. Martin, personal communication, July 30, 2005)

Job responsibilities. To hold staff members accountable for fulfilling their work responsibilities, you measure and monitor their ongoing performance—what they do every day in their jobs (Hersey et al., 2001). You hold them accountable for delivering the activities and services as designed for implementing your delivery system (Chapter 15). You oversee the development and monitor the implementation of work plans, such as calendars and schedules. You track the activities completed, the number of clients that have been served, how often, and to what ends.

Another means for holding staff members accountable is by tracking their attendance patterns, e.g., frequency of absences or tardiness. (Interestingly enough, tardiness is one of the biggest issues in the work place.) If supervisees are not there, they cannot be present with their clients. These patterns also indicate staff members' levels of commitment to their clients, jobs, agencies, and profession.

You hold your supervisees accountable for achieving their implementation and improvement objectives (Chapters 15 and 17). To carry this out efficiently, you establish patterns for your reviews of their progress towards attainment. Depending on the circumstances, you may do this weekly, monthly, or semi-annually. Frequency of these work reviews may vary among supervisees, depending on their levels of professional development. When working with staff members whose behaviors give indications of chronic impairment (e.g., depression, stress, burnout, unsatisfactory performance), you meet weekly. That is, when you are using your coercive or other harsh powers (Chapter 1) to guide supervisees to improve their work, you are advised to use more diligent surveillance techniques than with those who respond well to other power bases (Raven, 1993).

Use of time. To be efficient and ensure your staff members' efficiency, you hold them accountable for their use of time. There is a direct correlation between levels of productivity and percentage of work time spent on work. Without tracking their time use many cannot tell you where it goes. The best way for you and your supervisees to track their time use is through logs (Gysbers & Henderson, 2006). They "show you the truth about what you're doing with your time" (Mackenzie, 1997, p. 233). Useful time logs are those that are simple to keep up with, and require as little time as possible to record. An efficient log includes clearly defined boxes of relevant time increments and simple legends identifying categories of clients and recurrent activities that require only check marks or quick notations. Figures 16.3 and 16.4 are generic examples. Computerizing their use increases their ease of use and accuracy. To have them work for you, train your staff members in their use and monitor them frequently (Gysbers & Henderson, 2006).

There is great likelihood that you will have supervisees who have no control over their use of time. It is "difficult for some people [to] accept the reality that they themselves are to blame for many of their time problems" (Mackenzie, 1997, p. 7). They disavow their control. Mackenzie identified the 20 biggest time wasters (see Figure 16.5), and suggested hundreds of strategies for fixing the pesky problems. In counseling settings, scheduled clients missing appointments is an additional issue. Many of these are problems for administrative supervisors too.

FISCAL RESOURCES

The fiscal resources available to you and your department consist of the money for staff members' salaries and benefits, for renting facilities, for buying furniture, equipment, materials, supplies and printing, for paying for services and travel, and for providing inservice training, consultants, and continuing education. Staff members' salaries and benefits typically represent 80% of the department's total budget.

In order to get the money you need, you have to understand how the financial system works in your setting, i.e., where (or who) the money comes from, how you obtain it, what you can spend it on, and how. If you are a new administrative supervisor, you should anticipate that you are apt to need training in budget management, grant writing and data management (P.E. McDaniel, personal communication, September 26, 2005). If you own a private practice, you bear the legal burden of fiscal responsibility. If you are in an agency or large company, there is probably an individual or department that manages the financial affairs. In order to obtain and use your fiscal resources well, you should trust their expertise and work closely with them in such matters as developing your budget, acquiring money and implementing effective processes for managing it.

In most settings, the basis for earning money is the number of clients your department serves, or the number of hours you spend in counseling clients. Generating the income to support the counseling service delivery system presents the biggest difference between administrative supervisors in public or not-for-profit counseling agencies and those in a private business practices. "Businesses are paid for by satisfying the customer. . . . Service institutions, by contrast, are typically paid out of a budget allocation" (Drucker, 1974. p. 141), or by grants that target specific services or clients. Even in publicly funded service institutions, however, the quality and quantity of clients served impacts the amount budgeted for services. If you are in a successful private practice,

Figure 16.3 Counseling Department Counselor Daily Time Log

Date: _____

Counselor: _____

Time	Client Category	Ind'l Cnslng	Group Cnslng	Family Cnslng	Assessment	Cnsltng	Referral	Psych-ed	Prep/Doc
7:00 am									
8:00 am									
9:00 am									
10:00 am									
11:00 am									
Noon									
1:00 pm									
2:00 pm									
3:00 pm									
4:00 pm									
5:00 pm									
6:00 pm									

Figure 16.4 Counseling Department Counselor Weekly Time Log

Counselor: _____

Dates: _____

Counselor Time	Monday	Tuesday	Wednesday	Thursday	Friday
8:00 am					
9:00 am					
10:00 am					
11:00 am					
Noon					
1:00 pm					
2:00 pm					
3:00 pm					
4:00 pm					
5:00 pm					
6:00 pm					

Legend:
Client Category: (life stages) (diagnoses)
I: Individual Counseling
G: Group Counseling
F: Family Counseling
A: Assessment

C: Consulting
R: Referral
P: Psychoeducation
D: Preparation or documentation

Figure 16.5 The 20 Biggest Time Wasters

management by crisis
telephone interruptions
inadequate planning
attempting too much (more than is possible in the time available)
drop-in visitors
ineffective delegation
personal disorganization
lack of self-discipline
inability to say no
procrastination
meetings
paperwork
leaving tasks unfinished
inadequate staff
socializing
confused responsibility or authority
poor communication
inadequate controls and progress reports
incomplete information
travel
Mackenzie, 1997

you operate from a business plan that is the basis not only of your work, but also for generating funds (United States Small Business Administration, 2006).

Acquire Money

The sources of counseling departments' money vary from setting to setting, but the processes for acquiring it are similar. In order to be successful in getting optimum amounts of funds, you must understand the fiscal year of your agency, and prepare properly for each phase of its cycle. You project a budget for the upcoming year, ask for the funds, adjust the budget to match your appropriations, manage them and are accountable for their use. Being fiscally responsible is critical to your success as an administrative supervisor. Being fiscally irresponsible impairs your continuing ability to get money, and it could cost you your job.

Develop a Projected Budget

The budget is the instrument for you and the agency expressing and supporting priorities among services, staff, facilities and equipment, innovation and research, marketing and advertising, management and organization (Drucker, 1974). Your budget request reflects the priorities of your established service delivery system design. It identifies the amount of money needed in each of the budget categories to serve an anticipated number of clients through an anticipated number of staff members aiming to achieve implementation and improvement objectives. The history of the department's spending for the current year is a good place to start, but you identify areas where more money is needed, and where less. You include budget items that support future changes as well (Drucker, 1999). To help make the budget transparent for your staff members, you involve them in the budget development process. This helps them make sense of budget realities, and have a sense of ownership in the financial decisions affecting their work.

Obtain Funds From a Variety of Sources

Next, you seek to "obtain funds from a variety of sources" (Herr, Heitzmann & Rayman, 2006, p. 210). These might be allocations from the agency's budget, other departments and categories within the agency's budget, legislative entitlements, special project funding, grants, fundraising efforts, fees for services paid by third party payers, and fees for services paid by clients directly. Client fees are typically built on a sliding schedule. The ethical standards (ACA, 2005) suggest that in establishing fees, counselors consider the community standards—based on what other like-service providers in the community charge. Another important related principle is that when clients cannot afford a counselor's fee, the counselor is responsible for helping them find "comparable services at acceptable cost" (A.10.b).

You have to explain and justify your projected budget to the financial decision makers in each of your different sources. For all funding sources, "budgets are political statements" (Herr et al., 2006, p. 36) about their priorities. Explaining/justifying your budget requires you to exercise your political savvy and skills, as each budget decision demonstrates a level of support for the counseling department. It is your responsibility to present your budget honestly, but in the context of the potential funders' perspectives—i.e., one canned presentation will probably not serve all your purposes.

Within any agency or funding group, your budget request is merged with those from other, competing departments. You must be prepared to negotiate and make modifications as called for—usually trimming back. This process is complicated and difficult for the ultimate decision makers—e.g., publicly appointed or elected commissions or boards. It may take months. They, too, have to balance anticipated income and projected costs, but on a larger, more complex scale.

Manage Appropriated Fiscal Resources

The second phase of your being fiscally responsible is managing your department's money. You begin by adjusting your projected budget to match the real amounts you are appropriated or have earned, or you run the risk of spending more or less than you said you have planned use for. Nothing impairs the credibility of your next budget request more than inappropriate spending within the current budget. The adjusted budget is the basis for your operations throughout the fiscal year.

When unexpected expenses or windfalls come to your department, you follow the agency's adopted procedures for amending the budget. Agencies often require that you not change the bottom line of your department's whole budget, but give you permission to shift money among the categories. Again, you have to be able to justify your need to shift funds to the finance executive, and, depending on the scope of the change, the policy-setting body that is responsible for the agency's money, and who believed your original explanations.

Make Good Use of the Money

In order to make good use of appropriated money, you and your supervisees make spending decisions based on sound professional as well as economic considerations. Different funding sources have different rules and guidelines for what "their" money may be spent on, how it may be spent, and timelines for spending it. Agency decision makers set priorities for spending among budget categories, e.g., "Professional development holds a higher priority than travel." Your expenditures should also reflect the priorities of the department's design for the service delivery system.

You establish and communicate the principles for and rules associated with funds you allocate to your supervisees. You inform them of the agency's priorities and preferences, and are clear about your priorities for spending. You will probably have to acknowledge that some of the costs of providing your client services are borne by the supervisees themselves (e.g., for their own continuing education).

When money is allocated directly to staff members to spend, it should be distributed fairly—not necessarily equally—among the staff members. As always, your decisions must be explainable and defensible. In fact, one of the most sensitive issues you face is deciding between staff members' competing interests (Buller, 2004). Once you have allocated money to them, your supervisees should have autonomy in deciding how to spend it. Staff members who are allocated money must adhere to your rules and priorities, and be held accountable for using money appropriately. You ensure that they do.

Monitor and Track the Department's Money

In order to be fiscally responsible, you develop a system for accounting for your department's funds. You monitor (oversee the use) and track the actual status of the budget as a whole, and for each funding source and fund category. Different funding sources have different rules and procedures for accountability (e.g., reports, audits, compliance reviews). You need to know those of your agency and of other funders, and follow them.

Fiscal accountability processes involve many, detailed steps. Some of the steps in the budget management, purchasing, accounting and paying process, for example, are: receiving order requests from staff members (including the administrative supervisor); completing purchase requisitions; recording the requests, encumbering the funds (when the order is placed), receiving the item; authorizing payment; paying for the item; and directing the item to the individual who ordered it. To be conscientious, you not only track purchase orders, you sign-off on each one to ensure that it puts the money to good use and that the amount is reasonable. You also see that allocated money is spent and in a timely manner.

To be appropriately responsible, you keep books of the counseling department's use of funds, even if your agency's Finance Department also keeps them. Bookkeeping is the tool for tracking and monitoring the budget. It requires use of accounting practices to track the balance between the money that comes in and the money that goes out—the credits and debits. If you do it responsibly, it is not unlike keeping your checkbook.

You use forms and reports that facilitate management of the accounting system—this is definitely more complex than the typical personal checking account. Forms include purchase requisitions, invoices, ledgers and balance sheets. Reports include income statements and cash flow statements. "The balance sheet is a snapshot of a particular moment in time that shows total assets owned by the organization, claims (liabilities) against those assets, and the residual value in equity of the owners" (Newman, 2000, p. 149) or the fund balance in non-profit agency accounting.

To be fiscally responsible, you develop monthly reports of this status or review the ones provided by your agency. Reports may be developed by others, but you are still responsible for the money. You keep records of the money that comes in and the money that goes out in a computerized or hand-written ledger.

Hiring a support staff member with the technical expertise to help manage and monitor the details of bookkeeping allows you time to do other work, and yet get these tasks taken care of. Again, you maintain responsibility, but such a staff member facilitates your efforts. Good bookkeeping requires training in accounting practices, form use, and agency standards and procedures.

To be fiscally sound, you ensure that your department's purchased resources are used well. This entails attending to not only the human resources, as previously discussed, but also the fixed assets, materials, and supplies. You keep inventories of items that are fixed assets (e.g., facilities and furniture; office equipment, technology and communication devices), and those that are consumable (e.g., supplies and materials).

Fixed assets depreciate in value. You provide for their maintenance to extend their longevity. You assess the effectiveness and efficiency of acquired resources before they are replaced or displaced. You employ risk management practices to avoid circumstances that are potentially costly (e.g., allowing toner to run out and, thereby, damaging the printer). You often see to the details that allow for good resource use. As Clifford describes:

> I often find myself managing other areas of running our Center—everything from making sure the toilet paper is on the roll and the Ozarka water bottle is on the dispenser properly, to rent being paid and all the counselors having adequate insurance coverage. (August 14, 2005, personal communication)

Finally, while fiscal resources are essential to providing optimum services, they should not become your primary focus; providing services in the best interests of your clients should be.

Manage Being Underfunded

In my experience, initial budget requests typically are not fully funded. In fact, some administrative supervisors consciously request more money than they think they will get, thereby leaving room for negotiation. Some—maybe many—administrative supervisors feel that they never have sufficient funds to do what is wanted or envisioned. On the other hand, there are times when revenues available for counseling departments in either public or private agencies are very inadequate. They do not cover current needs, and, in fact, require severe cutbacks.

Revenue shortages may result indirectly from such societal causes as inflation or a decline in tax dollars. When a community's economy is troubled, individuals do not have as much discretionary money to spend on private counseling services. With policy or other political shifts, counseling may become a low priority in a multi-purpose agency. Grants are sometimes not reauthorized or refunded. Administrative supervisors, then, are required to make such adjustments as cutting 10% off the top of their current budgets, or reducing their staff costs by large percentages. Such cuts, particularly if they recur for an extended period of time, can cause counseling departments to be understaffed, and work in inadequate facilities with outdated equipment, and insufficient materials.

In responding to their departments' fiscal resources being severely insufficient, administrative supervisors have two basic choices. They can cope and make necessary adjustments, or they can leave the situation. The latter option is, typically, not desirable in that it entails losing one's job or abandoning one's clients and staff members. Some of these situations, however, do become untenable (e.g., requiring unethical practices). The profession's ethical standards suggest that if you are unable to change an unethical work situation, you should leave it (ACA, 2005; AMHCA, 2000). You also need to remain conscious of your vulnerability to liability for allowing malpractices.

Most economically challenging situations cause administrative supervisors to adapt. Because fiscal resources are finite (i.e., not expandable), it is essential that you operate within their limitations. While you modify what you can, you must maintain quality services for your clients and a professional climate for your staff. You make adjustments that do not jeopardize the validity of your original requests and long-term goals. The only way not to undermine the quality of your future is to ensure that your rationale for the cuts you make in the present is sound. You continue to strive to get as much funding as possible, based on sound justification.

To make large budget adjustments, you may have to alter the department's priorities, and change the design for the service delivery system. The severity of your cutback dictates the amount of your budget cuts. Typically, administrative supervisors decrease or eliminate costs associated relative to how essential they are to client-counselor working relationships. This order, on a continuum from least to most, may be consultants, continuing education, inservice training, services (e.g., for maintenance), supplies and printing, equipment and materials, furniture, rent, and salaries. Not attending to any of these over an extended period of time threatens the quality of the services. A harsh reality is the 80% of the budget that goes to staff salaries. When in dire economic straits, you make hard choices between downsizing your staff and letting the work environment deteriorate.

No matter the severity of the economic shortfalls, you manage what money you do have using the tools previously described, such as being accountable, ensuring appropriate and efficient spending, monitoring and tracking the money, and keeping accurate books.

You also attend to your staff members' morale. With or without money, you can create a great place to work through fostering healthy and meaningful interpersonal relationships, meeting individuals' values, and other non-cost items. It is essential that administrative supervisors provide honest information and rationale to help supervisees understand the depressed budget in light of the larger context (e.g., agency, community, funding sources). You do not blame those above you; in the eyes of your supervisees, you are one of "them" too. If you have been transparent with them throughout the budget development processes, your staff members' readiness for adjusting to the negative circumstances is improved. One year I developed three different budget proposals in sequence: one for a 10% across the board cut, one for maintaining the same bottom line as the department's previous year's budget appropriation, and one consisting of individual improvements for separate prioritizing of expenditures across the agency. Helping staff members follow that was quite a challenge! As often as possible, you engage them in the process and its decisions. You can ask them to help set priorities for necessary changes.

If you are in an agency with multiple departments and specialties, you will also experience shifts in relationships with your peers. Contributing to the usual turf-related tensions, you add competition for the same shrinking dollar.

Although this, too, has its challenges, it is wise to work hard to maintain the good will of your colleagues from other departments. If your budget is suffering because of lessening or lack of political support, it is wise to hone your advocacy and political skills—to work to shore up your political resources.

POLITICAL RESOURCES

Your political resources are those that support getting things done on behalf of your clients, service delivery system, counselors and other staff members, and agency. They include policies, such as local, state and federal laws, regulations and procedures, and the profession's statements of standards. They include people who pass such policies and standards.

Use Your Power Bases and Political Skills Effectively

Appropriate use of your power bases (expertise, information, referent, legitimate, reward, connection, coercive) combined with effective use of your political skills (e.g., communication, relationship building, negotiation, compromise, confrontation, consultation, conflict resolution, problem solving) supports your capacity to influence other people's behaviors, attitudes and values—to be a change agent. You consciously develop your political resources by learning the formal and informal power structures within and outside your agency. You, then, foster your relationships with key people, those whose support and other resources your department needs. Key people include your staff members, agency administrators, executives and board members, related professionals, clients, and other consumers (e.g., clients' family/support systems). You position yourself well by sharing your resources that others want (e.g., your expertise, fiscal or political support).

To be most effective politically, you use your power well. When you use a power base that is appropriate to a situation, it strengthens that power base. If you do not use a power base or if you misuse it, the strength of that power base is eroded (Hersey et al., 2001). You use your power bases to educate and empower key people to support your department as it seeks improvements that would better serve your counseling clients, and, in turn, help you achieve your mission and client objectives. An all-too-frequent example is when constituents opposed to counseling actively criticize the work of the department. It is your responsibility to work with your administrators and policy-setting board members to help them understand the expertise of counselors, and be ready to take supportive positions that are not in conflict with their own basic belief systems.

Develop Policies and Rules

By using your power bases, political influence and skills effectively, you are also able to enlist the support you need from policy- and rule-makers that results in the passage of policies and rules that support the values and purposes of the counseling department. By skillfully enlisting the support of administrators and colleagues, you are able to develop regulations and procedures that support your mission. This often entails your drafting such regulations and procedural guidelines. By enlisting the support of staff members, administrators, colleagues and policy-setters, you are better able to hold staff members accountable for adhering to ethical and other professional standards in their counseling work.

Use Information Channels

By developing information channels, you are able to use them for establishing the policies, rules, regulations and procedures and for promoting professional standards and principles. Having and communicating information is a source of power. You strengthen your relationships with staff members, co-workers and administrators by communicating information to them that they need, want and can use. By having information about what is happening in the agency as a whole, your staff members make more sense of their work context (Weick, 1995). By having information about the counseling clients, delivery system and staff, your agency co-workers and administrators develop better understanding of your department's mission and needs for support.

Manage Your Department's Reputation

Your ability to influence others—to use your power—is based on others' perceptions. The reputation earned by the counseling agency or department directly affects its support and, often, its funding. Thus, you and your staff members are responsible to recruit mission-relevant clients and build respected, professional reputations. Reputations begin with satisfied clients, but expand to include satisfied policy setters, funding agencies, potential investors, referral sources, and the local mental health and medical communities.

When you are politically adept, you understand others' counseling-related agendas well enough to assess their perceptions about your department, its services and staff members. By gathering this data systematically and objectively, you are able to develop and implement plans for improving your department's operations and enhance others' perceptions. Resnick (2004) recommends steps for developing a reputation management plan: first, you identify important areas for maintaining a good reputation (e.g., clients and client services); second, you identify key stakeholders for that topic area; third, you assess specific stakeholders' opinions or extract them from the original perception data; and, fourth, you analyze the data to identify the most significant issues, develop specific action plans to address them, and prepare tailored responses (Chapter 7).

Market

"I spend a great deal of time on marketing strategies" (S. D. Clifford, August 14, 2005, personal communication). Whether your department is publicly or privately funded, your purposes are well served by implementing marketing, advertising and public relations strategies (Drucker, 1998; Herr et al., 2006; Whyte & Martin, 2000).

There are ethical standards (ACA, 2005, C.3; AMHCA, 2000, Principles 1, 12 & 13), and, in some states, legal standards to guide your advertising practices (e.g., *Texas Administrative Code*, §681.49). Marketing is a form of advocacy—helping clients find and use the services they need. It also contributes to the public image of your department and agency. Again, you use specific messages as you target the agendas of different groups of people you want to influence.

SUMMARY

As a responsible administrative supervisor, you acquire, allocate and manage the human, fiscal, and political resources that support your department's clients and work. To do this, you develop your own resource management systems and understand those of others. You consult and collaborate with experts from disciplines that share responsibility for each of the resources (e.g., human resources, finance management, and public information departments).

SUPERVISORS' CHALLENGES AND RESPONSES

Supervisors' Challenges: Misuse of Resources

Many administrative supervisees misuse their work time. Some seem to be unable or unwilling to manage it; some are unable or unwilling to develop efficient organizational systems. Sometimes the result of these incapacities is their feeling stressed or burned out. One of the most prevalent concerns of supervisees is that their workloads are unreasonable. Many counselors, for example, believe that having lower caseloads would solve their issues. All too often they fail to take ownership of or fully develop their own systems for managing their time or organizing their work efficiently.

Supervisors' Responses

Effective administrative supervisors recognize that both time management and organizational systems are idiosyncratic. Individuals must find their own organizational styles, ones that are effective for them and meet professional guidelines (Borders et al., 1991). Administrative supervisors hold them as goals in supervision and performance improvement. They strive to help their supervisees understand that "We cannot manage time. We can only manage *ourselves* in relation to time. We cannot control how much time we have; we can only control how we use it. We cannot choose *whether* to spend it, but only how" (Mackenzie, 1997, p. 13).

As with other developmental issues, effective administrative supervisors' methods for helping supervisees depend on their supervisees' needs for directiveness. They work with individual supervisees, using approaches suggested by their assessed levels of professional development in the situation (Chapter 10). They consider the supervisees' levels of competence and motivations, and select appropriate responses. They draw upon the full range of their power bases, including suggesting resources or using rewards and sanctions. Sometimes they discipline supervisees who are stubbornly resistant to changing their ways (Chapter 4).

17

Improve Continuously the Counseling Service Delivery System

In establishing and operationalizing the vision, mission and goals of their counseling departments, and analyzing their current delivery systems in that light, effective administrative supervisors and their supervisees identify areas where improvements would enhance their client services. "Whatever an enterprise does internally and externally needs to be improved systematically and continuously" (Drucker, 1999, p. 80). It is an ethical responsibility of counselors to "attempt to affect changes" in policies or practices that are "damaging to clients or may limit the effectiveness of services provided" (American Counseling Association [ACA], 2005, D.1.h). Administrative supervisors are responsible for leading these changes (Falvey, 1987), risk-taking, causing innovations (Hersey, Blanchard & Johnson, 2001), creating and sharing knowledge (Fullan, 2001); and, thereby, continuously improve productivity, "one of management's most important jobs" (Drucker, 1974, p. 111).

To lead these improvements effectively, you understand about incremental improvements in a service delivery system; establish an improvement-oriented climate; guide your supervisees to make needed improvements; and manage the process they use in making these efforts. Your experiences in helping your clinical supervisees improve their clinical work, and in improving your own counseling and clinical supervision services and activities to better serve your clients and supervisees give you a foundation for carrying out these responsibilities.

UNDERSTAND THAT BIG CHANGES RESULT FROM MANY SMALL ONES

When you and your supervisees envision a re-designed service delivery system as an operational reality, the overall changes you need may be dramatic.

> Change is the engine which drives success. . . . Change. Here is a word that causes some to shudder, while others welcome it as an opportunity to make things better. But have no doubt—without change, . . . individuals . . . will stagnate, putting their future at risk. (Roberts, 2005, p. 8)

Energy to change stems from awareness of the discrepancies between the current reality and the new vision and design (Hersey et al., 2001).

Understand that it may take several years to achieve your vision, and be patient. As the Chinese proverb states, "The man who removes a mountain begins by carrying away small stones." You guide each of your supervisees to take steps toward the vision, to make incremental improvements that, when aggregated across the staff and over time, shift your delivery system to better match the design you desire for your clients. After 15 years of leading the development, design and implementation of a "new" delivery system, I still spent 8–10% of my time supporting staff members in accomplishing targeted program improvements (Henderson, 1999, 2001).

Incremental Improvements

Incremental improvements are first order changes, ones that are within individuals' control or influence. You support supervisees as they try to step out of their comfort zones and make changes in their daily job behaviors. Individuals' job performance is the result of decisions made moment-to-moment. "The sum of these tiny decisions—let's say a thousand a day—is your performance for the day" (Buckingham & Clifton, 2001, p. 57). These, of course, aggregate for the week and for the year. Thus, changing specific ways individuals do their jobs is how meaningful improvements happen.

> There's little meaningful difference in the innate abilities of star performers and average workers. Rather, the real differences turn up in the strategic ways top performers do their jobs . . . When companies promote such strategies systematically, individual professionals not only improve but also pass along the benefits to their colleagues and the company's bottom line. (Kelley & Caplan, 1993, p. 129)

You and your supervisees face the challenge of making these improvements while you are still carrying out your day-to-day responsibilities. Some of your supervisees may see it as trying to do two jobs at once—their current job and a future one. By making good use of opportunities that present themselves in the agency environment, you also facilitate changes (Gysbers & Henderson, 2006). For example, if the entire agency is shifting its focus to enhancing clients' career development, improvements in your career counseling services are supported by these broader efforts.

ESTABLISH IMPROVEMENT-FOCUSED ENVIRONMENTS

Set the Tone

To foster improvements, you "set the tone and pace, [and] . . . create an atmosphere" (Roberts, 2005, p. 8) that encourages and supports risk-taking. Your attitude encourages growth in others as well as yourself. You work with your supervisees to help them make sense out of changes that occur and will continue to occur in the department (Weick, 1995). You "establish an attitude of desire for change and receptiveness to suggestions for change" (Roberts, 2005, p. 10). When administrative supervisors want to encourage innovation by their employees, they establish:

> an environment characterized by incentives for learning and long-term achievements (cf. Erez, Gopher & Arzi, 1990). In this environment employees will be encouraged and motivated to be involved in highly challenging and risky [changes], with the expectations that achieving these [changes] may require some time and can be associated with temporal failures. (Fried & Slowik, 2004, p. 419)

As with other aspects of supervision, you facilitate your supervisees' growth by delicately balancing "challenge and support" (Standards, 1990, 4.8). You let your supervisees know you expect improvements, and that they will be evaluated on their commitment to carry them out. Supervisees are most willing to change when they trust you and feel secure in the supervisor-supervisee relationship. Acknowledge that change comes more readily for some of them than for others.

Establish Learning Communities

Another means for promoting comfort for your supervisees as they change their daily work behaviors is to build a learning community—a place where learning and growth happen continuously and comfortably. Enduring learning occurs through three interrelated activities: research, capacity building and practice (Senge, 1997); that is, from study, knowledge and skill development, and applications of new learning. "Learning occurs between a fear and a need" (Senge, 2004b, p. 5). Senge describes a:

> paradox of learning. When we claim we want to learn, we mean that we want to acquire some new tool or technique. When we see that to learn we must look foolish or let another teach us, learning doesn't look so good. . . . Only with the support, insight, and fellowship of a community can we face the dangers of learning meaningful things. (p. 5)

"Learning organizations are spaces for conversations and concerted action. In them language functions as a device for connection, invention, and coordination" (Senge, p. 4).

"Learning often occurs best through 'play,' through interactions where it is safe to experiment and reflect" (Senge, 2004b, p. 5). Through play, you encourage risk-taking, and see failure as learning opportunities—Senge calls them "surprises." When you and your staff are a community of learners, "surprises are seen as chances to grow, not as frustrating break-downs for which somebody must take the blame" (p. 4). A community of learners harnesses the intelligence and spirit of the group (Senge, 1997).

To underscore the importance of improvement, you spend time in staff meetings discussing new ideas, experiences, successes and surprises—theirs and yours. Improvement is a recurrent theme in formal and informal conversations, including your own progress toward improvement goals as well as those of your supervisees. You acknowledge your supervisees' new and improved accomplishments. You nurture "learning in context" (Fullan, 2001, p. 125), capitalizing on learning from the activities that are done, the relationships that exist, the ideas that grow out of supervisees' daily work. Fullan describes it as "learning in the dailiness of organizational life" (p. 130).

GUIDE SUPERVISEES IN IDENTIFYING AND COMMITTING TO IMPROVEMENT OBJECTIVES

You guide your supervisees as they identify and commit to individual improvement objectives. Together you identify what needs to be improved and what needs to be systematically abandoned (Drucker, 1999).

> Objectives are not fate; they are direction. They are not commands; they are commitments. They do not determine the future; they are means to mobilize the resources and energies of the business for the making of the future.... They are aimed at doing rather than good intentions. (Drucker, 1974, pp. 102–103)

Meaningful individual objectives are clear, well defined and measurable (Hersey et al., 2001).

Objectives for service delivery system improvement are different from goals (Chapter 15). Goals are general targets. Examples of goals are to increase the small group counseling services we provide, or to decrease the amount of client time we spend on paperwork, or to enhance our responsiveness to Mexican-American clients. Objectives are more specific than goals, i.e., it takes a collection of objectives to fully attain a goal.

Service delivery system improvement objectives are different from the performance improvement objectives discussed in the context of the *performance management system* (Chapters 10 and 13). The latter focus on the quality of supervisees' competence, motivation or commitment. Service delivery system improvement objectives are different than *implementation* objectives for maintaining effective and efficient aspects of the in-place system (Chapter 15). Objectives for *improving* the service delivery system focus on the quantity and effectiveness of the *services and activities* done with or on behalf of clients. You have to make these subtle distinctions clear for your supervisee. Sometimes they become confused because, while the outcomes are different, the process for developing and implementing them is the same (goal-based, action plan driven).

You facilitate your supervisees' moving forward successfully by targeting their efforts, ensuring that each objective has one simple purpose (Koch, 1998). An example of an activity improvement objective related to the first goal above is, "I will provide three process groups per week to help clients become more competent in solving relationship problems." One for the second goal is, "I will consolidate the reporting forms used by all staff members to eliminate redundancy." And, for the third, "I will change our intake procedures and translate our forms to accommodate our Spanish-speaking clients."

You also make distinctions for your supervisees between objectives with concrete timelines and exact measures, and "do your best" objectives, identified for complex jobs and requiring more latitude regarding time and accomplishment (Fried & Slowik, 2004). The latter are useful for innovation and exploration; the former for periods of application of knowledge already acquired.

Identify and Select Relevant Objectives

You guide your supervisees as they identify and select relevant objectives that, when achieved, will make high priority improvements in the system. "Here the concept is to identify better ways of doing business, removing waste and toppling the obstacles which stand in the way of change" (Roberts, 2005, p. 8). The service delivery system consists of interrelated activities. For individuals to identify ways to improve how they carry out their parts of the system, they examine the activities they do.

Your supervisees might be challenged to discern what objectives would make important changes in their own part of the service delivery system. A direct way to do this is to ask them to examine the quality of each activity for its effectiveness and efficiency—its relative value in contributing to achieving the department's mission, and its relative cost in spending their resources (e.g., talent, time). To encourage their thinking about improvements, you suggest they ask questions, such as, "Why am I doing this activity? Does it have to get done at all? Does it contribute to the business?" "Is there a faster (or more effective or better) way to do it?" "Are we doing tasks in the right order?" (Roberts, 2005, p. 9) A basic question related to their resource use is, "Am I using my time efficiently?" "Am I organized well enough to do this activity effectively *and* efficiently?" "Does this activity require a Master's Degree in counseling?" "Who else could do this job?" Some example questions to ask about establishing linkages with co-workers are, "What am I working on that relates to what someone else is doing?" "How does our work dovetail?" "How could we work together?"

Individual supervisees may need you to assist as they analyze the relevance, effectiveness and efficiency of what they are currently doing. One way you can do this is by using an analysis grid (Nickols & Ledgerwood, 2006). As displayed in Figure 17.1, the grid "is a simple 2 × 2 matrix constructed by examining the answers to two very basic questions: Do you want something? And Do you have it? Both questions can be answered Yes or No" (Nickols & Ledgerwood,

Figure 17.1 Analysis Grid*

	We Have It	
	/No	/Yes
Yes/	Yes/No *Small group counseling for young children* *Holding psychoeducational events for clients' significant others*	Yes/Yes *Individual counseling for young children* *Multidisciplinary client case conferencing*
We Want It No/	No/No *Completing clients' food stamp application forms* *Conducting "bed checks" in residence hall*	No/Yes Too much/Streamline *Writing client notes* *Attending staff meetings* Inappropriate/Eliminate (Displace) *Covering reception desk for lunch hour* *Moving furniture for different events*

* Adapted from Nickols & Ledgerwood, 2006

p. 36). Lists are built in each quadrant, typically by individuals separately, and, then, are aggregated into group lists. The first decisions made are identifying activities that are had or not, and whether they are wanted or not. The second set of decisions consists of clarifying what to do to improve the service delivery system. The examples in each quadrant of the figure are offered for illustrative purposes.

Improving your system may mean adding, augmenting, streamlining, displacing or avoiding activities (Gysbers & Henderson, 2006). If something is in the design and wanted (yes/yes), then the objective is to keep it. If something is not wanted and is in the design (no/yes), then the objective is to displace or eliminate it. If something is there, but there is too much of it, the objective is to streamline it. If something is wanted and not there (yes/no), then the objective is to add it. If something is neither wanted nor had (no/no), then the objective is to avoid it.

An example of adding a new, more valued activity is, "I will offer a new small group for grieving 6–8 year old children." An example of augmenting existing, valued activities is, "I will provide individual counseling for the 4–5 year olds in the small grief counseling group." An example of streamlining the time or effort appropriated to an activity is, "I will decrease the time I spend on making client notes to 1 hour a day." Improvements occur when you eliminate or displace non-counseling activities by delegating them to someone better suited. Displacement entails another person or department, and collaboration with those others is essential. They, then, have to accept the change, and the displacer has to work for a smooth transition. An example of an objective that targets displacing an activity is, "I will develop a protocol for the receptionist to use when answering phone calls that are part of the intake process" (Gysbers & Henderson, 2006).

Commit to Appropriate Objectives

You help your supervisees select objectives in ways that secure their commitment to accomplishing them. Setting their own objectives is motivating (e.g., Hersey et al., 2001; Huisken, 2006; Seijts & Latham, 2005). It allows them to have some power over their jobs and their professional working conditions (Davenport, Thomas & Cantrell, 2002). It liberates them (Hersey et al., 2001). Commitment to objectives is enhanced by their perceived importance and by "individuals' belief that they can attain" them (Fried & Slowik, p. 407).

You allow your supervisees as much autonomy as they can handle, given their developmental levels. Supervisees at high developmental levels handle a lot of autonomy over their objectives. They pick ones that are important to improving the department's services, and believe they can attain them. Unfocused supervisees often need direction in selecting important objectives, and encouragement about their capacity to attain them. Disengaged supervisees often need to be challenged to set appropriately high objectives, and encouraged to see their readiness to attain them. Supervisees at low developmental levels need to be directed to appropriate objectives, aided to see their importance, and encouraged to pursue ones they feel they can attain.

You guide your supervisees to aim for objectives that are at appropriate levels of difficulty, and yet are attainable (Fried & Slowik, 2004). Objectives may be set at minimum, actual or stretch levels (Huisken, 2006), or be safety, realistic or barrier breaking (Hersey et al., 2001). They may be performance or learning objectives (Seijts & Latham, 2005). The former relate to applications—e.g., I will see 20 more clients this year than last. The latter "focus attention on knowledge or skill acquisition" (p. 125)—e.g., I will learn how to terminate my groups in 6–8 weeks. "Managers might also consider strategically arranging the difficulty level of assignments for which employees are responsible, . . . appropriately balancing between easy and difficult assignments across time" (Fried & Slowik, p. 419).

MANAGE THE PROCESS FOR IMPLEMENTING OBJECTIVES

Improvement Process

For supervisees to operationalize your shared visions, you lead them through an ongoing, systematic process that promotes continuous improvement. They set service delivery system improvement objectives annually. Depending on the degree of challenge involved for a supervisee, one to three objectives per year is sufficient. As with implementation objectives, improvement objectives are written down.

While objectives are individual commitments, they also impact the work of the department as a whole. Identifying objectives for making small system improvements is done by individuals in the group context. In established learning communities or in team-oriented departments (Chapter 12), individuals may choose to work with other individuals on similar, related objectives. "General-systems-theory thinking [is] the mode of thinking that involves viewing a particular problem not in isolation, but as the problem is connected to, and therefore interrelated with, other problems" (Napier & Gershenfeld, 2004, p. 255). When your group is healthy, synergy catapults attainment of their objectives and goals—and yours. Share the collection of staff members' objectives with the entire staff, so that, while each individual is working on individual objectives, they are aware that they relate to the overall goals of the department (Chapter 15). Staff members also are better able to support each other's achievements.

Action Plans

In order to minimize the chances of you or your supervisees spending more energy or resources than is necessary, Koch (1998) advises workers to "Plan before you act . . . [and] Design before you implement" (p. 122). You collaborate with each of your supervisees as they define what they will do to achieve their objectives. You create, disseminate, and collect completed forms that support the action planning process. In developing action plans, supervisees think through *how* they will pursue objectives they have committed to (Chapters 10 and 13). They are tools that facilitate individuals thinking into the future, but with a foothold in reality. You supervise them, consistent with their assessed professional developmental levels, in developing their plans.

The action plans provide a means for staff members to be accountable to themselves, the department and you for doing what they say they will do. They also provide a basis for evaluating their levels of achievement of their objectives. One action plan is designed for each objective. You distribute and have staff members use a form that facilitates and records the process. Figure 17.2 provides a format we use that is easily completed.

In the first column, supervisees list the tasks they will do to achieve an objective in the order in which they will do them. These are listed as separate, discrete steps. If they envision working with someone else, they name them in the second column. Resources they think will be useful are identified in the third column. The fourth column identifies the targeted date of completion for each task. Hereafter, the form addresses completion. The actual date of

Figure 17.2 Counseling Service Delivery System Improvement Planning Form

Goal:

Objective:

Tasks/ Steps	People Involved	Resources	Timeframe	Date of Accomplishment	Results/ Comments	Follow-up Actions
1.						
2.						
3.						
4.						

Counselor's Signature: _____   Supervisor's Signature: _____

accomplishment of a task is recorded in the fifth column. Space is provided in the sixth column for supervisees to state the results or make other comments regarding the specific task. If subsequent actions are needed to complete the task, they are noted in the final column.

You encourage supervisees to be as creative as possible in developing their plans. Leading them through an initial brainstorming of possible steps to take helps them to generate robust plans. In some instances, you suggest specific tasks. As one new supervisor advises, "Don't be hesitant to put out new ideas and strategies for your staff" (Y. K. Steves, personal communication, June 16, 2005). Encourage supervisees to look outside themselves and their departments for ideas and resources (e.g., to their profession, or agencies). In a one-to-one conference, each of them submits their proposed action plans to you for review, approval, and support. At the end of the conference, both of you sign off on it.

As your supervisees implement their plans, you support them by monitoring and assessing their progress at regular, planned intervals. Monitoring does not need to be heavy-handed. Staff members work hard to succeed and are usually proud of their improvements, or they need some additional support from you. Establish timelines for monitoring their progress as it varies by a supervisee's professional developmental level. Impaired counselors may need weekly discussions. Star counselors may be self-directed enough to meet only quarterly or at mid-year. At the end of the year, you and your supervisees evaluate their levels of completion of each action plan, and degree of achievement of the objective. You also draw conclusions regarding the level of attainment of the targeted goal.

SUMMARY

In order to align the department's service delivery system with your vision, you lead supervisees in making incremental improvements. These entail individuals changing their daily work behaviors. You establish an environment that is improvement-focused and supports risk-taking. You guide your supervisees to identify, select and commit to individual objectives for improvement. You manage an ongoing, systematic process for guiding their implementation of action plans they developed to achieve their objectives.

SUPERVISORS' CHALLENGES AND RESPONSES

Supervisors' Challenges: Higher Order Thinking Skills

In guiding their staff members to develop service delivery improvement plans, administrative supervisors are challenged by their supervisees' inability to analyze their work activities systematically, to find the gaps between what they are currently doing and what is more desirable. Additionally, many lack creativity in finding ways to do things differently.

Supervisors' Responses

Challenge #1: Analyzing. Effective administrative supervisors teach their supervisees what "analysis" is and ways to do it. Analysis is breaking something into its component parts, and comparing and contrasting the parts against standards. An example of an exercise that guides supervisees to analyze their work is "Plusses and Minuses." In this exercise, individuals start with a piece of lined paper and divide it into three columns, titled "activities," "effectiveness," and "efficiency." In column 1, each person lists the activities that she/he does. In column 2, he/she rates the relative effectiveness of each activity by ranking each as compared/contrasted with each other. In column 3, they rate the relative efficiency of each activity in the same way. The least effective and least efficient, least effective or least efficient activities are appropriate targets of improvement objectives.

Challenge #2: Thinking creatively. It takes creative thinking to develop an action plan to achieve a new objective. If individuals already knew ways to improve activities, they would have done them. Therefore, their thinking must become "unstuck" (Napier & Gershenfeld, 2004, p. 319). Individuals may unstick their own thinking, but having the group of staff members work together broadens the number and ultimately the quality of the ideas that are generated. The task is to conceive of what a staff member could do to achieve a specific objective; it is not about what their objective should be.

The dyad or group is posed the question, "What steps could Patty do to add/augment/streamline/displace activity 'X'?" Examples of steps are 1st: talk to clients about their needs in this particular area; 2nd: re-design the activity; 3rd: arrange for a facility; 4th: develop worksheets; and on and on. Effective administrative supervisors often rely on one of the classic group techniques to bring out as many, different ideas as possible. They might rephrase questions, develop analogies, develop metaphors, line out different scenarios, lead the group in brainstorming (Remember the ground rules!), use a nominal group technique, conduct a round robin group, search for the wildest ideas the group can come up with, or do a synectics exercise (Napier & Gershenfeld, 2004).

18

Lead the Process to Plan, Design, Deliver, Evaluate and Enhance the Service Delivery System

To ensure clients are provided with the best services possible, administrative supervisors lead their staff members through a process to develop the activities and services for the year. In Chapter 15, a transformational process was described that began with building the foundation for the service delivery system (i.e., clarifying the values, vision, mission and goals of service delivery), and designing the priorities for and parameters of the department's work. The metaphor used for this process was building the foundation and internal structure of a house. It is recommended that that extensive process be reconsidered and redone every 5–10 years.

In Chapter 17, a process was described for annually making *improvements* in the service delivery system. In this chapter, an annual process is described for maintaining the responsiveness of the delivery system as a whole to its clients and to new trends in the environment—for keeping it *updated*. Here, the design decisions are more akin to determining whether to repaint or redecorate the house, and what furniture to keep or dispose of. Having not yet been addressed in this *Handbook*, your responsibilities in leading service delivery system evaluation are discussed also. Your experiences as a counselor and clinical supervisor in leading groups, and creating and evaluating client-appropriate interventions give you a foundation for carrying out these responsibilities.

USE A DEVELOPMENT PROCESS

Using the discipline of a delivery system development process better ensures the relevance, effectiveness and efficiency of the services and activities provided for clients each year. As depicted in Figure 18.1, it is a circular process, entailing planning, designing, delivering, evaluating, and enhancing the delivery system (Gysbers & Henderson, 2006).

Carrying out this process is best when all your department staff members do it as a team, having rich group discussions about client needs, learnings from evaluation data, creatively designing and redesigning activities, and fitting them into the timeframe of the year. To ensure staying in touch with your consumers, you also involve the department's advisors (e.g., the advisory group) and other agency administrators with a stake in your department's work.

Figure 18.1 Delivery System Development Process

You lead and are an active participant in redevelopment of the service delivery system. In participating, you fulfill several roles. You are a member of the staff, a member of the profession and responsible for upholding professional standards; and the link to your agency. Throughout the annual delivery system development process, you diligently keep your supervisees focused on implementing the department's operationalized vision, and true to your established values, mission and goals.

To be fully involved, you share your perspectives on the whole service delivery system and that of the agency, and provide information about the actual resources the department has to work with. You maintain open communication channels about the process and use your group process skills, and facilitate group risk-taking and decision-making. At the same time, recognize that you do not and should not have all the answers, but are a contributor to the creation of new ideas. As in other activities, you empower counselors and other staff members to contribute. It is their service delivery system.

PLAN THE UPCOMING YEAR

As one experienced, practicing administrative supervisor in counseling put it, "It is important to do department planning. . . . This helps in giving the department a unified mission (aligning activities, equity among [client subgroups], etc., and also helps in articulating to others the priorities for the department" (E. Zambrano, personal communication, June 14, 2005). Planning is a fundamental process used by administrative supervisors in counseling (Herr, Heitzmann & Rayman, 2006). To plan the service delivery system for the upcoming year, you lead supervisees in identifying new client needs and different ideas for meeting them, and by identifying, through evaluation, what worked well during the past year. You tie them together through a brief "SWOT" analysis.

Generate New/Different Ideas

Needs assessment. The department staff members begin these efforts by re-assessing the clients' needs. Society changes and within that the needs of clients change (Austin, 2002). This update does not have to be an exhaustive process—assuming the baseline needs assessment was thorough enough to be valid still. It should generate factual data, but can rely on a paper-pencil instrument or an input process. Process needs assessments involve consulting with experts, e.g., clients themselves, advisory groups, other services consumers, other specialists.

During the course of the year that was just completed, you and your supervisees learned much about the clients' needs as you provided services. A valid first step in reassessment is learning what the staff members learned from their clients, or lack of clients, their new or recurring issues. In reviewing this information and drawing conclusions from it, the need for new services became evident—"What pops out is that our kids need these groups: . . ., and not these: . . ." (M. L. Libby, personal communication, May 6, 2005). You note these, so that in the designing phase, you can reconsider them. You and your supervisees do not leap to conclusions, but base conclusions on careful and accurate analysis of data. Strive to accept reality and avoid defensiveness— even if pet projects are not needed.

Advisory group. As the planning efforts begin, seek input from your department's advisory group, whose primary task is to help keep your counseling services relevant to your clients. Typically, these groups ("committee," "council," "consumer panel") consist of clients, client representatives, client family members, other related service providers, and/or entities that refer clients to the counseling department.

For such groups to function effectively, you convene meetings regularly, but not often (e.g., quarterly). To keep them contributing, engage the members in meaningful discussions (Lees, 2004). It sets a tone of openness if you inform them how their previous ideas and suggestions were used. Ask them directly for feedback about current services, and for input about improvements or new ideas. It is essential to be cognizant of the various agendas individual members might have (Chapter 7). Some of these are idiosyncratic; others may have more general validity. Distinguishing between the two without embarrassing individuals is essential to a successful advisory group.

Administrative input. Your administrators often have feedback and new ideas from the agency's perspective about what might improve the department's services. You elicit their input directly. The best insights and inputs come when these relationships are based on trust. When they are trustworthy, administrators and executives are invited to be candid, and, perhaps, speak "off the record." If your relationships are not solid, seek their input, but use your best political skills. In these conversations, again, avoid defensiveness. You "seek first to understand" (Covey, 1989, p. 11). And, then, if it is appropriate, "seek to be understood" (Covey, p. 11).

Professional trends. As a professional, you identify trends in the profession that are relevant to your department's services (Cottringer, 2004). Professional standards are developed and refined continually. Counseling is still an emerging field. It is your ethical responsibility to keep your program aligned "with current guidelines and standards of ACA [American Counseling Association] and its divisions" (Association for Counselor Education & Supervision [ACES], 1993, 3.01).

Keeping abreast of new standards informs you and your supervisees as to service enhancements that are called for (e.g., ideas for implementing the mental health recovery model, using evidence-based practices, improving alignment with the American School Counselor Association [ASCA] Model for School Counseling Programs [2005]). Agencies change. They make (or do not make) policy changes. New funding sources are found (e.g., grants from foundations supporting mental health), or new funding mechanisms devised (e.g., new contractual agreements). These, too, have implications for improving your services.

Identify What Is Right Currently

While getting a lot of feedback, including or focusing on desired changes, it is important to identify what is relevant, effective, efficient, successful or important about what is currently being done—the activities and services to keep. These are probably candidates for fine-tuning, but they belong in the delivery system.

The evaluation done at the end of the previous year suggested what was done that worked and what did not. You and your supervisees considered this data in the enhancement phase of the process and made some tentative recommendations for the new year's delivery system. You bring these back to the table at this time.

The planning group(s) considers the level of achievement of implementation (Chapter 15) and improvement objectives from the previous year (Chapter 17), and their importance for the upcoming year. If they were successful, there will be logical next steps to be taken to incorporate them or expand them as permanent parts of the delivery system. At this point recommendations are made about specific enhancements or new improvement objectives. Final decisions, however, are made when the overall design is tempered by the reality of time—i.e., when you develop the annual calendar.

Draw Conclusions

The planning phase ends with your summarizing what has been learned from the search for new directions and ideas, and from understanding what has been right or not about previous activities and services. A way for you to facilitate drawing conclusions is to have the group do a brief "SWOT" analysis—a process described in strategic planning (McNamara, 1999). Through it you identify the strengths and weaknesses (SW) of the in-place system operations, and the opportunities and threats (OT) in the internal or external situation that might either enhance or hinder the department's ability to meet its goals. Through this exercise you and your supervisees determine what should stay (the baby), and what should go (the bath water). You begin to decide what you will add to replace what is being dropped (in the new, clean bath water).

DESIGN

Develop Your Department's Annual Calendar

To design the service delivery system for the year, you lead supervisees in building an annual calendar for their services and activities. With a yearly plan, there is much more likelihood that the department will achieve its goals and operationalize its vision than if it docs not. As one administrative supervisor in counseling advises, "Plan a full guidance program calendar or you will end up being given non-guidance tasks" (Y. K. Steves, personal communication, June 16, 2005), or you will end up not accomplishing your priorities and goals.

In planning the year, you and your supervisees consider the resources available for the upcoming fiscal year. Changes in resources occur frequently— sometimes from quarter to quarter, most often from year to year. If the resources are the same, have been added to or taken away, you must reckon with changes in the finite parameters. Finally, new initiatives are considered. Agencies stress new projects or themes, new grants with specific targets, use of new technologies, and new clients might be knocking at the door. These, too, are considered in yearly planning.

Developing the yearly calendar of activities clarifies in some detail who will be doing what with whom, when and where (Gysbers & Henderson, 2006). It brings together the uses of all the resources, and is an outline of the activities for each week or month. It allows each staff member to know his or her roles and assignments within the plan, and you can assist them in and hold them accountable for carrying them out. The department's services and activities will be done intentionally.

How to build a yearly calendar. As a team with your leadership, you, first, establish the priorities for the year, that also reflect the design established in the vision for the service delivery system (Chapter 15). You, then, collaborate, discuss, compromise, negotiate and create the plan. When led effectively, this is a very fluid, but fun and energizing process. New ideas for implementing activities and services are recorded for future reference. Maintain worksheets (e.g., easel pad tear sheets) in order to preserve group memory. When you do this well, a lot of ideas are generated.

Planning-oriented administrative supervisors in counseling suggest the following steps in calendar development:

1. Discuss mission and context information (e.g., clients' and consumers' needs/wants, agency's needs/wants, counselors' needs/wants).

2. Reaffirm/re-establish priorities and parameters:
   1. List parts of the delivery system (e.g., individual counseling, group counseling, assessment) and specific activities done the previous year in each part.
   2. Identify known events (basic system activities).
   3. Identify new events (improvements).
3. Guesstimate time needed to do each activity for specific clients.
4. Review past year's evaluations, especially the calendar, and discuss the accomplishments, real priorities and gaps, what was done/not done, and consider why the "not dones" were not done.
5. Reassess the balance of time (percentages) established for the various parts of the service delivery system (Chapter 15).
   1. Consider what really happened.
   2. Establish a realistic ideal that would best meet clients' needs and maintain the integrity of the services.
6. Prioritize activities within delivery system parts—to ensure the likelihood of doing the most important ones.
7. Develop prototype weekly schedule.
   1. Overlay ideal implementation of system parts and time reality.
   2. Develop a prototype weekly calendar by plotting activity slots having considered:
      i.   Things that can be done when clients are not present.
      ii. Client appointment times (set activities; easiest to schedule; busiest times).
      iii. Other direct service activities.
      iv. Staff responsibilities.
      v.   A realistic amount time for unplanned events (e.g., unexpected client distress or crisis).
   3. Assign individuals to develop their own weekly schedules for their caseloads and other responsibilities.
   4. Estimate numbers of clients to be served.
8. Plot anticipated activities on a yearly calendar.
   1. Consider "life cycle" of a year (e.g., "holiday blues").
   2. Use information from #'s 2–7.
   3. Plot #1 priorities for each system part, #2's . . ., #3's . . . and so on.
9. Develop plans for disseminating the calendar to interested others (e.g., agency administrators and executives, advisory group), and for developing new activities.
       (E. Zambrano & P. Henderson, personal communication, 1998)

Having staff members sign off on the calendar demonstrates their commitment to the overall plan. Based on this group work, individual staff members develop their own responsibilities to the system: job description (Chapter 12), implementation objectives (Chapter 15), performance improvement goals/ objectives (Chapter 10), and system improvement objectives (Chapter 17).

Solicit Administrative Support

Once the calendar is completed initially, review it with your administrators and agency executives in order to secure their support for its implementation. Strong administrative support enhances the probability that the plan is viable and will be implemented. You, then, post the approved calendar for staff members to use, and for clients, consumers, colleagues and others to see.

ENSURE DELIVERY OF THE PLANNED ACTIVITIES

Use the Calendar as a Management Tool

To continue to lead your supervisees as they implement planned services, use the calendar as a management tool. Remember: The calendar is a planning document and provides a guide. It cannot be etched in stone as unanticipated events occur within the department, the agency, or the community. To use it effectively, revisit it regularly, not only to monitor, but also to make adjustments. Zambrano (personal communication, 1998) recommends that the staff as a whole debrief their experiences and refresh the calendar monthly. You consider what was actually done, what was missed and why, and what to do about it. You begin planning for the upcoming month, and check on progress toward longer-range plans. Staff meetings provide a means for updating and coordinating activities. Review, debriefing and re-planning supports staff members' efforts to track and be accountable for their work. I estimated that I spent an average of 7% of my time on delivery system management during an average year (Henderson, 1999, 2001).

Allocate Resources

The calendar also provides a means for allocating budgeted monies and the use of materials, facilities and equipment in line with the design and plans. The discussions regarding actual implementation provide a vehicle for solving problems in a timely manner. You are able to facilitate staff members' implementation of new assignments. The process for identifying new activities ensures that they are appropriate activities to add to the system. Doing them well is critical to their ongoing success. The clarified expectations for staff members' use of time supports efficient time, caseload and resource management practices, facilitating your effective administrative supervision.

EVALUATE

Distinguish Between Types of Evaluation

Three different types of evaluation are conducted: of staff members' performance, client results, and the completeness and improvements in service delivery

(Gysbers & Henderson, 2006). Each looks at and evaluates staff members' and clients' work together from a different point of view. Evaluation of staff members' performance focuses on their past job-related *behaviors*. Evaluation of *client results* focuses on changes in clients that occurred as a result of the work. Evaluation of the service delivery system focuses on the *services* and *activities* staff members provided to help clients. All three look at past events. Each of the three is valid. All three are valuable. "Evaluating clinical practice through the measurement of clinical performance and clinical outcomes is becoming increasingly important" (Krousel-Wood, 2000, p. 233). Evaluating the level of implementation of the designed delivery system informs future operations (Gysbers & Henderson, 2006).

We discussed evaluating staff members' performance as part of the performance management system (Chapters 13 and 14). In your administrator role, a major responsibility is to evaluate not only the performance of each staff member, but also the work of the total department (Drucker, 1974; Gysbers & Henderson, 2006; Lees, 2004). Counseling supervisors understand "the meaning of accountability and the supervisor's responsibility in promoting it" (ACES, 1989; Standards, 1990, 9.1). For school counselors, it is an ethical responsibility (ASCA, 2004a, A.3.a. & D.1.c, d, & g.).

According to Drucker (1974), managers in service institutions need to impose discipline on themselves.

> They need to define *measurements of performance* . . . They need to use these measurements to *feedback* on their efforts, that is to build *self-control from results* into their system. . . . They need an organized audit of *objectives and results*, so as to identify those objectives that no longer serve a purpose or have proven unattainable. . . . They need a mechanism for *sloughing off* such activities rather than wasting their money and their energies where the results are unsatisfactory (pp. 158–159).

Design An Evaluation Process

It is up to you to design how evaluating client outcomes and delivery system activities will be accomplished, following the process outlined in Figure 18.2.

You are responsible for helping your supervisees make connections between the various elements of the evaluation process (e.g., gathering data, comparing

---

Figure 18.2 Designing an Evaluation Process

1. Discuss purposes of evaluation and who will receive the results.
2. Define the evaluation questions.
3. Determine applicable standards.
4. Decide what data will be gathered, how and when.
5. Design the evaluation procedures and instruments.

it to standards, and making recommendations). You and your supervisees defined standards as a group in planning the year (i.e., desired client outcomes, delivery system design and calendar, delivery system improvements, resource use). Each individual is accountable to all four of these sets of standards.

You hold each staff member responsible for developing and contributing her or his own data to the data collection, and for analyzing them. You hold the group as a whole responsible for collecting, analyzing, and drawing conclusions from the aggregated data (Herr et al., 2006). You, with your supervisees' assistance, develop reports of the information gleaned and conclusions drawn through evaluation. You, then, provide that information to your administrators, executives, other policy makers, and advisory groups. You use it in planning the next year.

Implement the Evaluation Process

Through the evaluation process, you and your supervisees seek to learn the answers to such evaluation questions as: What did our clients gain as a result of our services? How many of them were served? Did we do what we planned to do? How well did our service delivery system work? How effective were the delivery system improvements we made? Did we make all of them we intended to make? How efficiently did we use our resources? To answer these evaluation questions, you gather and analyze objective and subjective data in light of the established standards. You draw conclusions based on this comparison.

What did our clients gain as a result of our services? How many of them were served? Abernethy and Lillis (2001) state that:

> measurement systems that capture the results of clinical activities serve the accountability role well. They create an accountability for outcomes while at the same time enabling professionals to maintain their desired autonomy over the "means" associated with performing complex tasks. (p. 113)

According to Krousel-Wood (2000), outcomes for clients are "a measure of the end result of what happens to patients as a consequence of their encounter(s) with the health care system; a construct of quality that reflects functional status, clinical end points, satisfaction; and/or cost" (p. 251).

To answer the questions about which and how many clients achieved results, you and your supervisees have more complete information when you gather data throughout the year. Standards are set in planning the year for the number of clients that will achieve what number of results. In planning their activities and services (e.g., counseling sessions or series of sessions, psycho-educational activities, case management and consultation conferences), effective staff members identify outcomes they anticipate clients will achieve. Such outcomes are classified as cognitive, affective, behavioral or social. They determine how they will gather data to assess client results, such as objective measures, end-result questions, ratings, observations, anecdotal records, or self-reports. In evaluation, they determine how many clients they actually served and the percentage of them that achieved each of the anticipated outcomes. Ultimately they determine the percentage of their total caseload that achieved what level of what results.

Did we do what we planned to do? How well did our service delivery system work? To answer the question whether a staff member and the department as a whole did what they planned to do, you, again, use the yearly calendar as your standard. You gather data through monitoring calendar implementation throughout the year. You get the information you need by identifying the activities that were done and not done, and tracking the changes in the plans. These data reflect what was done—the *implementation objectives* for the delivery system. To determine how well the activities worked, you refer back to the outcomes achieved by clients in the activities, and the analysis about what those data imply. You draw conclusions based on this data about the effectiveness of various activities.

Other data reflected in the implementation of activities are those regarding the applications of staff members' *competencies*: which of their competencies were used and in what proportion. A related set of data is that regarding the balance of staff members' use of their time in delivery system implementation. You and your supervisees ask and answer how time was used by comparing this data to the standards set for time use in the design (Chapter 15).

You and your supervisees analyze the effectiveness and efficiency of the *delivery system* as a whole, applying the standards which you set in its development (Chapter 12). You ask such questions as: Did the delivery system operate as an organized collection of staff members, services, activities, and processes focused on helping your clients? Were there gaps where clients were lost or delayed? Did the activities that were designed to be interrelated actually interrelate?

How effective were the improvements we made? Did we make all of them we intended to make? You set standards for making specific improvements in the service delivery system at the beginning of the year (Chapter 17). Again, measurement of their effectiveness ties back to the results achieved by clients through these improvements. Another question you ask is whether all of the intended improvements were actually made. Your review of the implementation of the yearly calendar and the levels of completion of the action plan provides data. You draw conclusions about their value as contributions to the whole delivery system.

How efficiently did we use our resources? The center of evaluation of resource use is efficiency. Within this main evaluation question you and your supervisees ask two other questions: How beneficial was a particular resource or set of resources? Did the resource justify its expense? Applying the 80/20 principle to resource use (Koch, 1998) suggests that it is possible, maybe probable, that 80% of your resources are spent to support achieving 20% of your client outcomes. You apply the 80/20 analytical and thought processes to identify and solve problems related to the misapplication of resources.

You and your supervisees conduct cost-benefit analyses as a means for evaluating the efficiency of your use of resources. Cost-benefit analyses "refer to the ratio of costs of providing such services to various populations for specific purposes compared with the economic and, sometimes, social benefits derived from such services" (Herr et al., 2006, p. 64). Examples of data that support cost-benefit analyses could include how many of your clients were served through use of a particular material, facility, piece of equipment, or benefited as a result of its use. From the perspective of an agency, cost-benefit questions are asked about the percent of the value received by the agency resulting from the overall cost of supporting, for example, the counseling department as a part of the agency's service provision system.

Respond to External Evaluation

Most mental health services agencies are regulated, accredited, and/or funded by government or private sources that have policy and/or regulatory authority over them. In order to ensure their resources (i.e., funds, licenses, certifications) are properly, effectively and efficiently applied, these bodies conduct external evaluations. Agencies, their administrators, *and* administrative supervisors are held directly accountable to these sources for the services they provided and/or the money they spent. You share responsibilities not only with agency administrators and managers, but also with administrative supervisors charged with carrying out related functions. To be effective, collaborate and communicate well with your colleagues and the external evaluators to get the fairest results from these evaluations.

Some external evaluations are conducted annually, or on other cycles (e.g., 3-, 5-, 10-years). It is key that you understand the purposes of a particular external evaluation (e.g., compliance, monitoring, accreditation, certification, audit). The oversight agencies establish the evaluation standards based on the criteria and rules established in the original application process (Chapter 16), and that, typically, provide guidelines for how and what data are relevant. In some instances, they draw their own conclusions; but many times they want the agency being reviewed to develop their own as well. To be responsible, participate actively in this process in addition to providing the required information.

External evaluations by these authorities essential to agency survival are high stakes affairs. They tend to make administrators, managers and supervisors anxious. Patterson (2000) offers some good advice about what to expect (Figure 18.3) and how to prepare (Figure 18.4) for them.

Figure 18.3 Common Themes of External Evaluation

Quality services
Professional & administrative competence
Appropriate range of services
Consumer/patient rights
Public safety
Funding & resource allocation
Measurable goals & objectives
Accountability
Adherence to basic principles:
   Legal compliance
   Appropriateness of services to client population
   Acknowledgment of the regulatory process & standards compliance
   Linkage of processes with service delivery & funding

Patterson, 2000

Figure 18.4 Patterson's Top 10 Considerations for Preparation for a Regulatory Review

1. Know your agency and population.
2. Know state, local & federal laws that are applicable to your facility and its practitioners.
3. Know the manual and standards of the appropriate regulatory agency.
4. Prepare for review throughout the implementation year. It is an ongoing process.
5. Define your organization for the regulators.
6. Keep accurate and needed documentation.
7. Provide ongoing training, education, and supervision to your supervisees.
8. Understand & present the agency's commitment to quality.
9. Prepare for the survey process.
10. Know your department, staff, facilities and other resources.

Patterson, 2000

ENHANCE

In sound practice, you do not let the evaluation work end with drawing conclusions. The final step in the delivery system development process, and the first step in moving forward is to make recommendations based on the findings. You continue to lead the department team as they discuss their reflections on the year just ending. You and your supervisees generate many ideas for future enhancements. If you capture them, they are ready for consideration when planning the subsequent year (e.g., by using tear sheets, recorded notes). Two sets of thoughts inform future service delivery system enhancements: (1) recommendations based on the conclusions drawn in evaluation of the past year; and (2) new information that comes to light (Gysbers & Henderson, 2006). Your planning-designing-delivering-evaluating-enhancing cycle continues.

SUMMARY

Implementation of a process for developing your service delivery system is a continuous cycle. One phase flows into the next. Each phase informs the phase before it and after it. You are responsible for managing the cycle. You and your supervisees base service delivery on a planned calendar of activities. You use client outcomes and delivery system evaluation results in planning system enhancements for the next year. The result is a continuously developing and improving service delivery system, one that gets increasingly better at meeting your clients' needs and helping them achieve desired results.

SUPERVISOR CHALLENGES AND RESPONSES

Supervisors' Challenges: Persuasion

Administrative supervisors face several challenges in leading their staff group through the annual process of re-planning, re-designing, re-delivering and re-evaluating their departments' service delivery systems. Some supervisees resist adhering to accountability procedures (e.g., logging their time, tracking case progress, maintaining their schedules and calendars). Some feel threatened by the potential outcomes of the data collections. Some are not diligent about following procedures and maintaining their records.

Some supervisees are reluctant to spend their energy on the annual process. They do not appreciate the discipline required in systems thinking. They may be bothered by the repetitiveness of the process ("We just did this last year!"). Some may be fearful of or anxious about what changes will be expected of them in the ensuing year. They may be content with how the system worked the previous year and just want to change the dates to reflect the upcoming year. Some may be apathetic. They do not grasp the importance of continuous improvement to their ever-changing clients, and to their own ethical responsibilities.

Some administrative supervisors, in the face of resistance, are tempted to do the re-planning and calendar development on their own, without involving their supervisees. They may think that doing this themselves will be less bothersome to their staff members. For some supervisors, doing the annual plan themselves is a method of trying to control the outcome. They do not understand the point that, in order to maximize their work with clients, each member of the group must own the delivery system.

Supervisors' Responses

Effective administrative supervisors understand that to fully deliver services and activities that value clients, and fully address the defined mission (Chapters 2 and 15) takes time. They understand that "slow knowing" (Fullen, 2001, p. 122) by their supervisees takes patience on their parts. Small steps towards excellence are taken deliberately.

Until the system development process becomes the way of life for the department, improvement-driven administrative supervisors do a lot of persuading of their staff members to continue to come along. "An effective manager uses persuasion to induce others to accept what is required of them without intimidation or threat" (Fracaro, 2004, p. 3). This process is based on the premise that excellent work is the result of a team approach (Chapter 12).

The art of persuasion for administrative supervisors is based on good leadership skills. It is based on having meaningful relationships with staff members (Chapter 9), and on being competent, credible leaders with enthusiastic and optimistic attitudes (Chapter 8). "The trick behind successful persuasion is getting people to make decisions on their own" (Weiss, 2003, p. 3). Persuading individuals to do things that might not originally have been their ideas requires an individualized approach: one that considers an individual's needs and wants, values, strengths and weaknesses (Chapter 10). Effective administrative supervisors work hard to avoid putting their staff members on the defensive (Weiss).

Fracaro (2004) suggests steps to take in persuading staff members about large or small issues. To be intentional in persuasion efforts, he recommends that supervisors plan their persuasion attempts: know what they want to accomplish, gather their evidence, consider how it can best be understood, anticipate where resistance will come from, and consider the most appropriate power base(s) to use.

They, then, meet individually with key people, people who influence others—typically the leaders in the informal power structure. They attend to each individual's needs and points. After these meetings, supervisors meet with the whole group. Again, administrative supervisors present their case with the needs of the clients and the department as a whole in mind and invite discussion. They manage well the inevitable resistance that crops up in the group. They avoid using demanding or assertive postures and overselling. After each meeting, they consolidate information; present it back to the group on paper for discussion in the next meeting. The last steps are to arrive at consensus, and follow-up.

VI

Administrative Supervisors: Strive Continuously for Excellence in Fulfillment of Their Administrative Supervision Responsibilities

- Develop Continually Your Own Supervisory Competence

19
Develop Continually Your Own Supervisory Competence

In striving to best serve their clients, their supervisees and their agencies, effective administrative supervisors in counseling pursue development of their own professional competence throughout their careers. "Management is work, and as such it has its own skills, its own tasks, its own techniques" (Drucker, 1974, p. x). Effective, administrative supervisors continuously develop knowledge and skills (i.e., competencies) that support carrying out their five responsibilities (to and for their clients, agency, department staff, service delivery system, and themselves); performing their 10 functions (i.e., holding to a purpose, developing people, contributing to the agency, fostering change, learning, managing, maintaining professionalism, being accountable, using systematic approaches, and resolving problems); addressing their 18 job objectives (*Handbook* chapters); using their seven power bases (i.e., legitimate, information, coercive, expert, referent, reward, and connection); and fulfilling their four roles (i.e., supervisor, manager, leader, and administrator).

"Managers are the most expensive resource in most businesses—and the one that depreciates the fastest and needs the most constant replenishment" (Drucker, 1974, p. 379). Additionally, when you are continually learning and growing, you set "an almost irresistible example" for your supervisees (Drucker, p. 427). There is no formulated package or process prescribing a learning path for you (Fracaro, 2004, p. 3), but in very general terms, there are three different phases of development for practicing administrative supervisors: preparation, beginning, and continuing. Becoming a professional administrative supervisor entails moving forward through these three phases: i.e., getting the job and getting started do not mark the end of your education and learning, but rather the beginning.

This chapter describes what you need to do to prepare for, and to start off well in an administrative supervisory position, and what you can do to continue to be successful throughout this dimension of your career. It closes with a "Self-Audit" that is intended for your use as a reflection tool for considering the array of administrative supervision competencies and skills, and where you perceive your competence levels to be. Your experiences in pursuing continuous professional development as a counselor and clinical supervisor support your efforts to do the same in this professional assignment.

PREPARE FOR NEW RESPONSIBILITIES

Developing competence as administrative supervisors begins with your decision to pursue this goal, and includes learning from prior experiences and benefiting from formal pre-service education. An ideal career path is to have depth and breadth of successful counseling (Standards, 1990, p. 30) and clinical supervision experiences. To be realistic, learn about what the job entails and make a conscious decision that it is what you want to do. Reflect on how your background, experiences, professional beliefs and goals match the opportunities and challenges presented.

At this time, there are not many formal education strategies that target administrative supervision in counseling. Many current administrative supervisors have pursued leadership and management education programs offered in related disciplines and tailored their learning to work with counselors. Others have pursued doctorates in counselor education and supervision and tailored their learning to administrative supervision.

Pre-service and continuing education training is recommended for counseling supervisors (Borders & Brown, 2005), and required by the American Counseling Association [ACA] Ethical Standards (2005) and for the Approved Clinical Supervisor certification (Center for Credentialing and Education [CCE]). The education and training experiences recommended in the *Standards for Counseling Supervisors* (Association for Counselor Education & Supervision [ACES], 1989; *Standards*, 1990; Appendix A) and the related *Curriculum Guide* (Borders et al., 1991) can be applied to administrative supervisors. Effective training for new administrative supervisors in counseling includes conceptual and experiential components (Borders et al. 1991; Loganbill, Hardy & Delworth, 1982). It entails didactic instruction, group supervision methodologies, and exposure to actual administrative supervisors at work.

GET OFF TO A GOOD START

Developing competence as a *practicing* administrative supervisor begins your first day of work in your new position. Typically new administrative supervisors are eager, but awed by what lies in front of them. You soon learn that what you have already learned from your experiences "is a useful indicator of future success, but it is by no means the only one" (Brousseau, Driver, Hourihan, & Larsson, 2006, p. 121). "To avoid bad beginnings, we believe that new administrators must hit the ground *learning*, rather than running . . . and develop a *process for learning*, rather than reflexively focusing on tasks" (Jentz & Murphy, 2005, p. 738). You learn as much detail about your new circumstances as you can in a short period of time.

Formal training facilitates your development during the challenging start-up and transition phase. When offered, these training opportunities are typically provided by the employing agencies. Effective induction training extends throughout your entire first year, with agendas that match the calendar for your new activities (Henderson & Gysbers, 1998). Specialized training is sometimes offered; e.g., agencies' human resources departments often conduct training for new evaluators of personnel performance to ensure you know the legal policies and guidelines. One training for new university department chairs supports a self-managed process of conducting structured interviews with key personnel in their universities—their agencies (Miller & Butler, 2004–05).

Learn Realities

In the beginning, there are a lot of details to learn about your new situation, especially if you are in an agency that is new to you. There are a lot of resources to explore, and you need to peruse them in a short time. Because of your new responsibilities and perspective on your work setting, you will find it helpful to start by reading your agency's governance policies, operational manuals, personnel policies, and the like. You might get overloaded with information, but you will know what the playing field includes, and where to find the specifics later when you need them. Seek clarity about what your new boss's expectations are, and become "aware of how you can best serve your organization with the skills your boss recognized when he or she promoted you" (Cottringer, 2004, p. 14). You also are best served by being open with yourself and with the boss about your current, but temporary limitations. Knowing them helps you set your first competence development goals. It helps when you get the right mindset about being the staff leader, and model the behaviors you want to see in others (Cottringer).

Learn as much as possible from your predecessor. Sometimes these conversations are inconvenient, for example, if the predecessor has retired, relocated or been promoted. Sometimes they are uncomfortable if the predecessor was moved over, demoted or terminated. Predecessors can share information about policies, practices and system links that are or have been in place. They can share insights from oral history from their perspective and tenure. These hints and insights allow for continuity from what was to what is and to what will be. They can help you to be aware of possible pitfalls and problems, assets and opportunities. As a new supervisor, it is your responsibility to initiate these contacts.

You are challenged to learn about your new responsibilities, and about the changes in perspectives, roles and relationships associated with them. As you accept responsibility for all of the department's counselors and other staff members, all of the department's and agency's clients, and the whole counseling department service delivery system and its impact on the agency's operations and the community, your perspectives shift. The farther you move out from your individual counseling office, the broader your perspective becomes—the more of the forest you discern, and the more trees you see in the forest.

Part of the change in your perspective that leads to success as a new administrative supervisor entails a shift in your loyalties. As a professional counselor, your primary loyalty has probably been to the counseling profession. Effective administrative supervisors hold loyalty to their organizations as high a priority as loyalty to the profession (Tsui, 2005). Most often there are not direct conflicts between the two, but when there are you face new challenges and, even, ethical dilemmas. Making properly balanced choices is key. Remember, part of what the agency wants from you is to inform others of the counseling profession's values and standards. Some new administrative supervisors have difficulty dividing their loyalties.

> In every organization there are people who are true specialists and who ... do not see themselves as part of management either. They want to remain specialists and are not, fundamentally, much concerned with the whole of which they are a part. Their allegiance is to their technical or professional skill, rather than to their organization. (Drucker, 1974, p. 394)

Without properly balancing these loyalties, you are apt to not accept responsibility for large chunks of your job.

Almost as soon as you walk into your new office, you feel conflicting pressures exerted by those above, below and beside you (Chapter 6). They come from those who are happy and those who are unhappy with the situation as it has been. They come from those who want and those who do not want to change. They come from those who had and who have not had power or voice in the previous situation. "The moment of job entry always seems rich with the possibility for productive change ... Of course, reality quickly sets in" (Jentz & Murphy, 2005, pp. 737–738).

First and foremost, seek to understand and carve out your new role appropriately (Harris, 2002). According to one successful administrative supervisor of counselors, new administrative supervisors "already have comfort and competence in their service provider and program implementer roles. They need to have their leadership role nurtured" (M. L. Libby, personal communication, September 5, 2006).

With shifts in responsibilities, perspectives and roles, you learn that there are differences in the rewards associated with administrative supervisory work. They come through working with others to provide better client services. Achieving your goals has broader implications and takes longer to accomplish. You add efficiency, cost effectiveness, to your criteria for providing quality services. It is best if you were aware of this before you decided to accept the position.

Understand Changes in Relationships

Also before you accept an administrative supervision position, it is important to anticipate and accept the changes that will occur in your relationships with clients and with colleagues. Some of the most unhappy and ineffective administrative supervisors I have worked with are those who long for more direct contact with clients and for peer relationships with counselors. Successful administrative supervisors work consciously to build different, but meaningful relationships (Jentz & Murphy, 2005).

If you were promoted from within your counseling department, the shift in your relationships with your colleagues may be the first and a somewhat painful thing you notice. You shift from relationships of equals as peer colleagues and friends to ones of unequals based on your agency's hierarchy (Cottringer, 2004; Harris, 2002). These changes are the result of the dramatic shift in power bases and responsibilities from colleague to supervisor. If you change agencies when you advance your position, you come in as a newcomer-who-is-now-the-boss, and who is also unknown as a colleague (Henderson & Gysbers, 1998). As described in Chapter 9, your relationships are fundamental to all of your work.

Another shift required of you in your "transition from peer to boss involves learning new behaviors" (Curtis & Sherlock, 2006, p. 120) associated with your shift in roles. As one administrative supervisor of counseling supervisors notes:

> The major issue I have seen is shifting from a supportive role (counseling) to a supervisory role. For many of our [supervisory] staff, they have a difficult time being firm and directive with their staff. They tend to work too hard at supporting the staff—which actually twists into a form of enabling unacceptable behavior/performance. Related to this is the tendency to attempt to work so much from a "team" perspective that they paralyze themselves from making critical administrative decisions. Again, motivated from a perspective of support, they fail to lead the subordinate staff. (P. E. McDaniel, personal communication, September 26, 2005)

To be effective, you have to deepen your understanding of what it takes to "help counselors be better counselors" (M. L. Libby, personal communication, September 5, 2006).

Most often new administrative supervisors are confused as they face these shifts. It helps if you clarify and reclarify your answers to the following questions:

> Why did I become a supervisor? Why do my former colleagues treat me differently? Why do I feel caught in the middle—between my workers and top management? How do I use the skills acquired in helping clients in my new job of helping workers? (Tsui, 2005, p. 74)

In conducting their induction training for over 20 years, I learned that it is healthy for new administrative supervisors to process their confusion and ambivalent feelings. It is a priority for the induction period. If you find yourself in an agency that does not provide such training, you are advised to work through those issues with others that you select with circumspection. Mentors, predecessors, the bosses that hired you, and highly professional staff members can serve these purposes. They each have different perspectives, so using a variety of sounding boards works well. Jentz and Murphy (2005) advise new administrative supervisors to:

1. embrace your confusion,
2. assert your need to make sense,
3. structure the interaction[s],
4. listen reflectively to learn, and
5. openly process your efforts to make sense. (p. 738)

As an administrative supervisor new to an agency, I found it very helpful to hold planned and scheduled interviews/conversations with the counselors and executives who were keys to carrying out my responsibilities, both within my office complex and at external sites. Following a template of information I wanted, I gained a lot of data from a variety of perspectives. Jentz and Murphy (2005) describe this as "a prelude to making changes" (p. 738). They label it an entry plan and believe that it is best when it is transparent, with no hidden agendas.

Two seemingly different pieces of advice are offered to you, pointing out why proceeding cautiously at the beginning is imperative. On the one hand, "You don't have the luxury of the typical trial and error learning curve; you have to get it right—right away" (Cottringer, 2004, p. 13) because your supervisees and bosses want to get to know how you work and challenge—even test—you. On the other hand you are advised to avoid "jump reflex problem solving" (Jentz & Murphy, 2005, p. 740). "Many new beginnings go awry because newly appointed administrators . . . reflexively hide their confusion and try to appear decisive by acting quickly" (Jentz & Murphy, p. 738). These early decisions made in haste and without sufficient information may cause more harm than good. "Little changes can trigger surprisingly big repercussions" (p. 740). Lots of effort and reflection is required to "do no harm" to clients, supervisees or your agency. When you are new, you do not always grasp how your decisions will impact others and department or agency policies and practices.

Begin Honing Two Fundamental Competencies

As detailed later on in this chapter, effective administrative supervisors apply many competencies. Regardless of your agency or counseling specialty, two are fundamental to your success: decision-making and managing your work. Both are used in professional counseling, but the shifts in responsibilities, perspectives, roles, relationships and behaviors underscore their importance in being effective, efficient and successful in your new job.

Decision Making

Decision-making is "the first managerial skill" (Drucker, 1974, p. 465), and the basis for many other supervisory processes (e.g., problem solving, evaluating, goal-setting, planning). You make decisions in planning activities and the yearly or quarterly scheme for service delivery. You make them when there are problems to be solved. Problems come in every sphere of the job, e.g., ethical dilemmas, client issues, staff issues, department issues, conflicts, and so on. Effective administrative supervisors exercise their decision-making skills consistently, in small decisions and in big ones. Staff members and others are "comfortable in following the decisions of a leader that has demonstrated that he or she has employed those skills on a routine basis" (Leyden, 2005, p. 8).

As you transition successfully from being a non-judgmental, client-centered, supportive counselor and clinical supervisor to a leader, you learn that you have to, at times, be firm about adherence to rules, standards, policies and goals and, at times, highly directive. Based on both your harsh and soft power bases, the power behind your decisions is stronger; the choices, often, more directive. A "leader should be intentional about developing these skills" (Leyden, 2005, p. 8).

You need to use a sound decision-making *process*. A viable process supports your ability to "answer questions with confidence. When you are confident with your decision, the staff are more comfortable about following it" (M. L. Libby, personal communication, September 5, 2006). The decision-making process is well described by various disciplines and, essentially, entails 8 steps (Figure 19.1).

Understand the decision. When it is clear that you need to make a decision, determine what the specific choice is. "There are few things as futile—and

---

Figure 19.1 Eight Step Decision-Making Process

1. understanding what decision needs to be made,
2. applying relevant standards,
3. gathering information,
4. generating options,
5. evaluating alternatives,
6. making the decision,
7. acting on it,
8. evaluating its result.

Brousseau et al., 2006; Drucker, 1974, Forester-Miller & Davis, 1996; Leyden, 2005

as damaging—as the right answer to the wrong question" (Drucker, 1974, p. 471). The options are not always clear-cut.

Apply relevant standards. Consider the ethical, legal and professional standards that apply in the situation. There are also the standards you have established in determining your priorities for clients, services and staff (i.e., in the best interest of the clients (Chapter 2), the staff as a whole (Chapter 8), each staff member (Chapter 10), the department's service delivery system (Chapter 12), the agency (Chapter 5), and your own vision and values (Chapters 2 and 15). Keeping the "big picture" in view when making individual decisions better facilitates getting to where you want your department to be.

Gather information. Gather and synthesize information related to your choices. You are best at this when you are able "to decide what information to heed, what to ignore, and how to organize and communicate that which [you] judge to be important" (Gardner, 2006, p. 36). For example, consider the degree of relevance of the information, and the credibility of its source (Gardner, 2006). An experienced administrative supervisor in counseling recommends:

> Look before leaping . . . really means to not jump to conclusions too early . . . find all or as many of the facts as possible before moving forward. People come to you for many different reasons and with many different agendas. Some are not honorable and many are more complex than first realized at face value. (T. E. Miller, personal communication, June 13, 2005)

Generate options. In complex decision-making (e.g., how best to reprimand a supervisee), the more options you consider, the surer you are that what you have decided to do might be right. "The understanding that underlies the right decision grows out of the clash and conflict of divergent opinions and out of serious consideration of competing alternatives" (Drucker, 1974, p. 471).

Consulting with a peer mentor, boss, or other experienced supervisor helps you hone your thinking. For example, when faced with an insubordinate staff member, many new administrative supervisors' knee-jerk reactions are to fire the individual; but, as described in previous chapters, there is a logical and legal series of disciplinary actions to take. Unless the insubordination is harmful to clients, the first step is an oral reprimand and educating the supervisee about your perception of their specific behaviors or attitudes.

Evaluate alternatives. In addition to considering relevant standards, consider the short-term and long-term effects of the array of possible alternatives. Many a work-related decision ends up as "at best a choice between 'almost right' and 'probably wrong'" (Drucker, 1974, p. 470). "One alternative is always the alternative of doing nothing" (Drucker, p. 475). Sometimes, however, doing nothing can lead to deterioration or missed opportunities.

Make the decision. Take the time needed to make a decision, but begin the process quickly (Leyden, 2005). Good advice is to "Practice avoiding deciding too slowly and avoiding deciding too quickly or prematurely" (Leyden, p. 8). In making decisions with wide-ranging impact, engage the people who will be affected by your choice (e.g., the supervisees who will implement your decision) and strive for consensus among them. "Including staff in the decision-making process acknowledges that the managerial leader respects his or her staff's unique perspectives and knowledge base" (Curtis & Sherlock, 2006, p. 123).

> Where quick decisions are needed, you must make these decisions quickly and directively, authoritatively, and without much discussion. . . . On the other hand, if the situation has a long time span, . . . then greater patience is required and greater participative management, more explanations, more giving out of facts, more discussion of the facts and common agreement upon the conclusions. (Maslow, 1998/1962, p. 178)

Decision-making by committee can be painful and inconclusive. Typically, supervisees appreciate your maintaining the final "say-so". Arbitrariness as a regular habit is not (Bennis & Biederman, 1997).

Act on it. "An effective decision is a commitment to action and results" (Drucker, 1974, p. 476). Depending on the complexity of the decision and its subsequent actions, planning how you and your staff members will carry it out is essential.

To be effective, use a decision-making *style* that works for you. Some of the differences in styles have to do with how information is used in the process and how options are created for the decision. Some leaders gather a lot of information searching for the best answer. This process takes more time than the style of gathering key facts and moving quickly to an answer. In creating options, some leaders are single focused. They pick a course of action and spend their energy on making it work. The multi-focused leader generates a list of options and pursues more than one of them at a time. They spend their energy on adapting to the circumstances that arise (Brousseau et al., 2006).

Evaluate the results. Some time after a decision is implemented, evaluate whether you made the right decision or not—did it meet established standards? Did it allow you to accomplish appropriate—the best?—results? Did it cause something unexpected to arise? Was that a good or bad thing? Identify what you learned in the situation, and reflect on it.

Managing Work

For the most part, administrative supervisors work independently. To be successful, you need to be self-reliant, self-starting, and self-organized. Develop your own organizational style for accomplishing your work effectively and efficiently. "Organization design and structure require thinking, analysis, and a systematic approach" (Drucker, 1974, p. 523). New administrative supervisors often start by observing experienced administrative supervisors' personal systems and adapt them to suit themselves. It may take some experimenting to learn what works best for you to balance your new responsibilities, manage your time, plan and organize your work and offices, delegate, and manage your stress.

Balance responsibilities. You constantly juggle several work-related balls in the air at one time. Balance day-to-day management issues, problems, deadlines and operational details with taking steps toward your vision for the department (Brousseau et al., 2006). Adhering to the priorities for your work guides you in making it through this maze.

Ineffective supervisors may unbalance their work by spending too much time on their previous area of interest and competence—their former job responsibilities, or pay too much attention to low-yield projects. Effective supervisors work on things that count; work for more than money; are able to say "no;" read books and journals that will help them grow; decide things promptly; and do things that expand their abilities. They put pressure on themselves (Farrant, 2005).

Manage time. As discussed in Chapter 16, everyone's work is filtered through the reality of time. Managing your job means managing your use of time. One challenge to you is to balance properly your boss-imposed time, system-imposed time, and self-imposed time (Blanchard, Oncken & Burrows, 1989). You are especially in charge of managing the latter. Impose tasks on yourself that yield the most benefit to the overall purpose and priorities of the department's work. Supervisors who do not use time well tend to get caught up in "administrivia" or fail to block out interruptions—they react to whatever knocks on their door whenever, rather than guarding their private work time. Establish your own "rules" about your schedule and teach them to your supervisees. (Supervisees often need to learn to do this for themselves as well.) Use others (e.g., administrative assistants, secretaries) to help you guard your self-imposed work time by intercepting the interruptions (Farrant, 2005). If you have not had such help prior to this assignment, you may be amazed at how many of them they can handle for you.

Ineffective administrative supervisors lose time, often unconsciously, to excessive socializing and such things as reading only tangentially related mail and email, newsletters or journals on job time (Farrant, 2005). Being time-conscious and self-disciplined are a must! One suggestion is for you to raise your consciousness about where your time goes by logging how you spend it daily and tracking it weekly and monthly (as you will probably be asking your supervisees to do) (Mackenzie, 1997).

Plan. Plan your work and work for quality (Farrant, 2005). Planning allows you to spend time and energy not only on what is to be done, but how.

Anticipate the logistics, scheduling, and efficient use of the department's resources. Supervisors waste time by starting a task before thinking it through. Thinking through a project before starting on it saves you from making false starts and errors that delay the work. Another favorite time-waster that you can mitigate by planning is running or getting caught up in overlong meetings. When you call the meeting, plan the agenda and stick to it.

Pre-planning is essential to responding well to emergencies or crises. Anticipating them entails thinking through what would happen and assigning individuals to do what needs to be done. Anticipate also how you will protect the welfare of clients in emergency or non-emergency situations. Inform your staff members about how and when you will intervene in supervisee-client work that is endangering a client.

Use a yearly calendar. Use calendars as planning tools. In spite of there being some urgencies or surprises that cannot be planned, there are many administrative supervision activities you can anticipate. As described in Chapter 18, the major activities of the service delivery system are planned. These activities provide a baseline for your calendar. As they are the top priority, you plot their dates first.

The activities of the performance management system are also set in a timeframe (Chapter 13). While you conduct each of the system's activities with each of your employees, those with different assessed developmental levels need more or less emphasis on different ones (Henderson & Gysbers, 1998). Calendaring when these events will occur with each staff member helps you manage this essential responsibility.

Agencies have regularly scheduled events (e.g., regular agency-wide staff meetings, reporting due dates). You can calendar these. Your planned attendance at conferences and professional association events are calendared as well. A partial example of an Annual Administrative Supervision Calendar is displayed in Figure 19.2. Based on your yearly calendar, develop your weekly and monthly schedules to both guide and record your use of time.

Organize your work and your office. In order to organize your office, develop systems for record keeping, filing important documents, and budget accounting. Again, develop your own style for doing these tasks, and your systems should match your style—as long as they work. Having piles of items stacked waiting to be filed is an indicator that your filing system is not working. Having weeks' worth of expenditures not entered into your accounting system indicates it is not working. Having slips of paper with notes jotted on them for recording later means that your record-keeping system is not working.

One of the bad habits of supervisors is keeping too many or too complicated records (Farrant, 2005). Using efficient systems is essential to managing your work and that of the department. Sometimes they seem mundane and not worth your time and effort to think about, but when things get backlogged

Figure 19.2 Yearly Administrative Supervision Calendar (Partial Example)

Employment Month*	Client Activities	Self Delivery System Leadership Activities	Staff Performance Improvement Activities	Agency Activities	Professional Development Activities
January/ 1*	Open House	Activity schedule development Review service implementation goals	Individual job descriptions Individual action plans Orientation Ind prof dev goals	Final budget acct'g report for previous year Distribute staff budgets	Set professional development goals & action plans
February/ 2*	Advisory Council meeting	Staff team building	Live supervision: Counselors 1–4	Agency staff meeting	
March/ 3*	Clients evaluation of services	Monitor activity implementation	Live supe: Counselors 5–8	Annual Board report	Attend ACA/ ACES conference
April/ 4*			Live supe: Counselors 1–3 + needed follow-ups	Agency staff mtg Q'ly acctg report	Monitor professional development act plans
May/ 5*			Live supe: Counselors 4–6 + needed follow-ups	Dev Tentative budget request for next year	
June/ 6*	Advisory Council meeting Client services evaluation	Monitor activity implementation	Live supe: Counselors 7–8 Form/Self eval conferences	Grant renewal application Agency staff meeting	Attend Goal-related seminar

Month					
July/ 7*	Open House	Staff team building	Action plans monitoring confs	Quarterly acctg report Submit ten bud req State dep't mtg	
August/ 8*			Supervision: C's 1–3 + needed follow up	Agency staff mtg Present annual report to agency administration	
September/ 9*		Monitor activity implementation Audit report prep	Form/self eval confs Supervision: C's 4–6 + needed follow up	Auditors in-house	Monitor PD act plan Attend State Counseling Association conference
October/ 10*	Advisory Cncl mtg Holiday "blues" Community Workshop		Supervision: C's 7–8 + needed follow up	Quarterly acctg rep Agency staff mtg	Evaluate goal attainment level
November/ 11*	Client services eval	Staff team building			
December/ 12*	Terminating clients conferences Holiday party	Aggregate client evals Activity evaluation	Goal attainment confs Summ eval forms & confs & professional development goals	Final budget acctg Agency staff mtg	

* Depends on Fiscal Year

you and all of your staff members get slowed down. Doing troublesome or distasteful jobs first helps clear your mind and your "to-do list"!

Delegate. Delegate work appropriately. Delegating work that rightfully belongs to others—whether they are above or below you on the organization chart—helps you save your energy and time for your own work. Accepting your own responsibilities helps you do your job appropriately. One new administrative supervisor stated, "I am learning that I have to let go of parts of the program, or my staff will not grow" (L. M. Malloy, personal communication, June 13, 2005). Additionally, doing non-supervisory things can get in the way of your doing your supervisory functions, or it may lead to your spending time after regular work hours on them (Blanchard et al., 1989; Farrant, 2005).

You are able to delegate successfully when you feel that the person you are delegating to is capable of handling the responsibility, knows what to do, has the resources available to do it, knows the standards for its acceptable completion, and is committed to doing it. To delegate well you develop this mindset and trust others. Your responsibility is to be clear about *what* you want done, leaving the responsibility to them to determine *how* they will do it. Allow supervisees to develop their own projects and plans, and monitor their progress in ways that suit your needs and a supervisee's developmental level. Delegating to your supervisees has the side benefit of helping develop new supervisors.

Manage stress. As with all workers, you can become stressed, and, thereby, impair your effectiveness and efficiency. To be successful, manage your stress by keeping your life in balance. Covey (1991) identifies "four dimensions of the human personality: physical, mental, emotional and spiritual" (pp. 37–38) of a balanced life. Caring for your physical well-being entails rest, relaxation, exercise, and good nutrition. Mental well-being entails exercising your mind not only at work but also in your personal life through reading, having stimulating discussions with supervisees and colleagues, and pursuing learning opportunities. Emotional well-being entails letting go of problems and issues over which you have no control, using positive self-talk, and exercising your sense of humor. Social well-being entails having support systems, maintaining appropriate boundaries in and developing healthy and meaningful relationships within and outside of work. Hone your assertion skills, and control your work rather than letting your work control you.

CONTINUE TO BE SUCCESSFUL

In order to fully develop your career as an administrative supervisor in counseling, continuously strive to increase your effectiveness and efficiency. Recognize "that acquiring supervision competencies is a life-long cumulative, development process with levels of proficiency beyond competence" (Falender et al., 2004, p. 775).

You know this mountain. We all do. It is the psychological climb you make from the moment you take on a new role to the moment you feel fully engaged in that role. . . . At the summit of this mountain you are good at what you do, you know the fundamental purpose of your work, and you are always looking for better ways to fulfill that mission. You are fully engaged. (Buckingham & Coffman, 1999, p. 42)

As a professional and a knowledge worker "you know . . . you are making progress, when you realize how much more you need to learn" (Fracaro, 2004, p. 3). As one administrative supervisor in counseling expressed it, "I LOVE learning each day that I do not know as much as I think I do and being humbled and continuing to grow myself" (S. D. Clifford, personal communication, August 14, 2005).

Understand the Breadth and Depth of Administrative Supervisory Competence

Four broad areas of administrative supervision competence have been identified: conceptual, human, professional/technical, and self-management (Falvey, 1987; Hersey, Blanchard & Johnson, 2001; Buhler, 2005). Given the breadth of these areas, there is much for you to learn. Conceptual competence is the:

ability to understand the complexities of the overall organization and where one's own operation fits in to the organization. This knowledge permits one to act according to the objectives of the total organization rather than only on the basis of the goals and needs of one's own immediate group. (Hersey et al., p. 14)

It is also the ability to think critically. An:

administrator/manager spends much of his or her energy critically evaluating clients, staff, facilities, budgets, political situations, personnel, colleagues, organizational structures, strategic plans, and nearly every element of the work environment. Indeed critical thinking skills . . . are the very essence of skillful leadership and management. (Herr, Heitzmann, & Rayman, 2006)

Human competence is the "ability and judgment in working with and through people" (Hersey et al., 2001, p.14). Professional/technical competence is the "ability to use knowledge, methods, techniques, and equipment necessary for the performance of specific tasks; [it is] acquired from experience, education, and training" (p. 14). Competence in self-management is the ability to think and act with an eye to the greater good—effective client services, smooth working relationships with department and agency staff. Self-management includes self-care that allows an administrative supervisor to function at optimum competence.

Competence development reflects the spiraling process of all areas of complex learning (Borders et al., 1991). As a maturing administrative supervisor, seek to deepen your knowledge, add texture to your competence, and expand your repertoire of strategies. Strive to move "from vagueness to specificity, from superficiality to depth, from simplicity to complexity" (Henderson, Cook, Libby & Zambrano, 2006, p.129). Work to develop your:

1. sense of identity as a supervisor;
2. feeling of confidence as a supervisor;
3. degree of felt autonomy and/or dependence on others;
4. use of power and authority with supervisees, including the methods and process of supervisee evaluations;
5. degree of structure, flexibility, and variety of intervention;
6. focus on the needs of the supervisees and/or self;
7. degree of personal investment in supervisee and client success;
8. emphasis on and use of the supervisory relationship and the process of supervision;
9. degree of awareness and appraisal of the impact of self on the supervisory relationship and process; and
10. degree of realistic appraisal of competencies and limitations, coupled with an awareness and containment of personal issues, biases, and counter-transference reactions. (Heid, 1997, cited in Tsui, 2005, p. 147)

As you and the profession continue to grow, you "spend a great deal of time on keeping up with current trends and research in [your] areas of interest" (S. D. Clifford, personal communication, August 14, 2005). Supervisees surface an array of challenging issues. Given the infinite possibilities of different combinations of variables in the supervisor-supervisee-client-environment, consciously learn from each experience.

There are complex issues that permeate all spheres of your work that require ongoing and additional learning; for example, attention to diversity, and attention to legal and ethical issues (Falender et al., 2004). Indeed, the American Mental Health Counselors Association [AMHCA] Code of Ethics (2000) states that:

> Mental health counselors recognize the need for continued education and training in the area of cultural diversity and competency. Mental health counselors are open to new procedures and sensitive to the diversity of varying populations and changes in expectations and values over time. (Principle 7, C)

The array of new areas of learning to pursue grows daily. New issues emerge in society and are raised by clients or counselors. The profession advances. New directions are identified by the agency.

Recognize that You Have to be Self-directed

Maturing administrative supervisors, typically, direct their own professional development. You have few or no peers in counseling within the same agency, and your bosses have probably not been professional counselors. In any case, now they are overseers of several different programs and specialists. In some counseling centers, administrative supervisors are at the top of the organizational structure. Essentially many administrative supervisors apply the performance management system to themselves.

You do this well by being self-aware and self-analytical. Scrutinize your own job behaviors, attitudes and feelings, and continuously assess your own level of skill development in light of established standards. Accept and process feedback from others, and learn from evaluations of your performance made by your administrators and staff members (Curtis & Sherlock, 2006). Setting performance improvement goals and action plans annually (Chapter 13) allows you to be prepared to seize growth opportunities that come your way (Magnuson, Wilcoxen & Norem, 2003).

Use multiple strategies for increasing your effectiveness. Learn independently by reflecting on and consulting about your experiences. Read management and supervision as well as counseling books and journals. This *Handbook* is intended as a resource to help you learn about the multiple dimensions of your job. Scanning the references in it gives you some idea of how many and how varied the resources are! Many of these require you to filter them through the lens of an administrative supervisor in counseling. You can learn a lot from writing articles or books on your own or with other colleagues.

As I matured as an administrative supervisor, my approach to learning evolved. I learned that basic issues and problems repeat themselves (e.g., professional competitiveness interfering with collaborative work), but that different nuances need to be discerned (e.g., professional competitiveness morphing into professional jealousy, or professional jealousy turning into sabotage). In searching for new intervention ideas and strategies and not having many peers nearby, I often consulted my administrator or one from the human resources department, and read professional (research-based) and practical journals (practitioner contributed) from not only counseling, but also business, leadership, personnel or supervision sources.

Develop networks with other administrative supervisors both in and out of counseling. Professional associations of counseling and other mental health care workers and of supervisors provide such opportunities. Seek out opportunities for advanced education (e.g., advanced degrees), inservice (agency provided) or specialized training (using effective strategies in multicultural counseling). Recognize the needs of and benefits to your supervisees and clients as well as yourself for your development. However, as one supervisor of administrative supervisors noted:

Ironically I see [counseling supervisors] pass up opportunities for further training (not wanting to use program dollars that could be used for clients for their "own" benefit). They feel guilty if they use funds to better their abilities knowing that these funds could have gone to the clients. Funders tend to perpetuate this behavior through their emphasis on direct vs. administrative service expenditures. (P. E. McDaniel, personal communication, September 26, 2005)

Participating in supervision also helps you combat stagnation and maintain your forward progress. You benefit from individual or group supervision provided by your agency or through your own resources. Some agencies formally assign mentors from the ranks of experienced administrative supervisors. This allows you "to access the experts" (Y. K. Steves, personal communication, June 16, 2005). You may have to seek out individual colleagues and peers with whom to "consult, collaborate, celebrate" (D. A. Healy, personal communication, June 13, 2005), or identify your own mentor (T. Miller, personal communication, June 13, 2005). Meetings may be formally structured or informal get-togethers. Failing any of this, strive to conduct self-supervision as objectively as possible.

Ideally, you learned the processes of individual and group supervision of supervision in your previous role as a clinical supervisor. In larger agencies, peer groups of administrative supervisors in counseling might exist that provide resources and support for their members (Rezaie & Garrison, 2004). Meeting regularly (e.g., monthly) provides opportunities for discussing organization-wide issues as well as specific issues faced in supervision of staff members. When such groups are not organized by their agencies, ethical administrative supervisors form or join existing peer supervision of supervision groups (ACES, 1993, 3.03). If a supervisor of supervisors is not available to lead the group, a peer is designated for each or a series of meetings.

Group supervision is most effective when it is structured (Wilbur, Roberts-Wilbur, Hart, Morris & Betz, 1994). Planned supervision case consultations are appreciated by counseling supervisors as providing lots of insights and learning (M. L. Libby, personal communication, May 6, 2005). They provide opportunities to discuss and learn about strategies for practicing and supervising workers at different professional developmental levels and in different counseling activities. A case consultation format asks the presenting supervisor to answer three questions:

1. At what developmental level is/was this counselor in this supervision event?
2. How should I/could I have comport(ed) myself to intervene most effectively with this counselor on the clients' behalf?
3. Specifically, what should/could I do/have done to most effectively help this counselor in this supervision event?

Effective agendas also allow for discussion of impromptu issues and problematic or successful supervision cases (Henderson & Gysbers, 1998).

SUMMARY

This chapter closes the *Handbook* by looking at how you fulfill your professional and ethical obligations to continually and intentionally increase your work-related competence. You are given suggestions about how to prepare for and get off to a good start when the position is new to you, and how to anticipate the changes that will occur. Two competencies that are fundamental to your success on the job, decision-making and work management, were briefly described. Having started off well, you continuously improve in four major areas of competence; deepening your approaches to your work requires you to be self-directed. A Self-Audit tool is provided to help you discriminate your areas of need for improvement and their relative importance in your specific job.

SUPERVISOR CHALLENGE AND RESPONSE

Supervisor Challenge: Self-awareness and Direction

Administrative supervisors are primarily responsible for their own professional development. While standards for responsibilities are suggested in this *Handbook* and written job descriptions are typically available, standards for quality performance or evaluation instruments for them to use are not well described. They receive feedback from others that may or may not be relevant to the essence of their responsibilities. They may be evaluated on criteria that do not help them identify their needs.

Supervisors' Response: Self-Audit

To continue to develop as professional administrative supervisors in counseling, they determine their own needs—not necessarily wants—by assessing their strengths and weaknesses and being willing to more fully develop both. They conduct the OARS process (Chapter 10) for themselves. They observe their own behaviors in actual experiences and their effects on others; and draw just and honest conclusions about their levels of performance and professionalism.

Self-directed administrative supervisors consider the relative importance of each of the competencies needed to carry out their job responsibilities and relative need for development of each (Falender et al., 2004). A tool for guiding such self-reflection, based on the job responsibilities identified in this *Handbook*, is offered as an example in Figure 19.3. The purpose of the tool is to aid self-analysis and to support setting important and needed professional development goals each year. It was developed for use in the context of the *Handbook* and has not been researched to identify correlations, or establish validity or reliability.

The four sets of competencies are described by specific skills, synthesized from the literature and experience, and the essential elements of each skill provide a third level of specificity. A mental health care agency could adapt this as an administrative supervisor performance evaluation form by using the skills (i.e., the second level of specificity). In conducting a self-assessment, open-minded administrative supervisors strive for subjective objectivity (Barratt, 2006). The more information they glean from others' feedback and the more honest they are with themselves about their performance in various situations, the more grounded their self-judgments are.

In using the Self-Audit, administrative supervisors, first, determine the relative importance of each skill in carrying out their job responsibilities. Second, considering the feedback they have received plus their own performance perceptions, they rate their level of need for further growth in each skill set. They, then, analyze the information by drawing conclusions related to their data. The skills with the highest importance and the highest need are candidates for relevant professional development goals. A cluster of needs in one of the four competency areas suggests further development in that realm in order to enhance their effectiveness as administrative supervisors in counseling.

Figure 19.3 Self Audit*

Directions:
Rate yourself on a scale from 1–5, with 1 being highest and 5 being lowest, in each of the columns: "Importance" and "Need." Importance signifies how valuable the competency is/you think it would be on your/an administrative supervision job. Need signifies the level of your need for development in that competency. Draw conclusions that suggest the highest professional development priorities (i.e., high importance and high need for development) for you to increase your effectiveness as an administrative supervisor.

Conceptual Competencies	Importance	Need
Applies knowledge of principles based on:		
Counseling history, theory & research	1 2 3 4 5	1 2 3 4 5
Standards for professional practices	1 2 3 4 5	1 2 3 4 5
Standards of values, ethics & laws	1 2 3 4 5	1 2 3 4 5
Applies knowledge of principles based on related fields:		
Leadership	1 2 3 4 5	1 2 3 4 5
Management	1 2 3 4 5	1 2 3 4 5
Administration	1 2 3 4 5	1 2 3 4 5
Supervision	1 2 3 4 5	1 2 3 4 5
Is committed to clients, agency & counseling profession:	1 2 3 4 5	1 2 3 4 5
Has vision	1 2 3 4 5	1 2 3 4 5
Sets standards	1 2 3 4 5	1 2 3 4 5

Adheres to pertinent laws, policies & regulations	1	2	3	4	5		1	2	3	4	5
Synthesizes ideas & information from multiple sources:	1	2	3	4	5		1	2	3	4	5
Accepts reality	1	2	3	4	5		1	2	3	4	5
Gathers & processes information accurately	1	2	3	4	5		1	2	3	4	5
Analyzes information thoroughly	1	2	3	4	5		1	2	3	4	5
Applies findings from research	1	2	3	4	5		1	2	3	4	5
Understands the context & operational dynamics of the agency	1	2	3	4	5		1	2	3	4	5
Uses higher order thinking skills:	1	2	3	4	5		1	2	3	4	5
Comprehends, analyzes, synthesizes, evaluates	1	2	3	4	5		1	2	3	4	5
Thinks systematically and systemically	1	2	3	4	5		1	2	3	4	5
Creates	1	2	3	4	5		1	2	3	4	5
Is proficient in use of basic skills (reading, writing, arithmetic)	1	2	3	4	5		1	2	3	4	5

Human Competencies	Importance						Need				
Communicates effectively:	1	2	3	4	5		1	2	3	4	5
Expresses self clearly & appropriately orally & in writing	1	2	3	4	5		1	2	3	4	5
Presents self accurately	1	2	3	4	5		1	2	3	4	5
Listens/hears accurately	1	2	3	4	5		1	2	3	4	5
"Reads" others well	1	2	3	4	5		1	2	3	4	5
Communicates compliments & criticisms constructively	1	2	3	4	5		1	2	3	4	5
Is straightforward	1	2	3	4	5		1	2	3	4	5
Is appropriately assertive	1	2	3	4	5		1	2	3	4	5
Provides feedback directly	1	2	3	4	5		1	2	3	4	5
Is persuasive	1	2	3	4	5		1	2	3	4	5
Attends to diversity in work with clients, supervisees, colleagues & public:	1	2	3	4	5		1	2	3	4	5
Works effectively across cultures	1	2	3	4	5		1	2	3	4	5
Works effectively with individuals	1	2	3	4	5		1	2	3	4	5
of different ages	1	2	3	4	5		1	2	3	4	5
of different abilities/disabilities	1	2	3	4	5		1	2	3	4	5
Exercises power judiciously:	1	2	3	4	5		1	2	3	4	5
Uses authority	1	2	3	4	5		1	2	3	4	5
Uses power-base resources appropriately to supervisory situations	1	2	3	4	5		1	2	3	4	5
Disciplines staff members appropriately	1	2	3	4	5		1	2	3	4	5
Advocates for clients, staff members & counseling practices:	1	2	3	4	5		1	2	3	4	5

(Continued)

Represents them	1	2	3	4	5	1	2	3	4	5
Is concerned for their welfare & image	1	2	3	4	5	1	2	3	4	5
Communicates effectively with relevant publics	1	2	3	4	5	1	2	3	4	5
Applies political skills:	1	2	3	4	5	1	2	3	4	5
Works well with those in authority	1	2	3	4	5	1	2	3	4	5
Fosters relationships with key people	1	2	3	4	5	1	2	3	4	5
Understands formal & informal power structures of the agency	1	2	3	4	5	1	2	3	4	5
Works effectively within the context & dynamics of the agency	1	2	3	4	5	1	2	3	4	5
Understands the "big picture"	1	2	3	4	5	1	2	3	4	5
Uses an effective sense of timing	1	2	3	4	5	1	2	3	4	5
Manages interactions:	1	2	3	4	5	1	2	3	4	5
Ensures that interactions with & among clients are respectful	1	2	3	4	5	1	2	3	4	5
Ensures that interactions with & among staff members are respectful	1	2	3	4	5	1	2	3	4	5
Ensures that interactions with & among clients & staff members are respectful	1	2	3	4	5	1	2	3	4	5
Builds meaningful intraprofessional & interprofessional relationships	1	2	3	4	5	1	2	3	4	5
Conducts effective individual conferences	1	2	3	4	5	1	2	3	4	5
Conducts effective group meetings	1	2	3	4	5	1	2	3	4	5
Builds a team of the department staff	1	2	3	4	5	1	2	3	4	5
Applies knowledge & skills of group process	1	2	3	4	5	1	2	3	4	5
Continuously strives for complete involvement of each staff member:	1	2	3	4	5	1	2	3	4	5
Selects, places & inducts new staff members successfully	1	2	3	4	5	1	2	3	4	5
Assigns responsibilities to counselors appropriate to their training & experience	1	2	3	4	5	1	2	3	4	5
Is open to others' ideas	1	2	3	4	5	1	2	3	4	5
Motivates others to achieve:	1	2	3	4	5	1	2	3	4	5
Engenders motivation	1	2	3	4	5	1	2	3	4	5
Empowers others	1	2	3	4	5	1	2	3	4	5
Sets & maintains high standards	1	2	3	4	5	1	2	3	4	5
Sets clear goals & objectives	1	2	3	4	5	1	2	3	4	5
Works to resolve morale issues	1	2	3	4	5	1	2	3	4	5
Supports others	1	2	3	4	5	1	2	3	4	5
Maintains professional detachment:	1	2	3	4	5	1	2	3	4	5
Is objective	1	2	3	4	5	1	2	3	4	5
Helps others to manage stress	1	2	3	4	5	1	2	3	4	5
Balances task accomplishment & relationships	1	2	3	4	5	1	2	3	4	5

	Importance					Need				
Relates well with others:	1	2	3	4	5	1	2	3	4	5
Maintains a caring atmosphere	1	2	3	4	5	1	2	3	4	5
Fosters trust with & among staff members & clients	1	2	3	4	5	1	2	3	4	5
Has & enjoys a sense of humor	1	2	3	4	5	1	2	3	4	5
Cares for & about others	1	2	3	4	5	1	2	3	4	5
Manages conflicts:	1	2	3	4	5	1	2	3	4	5
Collaborates	1	2	3	4	5	1	2	3	4	5
Compromises	1	2	3	4	5	1	2	3	4	5
Negotiates	1	2	3	4	5	1	2	3	4	5

Professional/Technical Competencies	Importance					Need				
Is proficient & current in professional/ technical competencies of:										
Counseling	1	2	3	4	5	1	2	3	4	5
Supervision	1	2	3	4	5	1	2	3	4	5
Engenders continuous delivery system improvement:	1	2	3	4	5	1	2	3	4	5
Uses & facilitates others' use of the improvement process	1	2	3	4	5	1	2	3	4	5
Uses & leads others' use of goal-setting & planning skills	1	2	3	4	5	1	2	3	4	5
Manages human, capital & technological resources:	1	2	3	4	5	1	2	3	4	5
Acquires them	1	2	3	4	5	1	2	3	4	5
Allocates them	1	2	3	4	5	1	2	3	4	5
Monitors their use	1	2	3	4	5	1	2	3	4	5
Applies organizational skills:	1	2	3	4	5	1	2	3	4	5
Plans	1	2	3	4	5	1	2	3	4	5
Sets priorities	1	2	3	4	5	1	2	3	4	5
Manages own job responsibilities & time	1	2	3	4	5	1	2	3	4	5
Executes tasks	1	2	3	4	5	1	2	3	4	5
Directs & coordinates the work of supervisees	1	2	3	4	5	1	2	3	4	5
Delegates effectively	1	2	3	4	5	1	2	3	4	5
Is committed to professional development:	1	2	3	4	5	1	2	3	4	5
Has a model for counselor development	1	2	3	4	5	1	2	3	4	5
Continuously strives for optimal development of each staff member	1	2	3	4	5	1	2	3	4	5
Assesses professionals' needs accurately	1	2	3	4	5	1	2	3	4	5
Responds to professionals' needs appropriately	1	2	3	4	5	1	2	3	4	5
Pursues continuous self-development	1	2	3	4	5	1	2	3	4	5

(*Continued*)

	Importance					Need				
Uses supervisory interventions & techniques appropriately	1	2	3	4	5	1	2	3	4	5
Is decisive:	1	2	3	4	5	1	2	3	4	5
Uses a sound decision-making process consistently	1	2	3	4	5	1	2	3	4	5
Makes evaluative judgments fairly	1	2	3	4	5	1	2	3	4	5
Solves problems	1	2	3	4	5	1	2	3	4	5
Accepts responsibility for:										
Clients	1	2	3	4	5	1	2	3	4	5
Department	1	2	3	4	5	1	2	3	4	5
Agency	1	2	3	4	5	1	2	3	4	5
Own actions	1	2	3	4	5	1	2	3	4	5
Designs & implements effective & efficient systems:	1	2	3	4	5	1	2	3	4	5
For client management	1	2	3	4	5	1	2	3	4	5
For performance management	1	2	3	4	5	1	2	3	4	5
For service delivery	1	2	3	4	5	1	2	3	4	5
For delivery system development & improvement	1	2	3	4	5	1	2	3	4	5
For managing own work	1	2	3	4	5	1	2	3	4	5
Leads change:	1	2	3	4	5	1	2	3	4	5
Applies knowledge & skill of change processes	1	2	3	4	5	1	2	3	4	5
Takes risks	1	2	3	4	5	1	2	3	4	5
Manages uncertainty	1	2	3	4	5	1	2	3	4	5

Self-Management Competencies	Importance					Need				
Is self-aware:	1	2	3	4	5	1	2	3	4	5
Knows own values	1	2	3	4	5	1	2	3	4	5
Knows own talents, strengths & weaknesses	1	2	3	4	5	1	2	3	4	5
Holds high personal & professional standards	1	2	3	4	5	1	2	3	4	5
Consults with peers & colleagues	1	2	3	4	5	1	2	3	4	5
Is altruistic	1	2	3	4	5	1	2	3	4	5
Is cooperative & collaborative	1	2	3	4	5	1	2	3	4	5
Adapts style & competencies to those of others	1	2	3	4	5	1	2	3	4	5
Adapts style & competencies to the situation	1	2	3	4	5	1	2	3	4	5
Maintains appropriate boundaries in relationships	1	2	3	4	5	1	2	3	4	5
Is autonomous	1	2	3	4	5	1	2	3	4	5
Maintains own wellness:	1	2	3	4	5	1	2	3	4	5
Accepts reality	1	2	3	4	5	1	2	3	4	5
Is optimistic	1	2	3	4	5	1	2	3	4	5
Manages stress	1	2	3	4	5	1	2	3	4	5

Enjoys work	1	2	3	4	5	1	2	3	4	5
Is confident	1	2	3	4	5	1	2	3	4	5
Identifies professionally with administrative supervision & counseling	1	2	3	4	5	1	2	3	4	5

* Adapted from the following sources: Arredondo, 1996; Bloom, 1956; Drucker, 1974; Falender et al., 2004; Falvey, 1987; Forester-Miller & Davis, 1996; Fullan, 2001; Gysbers & Henderson, 2006; Henderson & Gysbers, 1998; Henderson & Gysbers, 2002; Hersey, Blanchard & Johnson, 2001; Khandwalla, 2004; Maslow, 1998/1962; Raven, 2004; Raven, Schwarzwald & Koslowsky, 1998.

Appendixes

Appendix A
Standards for Counseling Supervisors*

Core Areas of Knowledge and Competency

1. Professional counseling supervisors are *effective counselors* whose knowledge and competencies have been acquired through training, education, and supervised employment experience.
   The counseling supervisor:
   1.1 demonstrates knowledge of various counseling theories, systems, and their related methods;
   1.2 demonstrates knowledge of his/her personal philosophical, theoretical and methodological approach to counseling;
   1.3 demonstrates knowledge of his/her assumptions about human behavior; and
   1.4 demonstrates skill in the application of counseling theory and methods (individual, group, or marital and family and specialized areas such as substance abuse, career-life rehabilitation) that are appropriate for the supervisory setting.

2. Professional counseling supervisors demonstrate *personal traits and characteristics* that are consistent with the role.
   The counseling supervisor:
   2.1 is committed to updating his/her own counseling and supervisory skills;
   2.2 is sensitive to individual differences;
   2.3 recognizes his/her own limits through self-evaluation and feedback from others;
   2.4 is encouraging, optimistic and motivational;
   2.5 possesses a sense of humor;
   2.6 is comfortable with the authority inherent in the role of supervisor;
   2.7 demonstrates a commitment to the role of supervisor;
   2.8 can identify his/her own strengths and weaknesses as a supervisor; and
   2.9 can describe his/her own pattern in interpersonal relationships.

* First printed in *ACES Spectrum,* Spring, 1989. See also *Journal of Counseling and Development,* 69 (1), 30–32.

3. Professional counseling supervisors are knowledgeable regarding *ethical, legal and regulatory aspects* of the profession, and are skilled in applying this knowledge.

The counseling supervisor:

3.1 communicates to the counselor a knowledge of professional codes of ethics (e.g., AACD, APA);

3.2 demonstrates and enforces ethical and professional standards;

3.3 communicates to the counselor an understanding of legal and regulatory documents and their impact on the profession (e.g., certification, licensure, duty to warn, parents' rights to children's records, third party payments, etc.);

3.4 provides current information regarding professional standards (NCC, CCMHC, CRC, CCC, licensure, certification, etc.);

3.5 can communicate a knowledge of counselor rights and appeal procedures specific to the work setting; and

3.6 communicates to the counselor a knowledge of ethical considerations that pertain to the supervisory process, including dual relationships, due process, evaluation, informed consent, confidentiality, and vicarious liability.

4. Professional counseling supervisors demonstrate conceptual knowledge of the *personal and professional nature of the supervisory relationship* and are skilled in applying this knowledge.

The counseling supervisor:

4.1 demonstrates knowledge of individual differences with respect to gender, race, ethnicity, culture and age and understands the importance of these characteristics in supervisory relationships;

4.2 is sensitive to the counselor's personal and professional needs;

4.3 expects counselors to own the consequences of their actions;

4.4 is sensitive to the evaluative nature of supervision and effectively responds to the counselor's anxiety relative to performance evaluation;

4.5 conducts self-evaluations, as appropriate, as a means of modeling professional growth;

4.6 provides facilitative conditions (empathy, concreteness, respect, congruence, genuineness, and immediacy);

4.7 establishes a mutually trusting relationship with the counselor;

4.8 provides an appropriate balance of challenge and support; and

4.9 elicits counselor thoughts and feelings during counseling or consultation sessions, and responds in a manner that enhances the supervision process.

5. Professional counseling supervisors demonstrate conceptual knowledge of *supervision methods and techniques,* and are skilled in using this knowledge to promote counselor development.

The counseling supervisor:

5.1 states the purposes of supervision and explains the procedures to be used;

5.2 negotiates mutual decisions regarding the needed direction of learning experiences for the counselor;

5.3 engages in appropriate supervisory interventions, including role-play, role-reversal, live supervision, modeling, interpersonal process recall, micro-training, suggestions and advice, reviewing audio and video tapes, etc.;

5.4 can perform the supervisor's functions in the role of teacher, counselor, or consultant as appropriate;

5.5 elicits new alternatives from counselors for identifying solutions, techniques, responses to clients;

5.6 integrates knowledge of supervision with his/her style of interpersonal relations;

5.7 clarifies his/her role in supervision;

5.8 uses media aids (print material, electronic recording) to enhance learning; and

5.9 interacts with the counselor in a manner that facilitates the counselor's self-exploration and problem solving.

6. Professional counseling supervisors demonstrate conceptual knowledge of the *counselor developmental process* and are skilled in applying this knowledge.

The counseling supervisor:

6.1 understands the developmental nature of supervision;

6.2 demonstrates knowledge of various theoretical models of supervision;

6.3 understands the counselor's roles and functions in particular work settings;

6.4 understands the supervisor's roles and functions in particular work settings;

6.5 can identify the learning needs of the counselor;

6.6 adjusts conference content based on the counselor's personal traits, conceptual development, training, and experience; and

6.7 uses supervisory methods appropriate to the counselor's level of conceptual development, training and experience.

7. Professional counseling supervisors demonstrate knowledge and competency in *case conceptualization and management.*

The counseling supervisor:

7.1 recognizes that a primary goal of supervision is helping the client of the counselor;

7.2 understands the roles of other professionals (e.g., psychologists, physicians, social workers) and assists with the referral process, when appropriate;

7.3 elicits counselor perceptions of counseling dynamics;

7.4 assists the counselor in selecting and executing data collection procedures;

7.5 assists the counselor in analyzing and interpreting data objectively;

7.6 assists the counselor in planning effective client goals and objectives;

7.7 assists the counselor in using observation and assessment in preparation of client goals and objectives;

7.8 assists the counselor in synthesizing client psychological and behavioral characteristics into an integrated conceptualization;

7.9 assists the counselor in assigning priorities to counseling goals and objectives;

7.10 assists the counselor in providing rationale for counseling procedures; and

7.11 assists the counselor in adjusting steps in the progression toward a goal based on ongoing assessment and evaluation.

8. Professional counseling supervisors demonstrate knowledge and competency in client *assessment and evaluation.*
   The counseling supervisor:
   8.1 monitors the use of tests and test interpretations;
   8.2 assists the counselor in providing rationale for assessment procedures;
   8.3 assists the counselor in communicating assessment procedures and rationales;
   8.4 assists the counselor in the description, measurement, and documentation of client and counselor change; and
   8.5 assists the counselor in integrating findings and observations to make appropriate recommendations.

9. Professional counseling supervisors demonstrate knowledge and competency in *oral and written reporting and recording.*
   The counseling supervisor:
   9.1 understands the meaning of accountability and the supervisor's responsibility in promoting it;
   9.2 assists the counselor in effectively documenting supervisory and counseling-related interactions;
   9.3 assists the counselor in establishing and following policies and procedures to protect the confidentiality of client and supervisory records;
   9.4 assists the counselor in identifying appropriate information to be included in a verbal or written report;
   9.5 assists the counselor in presenting information in a logical, concise, and sequential manner; and

9.6 assists the counselor in adapting verbal and written reports to the work environment and communication situation.

10. Professional counseling supervisors demonstrate knowledge and competency in the *evaluation of counseling performance.*
The counseling supervisor:
10.1 can interact with the counselor from the perspective of evaluator;
10.2 can identify the counselor's professional and personal strengths, as well as weaknesses;
10.3 provides specific feedback about such performance as conceptualization, use of methods and techniques, relationship skills, and assessment;
10.4 determines the extent to which the counselor has developed and applied his/her own personal theory of counseling;
10.5 develops evaluation procedures and instruments to determine program and counselor goal attainment;
10.6 assists the counselor in the description and measurement of his/her progress and achievement; and
10.7 can evaluate counseling skills for purposes of grade assignment, completion of internship requirements, professional advancement, and so on.

11. Professional counseling supervisors are knowledgeable regarding *research in counseling and counselor supervision* and consistently incorporate this knowledge into the supervision process.
The counseling supervisor:
11.1 facilitates and monitors research to determine the effectiveness of programs, services and techniques;
11.2 reads, interprets, and applies counseling and supervisory research;
11.3 can formulate counseling or supervisory research questions;
11.4 reports results of counseling or supervisory research and disseminates as appropriate (e.g., inservice, conferences, publications); and
11.5 facilitates an integration of research findings in individual case management.

Appendix B
Ethical Guidelines for Counseling Supervisors*
Association for Counselor Education and Supervision

Adopted by ACES Executive Counsel and Delegate Assembly
March, 1993

Preamble:

The Association for Counselor Education and Supervision (ACES) is composed of people engaged in the professional preparation of counselors and people responsible for the ongoing supervision of counselors. ACES is a founding division of the American Counseling Association (ACA) and as such adheres to ACA's current ethical standards and to general codes of competence adopted throughout the mental health community.

ACES believes that counselor educators and counseling supervisors in universities and in applied counseling settings, including the range of education and mental health delivery systems, carry responsibilities unique to their job roles. Such responsibilities may include administrative supervision, clinical supervision, or both. Administrative supervision refers to those supervisory activities which increase the efficiency of the delivery of counseling services; whereas, clinical supervision includes the supportive and educative activities of the supervisor designed to improve the application of counseling theory and technique directly to clients.

Counselor educators and counseling supervisors encounter situations which challenge the help given by general ethical standards of the profession at large. These situations require more specific guidelines that provide appropriate guidance in everyday practice.

---

* Although these *Ethical Guidelines* have not been revised since their original adoption, they still suggest important standards for supervisors to consider in carrying out their work. Many of these standards are incorporated into the 2005 *ACA Code of Ethics*. ACA adjudicates any related ethical complaints; ACES does not. A current ACES task force is developing a document describing Best Supervision Practices that is intended to update this information (H. Glosoff, personal communication, 2008). These *Guidelines* are reprinted with permission from the Association for Counselor Education and Supervision, and can be retrieved from http://www.acesonline.net/ethical95guidelines.asp.

The Ethical Guidelines for Counseling Supervisors are intended to assist professionals by helping them:

1. Observe ethical and legal protection of clients' and supervisees' rights;
2. Meet the training and professional development needs of supervisees in ways consistent with clients' welfare and programmatic requirements; and
3. Establish policies, procedures, and standards for implementing programs.

The specification of ethical guidelines enables ACES members to focus on and to clarify the ethical nature of responsibilities held in common. Such guidelines should be reviewed formally every five years, or more often if needed, to meet the needs of ACES members for guidance.

The Ethical Guidelines for Counselor Educators and Counseling Supervisors are meant to help ACES members in conducting supervision. ACES is not currently in a position to hear complaints about alleged non-compliance with these guidelines. Any complaints about the ethical behavior of any ACA member should be measured against the ACA Ethical Standards and a complaint lodged with ACA in accordance with its *procedures* for doing so.

One overriding assumption underlying this document is that supervision should be ongoing throughout a counselor's career and not stop when a particular level of education, certification, or membership in a professional organization is attained.

DEFINITIONS OF TERMS:

Applied Counseling Settings—Public or private organizations of counselors such as community mental health centers, hospitals, schools, and group or individual private practice settings.

Supervisees—Counselors-in-training in university programs at any level who working [*sic*] with clients in applied settings as part of their university training program, and counselors who have completed their formal education and are employed in an applied counseling setting.

Supervisors—Counselors who have been designated within their university or agency to directly oversee the professional clinical work of counselors. Supervisors also may be persons who offer supervision to counselors seeking state licensure and so provide supervision outside of the administrative aegis of an applied counseling setting.

1. Client Welfare and Rights

1.01 The primary obligation of supervisors is to train counselors so that they respect the integrity and promote the welfare of their clients. Supervisors should have supervisees inform clients that they are being supervised and that observation and/or recordings of the session may be reviewed by the supervisor.

1.02 Supervisors who are licensed counselors and are conducting supervision to aid a supervisee to become licensed should instruct the supervisee not to communicate or in any way convey to the supervisee's clients or to other parties that the supervisee is himself/herself licensed.

1.03 Supervisors should make supervisees aware of clients' rights, including protecting clients' right to privacy and confidentiality in the counseling relationship and the information resulting from it. Clients also should be informed that their right to privacy and confidentiality will not be violated by the supervisory relationship.

1.04 Records of the counseling relationship, including interview notes, test data, correspondence, the electronic storage of these documents, and audio and videotape recordings, are considered to be confidential professional information. Supervisors should see that these materials are used in counseling, research, and training and supervision of counselors with the full knowledge of the clients and that permission to use these materials is granted by the applied counseling setting offering service to the client. This professional information is to be used for full protection of the client. Written consent from the client (or legal guardian, if a minor) should be secured prior to the use of such information for instructional, supervisory, and/or research purposes. Policies of the applied counseling setting regarding client records also should be followed.

1.05 Supervisors shall adhere to current professional and legal guidelines when conducting research with human participants such as Section D-1 of the ACA Ethical Standards.

1.06 Counseling supervisors are responsible for making every effort to monitor both the professional actions, and failures to take action, of their supervisees.

2. Supervisory Role

Inherent and integral to the role of supervisor are responsibilities for:

(a) monitoring client welfare;
(b) encouraging compliance with relevant legal, ethical, and professional standards for clinical practice;
(c) monitoring clinical performance and professional development of supervisees; and
(d) evaluating and certifying current performance and potential of supervisees for academic, screening, selection, placement, employment, and credentialing purposes.

2.01 Supervisors should have had training in supervision prior to initiating their role as supervisors.

2.02 Supervisors should pursue professional and personal continuing education activities such as advanced courses, seminars, and professional conferences on a regular and ongoing basis. These activities should include both counseling and supervision topics and skills.

2.03 Supervisors should make their supervisees aware of professional and ethical standards and legal responsibilities of the counseling profession.

2.04 Supervisors of post-degree counselors who are seeking state licensure should encourage these counselors to adhere to the standards for practice established by the state licensure board of the state in which they practice.

2.05 Procedures for contacting the supervisor, or an alternative supervisor, to assist in handling crisis situations should be established and communicated to supervisees.

2.06 Actual work samples via audio and/or video tape or live observation in addition to case notes should be reviewed by the supervisor as a regular part of the ongoing supervisory process.

2.07 Supervisors of counselors should meeting [*sic*] regularly in face-to-face sessions with their supervisees.

2.08 Supervisors should provide supervisees with ongoing feedback on their performance. This feedback should take a variety of forms, both formal and informal, and should include verbal and written evaluations. It should be formative during the supervisory experience and summative at the conclusion of the experience.

2.09 Supervisors who have multiple roles (e.g., teacher, clinical supervisor, administrative supervisor, etc.) with supervisees should minimize potential conflicts. Where possible, the roles should be divided among several supervisors. Where this is not possible, careful explanation should be conveyed to the supervisee as to the expectations and responsibilities associated with each supervisory role.

2.10 Supervisors should not participate in any form of sexual contact with supervisees. Supervisors should not engage in any form of social contact or interaction which would compromise the supervisor-supervisee relationship. Dual relationships with supervisees that might impair the supervisor's objectivity and professional judgment should be avoided and/or the supervisory relationship terminated.

2.11 Supervisors should not establish a psychotherapeutic relationship as a substitute for supervision. Personal issues should be addressed in supervision only in terms of the impact of these issues on clients and on professional functioning.

2.12 Supervisors, through ongoing supervisee assessment and evaluation, should be aware of any personal or professional limitations of supervisees which are likely to impede future professional performance. Supervisors have the responsibility of recommending remedial assistance to the supervisee and of screening from the training program, applied counseling setting, or state licensure those supervisees who are unable to provide competent professional services. These recommendations should be clearly and professionally explained in writing to the supervisees who are so evaluated.

2.13 Supervisors should not endorse a supervisee for certification, licensure, completion of an academic training program, or continued employment if the supervisor believes the supervisee is impaired in any way that would interfere with the performance of counseling duties. The presence of any such impairment should begin a process of feedback and remediation wherever possible so that the supervisee understands the nature of the impairment and has the opportunity to remedy the problem and continue with his/her professional development.

2.14 Supervisors should incorporate the principles of informed consent and participation; clarity of requirements, expectations, roles and rules; and due process and appeal into the establishment of policies and procedures of their institutions, program, courses, and individual supervisory relationships. Mechanisms for due process appeal of individual supervisory actions should be established and made available to all supervisees.

3. Program Administration Role

3.01 Supervisors should ensure that the programs conducted and experiences provided are in keeping with current guidelines and standards of ACA and its divisions.

3.02 Supervisors should teach courses and/or supervise clinical work only in areas where they are fully competent and experienced.

3.03 To achieve the highest quality of training and supervision, supervisors should be active participants in peer review and peer supervision procedures.

3.04 Supervisors should provide experiences that integrate theoretical knowledge and practical application. Supervisors also should provide opportunities in which supervisees are able to apply the knowledge they have learned and understand the rationale for the skills they have acquired. The knowledge and skills conveyed should reflect current practice, research findings, and available resources.

3.05 Professional competencies, specific courses, and/or required experiences expected of supervisees should be communicated to them in writing prior to admission to the training program or placement/employment by the applied counseling setting, and, in case of continued employment, in a timely manner.

3.06 Supervisors should accept only those persons as supervisees who meet identified entry level requirements for admission to a program of counselor training or for placement in an applied counseling setting. In the case of private supervision in search of state licensure, supervisees should have completed all necessary prerequisites as determined by the state licensure board.

3.07 Supervisors should inform supervisees of the goals, policies, theoretical orientations toward counseling, training, and supervision model or approach on which the supervision is based.

3.08 Supervisees should be encouraged and assisted to define their own theoretical orientation toward counseling, to establish supervision goals for themselves, and to monitor and evaluate their progress toward meeting these goals.

3.09 Supervisors should assess supervisees' skills and experience in order to establish standards for competent professional behavior. Supervisors should restrict supervisees' activities to those that are commensurate with their current level of skills and experiences.

3.10 Supervisors should obtain practicum and fieldwork sites that meet minimum standards for preparing students to become effective counselors. No practicum or fieldwork setting should be approved unless it truly replicates a counseling work setting.

3.11 Practicum and fieldwork classes would be limited in size according to established professional standards to ensure that each student has ample opportunity for individual supervision and feedback. Supervisors in applied counseling settings should have a limited number of supervisees.

3.12 Supervisors in university settings should establish and communicate specific policies and procedures regarding field placement of students. The respective roles of the student counselor, the university supervisor, and the field supervisor should be clearly differentiated in areas such as evaluation, requirements, and confidentiality.

3.13 Supervisors in training programs should communicate regularly with supervisors in agencies used as practicum and/or fieldwork sites regarding current professional practices, expectations of students, and preferred models and modalities of supervision.

3.14 Supervisors at the university should establish clear lines of communication among themselves, the field supervisors, and the students/ supervisees.

3.15 Supervisors should establish and communicate to supervisees and to field supervisors specific procedures regarding consultation, performance review, and evaluation of supervisees.

3.16 Evaluations of supervisee performance in universities and in applied counseling settings should be available to supervisees in ways consistent with the Family Rights and Privacy Act and the Buckley Amendment.

3.17 Forms of training that focus primarily on self understanding and problem resolution (e.g., personal growth groups or individual counseling) should be voluntary. Those who conduct these forms of training should not serve simultaneously as supervisors of the supervisees involved in the training.

3.18 A supervisor may recommend participation in activities such as personal growth groups or personal counseling when it has been determined that a supervisee has deficits in the areas of self understanding and problem resolution which impede his/her professional functioning. The supervisors should not be the direct provider of these activities for the supervisee.

3.19 When a training program conducts a personal growth or counseling experience involving relatively intimate self disclosure, care should be taken to eliminate or minimize potential role conflicts for faculty and/or agency supervisors who may conduct these experiences and who also serve as teachers, group leaders, and clinical directors.

3.20 Supervisors should use the following prioritized sequence in resolving conflicts among the needs of the client, the needs of the supervisee, and the needs of the program or agency. Insofar as the client must be protected, it should be understood that client welfare is usually subsumed in federal and state laws such that these statutes should be the first point of reference. Where laws and ethical standards are not present or are unclear, the good judgment of the supervisor should be guided by the following list.

(a) Relevant legal and ethical standards (e.g., duty to warn, state child abuse laws, etc.);
(b) Client welfare;
(c) Supervisee welfare;
(d) Supervisor welfare; and
(e) Program and/or agency service and administrative needs.

Appendix C
Multicultural Counseling Competencies and Standards*

I. **Counselor Awareness of Own Cultural Values and Biases**
    A. **Attitudes and Beliefs**
       1. Culturally skilled counselors have moved from being culturally unaware to being aware and sensitive to their own cultural heritage and to valuing and respecting differences.
       2. Culturally skilled counselors are aware of how their own cultural backgrounds and experiences and attitudes, values, and biases influence psychological processes.
       3. Culturally skilled counselors are able to recognize the limits of their competencies and expertise.
       4. Culturally skilled counselors are comfortable with differences that exist between themselves and clients in terms of race, ethnicity, culture, and beliefs.

    B. **Knowledge**
       1. Culturally skilled counselors have specific knowledge about their own racial and cultural heritage and how it personally and professionally affects their definitions of normality-abnormality and the process of counseling.
       2. Culturally skilled counselors possess knowledge and understanding about how oppression, racism, discrimination, and stereotyping affects them personally and in their work. This allows them to acknowledge their own racist attitudes, beliefs, and feelings. Although this standard applies to all groups, for White counselors it may mean that they understand how they may have directly or indirectly benefited from individual, institutional, and cultural racism (White identity development models).

---

* These first appeared in 1992, when they were published simultaneously in ACA's *Journal of Counseling and Development* (Sue, Arredondo & McDavis, *70*, 482–483) and in the *Journal of the Association for Multicultural Counseling and Development* (AMCD). Reprinted with permission from the American Counseling Association. They are also posted on the ACA website as the Cross-Cultural Competencies and Objectives, and may be retrieved from http://www.counseling.org/Files/FD.ashx?guid=8120574f-e1b2-4605-bd46-f7d459c0d851.

3. Culturally skilled counselors possess knowledge about their social impact on others. They are knowledgeable about communication style differences, how their style may clash or foster the counseling process with minority clients, and how to anticipate the impact it may have on others.

C. **Skills**

1. Culturally skilled counselors seek out educational, consultative, and training experience to improve their understanding and effectiveness in working with culturally different populations. Being able to recognize the limits of their competencies, they (a) seek consultation, (b) seek further training or education, (c) refer out to more qualified individuals or resources, or (d) engage in a combination of these.

2. Culturally skilled counselors are constantly seeking to understand themselves as racial and cultural beings and are actively seeking a nonracist identity.

II. **Counselor Awareness of Client's Worldview**

A. **Attitudes and Beliefs**

1. Culturally skilled counselors are aware of their negative emotional reactions toward other racial and ethnic groups that may prove detrimental to their clients in counseling. They are willing to contrast their own beliefs and attitudes with those of their culturally different clients in a nonjudgmental fashion.

2. Culturally skilled counselors are aware of their stereotypes and preconceived notions that they may hold toward other racial and ethnic minority groups.

B. **Knowledge**

1. Culturally skilled counselors possess specific knowledge and information about the particular group they are working with. They are aware of the life experiences, cultural heritage, and historical background of their culturally different clients. This particular competency is strongly linked to the "minority identity development models" available in the literature.

2. Culturally skilled counselors understand how race, culture, ethnicity, and so forth may affect personality formation, vocational choices, manifestation of psychological disorders, help-seeking behavior, and the appropriateness or inappropriateness of counseling approaches.

3. Culturally skilled counselors understand and have knowledge about sociopolitical influences that impinge upon the life of racial and ethnic minorities. Immigration issues, poverty, racism, stereotyping, and powerlessness all leave major scars that may influence the counseling process.

C. **Skills**

1. Culturally skilled counselors should familiarize themselves with relevant research and the latest findings regarding mental health and mental disorders of various ethnic and racial groups. They should actively seek out educational experiences that foster their knowledge, understanding, and cross-cultural skills.

2. Culturally skilled counselors become actively involved with minority individuals outside of the counseling setting (community events, social and political functions, celebrations, friendships, neighborhood groups, and so forth) so that their perspective of minorities is more than an academic or helping exercise.

III. **Culturally Appropriate Intervention Strategies**

A. **Attitudes and Beliefs**

1. Culturally skilled counselors respect clients' religious and/or spiritual beliefs and values, including attributions and taboos, because they affect worldview, psychosocial functioning, and expressions of distress.

2. Culturally skilled counselors respect indigenous helping practices and respect minority community intrinsic help-giving networks.

3. Culturally skilled counselors value bilingualism and do not view another language as an impediment to counseling (monolingualism may be the culprit).

B. **Knowledge**

1. Culturally skilled counselors have a clear and explicit knowledge and understanding of the generic characteristics of counseling and therapy (culture bound, class bound, and monolingual) and how they may clash with the cultural values of various minority groups.

2. Culturally skilled counselors are aware of institutional barriers that prevent minorities from using mental health services.

3. Culturally skilled counselors have knowledge of the potential bias in assessment instruments and use procedures and interpret findings keeping in mind the cultural and linguistic characteristics of the clients.

4. Culturally skilled counselors have knowledge of minority family structures, hierarchies, values, and beliefs. They are knowledgeable about the community characteristics and the resources in the community as well as the family.

5. Culturally skilled counselors should be aware of relevant discriminatory practices at the social and community level that

may be affecting the psychological welfare of the population being served.

C. **Skills**

1. Culturally skilled counselors are able to engage in a variety of verbal and nonverbal helping responses. They are able to *send* and *receive* both *verbal* and *non-verbal* messages *accurately* and *appropriately*. They are not tied down to only one method or approach to helping but recognize that helping styles and approaches may be culture bound. When they sense that their helping style is limited and potentially inappropriate, they can anticipate and ameliorate its negative impact.

2. Culturally skilled counselors are able to exercise institutional intervention skills on behalf of their clients. They can help clients determine whether a "problem" stems from racism or bias in others (the concept of health paranoia) so that clients do not inappropriately personalize problems.

3. Culturally skilled counselors are not averse to seeking consultation with traditional healers and religious and spiritual leaders and practitioners in the treatment of culturally different clients when appropriate.

4. Culturally skilled counselors take responsibility for interacting in the language requested by the client and, if not feasible, make appropriate referral. A serious problem arises when the linguistic skills of a counselor do not match the language of the client. This being the case, counselors should (a) seek a translator with cultural knowledge and appropriate professional background and (b) refer to a knowledgeable and competent bilingual counselor.

5. Culturally skilled counselors have training and expertise in the use of traditional assessment and testing instruments. They not only understand the technical aspects of the instruments but are also aware of the cultural limitations. This allows them to use test instruments for the welfare of the diverse clients.

6. Culturally skilled counselors should attend to as well as work to eliminate biases, prejudices, and discriminatory practices. They should be cognizant of sociopolitical contexts in conducting evaluation and providing interventions and should develop sensitivity to issues of oppression, sexism, elitism, and racism.

7. Culturally skilled counselors take responsibility in educating their clients to the processes of psychological intervention, such as goals, expectations, legal rights, and the counselor's orientation.

References

Abernethy, M. A., & Lillis, A. M. (2001). Interdependencies in organization design: A test in hospitals. *Journal of Management Accounting Research, 13,* 107–129.

Agard, A. (May 2005). Using objectivity. *Supervision, 66* (5), 11–14.

American Counseling Association (ACA). (2005). *ACA code of ethics.* Retrieved August 19, 2005 from http://www.counseling.org/Resources/CodeOfEthics/TP/Home/CT2.aspx.

American Counseling Association (ACA). (n.d.a.). *Advocacy competencies.* Retrieved February 9, 2006 from http://www.counseling.org/Resources/.

American Counseling Association (ACA). (n.d.b.). *Cross-cultural competencies and objectives.* Retrieved October 21, 2004 from http://www.counseling.org/Files/FD.ashx?guid= 8120574f-e1b2-4605-bd46-f7d459c0d851.

American Counseling Association (ACA). (n.d.c.). *Standards for internet on-line counseling.* Retrieved from http://www.counseling.org/Resources/.

American Counseling Association (ACA). (n.d.d.). *Who are licensed professional counselors.* Retrieved May 12, 2006 from http://www.counseling.org/Files/FD.ashx?guid=076eccaa-21e5-47ce-bed7-afddfabd3201.

American Counseling Association (ACA)—Task Force on Counselor Wellness and Impairment. (n.d.e). *Wellness strategies.* Retrieved July 3, 2005 from http://www.counseling.org/wellness95taskforce/tf95wellness95strategies.htm.

American Counseling Association (ACA)—Office of Public Policy and Legislation. (2006). *Effective advocacy and communication with legislators.* Retrieved May 1, 2006 from http:// www.counseling.org/Files/FD.ashx?guid=680f251e-b3d0-4f77-8aa3-4e360f32f05e

American Heritage Dictionary. (2nd college ed.). (1982). Boston: Houghton Mifflin.

American Mental Health Counselors Association (AMHCA). (n.d.) AMHCA.org—About Us. Retrieved August 21, 2005 from http://www.amhca.org/about/.

American Mental Health Counselors Association (AMHCA). *Code of ethics of the American Mental Health Counselors Association, 2000 Revision.* Retrieved August 21, 2005 from http:// www.amhca.org/code/.

American Rehabilitation Counseling Association (ARCA). (n.d.). *Certification standards of the commission on rehabilitation counseling certification.* Retrieved from http://www.crc-certification.com/.

American School Counselor Association (ASCA). (1997). *National standards for school counseling.* Alexandria, VA: Author.

American School Counselor Association (ASCA). (2004a). *Ethical standards for school counselors.* Retrieved from http://www.schoolcounselor.org/content.asp?contentid=173.

American School Counselor Association (ASCA). (2004b). *Position statement: Cultural diversity.* Retrieved January 11, 2005, from http://www.schoolcounselor.org/content.asp? contentid=249.

American School Counselor Association (ASCA). (2005). *The ASCA national model for school counseling programs* (2nd ed.). Alexandria, VA: Author.

Arredondo, P. (1996). *Successful diversity management initiatives: A blue print for planning and implementation.* Thousand Oaks, CA: SAGE Publications.

Arredondo, P., & Toporek, R. (2004). Multicultural counseling competencies = Ethical practice. *Journal of Mental Health Counseling, 26* (1), 44–55.

Arredondo, P., Toporek, R., Brown, S., Jones, J., Locke, D. C., Sanchez, L., & Stadler, H. (1996). Operationalization of multicultural counseling competencies. *Journal of Multicultural Counseling and Development, 24,* 42–78. Retrieved from http://www.counseling.org/Files/ FD.ashx?guid=735d18d6-2a6e-41bf-bd4a-75f4ce48a100.

The art and process of strategy development and deployment. (Winter 2005). *The Journal for Quality & Participation, 28* (4), 10–17.

Association for Adult Development and Aging (AADA). (n.d.). *Gerontological competencies.* Retrieved from http://www.uncg.edu/111jemyers/jem95info/docs/competencies.htm.

Association for Assessment in Counseling and Education (AACE). (n.d.). *Resources.* Retrieved from http://aac.ncat.edu/resources.html.

Association for Counselor Education and Supervision (ACES). (1989, Spring). ACES adopts standards for counseling supervisors. ACES Spectrum, 7–10.

Association for Counselor Education and Supervision (ACES). (1993). *Ethical guidelines for counseling supervisors.* Retrieved June 5, 2004 from http://www.acesonline.net/ethical95guidelines.asp.

Association for Gay, Lesbian and Bisexual Issues in Counseling (AGLBIC). (n.d.). *Competencies for counseling gay, lesbian, bisexual and transgendered (GLBT) clients.* Retrieved from http://www.aglbic.org/resources/competencies.html.

Association for Multicultural Counseling and Development (AMCD). (n.d.). *Multi-cultural counseling competencies.* Retrieved from http://www.counseling.org/Resources/.

Association for Specialists in Group Work (ASGW). (n.d.a.). *Best practice guidelines.* Retrieved from http://www.asgw.org/PDF/Best95Practices.pdf.

Association for Specialists in Group Work (ASGW). (n.d.b.). *Core group work competencies.* Retrieved from http://www.asgw.org/20020211%20Group%20Stds%20Brochure.pdf.

Association for Spiritual, Ethical and Religious Values in Counseling (ASERVIC). (n.d.). *Competencies for integrating spirituality in counseling.* Retrieved from http://www.aservic.org/Competencies.html.

Austin, D. M. (2002). *Human services management: Organizational leadership in social work practice.* New York: Columbia University Press.

Barratt, B. *Subjective objectivity: Evaluating students' writing.* Retrieved August 27, 2006 from http://home.alphalink.com.au/111umbidas/subjective-objectivity.htm.

Beck, D. (2005, June 27). Reason, emotions can be partners. *San Antonio Express-News,* pp. C1, C2.

Beckhard, R., & Harris, R. T. (1987). *Organizational transitions: Managing complex change* (2nd ed.). Boston, MA: Addison-Wesley.

Bekkers, V., & Homburg, V. (2002). Administrative supervision and information relationships. *Information polity: The international journal of government and democracy in the information age, 7*(2/3), 129–141.

Bennis, W. G., & Biederman, P. W. (1997). *Organizing genius: The secrets of creative collaboration.* Reading, MA: Addison-Wesley.

Bensimon, E. M., Ward, K., & Sanders, K. (2000). *The department chair's role in developing new faculty into teachers and scholars.* Bolton, MA: Anker Publishing.

Bernard, J. M., & Goodyear, R. K. (1992). *Fundamentals of clinical supervision.* Needham Heights, MA: Allyn & Bacon.

Bernard, J. M., & Goodyear, R. K. (2004). *Fundamentals of clinical supervision* (3rd ed.). Boston, MA: Pearson Education.

Bethune, G., Sherrod, D., & Youngblood, L. (April 2005). 101 tips to retain a happy, healthy staff. *Nursing Management, 36* (4), 24–29.

Bielous, G. A. (1998). Effective coaching: Improving marginal performers. *Supervision, 59* (7), 15–17.

Blanchard, K., Carew, D., & Parisi-Carew, E. (2000). *The one-minute manager builds high performing teams.* NY: William Morrow.

Blanchard, K., Oncken, W., Jr., & Burrows, H. (1989). *The one minute manager meets the monkey.* NY: William Morrow.

Bloom, B. S. (Ed.). (1956). *Taxonomy of education objectives, the classification of educational goals: Handbook 1. Cognitive domain.* New York: David McKay.

Borders, L. D. (1994). The good supervisor. In L. D. Borders (Ed.), *Supervision: Exploring the effective components* (pp. 23–24). Greensboro, NC: ERIC/CASS.

Borders, L. D., & Brown, L. L. (2005). *The new handbook of counseling supervision.* Alexandria, VA: American Counseling Association, sponsored by Association for Counselor Education and Supervision.

Borders, L. D., Bernard, J. M., Dye, H. A., Fong, M. L., Henderson, P., & Nance, D. W. (1991). Curriculum guide for training counseling supervisors: Rationale, development and implementation. *Counselor Education and Supervision, 31,* 58–80.

Bordin, E. S. (1983). Supervision in counseling: II. Contemporary models of supervision: A working alliance based model of supervision. *Counseling Psychologist, 11* (1), 35–42.

Brousseau, K. R., Driver, M. J., Hourihan, G., & Larsson, R. (Feb 2006). The seasoned executive's decision-making style. *Harvard Business Review, 84* (2), 110–121.

Buckingham, M. (March 2005). What great managers do. *Harvard Business Review, 83* (3), 70–79.

Buckingham, M., & Clifton, D. O. (2001). *Now, discover your strengths.* New York: The Free Press.

Buckingham, M., & Coffman, C. (1999). *First break all the rules: What the world's greatest managers do differently.* New York: Simon & Schuster.

Buhler, P. M. (2005). Managing in the new millennium. *Supervision, 66* (7), 20–22.

Building Team Performance. (July/Aug, 2005). *Harvard Business Review, 83* (7), p. 166.

Buller, J. L. (Fall 2004). Five case studies in budgeting. *The Department Chair, 15* (2), 10–11.

Bunch, L. K. (2002). Ensuring professionally relevant supervision and professional development: A state-level experience. In P. Henderson & N. Gysbers (Eds.), *Implementing comprehensive guidance programs: Critical leadership issues and successful responses* (pp. 193–198). Greensboro, NC: CAPS Publications.

Burge, J. (2006). STAR TEAMS. *Office Pro, 66,* 6–9.

Busick, J. (8/1/2006). *Safety Compliance Letter, 2468,* [Electronic Version]. 7–11. Retrieved August 12, 2006 from Business Source Complete.

By the numbers: Counselor impairment. (2005, October). *Counseling Today, 48* (4), 3.

Campion, M. A., & Campion, L. A. (January 1995). A practical checklist for content and organization. *HR Focus, 72* (1), 12–13.

Carbaugh, D. (2005). *Cultures in conversation.* Mahwah, NJ: Lawrence Erlbaum Associates.

Cebik, R. J. (1985). Ego development theory and its implications for supervision. *Counselor Education and Supervision, 24,* 226–233.

Center for Credentialing & Education, Inc. (CCE). *Approved Clinical Supervisor.* Retrieved August 26, 2005 from http://www.cce-global.org/credentials-offered/acs.

Coens, T., & Jenkins, M. (2000). *Abolishing performance appraisals: Why they backfire and what to do instead.* San Francisco: Berrett-Koehler.

Coleman, H. L. K. (2004). Multicultural counseling competencies in a pluralistic society. *Journal of Mental Health Counseling, 26* (1), 56–66.

Collie, A. J. (02/05/2001). Riley takes the Heat. *American Way,* 110–112.

Connor, P. E., Lake, L. K., & Stackman, R. W. (2003). *Managing organizational change* (3rd ed.). Westport, CT: Praeger.

Constantine, M. (1997). Facilitating multicultural competency in counseling supervision. In Pope-Davis, D. B., & Coleman, H. L. K. (Eds.), *Multicultural counseling competencies: Assessment, education and training, and supervision* (pp. 310–324). Thousand Oaks, CA: Sage.

Constantine, M. G. (2002). Prediction of satisfaction with counseling: Racial and ethnic minority clients' attitudes toward counseling and ratings of their counselors' general and multicultural counseling competence. *Journal of Counseling Psychology, 49* (2), 255–263.

Constantine, M. G., Arorash, T. J., Barakett, M. D., Blackmon, S. M., Donnelly, P. C., & Edles, P. A. (2001). School counselors' universal-diverse orientation and aspects of their multicultural counseling competence. *Professional School Counseling, 5,* 13–18.

Constantine, M. G., & Gushue, G. V. (2003). School counselors' ethnic tolerance attitudes and racism attitudes as predictors of their multicultural case conceptualization of an immigrant student. *Journal of Counseling & Development, 81,* 185–190.

Corey, G. (2001). *Theory and practice of counseling and psychotherapy.* Belmont, CA: Wadsworth/Thomson Learning.

Cottringer, W. (Jul 2004). From employee to supervisor. *Supervision, 65* (7), 13–14.

Cottringer, W. (2005a). Adopting a philosophy on conflict. *Supervision, 66* (3), 3–5.

Cottringer, W. (2005b). Being the kind of supervisor every employer loves. *Supervision, 66* (6), 8–10.

Cottringer, W. (2005c). Setting the standards. *Supervision, 66* (4), 6–7.

Cottringer, W. (2005d). Success as a supervisor. *Supervision, 66* (8), 6–7.

Covey, S. R. (1989). *7 habits of highly effective people: Restoring the character ethic.* NY: Simon & Schuster.

Covey, S. R. (1991). *Principle-centered leadership.* New York: Summit Books.

Curtis, R., & Sherlock, J. J. (2006). Wearing two hats: Counselors working as managerial leaders in agencies and schools. *Journal of Counseling and Development, 84* (1), 120–126.

D'Andrea, M., & Daniels, J. (1997). Multicultural counseling supervision: Central issues, theoretical considerations, and practical strategies. In Pope-Davis, D. B., & Coleman, H. L. K. (Eds.), *Multicultural counseling competencies: Assessment, education and training, and supervision* (pp. 290–309). Thousand Oaks, CA: Sage.

Daniels, J., D'Andrea, M., & Kim, B. S. K. (1999). Assessing the barriers and changes of cross-cultural supervision: A case study. *Counselor Education and Supervision, 38* (3), 191–204.

Davenport, T. H., Thomas, R. J., and Cantrell, S. (2002). The mysterious art and science of knowledge-worker performance. *MIT Sloan Management Review, 44* (1), 23–30.

David, F. R., & David, F. R. (2003, January/February). It's time to redraft your mission statement. *Journal of Business Strategy.* 11–14.

Davis, G., Chun, R., Da Silva, R. V., & Roper, S. (2004). A corporate character scale to assess employee and customer views of organization reputation. *Corporate Reputation Review, 7* (2), 125–147.

Day-Vines, N. L., Wood, A. M., Grothaus, T., Craigen, L., Holman, A., Dotson-Blake, K., & Douglass, M. J. (2007). Broaching the subjects of race, ethnicity, and culture during the counseling process. *Journal of Counseling & Development, 85* (4), 401–409.

Dellana, S. A., & Snyder, D. (2004). Student future outlook and counseling quality in a rural minority high school. *High School Journal, 88* (1), 27–42.

DeMars, N, (2006). The new loyalty: What bosses can expect (and what they can't). *Office Pro, 66,* 10–12.

Department of Labor. *Elaws—FirstStep employment law advisor.* Retrieved from http://www.dol.gov/elaws/firststep.

Deutschman, A. (May 2005). Making change [Electronic version]. *Fast Company, 94,* 52–62. Retrieved August 24, 2005 from Business Source Complete database.

Diamond, M. (Apr 2006). Organized for success. *Reeves Journal: Plumbing, Heating, Cooling, 86* (4), p. 68.

Drucker, P. F. (1974). *Management: Tasks, responsibilities, practices.* New York: Harper & Row.

Drucker, P. F. (Oct 5, 1998). Management's new paradigms. *Forbes.* Retrieved June 12, 2005 from the Business Source Premier database.

Drucker, P. F. (1999). *Management challenges for the 21st century.* New York: Harper Business.

Drucker, P. F. (2005). Managing oneself. *Harvard Business Review, 83* (1), 100–109. Retrieved May 30, 2006, from the Business Source Premier database.

Dye, A. H. (1985, November). *A dynamic view of the supervision environment.* Unpublished workshop material, Purdue University, Lafayette, IN.

Eby, L., Butts, M., Lockwood, A., & Simon, S. (Summer 2004). Protégeés' negative mentoring experiences [Electronic version]. *Personnel Psychology, 57* (2), 411–448. Retrieved July 13, 2005, from Business Source Premier.

Engels, D., Altekruse, M. K., Berg, R. C., Bratton, S. C., Chandler, C. K., Coy, D. R., Durodoye, B. A., et al. (2004). *The professional counselor: Portfolio, competencies, performance guidelines, and assessment* (3rd ed.). Alexandria, VA: American Counseling Association.

Ericksen, K. & McAuliffe, G. (2003). A measure of counselor competency. *Counselor Education & Supervision, 43*(2), 120–133.

Erwin, W. J. (Dec 2000). Supervisor moral sensitivity. *Counselor Education & Supervision, 40* (2), 115–127.

Esters, I. & Ledoux, C. (2001). At-risk high school students' preferences for counselor characteristics. *Professional School Counseling, 4,* 165–170.

Fago, J. (August 2004). Frequently asked human resources questions. *Illinois Banker, 9,* 28–29.

Falender, C. A., Cornish, J. A. E., Goodyear, R., Hatcher, R., Kaslow, N., Leventhal, G., et al. (2004). Defining competencies in psychology supervision: A consensus statement. *Journal of Clinical Psychology, 60* (7), 771–785.

Falvey, J. E.. (1987). *Handbook of administrative supervision.* Alexandria, VA: Association for Counselor Education and Supervision.

Farrant, D. (Jul 2005). Unproductive time drains. *Supervision, 66* (7), 15–17.

Fernando, D. M., & Hulse-Killacky, D. (2005). The relationship of supervisory styles to satisfaction with supervision and the perceived self-efficacy of Master's-level counseling students. *Counselor Education & Supervision, 44* (4), 293–304.

Fiedler, F. E. (1998). The leadership situation: A missing factor in selecting and training managers. *Human Resource Management Review,* Winter 98 (4), 335–350.

Fong, M. L., & Lease, S. H. (1997). Cross-cultural supervision: Issues for the White supervisor. In

Pope-Davis, D. B., & Coleman, H. L. K. (Eds.), *Multicultural counseling competencies: Assessment, education and training, and supervision* (pp. 387–405). Thousand Oaks, CA: Sage.

Forester-Miller, H., & Davis, T. (1996). A practitioner's guide to ethical decision making. Alexandria, VA: American Counseling Association. Retrieved November 15, 2005 from http://www.counseling.org/Files/FD.ashx?guid=c4dcf247-66e8-45a3-abcc-024f5d7e836f.

Fracaro, K. (Oct 2004). Modern management practices. *Supervision, 65* (10), 3–5.

French, J. R. P., Jr., & Raven, B. H. (1959). The bases of social power. In D. Cartwright (Ed.), *Studies in social power* (pp. 150–167). Ann Arbor, MI: Institute for Social Research.

Fried, Y., & Slowik, L. H. (July 2004). Enriching goal-setting theory with time: An integrated approach. *Academy of Management Review, 29* (3), 404–422.

Fullan, M. (1993). *Change forces: Probing the depths of educational reform.* Bristol, PA: Falmer Press.

Fullan, M. (2001). *Leading in a culture of change.* San Francisco: Jossey-Bass.

Fullan, M. (2002). The change leader. *Educational Leadership, 59* (8), 16–20.

Gardner, H. (Feb 2006). The synthesizing leader. *Harvard Business Review, 84*(2), 36–37.

Gaver, K., M.D. (2000). Mental health care delivery systems. In Rodenhauser, P., M.D. (Ed.), *Mental health care administration: A guide for practitioners* (pp. 31–52). Ann Arbor: The University of Michigan Press.

Gay, G. (2002). Culturally responsive teaching in special education for ethnically diverse students: Setting the stage. *International Journal of Qualitative Studies in Education (QSE), 15* (6), 613–629.

Ghoshal, S., & Bruch, H. (Spring 2003). Going beyond motivation to the power of volition. *MIT Sloan Management Review, 44* (3), 51–57.

Giannatasio, N. A. (Summer 2005). The discretionary function exemption: Legislation and case law. *Public Administration Quarterly, 29* (2), 202–230.

Glickman, C. D. (1981). *Developmental supervision: Alternative practices for helping teachers improve instruction.* Alexandria. VA: Association for Supervision and Curriculum Development.

Glickman, C. D., Gordon, S. P., & Ross-Gordon, J. M. (1995). *Supervision of instruction: A developmental approach* (3rd ed.). Boston: Allyn & Bacon.

Granello, D. H. (2003). Influence strategies in the supervisory dyad: An investigation into the effects of gender and age. *Counselor Education and Supervision, 42* (3), 189–202.

Gray, G. (2002). Performance appraisals don't work. *Industrial Management, 34* (5), 15–17.

Greengard, S. (S.G.). (May 1996). Making privacy a priority [Electronic Version]. *Personnel Journal, 75* (5), 76. Retrieved August 12, 2006 from Business Source Complete.

Groth, M. (2004, Fall). What do students want from us? *The Department Chair, 15* (2), 15–17.

Guiffrida, D. A. (2005). The emergence model: An alternative pedagogy for facilitating self-reflection and theoretical fit in counseling students. *Counselor Education and Supervision, 44* (3), 201–213.

Gysbers, N. C., & Henderson, P. (2006). *Developing and managing your school guidance and counseling program* (4th ed.). Alexandria, VA: American Counseling Association.

Hackley, S. (Nov 2004). When life gives you lemons: How to deal with difficult people. *Negotiation,* 3–5.

Harris, T. E. (2002). *Applied organizational communication: Principles and pragmatics for future practice* (2nd ed.). Mahwah, NJ: Lawrence Erlbaum Associates.

Hays, D. G., & Chang, C. (2003). White privilege, oppression, and racial identity development: Implications for supervision. *Counselor Education and Supervision, 43*(2), 134–145.

Helms, S. (2005). Designing a formative measure for corporate reputation. *Corporate Reputation Review, 8* (2), 95–109.

Hemre, A. (July/August 2006). Knowledge organizations and mission-based architecture. *KM Review, 9* (3), 10–11.

Henderson, P. (April 1994). Administrative skills in counseling supervision. In Borders, L. D. (Guest Editor), *Supervision: Exploring the effective components.* ERIC/CASS Counseling Digest Series. Greensboro, NC: Counseling and Student Services Clearinghouse.

Henderson, P. (1999, 2001). [Annual Reports]. Unpublished raw data.

Henderson, P., Cook, K., Libby, M., & Zambrano, E. (2006). Today I feel like a professional school counselor! Developing a strong professional school counselor identity through career experiences. *Guidance & Counselling, 21* (3), 128–142.

Henderson, P., & Gysbers, N.C. (1998). *Leading and managing your school guidance program staff.* Alexandria, VA: American Counseling Association.

Henderson, P. & Gysbers, N. (Eds.) (2002). *Implementing comprehensive guidance programs: Critical leadership issues and successful responses.* Greensboro, NC: CAPS Publications.

Henderson P., & Gysbers, N. (2006). Providing administrative and counseling supervision for school counselors. In Walz, G. R., Bleuer, J. C., & Yep, R. K. (Eds), *VISTAS: Compelling perspectives on counseling 2006* (pp. 161–164). Alexandria, VA: American Counseling Association.

Hermann, M. A., & Herlihy, B. R. (2006). Legal and ethical implications of refusing to counsel homosexual clients. *Journal of Counseling and Development, 84,* 414–418.

Herr, E. L., Heitzmann, D. E., & Rayman, J. R. (2006). *The professional counselor as administrator: Perspectives on leadership and management in counseling services across settings.* Mahwah, NJ: Lawrence Erlbaum Associates.

Hersey, P., Blanchard, K. H., & Johnson, D. E. (2001). *Management of organizational behavior: Leading human resources* (8th ed.). Upper Saddle River, NJ: Prentice Hall.

Herzberg, F., Mausner, B., & Snyderman, B. (1959). *The motivation to work.* New York: Wiley.

Hill, N. R. (2003). Promoting and celebrating multicultural competence in counselor trainees. *Counselor Education and Supervision, 43,* 39–51.

Hogg Foundation for Mental Health. (2006, March). Cultural Adaptation Proposals Sought. *Hogg Foundation News, 42,* pp. 1, 3.

How you can stay out of trouble. (2006, September 11). *Time,* p. 64.

Huisken, B. (May 2006). Top 4 ways to set goals. *JCK, 177* (5), 381.

Hurst, D. K. (1984, May-June). Of boxes, bubbles and effective management. *Harvard Business Review, 62* (3), 78–88.

Hyatt Diversity. Retrieved March 13, 2006 from http://www.explorehyatt.jobs/index95flash.php?docid=54&skipflash=true.

Jentz, B. C., & Murphy, J. T. (2005). Starting confused: How leaders start when they don't know where to start. *Phi Delta Kappan, 86* (10), 736–744.

Johnson, L. S. (2003). The diversity imperative: Building a culturally responsive school ethos. *Intercultural Education, 14* (1), 17–31.

Johnson, S. M.D. (1998). *Who moved my cheese? An amazing way to deal with change in your work and in your life.* NY: G.P. Putnam.

Kadushin, A. (July 1968). Games people play in supervision. *Social Work, 13* (3), 23–32.

Kadushin, A., & Harness, D. (2002). *Supervision in social work* (4th ed.) New York: Columbia University Press.

Kapp, M. B., J.D., M.P.H., & Mossman, D., M.D. (2000). Documentation for health care administrators. In Rodenhauser, P., M.D. (Ed.), *Mental health care administration: A guide for practitioners* (pp. 128–147). Ann Arbor: The University of Michigan Press.

Katzenbach, J. R., & Smith, D. K. (2005). The discipline of teams. *Harvard Business Review, 83* (7/8), 162–171.

Kell, B. L., & Mueller, W. J. (1966). *Impact and change: A study of counseling relationships.* New York: Appleton-Century Crofts.

Kelley, R. & Caplan, J. (1993). How Bell Labs creates star performers. *Harvard Business Review, 71* (4), 128–139.

Kemerer, F. R., & Crain, J. A. (1995). *The documentation handbook: Appraisal, nonrenewal and termination* (2nd ed.). Denton, TX: Texas School Administrators' Legal Digest.

Khandwalla, P. N. (2004, Oct-Dec). Competencies for senior manager roles. *Vikalpa: The Journal for Decision Makers, 29* (4), 11–24.

Koch, R. (1998). *The 80/20 Principle: The secret of achieving more with less.* NY: Doubleday.

Kramer, M. W. (2004). *Managing uncertainty in organizational communication.* Mahwah, NJ: Lawrence Erlbaum Associates.

Krousel-Wood, M. A., M.D., M.S.P.H. (2000). Outcomes assessment and performance improvement: Measurements and methodologies that matter in mental health care. In Rodenhauser, P., M.D. (Ed.), *Mental health care administration: A guide for practitioners* (pp. 233–254). Ann Arbor: The University of Michigan Press.

Kulik, C. T. (2004). *Human resources for the non-HR manager.* Mahwah, NJ: Lawrence Erlbaum Associates, Inc.

Kurpius, D. J., & Rozecki, T. (1992). Outreach, advocacy, and consultation: A framework for prevention and intervention. *Elementary School Guidance & Counseling, 26,* 176–189.

Ladany, N., Brittan-Powell, C. S., & Pannu, R. K. (1997). The influence of supervisory racial identity interaction and racial matching on the supervisory working alliance and supervisee multicultural competence. *Counselor Education and Supervision, 36* (4), 284–304.

Laschinger, H. K. S., & Finegan, J. (2005) Using empowerment to build trust and respect in the workplace: A strategy for addressing the nursing shortage. *Nursing Economic, 23* (1), 6–13.

Latham, G. P., Almost, J., Mann, S., & Moore, C. (Feb 2005). New developments in performance management. *Organizational Dynamics, 34* (1), 77–87.

Lees, N. D. (2004, Fall). Taking the department chair position seriously. *The Department Chair, 15* (2), 1–3.

Leong, F. T. L., & Wagner, N. S. (1994). Cross-cultural counseling supervision: What do we know? What do we need to know? *Counselor Education & Supervision, 34,* 117–139.

Leyden, T. (October, 2005). Middle management: Middle level musts! *TASSP NewsHilights,* 8.

Licensed Professional Counselor Act, Texas Occupations Code. §§ 503-001–003. (Acts 1999). Retrieved August 17, 2006 from http://tlo2.tlc.state.tx.us/statutes/docs/OC/content/htm/oc.003.00.000503.00.htm.

Linder, J. (Nov/Dec 2005). How do things really work around here? *Across the Board, 42* (6), 24–29.

Locke, D. C. (1990). A not so provincial view of multicultural counseling [Electronic version]. *Counselor Education and Supervision, 30* (1), 18–26. Retrieved December 8, 2005 from Academic Search Premiere database.

Loganbill, C., Hardy, E., & Delworth, U. (1982). Supervision: A conceptual model. *The Counseling Psychologist, 10* (1), 3–42.

Lopez, H. (2002). Seizing opportunities: Advocating for the development of a comprehensive guidance program. In P. Henderson, & N. Gysbers (Eds.), *Implementing comprehensive school guidance programs: Critical leadership issues and successful responses* (pp. 95–102). Greensboro, NC: CAPS Publications.

Luft, J., & Ingham, H. (1955). The Johari window, a graphic model of interpersonal awareness. *Proceedings of the western training laboratory in group development.* Los Angeles: UCLA. Retrieved June 14, 2006 from http://en.wikipedia.org/wiki/Johari95window.

Mackenzie, A. (1997). *The time trap* (3rd ed.). New York: AMACOM.

Magnuson, S., Wilcoxen, S. A., & Norem, K. (2000). A profile of lousy supervision: Experienced counselors' perspectives. *Counselor Education and Supervision, 39* (3), 189–202.

Magnuson, S., Wilcoxen, S. A., & Norem, K. (2003). Career paths of professional leaders in counseling: Plans, opportunities, and happenstance. *Humanistic Counseling, Education, and Development, 42* (1), 42–52.

Martin, W. F., Psy.D., M.P.H., M.A. (2000). Human resources in mental health care organizations. In Rodenhauser, P., M.D. (Ed.), *Mental health care administration: A guide for practitioners* (pp. 201–232). Ann Arbor: The University of Michigan Press.

Maslow, A. H. (1954). *Motivation and personality.* New York: Harper & Row.

Maslow, A. H. (1998/1962). *Maslow on management,* with Stephens, D. C., & Heil, G. NewYork: John Wiley and Sons. (Compiled and published in 1998 from Maslow's *Eupsychian Management* and other personal papers written in 1962).

Mayfield, J., & Mayfield, M. (2002). Leader communication strategies: Critical paths to improving employee commitment. *American Business Review, 20* (2), 89–94.

McGlothin, J. M., Rainey, S., & Kindsvatter, A. (December 2005). Suicidal clients and supervisees: A model for considering supervisor roles. *Counselor Education & Supervision, 45* (2), 135–146.

McIntosh, P. (1990, Winter). White privilege: Unpacking the invisible knapsack. [Electronic version]. *Independent School, 49* (2), 31–35. Retrieved February 27, 2006 from Academic Search Premiere database.

McMahon, M., & Simons, R. (2004). Supervision training for professional counselors: An exploratory study. *Counselor Education and Supervision, 43* (4), 301–309.

McNamara, C. (1999). *Strategic planning (in nonprofit and for-profit organizations).* Retrieved August 31, 2006 from http://www.managementhelp.org/plan95dec/str95plan/str95plan.htm.

Microsoft, Microsoft Windows 97, Word, Thesaurus.

Middleton, R. A., Stadler, H. A., Simpson, C., Guo, Y. J., Brown, M. J., Crow, G., et al. (2005). Mental health practitioners: The relationship between white racial identity attitudes and self-reported multicultural counseling competencies. *Journal of Counseling and Development, 83,* 444–456.

Miller, J. G. (2004). *QBQ! The question behind the question.* NY: G.P. Putnam.

Miller, R. & Butler, J. (2004–05). Training Program for New Department Chairs. Paper presented at Academic Chairpersons Conference: The Chair's Role in Empowering Change, Orlando, FL.

Mintzberg, H., & Heyden, L. V. D. (1999). Organigraphs: Drawing how companies really work. *Harvard Business Review, 77*(5), 87–94.

Napier, R. W., & Gershenfeld, M. K. (2004). *Groups: Theory and experience* (7th ed.). Boston: Houghton Mifflin—Lahaska Press.

National Board for Certified Counselors (NBCC). (February 4, 2005). *NBCC ethical code.* Retrieved August 27, 2005 from http://www.nbcc.org/extras/pdfs/ethics/nbcc-codeofethics.pdf.

National Board for Certified Counselors (NBCC). (n.d.). *The practice of internet counseling.* Retrieved from http://www.nbcc.org/webethics2.

National Career Development Association (NCDA). (n.d.a.). *Career counseling competencies.* Retrieved from http://www.ncda.org/pdf/counselingcompetencies.pdf.

National Career Development Association (NCDA). (n.d.b.) *Competencies for career development facilitators.* Retrieved from http://ncda.org/.

National Institute of Standards and Technology (NIST). (n.d.). *Baldridge National Quality Program: Health Care Criteria for Performance Excellence.* Retrieved December 28, 2006 from http://baldrige.nist.gov/PDF95files/200795HealthCare95Criteria.pdf.

Nelson, M. D., Johnson, P., & Thorngren, J. M. (2000). An integrated approach for supervising mental health counseling interns. *Journal of Mental Health Counseling, 22* (1), 45–59.

Neukrug, E., Milliken, T., & Walden, S. (September 2001). Ethical complaints made against credentialed counselors: An updated survey of state licensing boards. *Counselor Education & Supervision, 41* (1), 57–70.

Newman, R. G., Ph.D. (2000). Financial management. In Rodenhauser, P., M.D. (Ed.), *Mental health care administration: A guide for practitioners* (pp. 148–178). Ann Arbor: The University of Michigan Press.

Nickols, F., & Ledgerwood, R. (Mar 2006). The goals grid as a tool for strategic planning. *Consulting to Management—C2M, 17* (1), 36–38.

Northside Independent School District. (1997). *Guide to counselor performance improvement through job definitions, professionalism assessment, supervision, performance evaluation and professional development.* San Antonio, TX: Author.

Oncken, W., Jr., & Wass, D. L. (Nov/Dec 1974). Management time: Who's got the monkey? *Harvard Business Review, 52* (6), 75–80.

Organize for efficiency. (Oct 2004). *Supervision, 65* (10), 25–26.

Osborn, C. J., Dean, E. A., & Petruzzi, M. L. (2004). Use of simulated multidisciplinary treatment teams and client actors to teach case conceptualization and treatment planning skills. *Counselor Education and Supervision, 44* (2), 121–134.

Pack-Brown, S. P. (1999). Racism and White counselor training: Influence of White racial identity theory and research. *Journal of Counseling & Development, 77*, 87–92.

Parallels between performance management quality and organizational performance. (August 2005). *Supervision, 66* (8), 19–20. Retrieved August 19, 2005 from Business Source Premier database.

Patterson, R. F., M.D. (2000). Review mechanisms and regulatory agencies. In Rodenhauser, P., M.D. (Ed.), *Mental health care administration: A guide for practitioners* (pp. 76–100). Ann Arbor: The University of Michigan Press.

Pearce, J. A., II, & David, F. (1987). Corporate mission statements: The bottom line. *Executive, 1* (2), 109–116.

Pearson, Q. M. (2000). Opportunities and challenges in the supervisory relationship: Implications for counselor supervision. *Journal of Mental Health Counseling, 22* (4), 283–294.

Peters, P. (May 2002). 7 tips for delivering performance feedback. *Supervision, 61* (5), 12–14.

Pinsky, L. E., & Fryer-Edwards, K. (2004). Diving for PERLS: Working and performance portfolios for evaluation and reflection on learning. *Journal of General Internal Medicine, 19* (5), 582–587.

Pope-Davis, D. B., Toporek, R., Ortega-Villalobos, L., Ligiero, D. P., Brittan-Powell, C. S., Liu, W. M., et al. (2002). Client perspectives of multicultural counseling competence: A qualitative examination. *Counseling Psychologist, 30* (30), 355–393.

Popper, M. (2004). Leadership as relationship. *Journal for the Theory of Social Behaviour, 34* (2), 107–125.

Quealy-Berge, D., & Caldwell, K. (2004). Mock interdisciplinary staffing: Education for interprofessional collaboration. *Counselor Education and Supervision, 43* (4), 310–320.

Quigley, J. V. (1994, Sep/Oct). Vision: How leaders develop it, share it, and sustain it. *Business Horizons, 37* (5), 37–41.

Radtke, J. M. (Fall 1998). How to write a mission statement [Electronic version]. *The Grantsmanship Center Magazine.* Retrieved January 18, 2006 from http://www.tgci.com/magazine/98fall/mission.asp.

Ramsey, R. D. (Jul 1998). A supervisor's check-list for helping new employees succeed. *Supervision, 59* (7), 3–5.

Raven, B. H. (1993). The bases of power: Origins and recent developments. *Journal of Social Issues, 49* (4), 227–251.

Raven, B. H. (2-5-2004). *A glossary of terms related to interpersonal influence and social power.* Unpublished manuscript. University of California, Los Angeles, Department of Psychology, Los Angeles, CA. Received from author October 3, 2005.

Raven, B. H., Schwarzwald, J., & Koslowsky, M. (1998). Conceptualizing and measuring a power/interaction model of interpersonal influence. *Journal of Applied Social Psychology, 28* (4), 307–332.

Record retention: What to keep and what to toss now. (August, 2006). *HR Focus, 83* (8), 3–4.

Reichard, B. D., Ph.D. (2000). Managing organization behavior. In Rodenhauser, P., M.D. (Ed.), *Mental health care administration: A guide for practitioners* (pp. 179–200). Ann Arbor: The University of Michigan Press.

Resnick, J. T. (2004). Corporate reputation: Managing corporate reputation—applying rigorous measures to a key asset. *Journal of Business Strategy, 25* (6), 30–38.

Rezaie, J., & Garrison, C. (2004). Empowering the middle: The chair's role in the institution. *The Department Chair, 15* (2), 13–14.

Rigg, M. (1992). Increased personal control equals increased individual satisfaction [Electronic version]. *Industrial Engineering, 24* (2). Retrieved on July 13, 2005 from Business Source Premiere database.

Ritt, E. (2004, Fall). Crafting strategy that sticks: Aligning with institutional mission. *The Department Chair, 15* (2), 25–26.

Roberts, R. A. (2005). Success means change. *Supervision, 66* (4), 8–10.

Roux, J. L. (2001). Effective schooling is being culturally responsive. *Intercultural Education, 12,* (1), 41–50.

Salazar, C. F., & Abrams, L. P. (2005). Conceptualizing identity development in members of marginalized groups. *Journal of Professional Counseling: Practice, Theory and Research, 33* (1), 47–59.

Schlitz, D. (1978). The gambler [Recorded by K. Rogers]. On *Greatest Hits* [record]. Nashville: EMI America/Capitol Records.

Schwarzwald, J., Koslowsky, M., & Agassi, V. (2001). Captain's leadership type and police officers' compliance to power bases. *European Journal of Work and Organizational Psychology, 10* (3), 273–290.

Scott, C. L., M.D. (2000). Mental health law. In Rodenhauser, P., M.D. (Ed.), *Mental health care administration: A guide for practitioners* (pp. 101–127). Ann Arbor: The University of Michigan Press.

Seijts, G. H., & Latham, G. P. (2005). Learning versus performance goals: When should each be used? *Academy of Management Executive, 19* (1), 124–131.

Seligman, M. E., Steen, T. A., Park, N., & Peterson, C. (Jul/Aug 2005). Positive psychology progress. *American Psychologist, 60* (5), 410–421.

Senge, P. M. (Sept-Oct, 1997). Communities of leaders and learners. *Harvard Business Review,* 30–32.

Senge, P. (July 2004a). Building vision. *Educational Excellence, 21* (7), 16.

Senge, P. (Sep 2004b). Creating communities. *Executive Excellence, 21* (9), 4–5.

Senge, P. M., & Kaeufer, K. H. (Oct 2000). Creating change. *Executive Excellence, 17* (10), 4–5.

Siegel, C., Haugland, G., & Chambers, E. D. (2002). Final Report. *Cultural competency methodological and data strategies to assess the quality of services in mental health systems of care: A project to select and benchmark performance measures of cultural competency.* Center for the Study of Issues in Public Mental Health. Retrieved 3/3/2006 from http://csipmh.rfmh.org/projects/id9.shtm.

Smith, J. D., & Agate, J. (2004). Solutions for overconfidence: Evaluation of an instructional module for counselor trainees. *Counselor Education and Supervision, 44* (1), 31–43.

Standards for counseling supervisors. (1990). *Journal of Counseling and Development, 69* (1), 30–32.

Stanley, T. L. (2005). Can't we all just get along? *Supervision, 66* (6), 11–12.

Stanley, T. L. (Jul 2006). When push comes to shove: a manager's guide to resolving disputes. *Supervision, 67* (7), 6–7.

Staton, A. R., & Gilligan, T. D. (Mar 2003). Teaching school counselors and school psychologists to work collaboratively. *Counselor Education & Supervision, 42* (3), 162–176.

Staton, R. D., Ph.D., M.D. (2000). The national health care economic context of psychiatric practice. In Rodenhauser, P., M.D. (Ed.), *Mental health care administration: A guide for practitioners* (pp. 1–30). Ann Arbor: The University of Michigan Press.

Stoltenberg, C. D., McNeil, B., & Delworth, U. (1998). *IDM supervision: An integrated developmental model for supervising counselors and therapists.* San Francisco: Jossey-Bass.

Stone, G. L. (1997). Multiculturalism as a context for supervision: Perspectives, limitations, and implications. In Pope-Davis, D. B., & Coleman, H. L. K. (Eds.), *Multicultural counseling competencies: Assessment, education and training, and supervision* (pp. 263–289). Thousand Oaks, CA: Sage.

Sue, D. W., Arredondo, P., & McDavis, R. J. (1992). Multicultural counseling competencies and standards: A call to the profession. *Journal of Counseling & Development, 70,* 482–483.

Sue, D. W., & Sue, D. (2003). *Counseling the culturally diverse: Theory and practice* (4th ed.). NY: Wiley & Sons.

Sutton, J. M., & Fall, M. (1995). The relationship of school climate factors to counselor self-efficacy. *Journal of Counseling & Development, 73,* 331–336.

Synatschk, K. O. (2002). Ensuring professionally relevant supervision and professional development: A district-level experience. In P. Henderson & N. Gysbers (Eds.), *Implementing comprehensive guidance programs: Critical leadership issues and successful responses* (pp. 199–206). Greensboro, NC: CAPS Publications.

Tannenbaum, R., & Schmidt, W. H. (1973). How to choose a leadership pattern. *Harvard Business Review, 51* (3), 162–180.

Texas Administrative Code (TAC). Title 22, Part 30, Chapter 681, Subchapter B, Rule § 681.31.

Texas Administrative Code (TAC). Title 22, Part 30, Chapter 681, Subchapter C, Rules § 681.41–47, .49.

Texas Counseling Association. (2004). *Texas evaluation model for professional school counselors* (2nd ed.). Austin, TX: Author.

Texas Occupations Code. Chapter 503. Licensed Professional Counselors. Subchapter A, §503.001–.003.

Train managers and executives to avoid legal "danger zones." (Aug 2006). *HR Focus, 83* (8), 4–7.

Trotter, S. (2002). An aggressive advocacy plan: The state counselor association response to events in Missouri. In P. Henderson, & N. Gysbers (Eds.), *Implementing comprehensive school guidance programs: Critical leadership issues and successful responses* (pp. 103–114). Greensboro, NC: CAPS Publications.

Trusty, J., & Brown, D. (2005). Advocacy competencies for professional school counselors. *Professional School Counseling, 8* (3), 259–265.

Tsui, M. (2005). *Social work supervision: Contexts and concepts.* Thousand Oaks, CA: SAGE Publications.

Tuckman, B. W. (1965). Development sequence in small groups. *Psychological Bulletin, 63* (6), 384–399.

Tuckman, B. W. (1977). Stages in small-group development revisited. *Group and Organizational Studies, 2,* 319–427.

Uniform guidelines on employee selection procedures. (1978). Retrieved December 31, 2006 from http://www.dol.gov/dol/allcfr/Title9541/Part9560-3/toc.htm.

United States Small Business Administration. Business plan basics. Retrieved September 22, 2006 from http://www.sba.gov/smallbusinessplanner/index.html.

Vontress, C. E., & Jackson, M. L. (2004). Reactions to the multicultural counseling competencies debate. *Journal of Mental Health Counseling, 26,* 74–80.

Waugh, S. (May 2006). Solid performance reviews. *Supervision, 67* (5), 16–17.

Webster's Third New International Dictionary, Unabridged (2002). Merriam-Webster. Retrieved from http://unabridged.merriam-webster.com.

Weick, K. E. (1995). *Sensemaking in organizations.* Thousand Oaks, CA: Sage.

Weiss, W. H. (Jan 2003). Using persuasion successfully. *Supervision, 64* (1), 3–6.

White, V. E., & Queener, J. (2003). Supervisor and supervisee attachments and social provisions related to the supervisory working alliance. *Counselor Education & Supervision, 42* (3), 203–218.

Whyte, E. G., Ph.D., & Martin, W. F., Psy.D., M.P.H., M.A. (2000). Marketing mental health services. In Rodenhauser, P., M.D. (Ed.), *Mental health care administration: A guide for practitioners* (pp. 53–75). Ann Arbor: The University of Michigan Press.

Wiggins, J. D., & Weslander, D. L. (1986). Effectiveness related to personality and demographic characteristics of secondary school counselors. *Counselor Education & Supervision, 29,* 258–267.

Wilbur, M. P., Roberts-Wilbur, J. R., Hart, G. M., Morris, J. R., & Betz, R. L. (1994). Structured group supervision (SGS): A pilot study. *Counselor Education and Supervision, 26,* 26–35.

Zubizarreta, J. (Fall 2004). The learning portfolio: A good idea for departments. *The Department Chair, 15* (2), 19–21.

Index

Numbers in **bold** indicate Figure or Table

33, 36–8, 132, 204, **206–9**,
329–32; administrative
supervisors, **54**, 57, 198,
292–300, 301, **306–10**;
boundaries, 50, 57, 61;
development, 10, 127, 145,
201–2, **282**, **287–311**, *see also*
professional development;
incompetence, **15**, 41, 52,
56–7, 129, 130, 186, 212–14;
standards, **54**, 75; standards
use, **112**, 124, 131, 133,
159–66, 201–4, 214–16, 226–7,
237–8, *see also* professional
development; use in service
delivery, 29, **44**, 170–2, 204–6,
226, 228, 229, 280
competitiveness, 91, 92, 101, 103, 131,
173, 175, 249, 250, 253–4, 294,
303
complaints, 30, 37–8, 52, 56–7, 85, 105,
107, 143, 243, 322
compliance/non-compliance, 8, 11–17,
13, **15**, 50, 53, 54–8, 61–3, 68,
74–5, 149, 198, 199, 250, 281,
282, 322, 323
compromise, 11, 35, 67, 76, 80, 96, 104,
105–7, 150, 174, 175, 214, 254,
275, **309**, 324
conferences, 87; goal setting, 192;
individual, 28, 85, 86, 103,
186–8, 215–16, 279, 284, **308**,
317; job description, 189;
objective setting and action
planning, 266–8; performance
evaluation, 183, 190, 193, 197,
206, 209–12; professional
development, 87, 180, 196,
297, **298–9**, 319, 324; recording
forms, 189, 190, 190–1, 192,
206–8, 212, 241–3, **242**, 267;
scheduled supervision, 131,
140, 148–51, **149**, 155, 156,
190, 298–9; spontaneous

supervision, 55, 62–3, 140,
190; staff group, 30, 39, 40–1,
46, **54**, 60, 85–6, 87, 112,
172–9, **180**, 205, 219, 221, 226,
264, 266, 269, 271–3, 275, **308**,
317; *see* learning community
confidence: administrative supervisee's,
6, 73, 120, 130, 133, 155, 177,
233, 239; administrative
supervisor's, 62–3, 93, 145,
146, 202, 293, 302, **310**
confidentiality, 26, 28, 52, 53, 59, 75,
78–80, **207**, 318, 323;
administrative supervisors–
administrative supervisees, 57,
61, 125, 183, 189, 211, 212, 316,
326; clients, 26, 52, 318, 323;
personnel records, 211, 212,
318, 241–3;
conflict: interpersonal, 78–80, 90, 129,
131, 180–1; resolution skills,
86, 101, 102, 106, 176, 181, 254,
293, 294, **309**
conflicting: interests, 75, 93, 101, 177,
198, 290, 327; roles, 11, 76,
170, 324, 327; standards, 56,
74
confronting others: administrative
supervisees, 46, 69, 116, 130,
135, 146, 151, 162–3, 175,
200–1; outside the
department, 80, 92–3, 105–6,
254
Connor, P. E., 222, 227
Constantine, M., vii, 34, 35, 35, 42, **46**, 47
consultation, 75, 83, 104, 139, 142, 183,
229, **247**, 254, 273, 316, 317;
with administrative
supervisees re. clients, 39, 41,
57, 85, 150, **180**, **194–5**, **207**,
279, 326, 332; re.
administrative supervision
cases, 57, 116, 148, 153, 190,
203, 215, 241, 294, 304–5; for

Association; Association for
Counselor Education and
Supervision, Center for
Excellence in Education,
National Board for Certified
Counselors
evaluation, 277–8
evaluation, administrative supervisees
performance, 197–216, 202;
administrative supervisor
competence, 9, 86, 202, 206, -
211, 289, **306**, 309, 316, 319,
324; administrative supervisor
responsibility, 10, 13, 55, 75,
198, 199, 242–3, 289, 301, 302,
323, 325, 326; administrative
supervisor–administrative
supervisee relationship
impact, 57, 127, 130, 198, 239,
316, 332; evaluation anxiety,
200–1, *see also* administrative
supervisee anxiety; fair, 142,
164–5, 193, **194–5**, 201, 202–3,
206–8, 293, *see also* judging;
formative, **187**, 190, 192,
193–4, 212, 241; just, 16, 142,
190–1, 202, 203–5; purpose,
199, 212–16, 261, 318, 324–5;
relevant, 183–5, 202, *see also*
job description; self, 16, 241
evaluation, administrative supervisor
performance, 303, 305,
306–11, 310, 315, 316
evaluation, client results, **44**, 71, 72,
111–12, 113, 167, 227, 277–80,
281, 283
evaluation, external, 16, 281, **282**
evaluation, improvement, 151–2, 261,
266, 268, 280, 326
evaluation, service delivery system, 9,
44–5, 178, 271, 274, 276,
277–8, 280
evaluator bias, 203
excellence, 10, **12**, 23–4, 73, 111–21, 137,

147, 161, 164, 172, 175–6,
284
expectations, clients', 26, 27, 33, **42**, 332
expectations: administrative supervisee
improvement, 116, 151, 261,
283; administrative supervisee
performance, 58, 111–12, 125,
128, 148, 150, 152, 159, 183,
202, **206–8**; administrative
supervisee practices, 53, 58, 61,
277, 316, 325; administrative
supervisees' jobs, 3, 72,
188–90, 202, 210–11, 237–8;
administrative supervisors, 11,
29, 57, 73, 78, 80, 83, 100, 114,
221, 289, 302, 324, 325, 326; all
employees, 8, 27, 52, 113, 118,
172

F

facilities, 67–8, 126–7, 168, 174, 175, 245,
248, 251, 252, 277, **282**, 301
Fago, J., 241, 242
Falender, C. A., 300, 302, 305, **311**
Fall, M., 118
Falvey, J. E., ix, xi, 4, 183, 200, **311**
Farrant, D., 296, 297, 300
fatal flaws of administrative supervisors,
129
feedback: administrative supervisee
responses, 62, 149, 151, 185–6,
199–200, 201, 213; to
administrative supervisor, 87,
89, 90, 143, 151, 273, 274, 303,
305, 311, 315; administrative
supervisor to administrative
supervisees, **12**, 41–2, 54–5,
62–3, 130, 139, 140, 142, 151,
154, 164, 175, 185, 200, 213,
214; conference, 147–9,
210–11, **240**, 241;
environment, 88, 139, 151,
188–9m, 189–90, 278
Fernando, D. M., 133